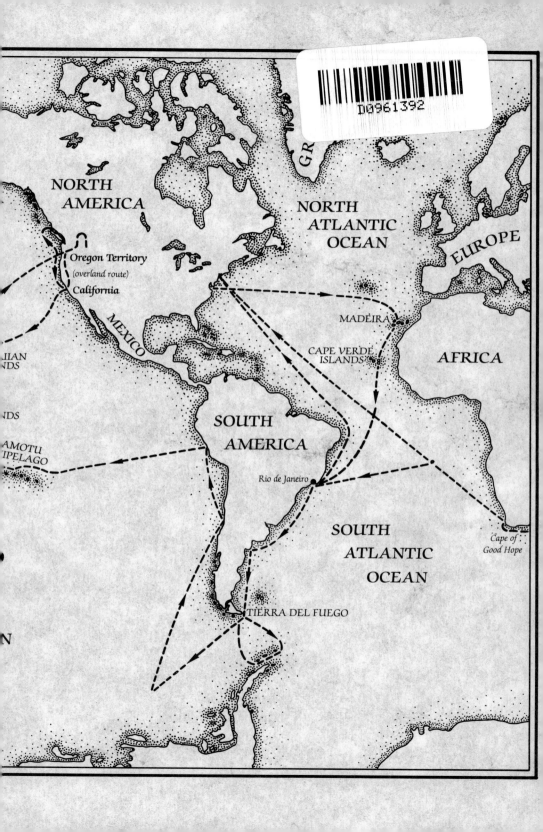

NORTH
AMERICA

NORTH
ATLANTIC
OCEAN

EUROPE

GR

Oregon Territory
(overland route)

California

MEXICO

MADEIRA

CAPE VERDE
ISLANDS

AFRICA

IIAN
NDS

NDS

AMOTU
IPELAGO

SOUTH
AMERICA

Rio de Janeiro

SOUTH
ATLANTIC
OCEAN

Cape of
Good Hope

TIERRA DEL FUEGO

N

William Reynolds as a young officer, miniature by an unknown artist. Courtesy Anne Hoffman Cleaver.

Voyage
to the
Southern Ocean

Voyage to the Southern Ocean

The Letters of Lieutenant William Reynolds
from the U.S. Exploring Expedition, 1838–1842

Edited by Anne Hoffman Cleaver and E. Jeffrey Stann
With an Introduction and Epilogue by Herman J. Viola

NAVAL INSTITUTE PRESS
Annapolis, Maryland

Library of Congress Cataloging-in-Publication Data

Reynolds, William, b. 1815.
*Voyage to the Southern Ocean: the letters of Lieutenant William Reynolds
from the U.S. Exploring Expedition, 1838–1842 / edited by Anne
Hoffman Cleaver and E. Jeffrey Stann; with an introduction and
epilogue by Herman J. Viola.*
p. cm.
Bibliography: p.
ISBN 0-87021-300-8
*1. United States Exploring Expedition (1838–1842)   2. Reynolds,
William, b. 1815—Correspondence.   3. Voyages around the world.
I. Cleaver, Anne Hoffman, 1914–   .   II. Stann, E. Jeffrey, 1944–
III. Title.*
G420.U55R49 1988

910.4'1—dc19   *88-10156*
                                                                       CIP

Designed by Moira Megargee
Printed in the United States of America

to

Patsy Haley Stann

and

William Jessup Cleaver

Saturday, August 18th, 1838

Let the day be registered and remembered —the Ships are off! *We* are "once more upon the waters." Farewell Home! Welcome the stirring scenes of strange Lands. May God in his watchful care preserve us from all dangers and return us in safety to those whom we love better than all the things of earth; and *they,* Oh, shield *them* from harm; give them health and peace; grant them every blessing, and in mercy to *us,* allow them *all* once more to see the wanderers from their firesides.

William Reynolds, first entry of Journal No. 1

Leaving the Fijis, August 1840

Two busy and eventful years have rolled away since this famous Expedition fairly sailed from the shores of our native Land. Alas! it is but the wreck of what it was; the best from among us have been taken away.

William Reynolds, first entry of Journal No. 2

Contents

List of Illustrations

Plates

Acknowledgments

This book began with a notice placed by Herman Viola in the newsletter of the National Genealogical Society in 1983. As head of the National Museum of Natural History's exhibition about the United States Exploring Expedition, he was seeking descendants of expedition members who might have objects or other materials of interest. One such descendant was Anne Hoffman Cleaver, who introduced him to the tremendous resources of the William Reynolds papers.

As work on the exhibition progressed, the value of William Reynolds's letters home from the expedition became increasingly clear, and the idea of publishing them arose. Anne Cleaver had long before begun the study of her family's papers, with the thought of using them as the basis for a history of American life in the nineteenth century: William Reynolds's grandfathers both fought in the Revolution; his father was a member of the delegation welcoming Lafayette to Lancaster in 1824; the four Reynolds brothers served in the Civil War; and his youngest sister lived until 1923. Nevertheless, she quickly responded to the idea of treating William's letters from the expedition as a story in themselves. Jeffrey Stann, a member of the exhibition team, also joined the project at this time.

The editors want to acknowledge Herman Viola's role in bringing them together and getting the project started. Although Herman's other commitments since then have prevented his acting as an editor, too, he has provided advice and assistance.

Many other persons have assisted us as we proceeded. At the Smithsonian, Richard Eyde, curator of botany, quickly developed a deep interest in all matters relating to the expedition and, perhaps because he is an alumnus of Franklin and Marshall College where most of the Reynolds papers now reside, to William Reynolds's role. Dick has been helpful at many points with locating sources, correcting facts, adjusting interpretations, and generally inspiring persistence. Harold Langley and Philip Lundeberg of the National Museum of American History have assisted with diplomatic and naval questions at various times during the past four years; other members of the Wilkes exhibition team offered assistance as well. Many individuals at the Smithsonian Institution Libraries helped in tracking down answers to questions, particularly the central reference and interlibrary loan staff, and Rhoda Ratner's staff at the Museum of American History branch.

At the National Archives, Richard Von Duenhoff and R. B. Matchette made the job of locating naval records simpler, just as Richard Gould did for diplomatic records. At the Library of Congress, John McDonough assisted with manuscripts relative to the expedition. Nearly every member of the very competent staff of the library's Geography and Map Division was helpful at one time or another. The untiring assistance of William Kane in examining vast numbers of records and documents at the National Archives and the Library of Congress to find those relevant to Charles Wilkes and the expedition was critical to the exhibition and, ultimately, to this book; Benjamin Pierce performed similar service with other sources in this country and abroad.

Australian Embassy science counselor John Cowan and librarian Pat Kay were both interested in responding to questions about Charles Wilkes's Antarctic claims. Excellent help was provided with Wilkes's papers at the Manuscript Department of Duke University Library by Mattie Russell, curator of manuscripts, and Sharon E. Knapp.

Charlotte Brown, college archivist at Franklin and Marshall College, was especially helpful. Besides arranging to have the Reynolds family papers organized and made available for use in a manner that greatly expedited our efforts, she was also responsive to other requests for assistance over many months.

The editors want to thank Anne Cleaver's cousin John H. K. Shannahan for permission to use his carefully prepared typescript of the Reynolds letters, which formed the starting point for getting the manuscript into automated form. It is also fitting to acknowledge the members of the Reynolds family who over the years kept these and other letters and documents intact and saw to their being deposited for posterity at Franklin and Marshall.

Finally, we should acknowledge the many persons at the Naval Institute Press with whom we have worked, beginning with Acquisitions Editor Paul Wilderson, and continuing with Managing Editor Laurie Stearns and others, as well as our copy editor, Trudie Calvert. Design Manager Moira Megargee made special efforts to turn these words into an attractive book. Their uniformly courteous and capable assistance has made publication a pleasure.

Editorial Method

In his eulogy of William Reynolds, Admiral C. R. P. Rogers stated that "to a ready command of the language, he united clear perceptions, a facile pen and elegant diction—he wrote well and with great strength" (Rosengarten 1880:11). Reynolds's fluid and vivid style captured for his family at home the drama and emotion of his adventures on the U.S. Exploring Expedition. He managed to write long and descriptive letters despite the frequent interruptions and cramped conditions of shipboard life and the relentless pace of surveying and other duties imposed while ashore. His style makes the editors' job easier.

The letters were transcribed from photocopies of Reynolds's letters to his family. The original manuscripts were consulted when faded or damaged portions were difficult to read. Similarly, photocopies of his journals and other family correspondence have been used, except those originals still in the possession of Anne Cleaver.

Editorial procedure has followed the expanded method, as described in the *Harvard Guide to American History*. Reynolds's spelling, grammar, and capitalization have been kept nearly intact. An exception has been made in capitalization. Reynolds often wrote certain letters—e, s, and i especially—in uppercase when beginning a word; they appear here in lowercase except when the context and Reynolds's own consistent practice suggest otherwise. Sentences always begin with a capital letter here.

Somewhat more liberty has been taken with punctuation. Reynolds used the dash, rather than periods, semicolons, and commas, to separate thoughts and phrases. In the interest of greater ease for the modern reader, the editors have sometimes replaced dashes with other punctuation and have ended all sentences with periods. Reynolds's frequent commas have likewise been reduced in number. Such changes have been kept to a minimum to preserve the flavor of the writer's style.

Abbreviations have been standardized in form and expanded except for those still in current use. Ampersands and &c are both spelled out. Raised letters at the ends of words have been lowered to the line of the text. Long paragraphs containing several topics have been divided.

Editorial comments and other interpolated matter appear in italics within brackets. Missing words and badly faded passages have been printed in roman type within brackets; if meaning is subject to more than one interpretation, a question mark is inserted. Minor slips by the writer have been corrected without notice.

In nearly every letter he wrote, Reynolds asked after family members and friends back home and commented on their doings. To avoid repetition, some of these passages have been deleted, as indicated by ellipses.

Reynolds sent letters at nearly every opportunity, even if he did no more than dash down a few lines to hand over to a passing ship headed home. Since he could never be sure how many of his letters would arrive, or when, he was thus assured of maintaining contact with his family. Most of his letters did arrive safely. No. 2, 12, and 18 did not, and the editors have supplied a narrative of the period from his journals or other sources, except for Letter No. 2, because there is no ostensible gap between letters No. 1 and 3. The section "Rio and After" supplies details on the period encompassed by letters No. 5 and 6.

The Letters

William Reynolds's letters from the U.S. Exploring Expedition—
which form the content of this book—and those written to him which
still exist were found in two attics in Fort Wayne, Indiana. The attics
belonged to the granddaughters of Lydia Moore Reynolds Evans, the
sister to whom most of William's letters were addressed: Katharine
Hoffman Kline (1876–1959) and Emily R. Hoffman Hoffman (1878–
1959). The nineteen surviving letters from Reynolds found in Fort
Wayne and the transcriptions made by Mrs. Kline's son-in-law, John
H. K. Shannahan, are in the Reynolds Family Papers (1765–1934),
special collection no. 92 in the Archives and Special Collections Department, Shadek-Fackenthal Library, Franklin and Marshall College, Lancaster, Pennsylvania. The answering letters written back to William by
Lydia and other family members are in the possession of Anne Hoffman
Cleaver of Westfield, Indiana, Emily Hoffman's daughter.

One of William Reynolds's letters—No. 19—strayed from family
hands and was found by one of the editors in the National Archives. The
letter is located in Area File 9, in the Naval Records Collection, Record
Group 45.

The Journals

On 13 September 1838, William Reynolds recorded in his private
journal that Captain Wilkes had ordered every officer on the expedition

to keep daily records to be sent to the commander weekly and to be presented to the Navy Department at the end of the cruise. Since his first voyage, Reynolds had been accustomed to keeping a journal to record his private thoughts. On hearing Wilkes's order, Reynolds concluded, "So I shall commence another [journal]—I cannot think of letting this go before any other eyes but those few at home."

This "other," official journal is entitled "Journal on board the Vincennes, Chas. Wilkes, Esq., Commander, Sea Account" and is referred to in the notes as "Public Journal." The volume includes Reynolds's service on other vessels as well until he left Rio de Janeiro on the *Porpoise*, homeward bound, on 22 May 1842.

Reynolds also kept up his personal journal writing. There are three volumes covering his service in the expedition. These are cited in the notes simply as "Journal" with the volume number.

The contrast between the public and private journals is clearly seen in the opening entries of each. The Public Journal is much like those kept by the other officers of the expedition: "August 18th 1838. At 2 P.M., the *South Sea Surveying and Exploring Expedition*, in Squadron, consisting of the Vincennes, Flagship; Peacock; Relief; Porpoise; Sea Gull and Flying Fish got under weigh and proceeded to sea with a light breeze." Journal No. 1 begins with a sense of the inner man: "Saturday, August 18th 1838. Let the day be registered and remembered—the Ships are off! *We* are 'once more upon the waters.' Farewell Home! Welcome the stirring scenes of strange Lands. May God in his watchful care preserve us from all dangers and return us in safety to those whom we love better than all the things of earth. . . . The morning after we sailed . . . the morning watch was mine and for the first time in my life, I held the trumpet and directed the movements of a ship. My ambition is fulfilled!" All of the journals are in the Reynolds Family Papers at Franklin and Marshall. The journals have been used to clarify and amplify references in the letters; they are also the principal source for the description of Reynolds's activities during the periods covered by two lost letters—No. 12 and 18—and by letters No. 5 and 6.

Most of the Navy Department records used are located in the National Archives (hereafter cited as NA). *The Records of the United States Exploring Expedition under the Command of Lieutenant Charles Wilkes, 1836–1842* are found in Record Group (hereafter cited as RG) 37 and published in National Archives Microfilm Publication M75. The first six rolls of M75 consist of Letters Relating to the Wilkes Exploring Expedition (hereafter cited as Letters WEE); the rest are journals of expedition members and court-martial records. Dozens of other documents concerning the expedition and its members, including private correspondence, are found in the Area Files, Naval Records Collection of the Office of Naval Records and Library, RG 45. These files contain miscellaneous papers donated by private individuals and are arranged by geographic area.

William Reynolds's official correspondence as a navy officer is found variously in Letters from Officers Commanding Expeditions, Squadron Letters, Logs and Journals of Vessels, and Officers' Letterbooks, all in RG 45, NA. Other navy records from the National Archives are cited in the bibliography.

Records still in the hands of the Navy Department which were useful include the ZB File, in the Operational Archives of the Washington Navy Yard; this biographical vertical file contains miscellaneous correspondence and other documents similar to the Area Files, as well as secondary information about officers' records prepared in response to public inquiries.

Other Sources

Other depositories consulted which are important to the expedition if not to William Reynolds specifically include the Wilkes Family Papers in the Manuscript Department of Duke University Library; the Papers of Charles Wilkes (1837–1847) in the Kansas State Historical Society, Topeka, Microfilm MS-53s; the Charles Wilkes Family Papers in the Manuscript Division of the Library of Congress; and the George Emmons Papers and the Henry Eld Papers, both in the Western Americana Collection, Yale University. The journals of selected other expedition members are cited in the bibliography.

In addition, there are a few sources frequently used but not always cited in the notes. First among these are William Stanton's *The Great United States Exploring Expedition of 1838–1842* (Berkeley and Los Angeles: University of California Press, 1975) and David Tyler's *The Wilkes Expedition, The First United States Exploring Expedition (1838–1842)* (Philadelphia: American Philosophical Society, 1968), the standard treatments of the Wilkes Expedition. Another is the recent *Magnificent Voyagers: The U.S. Exploring Expedition, 1838–1842* (Washington: Smithsonian Institution Press, 1985), edited by Herman J. Viola and Carolyn Margolis in conjunction with the exhibition by the same name at the National Museum of Natural History and later toured by the Smithsonian Institution Traveling Exhibition Service. Finally, many bits and pieces of Lancaster history and that of the Reynolds family and friends are scattered through ninety years of the Lancaster County Historical Society *Journal*.

"*My* proffession, above any other in the world. Hurrah! for the Exploring Expedition." This is how Midshipman William Reynolds initially expressed his feelings as a member of "the first, great national Exploring Expedition." Such exuberance was typical of the earnest young officer from Lancaster, Pennsylvania, during the three years and ten months he served with the U.S. Exploring Expedition of 1838–1842, commanded by Lieutenant Charles Wilkes. Reynolds was to have much to cheer about during his four years at sea, but he would have much to weep about as well. Indeed, few sagas of the sea embody more romance and excitement than the U.S. Exploring Expedition, our nation's first naval expedition and the only one under canvas.

Heroes all, the explorers met every challenge in what is recognized as one of the peacetime navy's finest moments. The squadron of six small ships logged 87,000 sea miles, surveyed 280 islands, and constructed 180 maps and charts, some of which were still in use as late as World War II. They also mapped 800 miles of the Oregon coast and surveyed some 1,500 miles of the Antarctic coast—an area known to this day as "Wilkesland"—thereby establishing the existence of the seventh continent.

In addition to a full complement of naval officers and crewmen, the expedition included nine civilian naturalists and artists called "Scientifics," whose job it was to collect examples of flora and fauna from the places visited. Their presence marked the first time in American history that civilian and naval personnel combined their talents and resources in a common effort. The effort proved so successful that the explorers returned home laden with the stuff of science—bird and animal skins, plants, rocks, minerals, gems, fish, reptiles, native artifacts. So vast and valuable were these collections that they led to the establishment of the National Museum of the United States at the Smithsonian Institution.

The expedition, which led to the emergence of the United States as a naval and scientific power with worldwide interests, was not completed without cost. The oceans claimed two ships—one with all hands. Other crewmen fell victim to native hostility, including two officers whose deaths provoked a brutal, hard-fought battle between club-wielding Fijians and sailors armed with muskets and pistols.

Fortunately, Reynolds realized he was making history and wished to share every detail with his family in Pennsylvania. Fortunately, too, he had a knack for writing, so his letters are fun to read. Besides keeping two journals—one private and one he gave to Wilkes at the end of the voyage (a requirement made of all officers on the expedition)—Reynolds wrote twenty-one letters to his family. These letters, which are published here for the first time, reveal an open-hearted, sensitive, and intelligent young man who loved his family, his shipmates, and his country. Only twenty-two years old when he set sail with the Exploring Expedition, Reynolds was flush with the patriotism and pride typical of Americans of his day, who believed themselves to be beneficiaries of a special destiny.

Besides the unique perspective they give us of the activities of the U.S. Exploring Expedition, the letters also provide invaluable information about a variety of other topics, many of them of special interest to naval historians because the young officer followed closely the activities of his superiors in Washington and he was forthright and vocal about such timeless issues as pay, selections for command, and promotions. In the peacetime navy of the 1830s the grand sea battles of the War of 1812 were a fading memory, but the aging veterans remained on active duty blocking chances for promotion and a parsimonious Congress continually sought to reduce the size of the fleet to save money. "All that I want, and all that the rest of us ask," Reynolds wrote in a moment of pique, "is for the Government to fit out the vessels we have instead of letting them rot, promote us who are dying for promotion, and send us to Sea in the rank we ought to occupy. Lieuts. over 50 and Midshipmen from 25 to 30—it is horrible, a sweep in the streets is better off."

Since his letters were written primarily to his sister Lydia, they contain considerable information that he presumed would be of special interest to her, and they abound with references to female dress and deportment, the food he ate, and the furnishings of the houses in which he stayed. Writing to his sister also gave him occasion to treat such personal subjects as love and marriage. Reynolds, after all, was a typical sailor. He appreciated a well-turned ankle and found the absence of female companionship to be the severest cross—besides Wilkes—of his four years at sea. Unlike many of his shipmates, however, he avoided the fleshpots that flourished in the seaports the expedition visited.

The letters also reveal much about how Americans viewed themselves in the late 1830s. Reynolds's often critical comments about other peoples are probably as much a reflection of his own prejudices and assumptions as they are objective statements about the natives of Tierra del Fuego, Tahiti, Samoa, Fiji, Hawaii, and the other exotic places on the expedition's itinerary. Although anthropology was not yet a science, the cultures and lifeways of the people the explorers met were of great interest to them and they collected as much as they could, from linguistic material to the human head being eaten by a Fiji cannibal—a sight that fascinated Reynolds as much as it disgusted him: "Oh! to look at that rugged skull and think that a day before it had contained a cunning brain. I have been used to rude and uncouth sights, but this one was too rude and discomposed me more than I can tell." Because Reynolds was able to articulate his impressions so graphically and eloquently, his letters have a dimension not normally found among literate seamen.

To help his family keep track of his letters, Reynolds numbered them. Of the twenty-one he wrote (plus a letter of introduction for one of the expedition surgeons) three never reached their destination; to make the narrative complete, the editors have replaced the missing letters with entries from Reynolds's journals.

It is little short of miraculous that so many of the letters did reach Pennsylvania because their delivery depended largely on trust and good fortune. Reynolds and his fellow explorers usually gave their mail to

American vessels bound for the United States. When those vessels reached port, someone would then deposit the mail in the local post office. Typical of such routing is Reynolds's letter of 4 January 1839, written in Rio de Janeiro and given to the brig *Volta* bound for Philadelphia. The letter bears a New York City postmark dated 9 March.

Letters to Reynolds enjoyed equally circuitous and chancy routing. Nonetheless, he continually exhorted family members to write and write often even though he realized many of their letters would go astray. Anticipating the end of the expedition, for example, he advised correspondents beginning in September 1840 to send their letters to Singapore, which the squadron expected to reach sometime between November 1841 and January 1842. "You must write by every chance to the Cape of Good Hope, and to Batavia or Sincapore, up to October 1841. Boston and Salem vessels are most numerous in the East Indian

John Reynolds, William's father, from a miniature.
Courtesy Anne Hoffman Cleaver.

Trade, and if you see none advertised, why be sure and send a package to the Navy Department and to the Lyceum at Brooklyn *every month,* and I cannot help getting some of them."

Considering all the hazards then as well as the possibility of loss since, it is remarkable that we have such a complete record of Reynolds's role in the Exploring Expedition. Fortunately, he came from a family of savers, who handed down his letters from generation to generation until 1962, when the collection was deposited at Franklin and Marshall College.

The choice of depository could not have been more appropriate because Lancaster is where William was born to John and Lydia Moore Reynolds on 10 December 1815. His mother's Scotch-Irish parents had emigrated there from County Donegal. His father's father, another Scotch-Irish immigrant, was an innkeeper in Lancaster County; his

Lydia Moore Reynolds, William's mother, from a miniature.
Courtesy Anne Hoffman Cleaver.

father's mother was descended from the first settlers in the county, French Huguenots named Ferree and Lefevre.

John Reynolds was a solid citizen and participant in community affairs. He had begun as a printer's apprentice, been the clerk of a newly formed Lancaster bank, captain of a volunteer infantry company, and county treasurer before purchasing the weekly *Lancaster Journal,* which he published from 1820 to 1834 from the family home on West King Street. During the years William served with the Exploring Expedition, his family lived in the Coleman house at Cornwall Furnace, about twenty miles north of Lancaster, where his father was occupied full time as guardian of his friend Thomas Bird Coleman's six children and their estate of iron furnaces and forges.[1]

The second of thirteen children—six boys and seven girls, of whom only nine lived—William seems to have been closest to his sister Lydia, about three years his junior. Of the Reynolds children, only William and a younger brother named John Fulton ventured far from their comfortable life in Pennsylvania. John entered West Point in 1837, was breveted for outstanding service in the Mexican War, twice crossed the continent during the troubles with Indians and Mormons in the 1850s, and was killed at Gettysburg.

The literary skills of the future explorer surfaced early. At age eight he sent his father, then serving in the state legislature at Harrisburg, a letter in a creditable hand describing affairs at home as his mother convalesced following the birth of her seventh child. "My Dear Father," he wrote, "you will excuse this first attempt I make in writing a letter though I may not succeed very well . . . my Mother can come downstairs a little and the nurse has left her and she moved the cradle in [the] nursery and she expects a great deal of trouble with so many noisy and disobedient children as we are." William also reported that his sister Lydia "can spell all the words in her lesson and I am in . . . weights in cyphering."

Relatively little is known of William's early life other than that he grew up in a warm and loving family and received an excellent

---

[1] *Unless cited otherwise, family information and quotations by William Reynolds are from records and correspondence in the custody of Anne Hoffman Cleaver, Westfield, Indiana. This material will eventually be deposited with the Reynolds collection in the Shadek-Fackenthal Library of Franklin and Marshall College.*

education for his day. By age twelve, he was attending John Beck's Young Gentlemen's Academy in Lititz, a Moravian village about eight miles north of Lancaster. The curriculum was broad: English, mathematics, science (in many surprising aspects), Latin, German, drawing and drafting, music, and sports. By age fifteen, he had applied for an appointment as a midshipman in the U.S. Navy, which he received on 17 November 1831, courtesy of Congressman James Buchanan, a friend of his father.

While awaiting his assignment, the aspiring officer went on a business trip for his father to collect money owed the *Lancaster Journal.* William went first to communities in Pennsylvania—Carlisle, Chambersburg, Harrisburg, Shippensburg (where he stopped at the grave of his grandfather Captain Samuel Moore)—before visiting Baltimore, Frederick, and Hagerstown in Maryland. His careful accounting to his father of his activities reveals remarkable poise and initiative for a fifteen-year-old.

Before returning home, Reynolds visited relatives in Philadelphia. There he received orders to report to the schooner *Boxer,* a warship of ten guns lying in Boston harbor. "He is delighted—it gives him new vigor," his aunt reported.

Eight days after his sixteenth birthday and en route to his first ship, William was again in Philadelphia. There he was fitted for his uniform: "The embroidery on the collar is gold; the buttons are large and plenty of them," he boasted. He called upon some of his father's friends, who gave him letters of introduction to prominent families in Boston. Indicative of his ingratiating personality, these staid Boston families received him warmly, cared for him when he was sick, helped outfit him, and in general made his stay in their city a memorable one for a young man from Lancaster, Pennsylvania. By Christmas Day he was in the Boston Navy Yard inspecting the *Boxer,* which he described as "a pretty vessel."

By coincidence, Lieutenant Charles Wilkes, who was later to figure so prominently in William's life, would also have reported to the *Boxer* for this cruise had he not contracted smallpox. Also coincidentally, the USS *Peacock,* a sloop of war carrying eighteen guns, sailed in company with the *Boxer.* The *Peacock* was later assigned to the Exploring Expedition, and Reynolds was to witness her destruction off the Oregon coast.

Reynolds returned to the United States in May 1834 on board the *Peacock* after an absence of almost three years in Brazil and Southeast

Asia. Upon receiving his warrant as midshipman from the secretary of the navy, he returned to Lancaster on a three-month leave confident that he now embodied the old navy adage "Go to sea a boy and you will come back a man"—a ladies' man. Warranted or not, he at least tried to uphold the navy's reputation in that regard for when he reported to the USS *Potomac,* a forty-four gun brig out of Boston, at the end of his shore leave, he asked Lydia to remember him "to all the young ladies" of Lancaster.

The *Potomac,* his largest ship to date, evidently enabled him to cut an even greater swath among the belles of Boston. "I have carried away more rings . . . from the ladies [here] than from those of Lancaster," he crowed. "I expect that a Mrs. Reynolds will arrive from Boston ere many years have elapsed. Naval men do stand so high among the ladies of this good city."

Although Reynolds was receiving "important instructions" on board the *Potomac,* he cut short his cruise so as to prepare for his examinations for the rank of passed midshipman. He returned to the United States on board the USS *Delaware,* seventy-four guns, in March 1836 and remained on leave until the following October, when he reported to the naval school at Norfolk.

William apparently did not spend all his leave in Lancaster, but his stay was long enough to deepen his rapport with his sister Lydia, now eighteen. Their letters to each other during the following winter indicate a close friendship and easy camaraderie. William sometimes enclosed confidences on "private" sheets (these are still private because they no longer exist). His first letter home from Norfolk, dated 30 October, is especially interesting because it contains his first reference to Rebecca Krug, his future wife. "I should consider it very strange, improper, malicious, unladylike, ungentlemanly, in any one to say, from seeing you with Miss Krug, that her and I were engaged," he wrote. "Why good God, it's absurd to think of such a thing; no one would say so and if they did, why then, what matter who would believe them on such a foundation. No," he advised Lydia, "it will be very wrong with you to shun her on that account—*do not do so.*"[2]

---

[2] *George Hopson Krug, tanner and banker, and his family of two daughters and three sons lived down West King Street from the Reynolds family. Rebecca, a gregarious and handsome young woman, was never in want of suitors, whether in town or on her frequent visits with relatives in Philadelphia and Pittsburgh.*

Because there was as yet no naval academy at Annapolis, student officers of Reynolds's day received practical experience first—in his case three years, ten months, and nine days at sea—and naval theory later. For him, this meant reporting to the school at the Gosport Navy Ship Yard in Norfolk, where he received eight months of instruction. While at the school, Reynolds and his fellow students lived in nearby boardinghouses. His was operated by the sister-in-law of his captain on the *Boxer.* His roommate was John Quincy Adams, a member of the great Adams family of Massachusetts, who had been named after his illustrious uncle; in an adjoining room was William May, who was to become his best friend on the Exploring Expedition. Reynolds claims he took his studies very seriously, becoming a "perfect anchorite," and sticking strictly to his study of the "immaculate Bowditch," the midshipman's "bible."[3]

After a short visit home, Reynolds reported to Baltimore at the end of May 1837 with forty-four other midshipmen to appear before an examining board of senior officers. The candidates had only fifteen uniform dress coats among them, which they shared for their appearances before the board. The examinations were to be given in the order in which the midshipmen entered the service. Reynolds—thirty-third in line—calculated that he would have to stay in Baltimore one month. Rooming with Adams and May at a boardinghouse that charged $11 a week, Reynolds impatiently waited his turn, which came on 15 June. He was examined, certified, and received his warrant as passed midshipman a week later. Neither Adams nor May passed on the first attempt.

The following November, Reynolds reported to the Philadelphia Navy Yard for duty on board the newly commissioned USS *Pennsylvania*, 120 guns, the dreadnought of the American navy. He spent a month helping to ready "the largest ship in the world" before sailing with her to Norfolk, where the vessel received *"a tumultuous welcome."* On 17 January 1838, he was given leave and returned to Pennsylvania.

After another extended visit with his family, Reynolds received orders to report to the Depot of Charts and Instruments in Washington, where he met Charles Wilkes for the first time. The depot, predecessor of the Navy Hydrographic Office, had been established in 1830. Wilkes

---

[3] *Nathaniel Bowditch, distinguished mathematician and astronomer, published in 1801 his* New American Practical Navigator, *which became the standard treatise for seamen.*

took charge three years later. His first action was to move the office to his home on Capitol Hill and, at his own expense, erect an observatory with a transit made in England for the U.S. Coast Survey. As superintendent, one of his greatest contributions was to establish standardized procedures for rating and testing chronometers for the U.S. Navy (Leonhart 1985:193). By coincidence, on the same day Reynolds reported to the depot, 20 April 1838, the president approved the appointment of Wilkes as commander of the Exploring Expedition.

How or why Reynolds received the appointment to the depot is unknown, but he quickly became a great admirer of Wilkes and began thinking seriously about joining the expedition. "I am in the hands of fate," he wrote on 1 May. "I am now wavering in the balance, a feather will turn the scale. . . . I am now desirous to go Exploring. I like Lieutenant Wilkes very much, which is important (to me)." He also liked the idea that the expedition would "partly follow in the footsteps and partly go beyond the adventurous researches of the immortal Captain Cook, whose narration has always possessed a romantic charm for me. May ours be a different fate from his!" Thus, Reynolds reasoned, "as regards the commander and the cruising ground . . . I am perfectly satisfied."

The young officer found even more satisfactory the news that the passed midshipmen would perform the duties of lieutenants. "The *watches* will not come *every* night, and I shall have attained almost the height of my ambition 'when I take the Trumpet and direct the movements of the ship.' " All in all, Reynolds viewed the expedition as an agreeable and profitable way "to pass away my years of probation"—"more agreeably because my duties will be of a higher order; more profitably, because it will make me a seaman."

Despite all the points in favor of joining, Reynolds was still undecided a week later. His plan, he informed Lydia, "remains fixed almost, and that is to link my fortunes, sink or swim, with the Exploring Expedition. A little longer and I shall know. Two years and a half will soon pass away on that cruise, and I may hope to be an interesting person, for a very little while, if I should return." The decision was obviously not easy to make because on 13 May he still had not committed himself, although he was about to do so: "I cannot give up the Exploring Expedition. I shall offer myself to Captain Wilkes today or tomorrow, therefore be ye all prepared." Actually, it was two more weeks—28 May—before Reynolds made the official announcement: "I am as one of the Explorers. The Ex. is to sail before the 10th of August; I shall be very busy, I do not know when I can come home. I will want more red flannel shirts and drawers made. . . . Save my white hat. I will take it, as we will be much in the hot latitudes also."

His letters were now less frequent. One reason was the press of business as the time of departure drew near; another was his friend May, now a passed midshipman, who had also signed on with the expedition. Reynolds was virtually adopted by May's family, which lived in Washington. "I believe I have supped there every night for the past two weeks," he informed Lydia on 17 June. Wilkes also kept the young officers busy. Every third night, Reynolds and May assisted him at the depot as he recorded the movements of the pendulum and observed the transit and altitudes of the stars. "This is something new to me, and of great interest [although] . . . it is sunrise before we finish," reported Reynolds, whose admiration for Wilkes seemed to increase with each passing week. "I like Captain Wilkes very much; he is a most wonderful man, possesses a vast deal of knowledge and has a talent for everything."

The closer the time came for embarking, the more excited he became. "Nothing will tempt me to leave the Ex.," he exclaimed, "the prospects are too delightful, too flattering. 'My heart is with the Heathen, let me go.' "

On 7 July, a month before the expedition was to sail, Reynolds returned home on a week's leave. He picked up a supply of red flannels, calico shirts, and other sundries, wished his family well, and left for Norfolk. The one person he missed seeing was Rebecca Krug, who was attending a cousin's wedding in Pittsburgh.

Reynolds's original orders were to the gun brig *Porpoise,* but before the expedition left he was transferred to the *Vincennes,* a sloop of war of the second class pierced for eighteen guns and the squadron's flagship, commanded by Wilkes. Although Reynolds had very much wanted the change and considered himself lucky to receive it, he was to regret the transfer.

Despite its importance, the expedition is relatively unknown today. Even the colorful and controversial Wilkes is remembered primarily for his role in the *Trent* Affair during the Civil War, when he removed Confederate diplomatic agents from a British vessel in international waters.

The expedition traced its origins to the early nineteenth century, when various mercantile and scientific interests merged to persuade Congress to launch an exploring expedition to the Pacific. Although Congress passed the resolution in 1828, the expedition did not set sail until a decade later. Officially known as the United States South Seas Exploring Expedition, it was commonly called the Exploring Expedition or the Wilkes Expedition. One wit dubbed it the "Deplorable Expedition" because of the seemingly endless delays and controversies that surrounded it. There were squabbles over the number and types of ships, the choice of commander and the scope of his authority, and the size and background of the scientific staff.

Wilkes was not the navy's first choice to lead the expedition. Of forty lieutenants in the service, thirty-eight had had more sea duty. What he lacked in experience, however, he more than made up for in vision, intelligence, and determination. His sense of mission and national pride dictated high standards of performance and accomplishment, and he gave the expedition its distinctive stamp. But he was not without flaws. He was aloof, brooding, and always sensitive to marks of disrespect. He was also a strict disciplinarian who ran a taut ship—too taut, some insisted. Reynolds, for one, came to dislike him intensely. Wilkes later claimed that he cultivated the image of a "martinette" because it carried with it "authority" and "obedience to command" (Wilkes 1978:391). Regardless, despite difficulties of personality, he guided the expedition through awesome hazards and demonstrated considerable leadership as well as scientific skill. Even his worst detractors could not deny that Wilkes had driven himself harder than he had driven his ships and men.

Second in command, on the *Peacock*, was Lieutenant William Hudson. At forty-four, he was four years older than Wilkes and the senior officer in years of service.

The squadron started out with six ships. Besides the *Vincennes* and the *Peacock*, these were the brig *Porpoise*, the supply ship *Relief*, and two virtually identical schooners, the *Sea Gull* and the *Flying Fish*. Modifications were made to most of the vessels to prepare them for the anticipated stresses of an expedition to polar waters and to accommodate the nine civilian scientists who sailed with the squadron.

The scientifics were young (average age thirty-two), enthusiastic, and talented. Most were academically trained, and several went on to become giants in their fields. James Dwight Dana, the most gifted of the group and already the author of a major work on mineralogy, became one of America's most distinguished scientists. The others were Horatio Hale, philologist; Titian R. Peale and Charles Pickering, naturalists; William D. Brackenridge and William Rich, botanists; Joseph P. Couthouy, conchologist; and Alfred T. Agate and Joseph Drayton, artists.

Although the age of sail evokes romantic images, Reynolds's letters suggest that life as a member of the expedition left much to be desired. Scientific, commercial, and diplomatic objectives may have inspired the enterprise, but traditional naval discipline and custom—including flogging and the regular issue of grog—were the order of the day. The ships were small and crowded and the time between ports often weighed heavily. Since the only way to keep meat and poultry fresh was to keep it live, the decks the first few weeks after leaving port often resembled barnyards, complete with the accompanying litter and stench. The problem became even more acute when departures were delayed because the livestock had to remain on board even though, as Reynolds once grumbled, "which time they would have spent more profitably on the Shore." Exotic fruits, native dishes, and fresh fish and game were occasionally available, but the traditional shipboard diet of salt pork, bread, water, and such antiscorbutics as sauerkraut and pickles prevailed.

Life on board ship was not completely spartan. The officers, as these letters indicate, could give their quarters a personal touch. Few, however, went to the lengths of Reynolds and May, whose cabin on the *Vincennes* featured curtains, rugs, and other nonregulation furnishings.

Despite the homey decor, there was no substitute for news from home. Perhaps the most persistent theme in these letters is the hunger for mail and newspapers. When mail reached a ship, virtually all activity ceased. Reynolds once reported his pleasure at obtaining American newspapers "less than 80 days old" from a ship that came into Honolulu from Mazatlán. It was not uncommon for a year and a half to pass before a letter home received its response. "Only think, your *last dates* are *now ten months old* and it will be *more than a year before* I can think of *another letter from Home; do write and send many papers*," Reynolds pleaded in his letter of 21 September 1840, written in transit between Sydney and Oahu. In truth, for all hands, four years of absence—one year longer than anticipated—proved an extraordinary sacrifice, depriving their families of needed support and making particularly bitter the official indifference that met the expedition's return in 1842.

Combining naval and scientific objectives was not always easy, but for the most part the two groups worked well together. Although Reynolds seemed to be genuinely enthusiastic about the work of the scientifics, his attitude was not always shared by his fellow officers. Some derided the scientifics as "clam diggers" and "bug catchers"; others resented the additional workload they represented, such as the need to ferry them from ship to shore so they could collect specimens from the islands the squadron surveyed. Even Wilkes, who took the expedition's scientific objectives seriously, eventually became vexed by the noxious odors that emanated from dissected creatures and prohibited their study below decks.

Since Reynolds was an avid chronicler of all aspects of the expedition, his letters provide a detailed description of the itinerary, and there is no need to elaborate on it here (Appendix A). The explorers set sail from Hampton Roads, Virginia, on 18 August 1838.[4] The first important stop was Orange Harbor at Tierra del Fuego, which Wilkes used as a base for his initial attempt to explore the waters around Antarctica in February 1839. Leaving the *Relief* and *Vincennes* behind, he took the rest of the squadron south, where he found enough indications of land to justify a more extended attempt the following year.

Wilkes planned to have the squadron reunite in Valparaíso, Chile, but only five ships reached port. The *Sea Gull* disappeared somewhere between Orange Harbor and Valparaíso never to be heard from again. The loss was a devastating blow to morale, and the memory of their missing companions haunted the explorers as they continued their voyage. Meanwhile, Wilkes had decided the *Relief* was too slow and would keep the expedition off schedule so he ordered her home by way of Hawaii and Australia, where she was to offload supplies which the remaining ships would pick up when they arrived there the following year. For much of the expedition, therefore, the squadron consisted of only four ships.

The explorers reached the first Pacific islands, the Tuamotu group, in August 1839 after almost a year at sea. The main order of business was

---

[4] *The following information on the expedition is adapted from Viola and Margolis 1985:9–23.*

surveying, which Wilkes developed to a fine art using the triangulation method he had perfected earlier in his naval career during a survey of Georges Bank. The squadron gradually worked itself through the coral islands—the Disappointments, Tahiti, Samoa—completing its work by the end of November 1839 and then proceeding to Australia for another probe into Antarctic waters.

Leaving the scientifics to explore Australia and New Zealand, Wilkes took the four remaining vessels on what was to become the expedition's finest but most controversial achievement. The ships and crews suffered terribly from the harsh conditions. Each vessel had difficult moments, but it was the *Peacock* that came closest to a watery grave. On 23 January 1840, she went stern first into an iceberg, broke the rudder, and parted the starboard wheel rope. Unsteerable, the vessel drifted into a huge ice island and broke the stern davits, stern boat, and spanker boom. At the same time she became trapped by floating ice. Providentially, a narrow channel opened, and Captain Hudson and the crew worked for more than twenty-four hours to pull the stricken vessel to the safety of open water. Reynolds, who was now assigned to the *Peacock*, not only described the harrowing ordeal for his family but also sent them a drawing of the scene by the ship's surgeon, Charles F. B. Guillou, the first drawing of an Antarctic scene to reach the United States.

Despite this bad luck, the *Peacock*—and Reynolds—get credit for the expedition's first landfall. Reynolds and his shipmate Henry Eld often spent their free moments in the rigging hoping to be the first to sight land; their diligence was rewarded on 16 January. To their dismay, however, the sighting was not recorded in the ship's log. In fact, it was not until 19 January that a landfall was recorded in the log of the *Vincennes*. This proved unfortunate because a French exploring expedition under Admiral Dumont d'Urville was in approximately the same waters at the time and recorded making a landfall the same day as the *Vincennes*. Nevertheless, scholars have since credited the Exploring Expedition with the first landfall. More significant, however, the expedition was able to establish the continental proportions of Antarctica, based on a survey of some fifteen hundred miles of the coast.

The next major surveying task involved the Fiji Islands. There Wilkes investigated the murder in 1834 of ten members of an American ship by a Fiji leader named Vendovi, brother of the king of Rewah. Hudson invited the king and his family on board the *Peacock* and then held them hostage until Vendovi surrendered, which he readily did the following day. Upon admitting his role in the murders, Vendovi was made prisoner and told he would be taken to America, where, Reynolds declared, he would learn "that to kill a white man was the very worst thing a Fegee man could do."

Shortly thereafter, Fijians on the island of Malolo attacked a small surveying party that had gone ashore to purchase food. Two officers, one of them Midshipman Wilkes Henry, nephew of the commander, were killed. Wilkes retaliated by destroying the two principal towns on Malolo and killing some eighty natives.

Except for the violence, the explorers were proud of the work accomplished in Fiji. They corrected a number of errors on existing charts, made impressive additions to their growing collections of natural history specimens, and learned firsthand about the existence of cannibalism, a practice about which they had heard many rumors but had generally discounted. The evidence was obtained by officers on board the *Peacock,* when a native visited the ship while eating flesh from a cooked human head. "Every one on the Ship was affected with a nervous and terrible feeling of mingled horror and disgust," Reynolds reported. Disgusted though they may have been, the scientifics purchased the head for their collections.

After a welcome respite in the Sandwich, or Hawaiian, Islands, the squadron planned to rendezvous on the northwest coast of North America. Once again misfortune intervened, however, when the *Peacock* struck a sandbar while attempting to enter the mouth of the Columbia River. The crew survived, but the ship and its scientific collections were lost. Although Reynolds lost most of his belongings because they were still on board the *Peacock,* he was not directly involved because he had been reassigned to the *Flying Fish* when the squadron left Hawaii. Nevertheless, he witnessed the last moments of the beloved *Peacock,* which he described in graphic detail for his family: "We have *all* got *safely away* from the Columbia River, for which I thank God!"

Because of the loss of the *Peacock,* Wilkes had to abandon plans to proceed to Japan. Had he done so, the expedition might well have succeeded in opening that island country to the West more than a decade before the Perry expedition. This would have been of small comfort to the explorers, who by now merely wanted to get home. Some wits had already renamed their enterprise the "Everlasting Expedition."

In addition to conducting extensive surveys in what was soon to become Oregon Territory, Wilkes sent a party overland to California (then still part of Mexico). Wilkes picked this party up in San Francisco Bay after completing his surveys along the Oregon coast and then proceeded to Oahu with the *Vincennes, Porpoise,* and *Oregon*—a merchant vessel purchased in Astoria to replace the *Peacock.* In Hawaii, these vessels met with the *Flying Fish,* which had sailed there directly from Oregon. From there, Wilkes set a course for the United States, which virtually meant circling the globe.

The return voyage was anticlimactic. En route, the explorers visited South Africa after the Philippines and Singapore, where Wilkes sold the *Flying Fish* because it was no longer seaworthy.

Once into the Atlantic, the voyagers expected Wilkes would set a direct course for the United States. He did so for the *Vincennes* but sent the *Porpoise* and *Oregon* home by way of Rio de Janeiro to pick up additional scientific specimens—five small containers of minerals, shells, bird skins, and plants, as it turned out. The officers felt the detour was ordered to give the *Vincennes* the glory of returning home first.

By now, Wilkes had managed to alienate most of his junior officers, including Reynolds. "[He merits] hanging, only that he deserved impaling, long long ago," Reynolds confided in his private journal. As is described in the epilogue, the junior officers had their revenge when the squadron reached home.

*Voyage
to the
Southern Ocean*

My dear Sister

Letter upon Departure

Norfolk
August 12th 1838

Lydia[1]

. . . The Ships are down at Hampton Roads, all of them; the first move of the Exploring Expedition has at length been made. The Squadron is increased by the addition of two Pilot Boats purchased at New York.[2] Passed Midshipmen will command them; I wish my rank would entitle me to one. 'Tis something to be a Captain, and those Boats are large, beautiful and swift—perhaps I may return *Captain* Reynolds. I have not slept on board yet, having

[1] *Lydia Moore Reynolds (1818–1896) was the eldest sibling at home. Sam was working in York County; the rest, except for the two youngest, were away at school. Lydia seemed always to have played the "responsible" role— confidante to her brother Will, amanuensis for her busy family, housekeeper during her mother's final illness and after. Her marriage in 1846 to Cornwall ironmaster Nathan Evans took her away from her active family and friends to the wilds of northwestern Pennsylvania and the management of floundering Lucinda Furnace (Letter No. 15, n. 47). Three of their four children were born there, and, as William wrote her in the 1850s, she was as much an exile as he, invalided in Hawaii. After the sale of Lucinda in 1858, her husband tried farming in Chester County, Pennsylvania, an iron furnace in Ohio, an iron foundry in Fort Wayne, Indiana, and, finally, retirement as a gentleman farmer outside West Chester, Pennsylvania. Here Lydia was close to her family again, but her life was never as easy as her sisters'.*
[2] *The* Sea Gull *and the* Flying Fish; *for the ships of the squadron, see Letter No. 1, n. 1.*

Lydia Moore Reynolds, William's sister.
Courtesy Anne Hoffman Cleaver.

been most busily and arduously engaged in expending $1000 for the mess and $600 for myself. We have a great many stores, and I flatter myself that the mess over which I preside will be most respectable, tasty and somewhat stylish.[3] When I get my room arranged, it will be carpeted, cushioned, curtained (one set crimson dama[s]k, one white), mirrored, silver candlesticked, etc., etc., etc.—a little *boudoir*, most exquisitely luxurious in its arrangements. I like the associates we shall have during the cruise—these enthusiastic Artists, and those

[3] *It was then the custom on navy ships for officers to make their own eating arrangements. The wardroom officers and groups of six to eight junior officers in steerage would pool their money to buy food, supplemented by flour and other staples available from the ship.*

headlong, indefatigable pursures [*pursuers*] and slayers of birds, beasts and fishes, and the gatherers of shells, rocks, insects, etc., etc. They are leaving their comfortable homes, to follow the strong bent of their minds, to garner up the strange things of strange lands, which fact proves that the ruling passion is strong in life.

Titian Rembrandt Peale, the great Naturalist, is with us; he is most devoted to his favorite pursuit and has passed the greatest part of his life time in hunting subjects to preserve. He was with Major Long over the Rocky Mountains, has been in Canada after the moose, etc., and to South America after other things, he is perhaps the most scientific slaughterer of living hanimals [*sic*] now existing.[4] The other Scientifics are said to possess talents and much zeal in their respective pursuits. We, the ignoramuses, will no doubt take great interest in learning the origin, nature and history of many things, which we have before regarded with curious and admiring eyes.

I see before us an intensely interesting cruise and a career of wild and exciting adventure; may we go safely through all danger, and return with knowledge that will be useful to the world and that will gratify those whom we love best, at home.

I have purchased two Journals of 5 quires each; if I fill them, I trust I shall make a perusal interesting. . . .

Sunday evening

The Captain, Mr. May and Mr. Carr[5] arrived this morning. I am on shore for the last time, settling the mess accounts. Today we had

[4] *Titian Ramsey Peale (1799–1885), from Philadelphia, one of the expedition's naturalists and the youngest son of portraitist, revolutionary, early museum organizer, and naturalist Charles Willson Peale (1741–1827). One of Titian's older brothers was artist Rembrandt Peale (1778–1860). An excellent marksman, Peale had gone on bird and other collecting expeditions to Georgia, Florida, and Colombia between 1818 and 1832. He had acted as assistant naturalist and painter on the expedition to the upper Missouri and Rocky Mountains led by army engineer Stephen Long (1784–1864) in 1819–1820. Beginning in the late 1840s, he served for twenty-three years as a patent examiner in Washington (Watson 1985:47–59).*

[5] *Passed Midshipman William May was Reynolds's cabinmate and close friend from naval school at Norfolk. Born of a prominent Washington family*

the first meal on board in the steerage; all hands have been living together previously. Tuesday night or Wednesday morning we go to Sea.

I am perfectly charmed with every thing on board, and have the most glowing hopes of a glorious cruise, nothing could tempt me to withdraw. I am wedded to the Expedition and its fate, sink or swim. . . .

Give my most affectionate love to everyone at home and remember me most kindly to those who may inquire about me. When you write, your letters must be very lengthy and always send newspapers with them. Good bye and do not let Elly forget her brother.[6]

William

[*Outside wrapper:*] Miss Lydia M. Reynolds
Lebanon
Pennsylvania
by Hably [*Hubley*] Jenkins

(his father, Frederick [1773–1849], was family physician of President George Washington and a leading citizen), May had been appointed midshipman in 1831 through senatorial influence. While serving in the West Indies in 1835, he and Augustus Baldwin (Letter No. 15, n. 53) had faced each other in a duel—one of several May fought during his career. He was twice wounded in action, once as a midshipman in Sumatra and later, seriously, at Tabasco during the Mexican War. He later rose to the rank of commander shortly before his death in 1861 at the age of forty-seven, having suffered from ill health since the expedition (Topham 1930; Bauer 1969:116; ZB).

Overton Carr, one of the lieutenants assigned to the Vincennes, was described as "stout and healthy, diligent, indefatigable and successful" by the principal of the Washington Catholic Seminary in an 1827 letter of recommendation to the navy. During 1854–1855, Carr commanded a survey expedition to the Rio de la Plata. He apparently retired from the navy in 1861 as a commander (ZB).

6 *William's sister Eleanor was three years old. See Letter No. 9, n. 13.*

Letter No. 1

Vincennes at Sea, Thursday Evening
August 30th 1838
Lat 37° N.
Long 54° W.

The other day when dining with the Captain he remarked "that in less than a month, he hoped that we would have a plentiful supply of Fruit and *Grapes.*" Now these latter flourish in Madeira and we have come to the conclusion that to Madeira we are bound, first, and then to Rio de Janeiro. I make a commencement, to take advantage of any opportunity that may offer.

We have had some bad weather since we sailed but now it is charming, the sails asleep, the breeze moderate, the moon bright, the Sea smooth as a summer lake, the sea sickness of the "Green ones" is over and every one has a smiling face *and* a good appetite.

The Relief Store Ship being too dull a Sailor, we parted company with her some days ago, directing her to "make the best of her way to Rio, direct." Poor fellows! they will miss the delicious times which we hope to enjoy in the Sunny Ile of Madeira. The Peacock and Flying Fish (Pilot Boat) separated from us the other night in a Blow, and we have not fallen in with them since. The Brig Porpoise and Schooner Sea Gull are with us now.[1] We spoke a vessel bound home when a few days out and I suppose you saw her report in the Papers.

[1] *Of the six vessels that began the cruise, the sloop of war* Vincennes *was the largest at 700 tons and 127 feet in length, with a complement of 190 persons. The sloop of war* Peacock *was next at 559 tons and 118 feet, with a*

The Scientifics have had one chance since we sailed. On a calm day many fish were around us, and we caught them in numbers. Instead of consigning them instantly to the cooks, the Scientifics went at them with the utmost eagerness and relish, dissected them, found out many mysterious things in the stomach etc., talked over many hard names, and then took drawings of the whole and the parts; all they did was Greek to us, but somewhat interesting, and I look forward to much that will be novel and pleasing in the result of their performances.

I went in a Boat on that day, among the masses of Gulf Weed to catch small fish. We were fortunate in getting two tiny fellows, the most diminutive I ever saw in the great Ocean; some large Dolphins we caught also and if we admired the changing of the bright tints of their bodies, as they gasped away their lives, we likewise did justice [to] their flavour after death. In our little boat we pulled from Ship to Ship, passing the compliments of the day and making a little excitement. The Captain's orders were that "every officer of the deck" shall alter the Ship's course and perform all manoeuvres that may be necessary to aid and facilitate the projects of the Scientific Gentlemen. I expect we will *square away* after a whale, or make sail after a runaway shark or chase a Devil fish to leeward, and do a great many things that were never heard of before, nor would be now, were it not for the Scientifics: here's success to them, may they have a large book to publish when we return.

We have formed a Boat Club among us: the "Antartic Boat Club." We have a very sailor like uniform[2] and I anticipate many pleasant

---

complement of 130. The supply ship Relief *was third in size at 468 tons and 109 feet, with 75 men. The fastest sailor was the two-masted brig* Porpoise *(224 tons, 88 feet, with 65 men). The squadron was completed by two converted pilot boats brought along for surveying work in the Pacific islands: the* Sea Gull *(110 tons, 74 feet) and the* Flying Fish *(96 tons, 70 feet), both with complements of 15.*

   [2] *Navy regulations did not specify official uniforms for enlisted men until 1841, but procurement of seamen's clothing by contract did tend to standardize their apparel before that time. Seamen typically wore a black brimmed hat, short jacket with brass buttons, white blouse with blue bib, and full white trousers, when in dress uniform (Tily 1964:74–97). Their daily dress, without bib and jacket, is depicted on page 242.*

Charles Wilkes, by Thomas Sully. Courtesy U.S. Naval Academy Museum, Annapolis.

trips in the Boat bearing the name of "*White Hankerchief.*" When we were voting for the name, I put in a certain fair one's, whom you wot of; two others were guilty of the same, but the First Lieutenant's *White Hk* carried the vote most enthusiastically and we poor fellows were in a glorious minority; the names we gave were Julia, Virginia, and —— guess.[3] We, the officers, form the crew of the Antartic Boat Club, of the Boat White Handk. When we wish to visit any interesting spot, to go on shore on any particular occasion, and to do many other things, we will don our uniform, take to the oars and pull away. Much fun will we have in the "White Handkerchief"; all of us have some reminiscence attached to one of those delicate articles, and we are satisfied with so general a name, though it was given exclusively in compliment to the first Lieut.[4]

[3] *No doubt William's future wife, Rebecca Krug (Introduction).*

[4] *Thomas T. Craven (1808–1887) was first lieutenant of the* Vincennes *until the squadron left Chile in June 1839. He was detached in Valparaíso to*

And I am officer of the Deck, and my present ambition is gratified in having the trumpet and directing the movements of a Ship; I did not expect the honor nor should I have had it elsewhere for two or three years. I cannot explain to you the feeling; for though we only take advantage of or oppose the wind and waves, it seems as if we directed them: "thus far shall thou come and no farther, here shall thy present course be staid." To handle the fabric with exquisite skill, to have hundreds move at your bidding, to run in rivalry and successfully with the Squadron and passing vessels, to laugh at the wind and bid defiance to the waves, ah! the excitement is good and glorious, and the goodly prospect of strange Lands and wild adventure that is before us. *My* proffession, above any other in the world. Hurrah! for the Exploring Expedition!

I belong to that Division of the Crew which will be employed in all excursions on Shore; if there are any rows, we will have to settle them, and when the Scientifics make journeys inland *we* will accompany them for protection. We are drilling the men to the use of the musket, to march and counter march. *Jim Gibson* is 1st Lieut. of my squad, and I hope for much fun and more information during the trips we shall make in this way in strange lands. Not one cloud dims my future now; the cruise promises to be one of extraordinary delight while it lasts, and one to which I can always refer with pride and pleasure when it is over. James Gibson is very well and is perfectly correct in his behaviour—he is one of the Petty Officers; at Litiz we were equals![5]

---

await the arrival of the Sea Gull *from Tierra del Fuego. Craven, whose grandfather Thomas Tingley had been commandant of the Washington Navy Yard and whose father had also served as a purser and storekeeper, had been with Reynolds on the* Boxer *and the* Peacock *in 1832–1834. He later commanded the* Porpoise *in slave trade suppression off Africa and was commandant of midshipmen at Annapolis. After the Civil War, he went on to become a rear admiral and to command the navy's North Pacific Squadron based in California, where Reynolds, commanding the* Lackawanna *in the Pacific, served under him as a captain in 1868–1869 (Reynolds 1868; C. Reynolds 1978:83–84; ZB).*

[5] *James H. Gibson, listed as a carpenter in navy records, had evidently been Reynolds's classmate in John Beck's school in Lititz. Gibson was a relative of the Hubley family of Lancaster, but his mother lived near*

I often talk over old times with him in our night watches and for the life of me, I cannot help calling him *Jim* as I used to do in times gone by. I hope when we return to persuade him to leave the service and try to be mate of some merchant man.

Ah, you should see my State Room. On either side of it are couches covered with Blue damask running the length of the apartment; these are for lounges by day, for beds at night, when the sheets are substituted for the Blue covering. White and crimson curtains hang around the Bulkhead; the Bureau has a handsome cover and the Mirror is beautiful; the Candlesticks are plated and kept as bright as silver; a *Brussels* Carpet hides the deck and some soft mats yield most luxuriously to our tread. Various other elegancies adorn the room, and last though not least, the two occupants, May and myself. And the wash stand is an ornament and its furniture—white, with sprigs of green and gilt—is in perfect taste. Bowie knives, pistols, cutlasses etc. displayed in different places and figures, give the man of war finish to the whole. Would you were here to see all of us, to look upon the Ocean and the white sails upon its waters, and to step ashore with me at Madeira. Alas! those unfortunates who live on shore, they see nothing, nor are they ever alive to some of the finest feelings of our nature. The words of the Psalmist are true—"They who go down to the Sea in Ships see the wonders of the deep and the great works of the Lord."

Monday, September 3rd 1838
Long 42

This morning my watch was from 4 to 8, my favorite one. I love to see the stars disappearing one by one before the grey light of day['s] dawn, the brightening of the eastern sky, the masses of gorgeous clouds, the golden speck in the horizon as the sun first shows himself, which grows gradually into the full and fiery globe when he is entirely above the water; ah! day break and sunrise upon the

---

Columbia, ten miles west of the city. Curiously, his name is not found in the later lists of officers and petty officers Reynolds kept in his Journal No. 1. Charles Erskine (1985:26) refers to a fellow seaman James H. Gibbon being rated a coxswain when the squadron left Madeira. Reynolds always spelled Lititz in the original German manner, Litiz.

ocean. Would you were here to look and to be charmed as you gaze with me.

Sail ho! from the mast head, and crossing our course, comes on a Gallant Ship; she is English. We near each other, we are alongside, those who never met before nor will again now hold a brief communion; the news and hearty greetings are interchanged, and the companions of a moment are separated. On the deck of the Englishman were two lovely women and some children, returning to their homes: I could discern their features plainly with the glass; there they stood, among the group of Gentlemen, their hair unconfined and floating in the breeze, their morning robes loose and graceful, looking like Sea Nymphs just arisen from the deep. 'Twas a sudden but most pleasing apparition, and that meeting forms another incident which I can recal with feelings of delight. It sets one all in a fever to *see* females at Sea. At Madeira I hope to enjoy myself much and shall endeavour to find the blue eyed Louisa whom I saw there three years ago.[6]

It is so strange to me to look around and find none but youthful faces among the officers—a young Captain, with boys for his subordinates—no gray hairs, no veterans among us. None of those 'hard a weather' characters, of whom there are generally more than one on board our ships. We are all in the Spring time of life—may we live to reach its winter.

Thursday Morning

All day yesterday we were cruising about to look for an Island said to be near our position. We sailed *over* the place marked on the chart, but neither saw nor *felt* any thing of the Island. But the alteration in our course was productive of a novel and interesting sight. We descried a long, dark and low object on the surface of the water and steered directly for it. The news, a wreck! a wreck! went

[6] *Reynolds evidently stopped at Madeira during his second navy cruise in 1834–1836. According to his letters, the* Potomac *sailed from Boston to join the ship of the line* Delaware *off Gibraltar to await word from the French government about payments on claims for American shipping damaged during the Napoleonic Wars. The squadron then proceeded to the Mediterranean, where in October Reynolds transferred to the* Delaware *for the return home.*

quickly through the Ship and soon all hands were on deck. Any trifle causes excitement at Sea, but such a cry stirs the blood to an unusual pitch. Glasses were in requisition and eyes were straining to make out the true character of the floating mass. Some could distinguish the mast and timbers, and several swore positively they saw people standing up and waving signals. We were in a perfect fever to have all doubts solved: nearer, nearer we came to it, and opinions changed. At length, to a certainty, all agreed it was a tree and so it was—a Giant tree: the limbs whitened by exposure and standing perpendicular were what had seemed to us *masts* and *men*.

We sent two boats to catch fish, for myriads of them are always found about floating things, and hove the Ship [to], to wait their return. The other vessels followed our example and the scene became highly animated. The shouts of officers and men, and the quick movements of the boats, the glancing harpoons, and the leaping fish (do not laugh, fish do leap, and their whole lengths out of water), the huge tree rolling among the mimic waves, the large Ships in the majesty of repose, crowded with eager faces, the saucy Schooner [*i.e., the Sea Gull*] dashing here and there with a graceful beauty in her motion and appearance that is indescribable, but which to the eye of a Sailor is lovely to behold. Ah! that Schooner, she is the sweetest craft that ever swam; the English will look upon her with jealous eyes.

The tree we supposed to have come from the Mississippi, set by the Gulf Stream. I have a piece of it and I intend to let nothing that is curious slip by me this cruise without procuring it if possible. The Scientifics have made another haul and it is most curious to see the patient manner in which they toil, toil, seemingly for trifles, giving up their whole soul to their employment. On calm days, they drag scoop nets on board, and as the ocean is teeming with living things, they find many, the most minute and beautiful to look at, and having every thing that is wonderful in their character to hear of, by the aid of microscopes eggs etc. almost invisible to the eye are found to possess rare beauty. The Artists copy every thing from life and to watch them is another source of gratification.

We have on board the Histories of all the French and English expeditions to the Seas we are to visit. The works were published by the respective Governments in superb style, full of plates, colored and plain. I have been looking over them and only wish that we were *now* among the *Islands:* ah! we shall have a glorious time, wilder than the romance of imagination.

A New Zealand chief is on board, we are to leave him at *his Home*, from which he has been absent 9 or 10 years! He is civilized in a manner, eats cooked meat, and has some idea of a God! Whether he will relapse into his old habits when he is again among his countrymen, is a query? I shall watch him closely. He was exhibited over the U.S. and we often have him to dance and sing after the manner of his nation—'tis as good as a play. And better than one, to talk with him about his youthful days, his feelings on leaving home, his impressions on landing in America and the change which came over him when he was able to think and reason for himself. Something of human nature can be learned from a Savage, from a cannibal New Zealander; only think! a cannibal, how Robinson Crusoe like. And his face and body are tatoed [*tattooed*], just the same as the pictures in the Penny Magazine represent.[7] Well, we shall find people as interesting from their rude and primeval habits, living in Lands where the white men have never trod, before the cruise is out; and once more, "here's to the future!"

We keep up the good old custom of the Sea, in celebrating Saturday night: Sweet hearts and wives, the theme! Fancy us all, removed from the spells of woman's presence, but in all our hearts doing reverence to the memory "of those we've left behind us." The verses (which you can find in my book) commencing with "as slow an Ship, her foamy track" etc. are read as the commencement, and the burthen of the song is the toast; then comes "Sweet hearts and wives," and afterwards out of respect to the 1st Lieut. the "White Handkerchief"; then come many silent ones too dear and precious to be breathed aloud. There are but *three* married officers on board; nearly every one of the others has left his heart behind him.

[7] *In his* Narrative of the United States Exploring Expedition, *Charles Wilkes (1845, 2:401) identifies this man as John Sac or Tuatti. Sac was used as interpreter on some of the Pacific islands by the squadron until being discharged in Honolulu in October 1840; he had decided not to stay in New Zealand.*

September 15th, 2 P.M.

Just now the most strange, wild and appalling thing occurred such
as I never heard of before and hope never to witness again. I had the
forenoon watch, we were sailing along with a glorious breeze right
aft, running 9 or 10 knots, several strange vessels in sight and the
Ocean with its breaking waves so beautiful as to call all the Scientifics
on deck to look and admire. At 12 the Captain told me to make more
sail and chase a Brig that was ahead; we all felt elated and excited
from the speed at which we were going and the way in which we
were leaving every thing astern of us. I gave the necessary orders,
and looking aloft, I saw that something was wrong with the Main
Top Gallant Sail (the next to the Loftiest on the centre mast) and
called out, "to let go the M.T.G. Buntline," at the same time
bellowing to the man on the Top Gallant Yard to over haul it. The
force of the wind blew the sail out full and when the rope was let go,
it went so quickly that it caught the poor fellow around the neck
several times and swung him off his foothold; one awful cry came
from his lips, another came from the Boatswain, who was the first to
see him from the deck; both unearthly in their tones, such cries as
would almost wake the dead; there *hung the man* swinging to and fro
with the roll of the Ship, his form showing terribly distinct against the
clear sky. The sight was most horrible to all and to me! from whose
lips *were* to come the orders, when any thing *could* be done. Thank
God! I did not lose my presence of mind. I was not confused, but did
we haul on the rope, it would be to choke him instantly; did we slack
it, he would be dashed to the deck. *There he hung!* A moment before
my voice had been in his ears, and in executing my orders, he was
meeting his death. Neither could we then clue up the sail, but as the
rope which held him gradually slacked, he came below the sail,
which I immediately took in; by this time many of the men had gone
aloft, the rigging was alive with them; and now the sail was in, they
caught his body, but for a moment and it was torn from their grasp.
Again they have him, again the Ship rolls, the rope jerks, but the
hold is firm, and the rope is cleared from his throat. Thank Heaven,
he is saved, came from the lips of many below; *he is dead!* was uttered
in husky tones from aloft; his face was black, and to his rude
shipmates he shewed no signs of life. Can you imagine the scene; the

Ship careering onward, unconscious of the tragedy she was the stage of, and the hundreds upon her decks, with their souls harrowed to the quick by the dreadful spectacle they were beholding.

The man was lowered down into the Top, and miraculous to relate, recovered his senses. The rope had been around his jaw, and the *back* of his head, and had stopped his breath, instead of breaking his neck. He was somewhat bruised, but is now doing well. As the men told him when the Doctor quitted his side, "he was not born to be hung, or he would not have missed so good a chance." Sailors will have their joke, even in affairs of Death and danger.[8]

Do you know what it is to *lay out* on a Ship's Yard, a spar about as large as one's body, at a giddy height above and over the boiling Sea: and not steady then, but pitching and tossing most fearfully with the motion of the Sea; a rope for your foot hold, another for your hand to grasp and then to work, when you are out to the extreme end, forty feet clear of the Ship, the water far beneath you? Perhaps you do not. And it a matter of great Surprise to *our* Landsmen on board, and to all on first going to Sea, to see the men as much at their ease aloft as if they were in a comfortable parlour. 'Tis custom makes them so. *Something* like eel skinning though, *"nothing* when you are used to it."

Funchal Roads, Tuesday, Sept 18th

I must change the subject, to one that may be more interesting. Sunday morning at 8 we made Madeira,[9] run along the Land all day, having the greatest succession of beautiful prospects as we went onwards. Description fails, it is impossible to convey to you any idea of the bewitching scenery. But conceive ravines, bridges, rushing waters, vineyards on the smooth sides of the mountains, churches, convents, fortresses, cottages, palaces, gardens—"all in sweet confusion scattered"—a clear sky, a calm ocean, many vessels and a long range of high land and possibly you may have a *faint* vision of the alluring sight then and now before *me*. I have been on shore; I

[8] *The hapless sailor was George Porter, a maintopman. Porter survived this incident only to die of dysentery near the straits of Sunda in March 1842 (Wilkes 1845, 5:415).*

[9] *Madeira is situated about 350 miles off the coast of Morocco. The islands had been a Portuguese colony since 1418.*

knew nothing of Madeira from my recollections, my visit had been so brief and hurried. Now I know it is a place I should like to pass some time in. Confound the thing, I will try to tell you what it looks like, but I have not time to arrange words, thoughts or sentences, so excuse me if I [Draw?] loosely.

The Squadron minus the Relief are at anchor 1/4 of a mile from the landing. The shore makes a semicircular sweep, the two horns or extremities being to Seaward of us. The Land rises abruptly in some places, in others by a succession of gentle ridges, to an altitude of from 2 to 5000 feet; it is much broken by wild ravines, down which the rain reaches the bay in the winter season. There is also table land on the summit, which is irregular, surface and height. Every spot excepting in the ravines is cultivated with the vine or grain, and innumerable houses dot the hillside.

The town stands close on the water's edge and is built up some 7 or 800 feet; it is walled in and fortified along the whole front towards the water, the entrances through strong and narrow Gates. Forts perched on commanding and picturesque sites look down with a surly air, and add much to the picture by their own appearance and the strong contrast they show to the quaintly built churches and convents by their side; the weak near to the strong. The architecture of all the buildings is of the olden style and perched as they are among the rocks and rude hollows they have a Barbaric Saracenic air that reminds me of the South of Spain and the opposite Shore of Africa, where yet are the traces of the Moors. The rich vineyards show well over the sunny hills, some places they stray down for a little ways in to the ravines. The streets are narrow, winding, precipitous mostly, level seldom; they are paved with pebles small as a boy's hand, well driven in to the clay beneath and so arranged as to make a rough mosaic. What labour and perseverance were requisite to finish them. Three or four walled up, deep canal like chasms or gorges pass from the ravines through the town as conductors of the waters—art has built the wall, nature forced the channels; art has not tamed nature, and these same passes are rugged enough. Huge rocks that weigh many tons, brought by the torrents from above, lie all along the bottom and the beach is covered with the like deposits. A small stream was trickling through, barely sufficient to wet the clothes for the women, who were washing. Streets and houses run right along the verge of these conduits; communication is sustained by means of high bridges.

To look up one of these beds from below and trace its wild and torturous course from the summit, catching here and there a glimpse of a waterfall, with the many bridges rising one above the other, the avenues of stately trees, the crowded houses and crowds of people, and the bottom with its piles of rocks—you have before you a strange mixture of scenery. I stood on the lower bridge where I had a clear view aloft and out to sea. Long I remained for I was charmed as I looked and I thought I should like to witness the terrible grandeur of a storm in the winter, when the now almost dry channel would be the course of the torrent as it came down.

I rode up to the top of the mountain: oh I wish you had been here. 'Tis a pity that your rides to elevated spots should be confined to the mine hill.[10] The Road is almost *"up and down,"* but that is the sea phrase for *perpendicular.* The one which we went up was paved all the way, like the streets, running right through the Vine Yards. I never before saw so much of the picturesque, of the beautiful in miniature, intermixed with the grand and sublime, in scenery. A high wall, built up some 10 or 15 feet to the level of the vineyard, bounded the road on either side, and rising terrace fashion. The vines overhung the walls and the clusters of tempting grapes seemed ready to drop into our mouths. Little streams crossed the road, large trees grew on the banks—the chestnut, poplar, and weeping willow looked like home. But many were the pictures that would have charmed an Artist, for they fascinated us—the cottages peeping from the sheltering vines, the groups of peasantry, men, women and children, gathering the luscious harvest or lounging over the walls to look at the strangers, the winding paths that struck off from our road at intervals over the rocks and down into the valleys beneath, the mansions of the rich seated in the midst of splendid Gardens, oh there were so many beauties in the ride that I despair of telling you them all. So many little spots, so simple in their loveliness, and having cast around them the witchery of all that we deem poetical and romantic. The vines grew over trellice work and completely

---

[10] *Cornwall Furnace was adjacent to the ore banks known as Big Hill, Middle Hill, and Grassy Hill.*

shade the ground beneath them; under their wide spreading branches, the cottages are built, and they, like the people, partake of the character of the country: they do not seem the work of hands, but as if they had been placed there by the great architect of [the] whole. I never could fancy love in a cottage before; here it might exist. The Island is shut out from the world and those dwellings are so secluded, so peaceful looking, that one thinks ill could never come near them, that there the bad passions of men would never find a vent. I wish that you were all here to see.

Looking back, we saw the town immediately below us and the blue ocean so vast in expanse that we could scar[c]e tell where sky and sea met: from a great height, the ocean always seems a part of the clouds. We reached the church built by the pious who travel up and down the mountain; the materials were all carried up from below, and nothing but superstition would have accomplished the task. There is a loveliness in this same superstitious religion: they who believe in it, place in it all their hopes, give to it all their means. They would starve rather than the Shrine of their saints should be dishonored; they worship the holy martyrs with an affection more than human, and devote much time and money to the adornment of their Shrines—alas! that they should be wrong!

From the Terrace in front of the Church the view was magnificent; the range of the Island and all it[s] broken but most beautiful features was spread out before us, and all around, ay farther than the eye could reach was the glorious Sea, *our home!* At that moment all seemed glowing and joyous, the very waves (as Mr. Bulwer[11] says) wore a golden and happy smile. And there were the Ships that are to hold us for so long—that are to carry us over the world—far, far, down they were dwindled almost to insignificance.

On we went up to the summit and the road which had hitherto been paved and though steep and winding, not dangerous, at least to our sure footed beasts, now was no road, but a way—paths cut spirally and zigzag, broken and rough, running along the verge of precipices that almost made one dizzy to look down, crossing the ravines over bold bridges, and turning so short that the horse's head

[11] *Edward Bulwer-Lytton (1803–1873), English novelist, also dramatist and politician, the first Baron Lytton.*

would be around one corner and his tail the other. And yet over these places we went often at full speed, so fast that we shook off the guides' hold of the horses tails. Each owner accompanies his nag, and by aid of long poles and a grip on the nag's crupper kept close by us all the way. But when we flew over the stones and up the fearful acclivities, they could not retain their hold and we left them astern. The excitement of such a ride is most glorious. I had the lead, for my charger bore himself most gallantly, the *Purser* was next,[12] and a whole troop behind. More than once I stopped to see the train, some coming slowly down an abrupt descent, others thundering over the bridge that crossed a chasm, and some coming close in my wake. Mazeppas' ride was a trifle,[13] and yet the horses never faltered, never stumbled, never fagged—the guides assuring us they neither wanted water or rest. On, on, we sped, pausing occasionally to enjoy the view. The wind came sweeping down the gorges of the mountain, and when we turned suddenly, it struck us with great force—away went caps, and sometimes almost riders too. And the waterfalls that we more than once passed over and often saw in the distance, they were grand, and the little villages, and the endless succession of vineyards, and the emerging from narrow defiles to a clear and open view, and the wondering looks of the peasants as we dashed by them, and the amazing jabber of the guides, and our own merry talk and laughter, and the rich valleys that were not ravines, and the ornamented and spacious dwellings and grounds of the wealthy, all these made the ride one which I shall long remember with delight, and may perhaps repeat.

We went to the Convent, and I purchased the prettiest flowers that I could find. The nuns did not have much of a collection on hand, and mine are not so beautiful as many that I have seen. Still I think when you see them, you will be tempted to try if they have any odour; but you will have to wait three long years first.

[12] *The purser of the* Vincennes, *Richard Russell Waldron. Apparently a native of New Hampshire, he had served in the navy since 1835; Waldron died in 1846 (ZB).*

[13] *Ivan Mazepa (ca. 1640–1709), a Cossack leader whom legend said was tied onto a wild horse as a youth and sent into the steppes by a jealous husband. Byron depicted this ordeal in* Mazeppa (1819).

This time we saw a nun, who was young and most lovely; her eye was one for a kindly glance of which one might almost die, at least one who has been at Sea a month. She was beautiful, Sister Genevieve, and her voice was so sweet, for she talked with us through the medium of the guides. Her pretty hands worked the flowers that were now to pass into sacrilegious palms. Two grated doors separated us, forbidding the practicability of a touch, but her face just filled in between the bars and it was a lovely picture, though set in an iron frame. The eternal little revolving hole in the wall, which had one opening which they turned inside and placed in it the articles and then turning it around, they came out to us—jealous care. If I was Captain of one of the Pilot boats, I should certainly carry her off, that dear Sister Genevieve. She looks as if she ought not to be a nun, although the nun's garment became her beauty well.

An elder nun who was there all the while was of commanding stature, dignified and stately, with her features composed to marble like stillness. She was one from whom all feelings, save those of rigid devotion to her vows, had departed; her decorum was austere. Calm and placid she remained while we were making selections, but a half smile crossed her features as the money jingled in her hand. She returned one Dollar which she said was not *"buono"*—mammon had not yet been driven from her heart.

The younger, the lovely one, into whose face I gazed because I could not resist the charm, and she had not enough of the nun in her to withdraw, well she gave us some sweetmeats of her own preserving—ah charming Genevieve. I shall never see you again, you have been the passing vision for a moment—of your early life or of your later years I shall never know. May they be happy.

Had I been an artist I should have sketched them as they stood or sat in their mournfully simple dresses behind the grated door. What a host of thoughts nuns and convents bring through our minds. Ages past sweep dimly by us; and to be in one, face to face with the reality—ah, you will never know the charm of such moments as these, your lives are all too tame at home. And yet at times I think I could live among you always, if—but the thought is vain, and transient, and goes almost as soon as it comes. This cruise I could not relinquish. I see in the future too much that will be exciting, that will be delightful, and when it is over, Europe must be traversed by my footsteps. When that is accomplished, who knows what will happen then. I am afraid I shall be a wandering bachelor all my days.

I must break off, and you must depend on my Journal or my next letter from Rio for more [stuff?] if you be not tired of all this. I could write for a week about Madeira, but you may think yourself lucky to get off with four sheets of prating.[14] An American Brig will sail tomorrow for New York—the Cazenove.

[*Later*]

I have written every spare moment that has offered and now have not more time; the Brig sails this evening in a few hours from now, and I am relieved for a short time to finish my letter; it is my watch on deck. You shall have a long yarn soon again, and more afterwards, unless you write me that I am tedious.

We are perfectly happy on board here. The Captain is all he should be and all the rest are like him; and we are so comfortable, you should see my room, it is the admiration of every one; and we live so well, and we look forward to so much of interest and pleasure.

I forward the Feather flowers by a Gentleman passenger, who will deliver them to Mr. Edward Coleman.[15] I directed them to his care, knowing no one else, and have written to him to excuse the trouble given. I hope you will get them safe; they are for no one in particular, to be preserved until I return. And now Good bye, my best love to you all and my best wishes. Kind remembrances to all friends of both sexes young and old; mention of them all when you write. I shall expect long letters from you by the Store Ship which is to sail in November; what she brings we will get in April at Valparaiso.

[14] *Reynolds described Madeira for some twenty-eight pages in his Journal (1:6–34).*

[15] *Edward Coleman (1792–1841), good friend and business associate of John Reynolds, was an older brother of Thomas Bird Coleman, mentioned in the Introduction. Two short-lived Reynolds babies were named for him. Coleman lived in Philadelphia, a convenient address to send packages.*

Do not let Elly forget me. I will write to Rebecca Myer, as I promised, when the flight of time will make a letter more acceptable.[16]

Adieu, God's blessing be with you all,

William

Lydia M. Reynolds
  Sep. 20th 1838

[*Inner wrapper:*] The Brig Cazenove which takes this letter will also take the Feather Flowers. A passenger will have them delivered in Philad. Their value is $4.00, if any customs house duties are to pay.
[*Outer wrapper:*] Brig Casenove
                    New York
[*Postmark:*] New York, November 10 [17]

---

[16] *Rebecca Myer was Rebecca Krug's cousin. While visiting Cornwall, she had added a postscript to Lydia's last letter (4 August 1838) reminding William of his promise to write her. She also noted that "Our friend 'Jane' [Rebecca Krug] returned from the west last week"—her trip to Pittsburgh mentioned in the Introduction—and teased him for giving her no message for Jane, especially as she had delivered Jane's message to him. As far as is known, the only personal letters William wrote from the expedition were to his family.*

[17] *Lydia's answering letter of 18 November was received in May 1839, in Valparaíso: "If you do not stop writing till I tell you, you may write forever." She wrote of her summer travels with her parents and the Coleman girls to Philadelphia, New York, and West Point, where they visited cadet John, who was "very well and very much grown and very glad to see us."*

Letter No. 3

U.S. Ship Vincennes. At Sea.
Tuesday Evening
November 20th 1838. Lat 21° 18' S.
Long 36° 56' 15" West. 8 P.M.

My dear Sister Lydia,

       As we are now within a few days sail of Rio de Janeiro, I think it is high time for me to make a commencement. I cannot in my heart neglect writing to you, for it is one of the greatest pleasures I enjoy. I only wish I could steal upon you about the time when this shall reach you. Time! how it speeds—four months gone since I left home—3 months and four days since the Squadron sailed from Hampton Roads! I have not had one heavy hour—the moments fly, and the cruise will be over before we are aware of it! As yet, we have scarcely deviated from the common routine of cruising ships; it is only in anticipation that we feel as "Explorers." True, we have been searching for supposed Rocks and Shoals, and although we could find no traces of them, we had some days of interest and excitement while looking for them.

    We have spoken many vessels and always requested them to report us. Perhaps you may see the notices in the papers. By the English Ship "Crusader" from the East Indies for London I sent a few hurried lines which I hope will find their way to Cornwall in the "Great Western"[1] or the "Victoria." We fell in with her to the

---

[1] *Reynolds's second letter never reached his family. The English steamship* Great Western, *especially built for transatlantic passage by Isambard Brunel, had helped to inaugurate a new era in fast coal-powered ocean travel only a few months before the expedition left the United States.*

Southward of the Cape de Verd Islands and as they had been a long while out, presented them with fruit and some vegetables, though it were giving our blood to do so!

We remained a day at Port. Prayo, the principal harbour in the C. de V. Islds.[2] The town has the most wretched, starved, sandy appearance! The houses seem naked and rude, the streets *narrow deserts*, the people miserably poor and famine stricken, while the multitudes of swine that were roaming about gave every evidence of good keeping. They were the only things that appeared fat—or living! The Town stands on a bluff sandy ridge. In the rear of it is a beautiful valley, rich with growths of cocoa nut and plantain trees, gardens of Indian corn, and a rivulet winding its course through. Hundreds of canary birds were singing in the groves, making sweet and joyous music. In the distance were some half verdant hills—what a contrast to the dreary town above on its rough eminence. And for a *while* Ocean was shut from our view. We rested in the shade of the broad leaved trees, on the fresh turf, by the running waters. We slaked our thirst with the cool milk of the young cocoa nuts, a most delicious beverage in sultry climes. We scaled the rocky heights and regained the Town. Monkeys were numerous and several purchased. The Military seemed to be rather deficient, both in arms and clothing; the display of what they *did* possess was most ludicrous.

We dined at the Consul's, the American Consul's, "Mr. Ferdinand Gardiner."[3] He is rather a rude Christian and is the only one who can read or write English in the Islands. He has no society but a few time worn Portugese whose ideas are limited enough—a pleasant life he *must* lead. The inhabitants of the Island were in a state of starvation some 4 or 5 years ago, as you may remember, and were relieved with provisions sent from the U. States.[4]

[2] *The Cape Verde Islands are situated about three hundred miles west of Senegal and fifteen hundred miles southwest of Madeira. The islands had been a Portuguese colony since 1462. Praia was the capital and principal city.*

[3] *Frederick Gardner from New York served as U.S. consul at Cape Verde between 1837 and 1841.*

[4] *Limited and irregular rainfall has given the Cape Verde archipelago a history of recurring drought. In the famine of 1830–1833, which wiped out one-third of the population, fund-raising efforts were held throughout New England, stirred by the efforts of the U.S. consul at Cape Verde. Congress*

Since leaving the C. de Verd, we have had rather a monotonous time—light winds and plenty of rain. Crossed the Line without any ceremony or humbug, and here we are! But now I am writing on the 23d. Yesterday we made Cape Frio, a headland to the Northward and Eastward of Rio,[5] and spoke an American ship 51 days from New York: 45 days *later* than ourselves. What a happy treat it would have given us to have found *letters*! We received some papers as late as the latter part of September but they contained no news. I suppose every one in the U.S. thinks that *we* are off Cape Horn by this time, but the delay has been necessary and Captain Wilkes says that we have time enough. He wished the crews to become well disciplined and drilled before he could venture with them among the perils of Southern Latitudes.[6]

We shall be at anchor in the harbour to night. I regret that we will not be able to make our *entree* by day—I long to look upon the glorious beauties of the Bay. It is now noon, we are 10 or 12 miles distant, the breeze is light, and the weather misty; it will be dark when all hands are called "to anchor."

Ah! but when we anchor in some quiet creek, the interior of some beautiful Island, where the white man has not been, where men and

---

also provisioned eleven ships for the relief of the islands (Machado 1976:22; Ribeiro 1960:319).

[5] *Cabo Frio, a headland about one hundred miles east of Rio de Janeiro.*

[6] *Reynolds's opinion of the commander's strategy changed radically in hindsight. Immediately upon his return to the United States, Wilkes addressed the National Institute for the Promotion of Science in Washington, on 13 June 1842. This address (Wilkes 1842b), Wilkes's testimony at his court-martial, and his five-volume* Narrative of the United States Exploring Expedition *published in 1845 were criticized by Reynolds in a manuscript of seventy-eight pages (hereafter referred to as the "Critique"). Obviously prepared at considerable effort and with collaborating opinions from other expedition officers, the "Critique" appears to have been written for publication, but apparently never was printed. In it, Reynolds asserted (pp. 4–5) that Wilkes's instructions were " 'to shape his course for Rio de Janeiro; and to look for Vigias [i.e., shoals] South of the line' " and that "a fair passage to Rio may be made in 40 days; the Squadron were 30, in getting to Madeira." The* Vincennes *arrived at Rio "97 days out from the United States."*

women and everything else exist in primitive simplicity—will it not be sweet? It will! Would that you could be there also!

We expect to remain a month in Rio de Janeiro, engaged in overhauling the vessels—for they were fitted out most rascally at Norfolk, doubtless with a view to retard the Expedition—and making Astronomical, Magnetic, and all other kinds of observations. The Naturalists, Artists, Conchologists, Geologists, and Mineralogists will have a splendid field to exercise their pursuits in—Brazil is rich in subjects of all those sciences.[7]

Sunday, November 25th

What a prophet I was. We did anchor on Friday but as it happened *before* sundown. The weather was hazy and the splendors of the Bay were partly obscured, but the night was clear and beautiful, a bright moon and myriads of stars. Mine was the first watch; the evening previous I had had the first watch also. I felt the contrast most strongly and it is these changes that make the Heaven of a Sailor's life. On the one evening, the Ship was at Sea, the weather lowering, the land near, throwing upon me more responsibility than usual. And indeed, we had a very narrow escape from what would have proved a serious accident.

The lookoutman reported to me a vessel crossing our track—I went forward and there was a large Brig close to. It was her place to have altered her course, and supposing she would do so, I held on, fearful that if I deviated any and she likewise that we would run foul. She came nearer, so near that I could hear the water rippling under her Bows. I had a lantern held up; the Brig displayed one also, but kept on—a minute more and there would have been a crash. Thinks I, it will not do to stand up on rights now, so I hailed, "Brig ahoy." The answer followed immediately—they were on the watch. So I

[7] *Reynolds refers to the decade of controversy regarding the purposes, funding, leadership, and equipping of the expedition; the Board of Navy Commissioners, which controlled the outfitting of ships, was even suspected by Wilkes and others of trying to sabotage the expedition by approving inferior workmanship on the vessels. The naval officers had responsibility for conducting geodetic and other observations of interest to navigation and commerce; in addition, they assisted the "scientifics" in their field work when necessary.*

ordered our own helm up and told him to *"Keep his luff"*—and this in a twinkling—the Ship's head went rapidly off and the Brig passed slowly by us—so near, that I could have hove a biscuit on board her. I drew a long breath and felt wonderfully relieved when we were all safe.

The whole thing had occurred and passed so quickly, that I had not had time to call the Captain. He knew nothing of it 'till it was over, while it is customary and necessary to let him know, the instant a strange sail is discovered either in the night or day time. I never saw two vessels in such startling proximity to escape free and am thankful that I did not lose my presence of mind. I should have been ruined forever if I had faltered or gone wrong; the consequences would have been terrible to me and perhaps fatal to some lives on board either [*ship*]. My seamanship would have been disgraced—and to *you* I will say that I can take some credit to myself for having been perfectly cool, for having held on my course until I could hold on no longer and then altering it just in the nick of time.

Well, after such a night, what a change to be on the succeeding one quietly at anchor in a safe and spacious bay amidst ships of all nations, many of our own, having news and meeting with old friends, a *fresh* breakfast, and a visit on shore to be enjoyed on the morrow. Cannot you imagine of the exceeding delight?

The Relief has not been heard of. We can scarcely conjecture what has befallen her, almost one hundred days since we sailed from U.S., time enough to have gone to *Canton*. And yet the Relief was the crack vessel of the old lot, far superior to the two Barques—oh yes, whatever were the alleged faults of the Barques, the Store *Ship* was faultless.[8] She *is* a craft to go exploring, certainly—more than one quarter of a year, sailing 6000 miles over a clear and much frequented Ocean with no pursuits to occasion the least delay. Mercy! we shall all starve if we do not look out sharp; the *Relief* will come *too* late. It is a happy thing that the Exploring Squadron did not sail as it was organized at first. I think the nation would have been put to shame.

[8] *The original squadron approved by President Andrew Jackson in 1836 included the frigate* Macedonian *and four other vessels built especially for Antarctic cruising. In addition to the store ship* Relief, *there were the bark* Consort, *the brig* Pioneer, *and the small schooner* Pilot. *The three last proved such poor sailors that they were replaced, as was the* Macedonian *because it was too large for use in island surveying (Chappelle 1949:390).*

In reading the histories of former Expeditions, English, French and Russian, I find that those Commanders were always selected who possessed the requisite scientific attainments, whose varied and extensive knowledge and peculiar talent would enable them to direct and carry on *all* the operations, and to judge on their merits. Now, none of the first named officers to the command of this Expedition were in the slightest degree acquainted with any higher branches than plain and practical Astronomy and Navigation, and the nautical parts of their proffession. They would have been completely at a loss what to do, and the American attempt at exploration etc. would have been a laughing stock to all nations. For a discovery voyage, these men might have done very well; they may have been gifted with essential qualities by nature, been full of ardour and perseverance, capable of undergoing and surmounting trials and dangers and all that sort of thing. But then they had never paid the slightest attention to any of the learned sciences and were utterly ignorant of the uses and construction of the more delicate instruments required in experiments absolutely necessary to be performed, appertaining to the magnetic needle etc. etc. etc.

Now take Captain Wilkes; he has long been distinguished for his varied scientific talent, he has devoted his life to that kind of study, has sought instruction in the observatories of Paris and London, and may rank himself among the enlightened few who are the geniuses of the age. He is familiar with the abstract sciences, the results of which go toward determining the laws and mysteries of nature. When in England and France, he was thrown much in company with Parry, Ross, Franklin, Back, Beechy, Beaufort, and others distinguished for their adventurous devotion to such cruises, as well as many citizen members of the learned societies.[9] From these, he obtained much and useful information, such as will prove of the greatest benefit to him now—the weight of their advice and experience, given with the

---

[9] *Wilkes had been sent to Europe in 1836 to collect instruments for the expedition, when the squadron was under the command of Thomas ap Catesby Jones. While in England, he consulted with a number of leading scientists and explorers. William Edward Parry (1790–1855), John Ross (1777–1856), John Franklin (1786–1847), George Back (1796–1878), Frederick William Beechey (1796–1856), and Francis Beaufort (1774–1857) were all British Arctic explorers and naval officers.*

utmost openness and sincerity. He has received very handsome letters from the most eminent men congratulating him on his appointment and wishing him the most happy success.

So, considering every thing, I think the circumstances which caused the delay and eventually the breaking up of the original Expedition were most fortunate and especially intended for the purpose of bringing Captain Wilkes. Long life to him! to the commander. I do hope that luck will befriend us and, barring accidents, we may do well—we may accomplish something which will do honor to the country and afford us gratification to remember during our lives.

We have seen papers as late as October 1st and notice that the attack upon the Navy in the Globe has caused much discussion and censure. Such a *thing!* as Mr. *Blair* to talk in *that* strain—fie, for shame! It is perfectly amusing to hear that fellow, devoid of all honesty and conscience, endeavouring to make Navy officers out a set of bloodsuckers, money seekers, when every one knows that they are a class of men who earn their money like horses and spend it like asses. It won't do, Mr. Blair—the falseness of your assertions stares you in the face. You receive your thousands; pray allow the poor Navy officers to receive *all* that the *Law* grants them. The greatest possible care is taken never to pay them more; would that the same existed in the other departments—in that which pays you.[10]

---

[10] *Francis Preston Blair (1791–1876), journalist, adviser to Andrew Jackson, and in later years founder of the Republican party, edited the influential* Washington Globe *during the 1830s and early 1840s. An editorial of 1 August 1838 defends Navy Secretary Mahlon Dickerson (1770–1853), then leaving office, against the many complaints over the manner in which he had handled preparations for the Exploring Expedition; according to the writer, navy discipline was at a low ebb and, referring to naval officers, "it is impossible to make heroes of men who adopt the maxims and principles of cobblers and tinkers." Another editorial on 9 August accused naval officers of having placed "love of money" ahead of "love of glory" and cautioned that they "must depend more on their own merits and services . . . less on becoming the toadeaters and hangers-on of members of Congress." (See also issue of 10 July.) Blair's son James L. Blair was a midshipman on the expedition; his naval service extended from 1836 until his resignation as a lieutenant in 1851 (ZB).*

I saw a notice of the Inspectors elections in Pennsylvania, but could not tell which party had the majority.

I wish you to number your letters as you write, so that I may know if any have gone astray. I will do the same, this one being No. 3. The Store Ship was to sail on the 15th of November and proceed to Valparaiso.[11] If I do not get long letters by her, I shall be in utter despair—you *could not* have neglected that opportunity. And I hope you will be sure to send ones in two or three months to the Department and Naval Lyceum.[12] And many letters by the *two other Store* Ships which are to sail in the two coming years, one for Singapore and one for the Sandwich Islands. During the third year of our absence, you must search the papers for notices of vessels sailing for Rio de Janeiro and write me by *every one* of *them,* so that *as we return* I may find many letters and papers and news that will gladden my heart.

Yesterday two letters came by a Boston Brig for the Sailing Master of this Ship, a young Passed Midshipman of 3 or 4 and 20 years of age; he received them with a smile but in a moment he was in an agony of grief, for *both his babes were dead,* and *he away!* His young wife had written them, and even in her deep and heavy affliction had not forgotten to *endeavour* to afford *some* consolation to her equally bereaved husband; but the blow unmanned him quite. His joyous anticipations and happy feelings when breaking the seal had been too awfully changed to sudden and bitter woe. Poor fellow, three years must elapse ere he can return, and then when he seeks his children, he must know his way towards their *Graves!*

[11] *The Exploring Expedition was to be provisioned through a series of store ships, one of which was to set out from the United States each year to leave supplies along the squadron's expected route.*

[12] *Organized by Captain Matthew C. Perry and other officers at the Brooklyn Navy Yard some five years earlier, the United States Naval Lyceum was an organization devoted to improving the education of naval officers. Before the Naval Academy was established at Annapolis in 1845, the lyceum—through its library, museum, lectures, and related publications—was an important influence in the training and professional development of officers (Paullin 1907). The directors of the lyceum had played a role in planning the Exploring Expedition, and the squadron's second in command, William Hudson, was associated actively with the organization.*

I shall never be married if I follow the Sea. To get a wife I must quit the Ocean and I rather think I shall remain a Rover all the days of my life. Who knows! We will see when the cruise is up; *then* or never! Perhaps I shall be so full of honors and glory that I will require some one to share them with me. But if there ever be a Mrs. Reynolds, I shall love her too well to leave her—the Navy must go by the board.[13]

I have written away in my Journal and shall continue to do so, though I know that no one will read half the nonsense which I commit to paper. But I *cannot* stop to think or to arrange, or to select, or to condense—down go my feelings, right or wrong, wise or foolish, well expressed or at the expense of the King's English. If I live to be an old man, I may reap many an hour's amusement by the perusal of these records of my youthful and vagrant days. If I *should slip my cable* in any sudden blow, why they will constitute the only legacy I shall have to leave and will serve to remind *you all* of one who with all his foolish waywardness loved and loves you well! . . .

I will write to you when occasions offer from here, and by the way, my Birth day will come while we remain. I believe I am never to have one at home again nor to pass another Christmas with you while the family hold together. This will be the seventh one and I away; the eighth, ninth and tenth must go by. Mercy—I shall be twenty six! ere I see you again, and then I shall *not* want to count Birth days any more. They will tell melancholy facts such as I shall not repeat to the Ladies. I hope I will look young, but fear I shall be weatherbeaten, ugly, broken down. . . .

The Relief came in last night, the 24th, having been just *one hundred days* out. She has had light winds and calms. She arrived at

---

[13] *Reynolds had written in his Journal (1:77) on 17 November, the seventh anniversary of his appointment as acting midshipman, that he had seen five years and seven months of active duty and only seventeen months of leave; adding the three years anticipated on this cruise, he asked "what would a wife say to have but one year in ten of her husband's company. It will not do. There will be no Mrs. William Reynolds."*

the Cape De Verds just 10 days after we left there. Two of her Passed Midshipmen are so unwell that they will return home.

I have not been in a lively mood lately and am not now much "in the vein" for writing. So you must excuse dullness this time and perhaps the next may be of a merrier tone. . . .

Do not let the within wording, *"for the support of my family"*! cause a smile at my expense. The expression is according to the form of the Law and cannot be altered, as the favour is solely intended for such purposes, but there are exceptions allowed. I send this Allotment home because I know I can live as well upon $60 a month as upon $100. If I have the latter at my command it would very likely go. I should spend it all, and so I will deprive myself of a portion.

Father can act his pleasure in drawing the money or allowing it to remain until the time is up, just as he thinks best. If he has the slightest occasion for the use of part or the whole of the trifling sum, it is quite at his disposal and I hope he will oblige me by taking it. It might as well be employed as to remain Idle!

A duplicate copy I will send by another vessel, which is to be destroyed if the enclosed comes to hand!

This will go by the Brig Eagle for Philadelphia and you will get it in the latter part of January. At that time we shall be some where South of Cape Horn, busily employed in the midst of snow, cold and Ice bergs!

I trust that you will remember to be particular and minute in your letters. Write long ones, tell me all about every one—of Grandmother,[14] who I hope keeps her health, and every one in whom I have the least interest. Then while I read, though I be thousands of miles away, I can for a few moments imagine myself in your midst. And *do* write *often*, for your letters will be to me as the

---

[14] *Jane Fulton Moore (1768–1847) was widowed in 1795, when her daughter Lydia was less than two years old. She became part of the Reynolds household upon Lydia's marriage to John Reynolds in 1813. When the family moved from Lancaster to Cornwall, granddaughter Lydia wrote, "I believe [Grandmother] is willing to go with Father and Mother anywhere" (19 March 1837).*

cool spring is to the parched and weary traveller in the deserts. They will be so grateful and will afford me the most happy and sunshiny hours I shall enjoy while I am away. . . .

And now with blessings and fond wishes for you all, adieu

Wm. Reynolds

Miss Lydia Moore Reynolds

[*Outside wrapper:*] for Brig Eagle
                    for Philadelphia

Rec. February 3rd 1839[15]

---

[15] *Lydia's answer of 17 February 1839 reached her brother in September, at the Sandwich Islands: "I wish you could have come in upon us when we received it, though we were very quiet. Mother was asleep in her chair, Father on the sofa and I reading by the fire. We were all up in a moment and very much rejoiced." She told of the seven-week visit she and Aunt had made that winter: "I saw almost everything that is to be seen in Phila." Rebecca Krug had been in the city also, and "she was much admired. She looks uncommonly well this winter." William's feather flowers from Madeira "arrived safely, on New Year's Day, quite a handsome New Year's present. They are the most beautiful I ever saw." Lydia concludes much as in all her letters: "The family unites with me in love to you and may God bless and protect you and return you to us in safety is the prayer of Your affectionate Sister, Lydia."*

$$\mathcal{Letter\ No.\ 4}$$

Tuesday, December 4th 1838
Island of *"Enchados,"* Rio de Janeiro

My dear Sister,

I am writing in a room in that old Convent building which you will find mention made of in the Journal at home—the same place wherein we lived when the Schooner *Boxer* was being "hove down."[1] Then it was in the most ruinous decay; now the ceilings, floors, windows, doors, places are replaced and repaired, and the work is going to make the edifice a habitable dwelling house. The Chapel will remain, the Altar pieces have been renewed, and it will soon shine with something like its former splendor. The plan has not been altered; the court yard is yet in the centre, bounded on all sides by the walls and the long corridors. And narrow winding passages, the many rooms and steep flights of stairs admirably calculated to endanger one's limbs and neck, the belfry and

[1] *Reynolds refers to his first cruise (1832–1834), aboard the USS* Boxer. *After calling at Liberia, the* Boxer *was based on the Brazil station before proceeding in November 1832 to Java. While the ship was being completely overhauled on this same island of Enxadas during August, the officers and men lived in the upper part of the monastery described here. Reynolds's journal from this early voyage does not survive.*

Enxadas is an islet situated at the mouth of Guanabara Bay facing Rio de Janeiro; Lieutenant Wilkes had arranged through the Brazilian Foreign Ministry to use it as a base for conducting meteorological and other observations.

the turrets and the dungeons under ground, all mark the characteristics of the monastic buildings of some centuries ago.

The Officers and Men of the Porpoise Mess and Sleep in the different apartments while their vessel is being fumigated and smoked out to kill the rats and cockroaches. The Officers whose routine of scientific duty calls them daily to the Island also make their quarters in the building, as Captain Wilkes has hired the whole Island. And the tents are spread, and the portable houses for the Instruments are put up, and the Instruments are fixed in their stands, and the Carpenters and Armorers, and Sailmakers and riggers with their busy gangs are at work, and there is a hum and a life and a stirring spirit pervading the usually quiet Island.

[*Inverted:*] (Note: It is now midnight. Every one is asleep and I am alone in a large chamber! The night is cloudy and only one person required to watch; hourly, I take the Tide Staff, Barometer and Thermometer.)

Sunday was the King's, or rather the Emperor's Birth day.[2] His Imperial Majesty was pleased to become 14 years of age on that day and great was the *row* that was raised upon the occasion. On the water, the men of war and the merchant Ships were all gaily "dressed" with Flags of various nations and party coloured signals and flaunting streamers like the scarfs and ribbons of a *Belle!* Salutes were fired, making a tremendous din, and the Bay was covered with a multitude of Boats passing swiftly to and fro; I landed at 11 o'clock—the whole population seemed to be in the streets or at the windows, a most miscellaneous throng of miscellaneous complexions. One could easily see from the bustle and preparations that the day was to be one of unusual rejoicing. The *lower stories* of *all* the Houses in the two streets through which the Emperor was to pass on his way from his Country Palace to the Imperial Residence in the City were hung with blue and crimson damask, bordered and fringed with gold lace and rich according to the circumstances of the householders, each one adorning his own premises. The windows far as you could see were crowded with the fair dames of the Land—a radiant and bewitching relief to the sheening splendour around them. Where the

[2] *Dom Pedro II, emperor of Brazil, 1831–1889. The country was governed by a regent until 1840.*

two streets met each other at right angles, a Triumphal Arch was
raised and here the Emblem Flags of almost every country under the
Sun were displayed, reaching across from roof to roof and forming a
waving and a beautiful canopy. On came the procession. The body
Guards mounted and the body guards on foot, then the gorgeous
carriage that contained the magnificent Emperor boy drawn by eight
horses, the Postillions, Coachman and Footmen, all covered with gold
embroidery, then more Guards, and the coach with the Sisters two,
and two maids of honor. Loud *"vivas"* rent the air, *"Viva, Don Pedro
the 2d!"* and the music sounded, and the kerchiefs waved, and
flowers and laurel wreaths were showered like rain upon the cortege.
And bowing and smiling, and doubtless proud and happy *the child*
moved on. His young heart must have been filled with rapturous
joy—he! the object of all this loyal devotion, the cause of the
glittering show!!

I preferred to look at *his Sisters* and their attendant Ladies, for they
were a group of loveliness; and had *I* hurrahed, it would have been
for *them!* Then came the mass of military, Foot and Dragoons, and
they formed in the Palace Square and fired "feu de joie," and went
through all kinds of evolutions much to the admiration and applause
of the crowd. The Captain and many of the Officers were presented
to his Imperial *High*ness, but I could not think of going through a
ridiculous ceremony before a *boy*. At night, "the scene was changed"
and such a change! Oh night! And now again, *first* from the *water*, the
effect was most brilliantly grand. The Moon was up and at her full,
and it seemed as if the Stars had deserted the Heavens and were
besprinkled over the Shore, for lights shone bright and clear in every
quarter: in long lines along the beaches and around the curves of the
Bay, over the hill sides and on the hill summits, on the lofty towers
and on the still higher crosses of the many churches; wherever
ingenuity could place and taste suggest. And hereaway was a mimic
fortress with battlemented walls, and there an arch of fiery light
showing strongly against the dark green of the back ground. And the
stately ships and the dancing boats displayed their lamps; among the
black masses of rigging and the spars, and in the latter [*i.e., the boats*],
gliding swiftly over the waters.

Fancy yourself before that Triumphal arch now all illuminated,
under the canopy of flags, and in the midst of a most enthusiastic

crowd (where there were many sweet faces) and looking up the "Rua St. Pedro" (or St. Peter's Street) through which the Emperor made his way in the morning. It is more than a mile in length, it is thronged with people of all classes and all colours, and throughout this long vista the lights are hung in fanciful array—brilliant, glaring, intense! portraying various devices and shining strong as the Sun at noonday. The Houses are still clad in their splendid livery, looking infinitely more sumptuous and rich than by day. Bands of music are playing. And the superb effect of the whole heightened exceedingly, made into a scene of enchantment most glorious and delightful to behold.

In an open square that broke away from the street, cocoa nut trees were planted and amidst the branches colored and illuminated globes were hung. On lines that ran all round the square and horizontally across from the corners were once more the thousand National Flags, those of rival and distant countries side by side. In the centre of the square a miniature castle was raised, from whence the band set forth their stirring strains, and here as in the two streets the crowd was immense. Balloons were sent up, from which rockets detached themselves at various heights, gleaming like meteors through the air; finally the balloon reaching so far above the earth as to seem a star in the Heavens would take fire, and the mass come blazing and crashing to the ground. I could not tear myself away and deep into the night Simon Blunt[3] (bless his honest heart) and I wandered about, giving way to the pleasing and happy feelings that were suggested by the rare and manifold splendors that every where met our eye.

The evening was soft and mild, there was no rude and chilling air, no breath or wind to disturb the exposed and burning tapers. The Ladies were without bonnets and in light dresses—no fear of cold, no dread of shivering ague. There was a charm in the balmy night, and young and old gave up their souls to enjoyment without alloy. As I was going to the Landing for a boat, the Emperor and his cavalcade of Dragoons and mounted servants carrying torches went clattering through the streets on the way to the Palace in the country. The show

---

[3] *Passed Midshipman Simon F. Blunt, a Virginian, who was assigned first to the* Porpoise *before transferring to the* Vincennes *at Orange Bay. Blunt was to leave the expedition in Honolulu in 1841; see Letter No. 19 (ZB).*

was ended and on the morrow the every day affairs of life would
resume their sway.

Wednesday, December 19th 1838

We shall pass our Christmas at anchor. I think that we shall not
sail from here until after the 25th. I have been so busily employed as
to prevent me from attempting to put pen to paper, but now I must
make an effort—a vessel sails on Friday.

The experiments and observations have been going on successfully
and unceasingly. A week more and they will be concluded. The
Peacock and two Schooners went to Sea a few days ago to measure
the distance to Cape Frio. The Relief sailed this morning, to be in the
advance. We shall meet some where to the Southward. I do not know
where we shall touch at first, or what will engage our attention
until April; the same annoying mystery is preserved regarding our
movements as is the case in all squadrons or vessels. One never is
aware whither he is to be carried, until after being at Sea some time
the destination leaks out.

Well, I expect a rough and hard season—plenty of work, no play,
and freezing weather which will chill us awfully after leaving this
burning clime. Ten days, twenty days, and we will be in the very
latitudes of storms and Ice bergs. *You* will all be cozy and comfortable
around that coal fire, the lamp lit and the newspapers spread out. No
watches do you keep, no exposure, worse than a ride in a sleigh will
subject you to, do you undergo. Let gales blow and snow fall, you
turn in your bed and hug the blankets closer. *We* must *strive* to keep
the "frail planks" together, to keep our *home* afloat; for us there is no
rest and but little comfort. Each day brings the same toils, the same
dangers. Physically we suffer much and, almost totally deprived of all
intercourse with those we love, we suffer more.

But then even *you* would forget all those ills, think lightly of them
when over, and be ready to launch anew into them, for the sake of
tarrying in the glorious places where *we* find our rest. Oh! could you
have ridden with me a few evenings ago. The miniature scenery in
Madeira charmed us; here the features are more majestic—more of
nature, less of man's encroachments. I cannot say a word about
it here. I'll try in my Journal when I have leisure to think. All is
bustle and din around me. Caulkers and Carpenters are noisy and

John Fulton Reynolds, William's brother; daguerreotype taken in Mexico in 1846. Courtesy Anne Hoffman Cleaver.

preparations for sea are going on briskly. I am often interrupted, and you must take this letter as the production of *such* moments and thank me for snatching them to devote to you. April, April! how I look forward to that month: *then* I will get your letters though they will be half a year old. They will tell me of *your grand tour*, that most memorable jaunt! Why should not *I* go to the Southern Pole if *Mother* journeyed *so far North* as West Point? I trust she will make many more trips, to Boston or Niagara, or somewhere, so that she travels. For like Mrs. John Gilpin, her excursions have been few.

In *my* Journal you will find recorded every thing eventful which happens to me. You keep none and how much will pass in your circle that I will know nothing of! I have caught myself oftener in sad and thoughtful moods since leaving home than ever before. And I scarcely know why, unless it be because I am getting so *old*—my 23d Birth day has gone by. I begin to perceive that there is an *old age* to live for, a fact which has not often troubled my mind hitherto. To enjoy the present at whatever expense was all that I cared for. Often and unconsciously I find myself singing that old sailor's catch

> "And when I do return again
> Unto my native Shore
> I'll marry my sweet Nancy
> And I'll go to Sea *no more!*

But what is the use? The stirring action and adventure that we shall so soon be in the midst of will have a healthy effect and drive me from idly dreaming to happy and beneficial exertion.

I have been in excellent health and am perfectly happy in this Ship. Comfortable as circumstances will allow on ship board, I luxuriate in my sanctum sanctorum, my elegant state room. And the mess has flourished under my auspices until it has the fame of being in the best order of any in the Squadron, save our own ward rooms. The money goes, flies; we live well and in such good and, for a steerage, elegant style, that I wish you were here to see. I should like to have a *certain set* of you for *my* guests, that you might witness the effects of my taste as displayed in the economy of my table and in the active and respectful attendance of the boys. I flogged them into good servants, which they may thank me for; and with my messmates, they give me absolute power and never interfere. My Kingly office as Caterer is troublesome, but almost any one has a pride and a pleasure in carrying his own ideas into operation and witnessing the effects, especially when means are plenty and authority despotic—when there is no opposition and when every one must bow to your imperial will.[4]

[4] *The food in each mess was prepared and served by cabin boys under the supervision of one of the officers known as the caterer, who also purchased the food on shore. In his autobiography, Charles Wilkes described his own experience as caterer while a junior officer (1978:125–28).*

Power is pleasant to most men. It is natural to wish to Lord it over our fellows and it is gratifying to one's self pride not only to meet with respect and obedience, but to be able to command it. On shore all these Anti American notions go out of my head; on board Ship they must return. I only hope that I exercise my slight privileges in this way—with discretion. I may be wilful, but never tyranical; and the good feelings of the men towards me on board every ship in which I have sailed tells me that my errors have mostly been on the lenient side.

I send the *duplicate* copy of the allotment in this letter. And again I hope that Father will consider the money as much his as my own.

Do not fail to write every two months at least by the Department and Naval Lyceum. They are aware of the times we shall be at the different places and will forward mails for us frequently. The more letters you send, the more chances I shall have of getting at least one or two.

Several parties and balls have been given on shore, one by Mr. the Hon. Wm. Gore Ousely, the English Minister; his wife is a daughter of Van Ness of Washington City.[5] I did not attend either of them, for I do not feel in the least inclined to gayety of that kind. The fact is that a change from Shipboard to a room full of Beauty and alive with mirth produces an after effect that is shockingly disagreeable; one almost goes crazy. The transition from the rough forms on board to the delicate and graceful company of females is most delicious, but especially when one has been for months deprived of even the sight of a petticoat. Feelings are awakened that had better slumbered, and when the intoxicating pleasure is over, when the dark curtain of separation falls, we go back to our masculine associations, saddened with the recollection that for us, indeed, such "angel visits" are few

[5] *Sir William Gore Ouseley (1797–1866) had been appointed British chargé d'affaires in Brazil the previous year, after serving six years as secretary of the legation in Rio. Accomplished in languages and the classics, he had some years previously been attaché in Washington, where he had written a book highly favorable to U.S. institutions. His wife Marcia (d. 1881) was the eldest daughter of Cornelius P. Van Ness (1782–1852), a New Yorker and former governor of Vermont, supporter of Martin Van Buren and Andrew Jackson, and minister to Spain. It was Marcia's uncle John P. Van Ness (1770–1847) who was a former congressman and prominent banker and then mayor of Washington, D.C.*

and far between! To save myself from vain regrets, I deny myself the moments of enjoyments—that is I have done so *here*. Heaven knows *when* next and *where* we shall meet with Christian women, and then I suppose I shall go with the current. Nolens volens.

A slaver was sent in here the other day, a prize to a British Sloop of War. 300 slaves on board, the small pox raging terribly, and 12 killing themselves after the capture thinking they had changed masters only to be eaten! The English make many captures, but they do not better the condition of the negroes one whit. They confiscate the vessels and if resistance has been offered hang the Captain and his crew—but the cargo! They are kept on board until the court consider on the case and condemn the craft as a lawful prize. Then they are taken on Shore and hired as apprentices to the highest bidder. Negroes are numerous as the sands on the Sea Shore and are daily in the streets with scarcely any notice taken of them. Well, a man has hired some of these captured blacks; he takes a dead body when he finds one, swears that it is such and such a one, his apprentice whom he had bid off at the English sale; the registry is made and the poor bona fide apprentice, still living, becomes a slave for life. He knows nothing—who is there to aid him or to correct the horrible fraud? No one, and his lot is the same as if he had been sold into slavery by those who tore him from his home. What sweet fellow creatures we have in this world and how pleasant and amiable are their ways.

Slaves are brought here by the thousands. I pass by three or four vessels as I go on shore that I know to be in the Slaving trade, from their rig and build. They anchor in some bay near the Harbour when they are full and send the slaves in by night in fast pulling canoes. The sufferings of the negroes on board these slavers are too dreadful, too foul and revolting to write of. The reality is worse than the imagination can well conceive of; but brought right under one's eye, when you find yourself side by side with one of these floating Hells with all the unnatural and aggravated cruelty and misery staring you in the face, then you can see, and feel, and weep, that these things be![6]

[6] *The slave trade had been outlawed by Great Britain, the United States, and other countries by 1820; Brazil agreed to stop importing slaves after 1829. Nevertheless, the trade continued and though the U.S. Navy made*

And *you all*, in that quiet Home. What see you of the horrors of life? Of the evils, every one may taste. Many may enjoy the sweets; and better is it for those who quietly and peacefully pass the even tenor of their days remote from the scenes of those deeds which blacken and degrade man's history.

And why is it I have spun my yarn out so long? You must be amused at my miscalculations when my letters embrace many dates! On Wednesday, I thought the vessel which will carry this would have sailed on this morning. She will go to morrow or Sunday and I have found more time to write. Yesterday was my day's duty on board the Vincennes—from 8 in the morning until 8 in the evening I was, with the exception of one hour, on deck carrying on all kinds of duty, worrying with the Brazilian Carpenters and Caulkers, and playing the deuce among our own men. Up at 4 this morning and on deck until 8, and now ashore on the old Island until 9 o'clock to morrow, all the work to attend to without any help.

Every hour I sally forth from the house and make the grand tour of the Instruments—first a "Barometer and Thermometer" in a house near the "Pendulum and clocks"; then a "diurnal variation machine" in a room alone; then the Tide Staff; then "a Thermometer with black sheep's wool around the bulb and another plain," both exposed to the Sun's rays—"to ascertain the Solar intensity"—then "the Dip of the Needle"; then "two other Thermometers in the air, but in the shade"; then "two other diurnal variation concerns" and finally a

---

some attempts to interdict slavers—William Hudson served with the West Africa Squadron as a midshipman during the 1820s—the Royal Navy took a more active role in stopping it. These efforts had only limited success: between 1835 and 1839 the Royal Navy's South American squadron interdicted only eleven of the estimated three hundred voyages made by slavers to Brazil, which landed some 125,000 slaves. Once captured, Brazilian slavers were escorted to Liberia or to Rio and turned over to Anglo-Brazilian joint commissions. If a ship was condemned for slaving, it was sold at auction and the slaves released to local authority. In Brazil, such slaves were apprenticed out and often ended up in slavery again (Bethell 1970:122–50, 380–83). For an account of U.S. Navy activity on the Brazil station during 1841–1842, see Johnson (1959). The Brazilian slave trade was not finally suppressed until 1851; slavery was abolished in 1888.

"Thermometer in the house." All these I observe and note, at the expiration of *every hour* in the twenty four.[7] When the other vessels were here the task was a light one; but now, but one officer can be spared to attend here. The marine corporal calls me when the hour strikes and my time and rest are of course eternally disturbed. Still I take the intervals to write away to you. Whether you will take the same exceeding pleasure in the reading that I do in the writing, I do not know; I hope you will. 'Tis 5 P.M., the bells are tolling in the City for some saint's holiday, and I must be off on my round.

Well, I have come back. The day has been sultry in the extreme, the black wool Ther. 114°. The Island is but sand and rocks, as arid as a Desert; but the prospect around is lovely as an Eden. The green Isles, the distant Mountains, the far spreading Bay, the verdant Shores, the multitude of Shipping, the Town—convents, fortresses, villas, Palaces, all in mingled beauty meet the eye.

Our officers have scaled the "Sugar Loaf," hitherto considered an almost impracticable feat; passed the night there and kindled a fire, which setting the Shrubbery in a bright and towering blaze, brought all Rio out in wonder to see. I had duty and could not accompany them.[8]

If I be not too sleepy during the night, I will scribble more; now I want rest, 'tis Sundown. The moon is up and her silvery light plays over Shore and Bay; let me but step to the window, that old arched

[7] *The collection of instruments in the "observatory" set up and manned at Rio and elsewhere by the naval officers included a pendulum on which the effects of gravity helped to determine the shape and mass of the earth; a "diurnal variation machine," which measured the intensity of terrestrial magnetism; and a compass needle of which the angle or "dip" from the horizontal measured magnetic latitude.*

[8] *This was the second time that Passed Midshipman George Emmons and Lieutenant Joseph Underwood had climbed the Sugar Loaf. After their first ascent, Wilkes complained that they had not advanced the scientific purpose of the expedition by taking measurements from the mountain, causing them to make the arduous climb again. After the voyage, Reynolds described this incident as an example of the commander's arbitrary and unfair behavior because the two officers had intended to offer to return to the top with instruments if their first climb showed it was possible but were forestalled by Wilkes's quick complaint (Critique:5–6).*

window which opens on the balustrade, and I look forth upon a scene that may well tend to drive sleep from my eyes.

It is now the witching hour of midnight and all is hushed; it is 10 o'clock with you. How different has your day been from mine and you are sleeping sweetly and undisturbed. Well, I must ashore in the morning to buy stores, in the afternoon I shall ride, and when I get on board I will have the middle watch to keep—no rest for 48 hours. No wonder seamen show the marks of premature age, toiling night and day at most irregular periods, sleep broken in upon nightly, bad food at times, exposure to the worst of weather and going rapidly from the extremes of one climate to another. One's frame cannot stand uninjured. We should be nursed well when at home and we should be as tender of ourselves as possible when away, which we are not.

And now once more good bye. I will write again ere we leave and give you any intelligence of our movements that I can hear of, but you must not tell of it for the Secretary has expressly forbidden any one in the Expedition from making public our doings. You will remember this and not bring upon me the censure of the Captain and the Department.

The kindest love and remembrance to you all from your Brother

William

I wish you to send me the measure of Father's head; I want to bring him some peculiar hats that will suit him to wear in summer.

[*Inside wrapper:*] I hope you have received the Flowers and Letter by the "Cazenove" from Madeira, the letter by the Englishman at Sea, and one from here when we first came in—this being the 4th.

[*Outside wrapper:*] Brig L'Orient, for Philadelphia

[*Postmark:*] Philad., Mar. 27

$$\mathcal{L}etter\ No.\ 5$$

U.S. Ship Vincennes
[*Rio de Janeiro*]
January 4th 1838 [*1839*]
Saturday Evening 9.30

My dear Sister,

Delay after delay has occurred to detain us here until now. We will sail at daylight, but for where I know not yet. There are rumors about the Columbia River, the South Shetlands, and other places—but all is glorious uncertainty.

Sunday Morning

I was cut short last evening. Now we are underweigh and shall be at sea by 2 P.M. if the breeze holds. I will keep the letter open until the last moment and give you the last sigh, the last thought, the last blessing, ere we go into Lands unknown.

The time has come—good bye, a long farewell. Write and remember me, and speed the time until I am again among you.

William

Lydia.

[*Inside wrapper:*] No. 1 letter from Madeira with flowers by Brig
Cazenove.
No. 2 by English Ship Crusader, for Liverpool.

No. 3 from Rio de Janeiro by Brig Mary for Philad.
No. 4 from Rio de Janeiro by —— for Baltimore.
And this No. 5—hope you have had all.

Received No. 1 from Madeira with flowers Nov. 10th
Received No. 3—4th February
Received No. 5—9th March

[*Outside wrapper:*] Brig Volta for Philadelphia

[*Postmark:*] New York, Mar. 6

Letter No. 6

Vincennes at Sea
10 days from Rio de Jan.
Lat. 34° South

My dear Sister,

  By a Barque we have just run alongside of, I send *one* line to say that I am well.

We are to put in to Orange Bay in Terra del Fuego and to tread on the verge of Cape Horn itself. Perhaps we may venture South as far as we can with out "let or hindrance" and shall be in Valparaiso in March when I shall be happy in the receipt of your letters. Please remember and make nothing public regarding our destination, which I may write to you. I shall be ruined if you do. God bless you. Write often to your Brother.

William

L.M.R.

[*Outside wrapper:*] Barque Leader at Sea

[*Postmark:*] New York, Apr. 10

Rio and After

Despite the brevity of letters Nos. 5 and 6 and the apparent long hiatus between the last entry in Letter No. 4 (22 December 1838) and the opening date of Letter No. 7 (22 May 1839), this period is covered by the letters in almost as much detail as in Reynolds's Journal, which, no doubt, was used as source material.

As for the stay in Rio, what can be known of it is almost solely from Letter No. 4. The Journal's last entry there is 1 December; the next is 24 January, at sea. An entry of 26 November in the Public Journal is followed by one some time in January, at sea, when a slight recapitulation is attempted. Reynolds does indicate some annoyance, in the Public Journal, with the extensive repairs required for the *Vincennes*. "The fit out at the Norfolk Navy Yard was bad, miserably defective. This subjected us to much trouble, expense and delay" (1:18).

On 24 January 1839, at sea, Reynolds wrote in his Journal, "I have not felt like writing since we sailed. I have been in strange humours, in such fitful moods as to prevent me from quiet thought or feelings." On 7 February: "Time goes. I have left a wide gap, but actually I have not been able to write a line. . . . Sunday, January 6th we left our moorings and stood down the Bay with a light breese from the land. This Ship and the Peacock ran into an English Slave Brig (a Prise with her human cargo yet on board not disposed of), but got clear without damage and with little delay. We were much mortified, because the thing looked lubberly and right in the very face of every body, among all the men of war. It was the first mishap of that kind that I ever witnessed occur to an American man of war."

Shortly after the squadron's final departure from Rio on 9 January, the intelligence leaked out that they were bound for Orange Bay. On the nineteenth, they learned they were to touch in at the Rio Negro. Perhaps impatience with delay and secrecy and some doubt as to the naval competence of the commander contributed to Reynolds's "strange humours."

On 18 January, Reynolds boarded the whaler *Leader* from Westport, Massachusetts, spruced up "to show them a cleanly looking individual, a sight I knew they had not met with for months." The hearty-looking, rather greasy captain offered the officers tumblers of lemon juice, while he enjoyed his rum, and received their letter bag—including William's Letter No. 6.

[*Pages 1–4 missing*]

[*Valparaíso*]
[*22 May 1839*]

We sailed from Rio de Janeiro on January 4th expecting to proceed direct to Valparaiso without making any stoppage on the way, hoping that 50 days would carry us there and give to us our letters from *Home!*

About a week out a piece of intelligence leaked out which of course was a surprise to all of us. We were to make a survey of the "River Negro" in 41° Lat South and 62° West Long, somewhat to the Southward of Buenos Aires—the River being the boundary between Patagonia and the Argentine territory.[1] But this duty was not to delay us long, and it completed, we knew of nothing else that could detain us. When we left Rio, we were in utter ignorance of our destination, except as far as *our own* conjectures went. Not a hint had been given from head quarters, a silence and mystery deep as the grave was observed by the Captain regarding our movements, and he more than once enjoined us to preserve the like secrecy in our communications home of even *where we had been*, which of course is a thing not possible—letters *must* have a date. (And here let me again beg, that you will never allow any part of my writing to gain publicity. Show my letters to *no one* who will be likely *even* to *speak* of the contents; otherwise I shall get into trouble and disgrace.)

[1] *Patagonia was then Indian territory and was not to be integrated politically into Argentina for another forty years.*

Jan 26th we arrived off the River and commenced operations at once. The coast is low and sandy, the River narrow and difficult of approach from the many shoals off its mouth, and the anchorage in the Roads altogether unprotected from the Sea. An insignificant town stands on the River bank, 20 miles from the Ocean, and offers no inducements either in the commercial line or for the purpose of refreshment to Sea going Ships. *Why* we were ordered to survey it, I cannot imagine.

The Governor was much alarmed at the approach of the Squadron. He thought us French vessels under false colours with a design of taking the place.[2] The pilots were withdrawn from the Shore, the women, children, and *other cattle* sent off into the interior, and all the preparation in his power made to defend the town. He was happy to be undeceived and was exceedingly courteous and accommodating.

The weather was so bad and the situation of the shoals so unprotected and dangerous, that the survey was attended with much risk. Several of the Boats had narrow escapes from being swamped and once I would scarcely have given a pin for *my* chances for life. However, I have often seen that "all's not lost that's in danger," and more than once have experienced the comforting truth of that observation, "a miss is as good as a mile."

Four or five days passed, and we were nearly through the work and were taking advantage of a fine sunshiny morning to finish, when a thick fog came up suddenly, enveloping Ocean, Land, Ships, Boats and all, of course putting a stop to the proceedings. I was in a small boat at the time, about 5 miles from the Vincennes and 1 mile from the Porpoise. I could see neither of them and was without a compass to steer by. I made for the Brig as she was so near and after pulling some time, I had the satisfaction of finding myself close to her and was happy when I put my feet on her decks.

[2] *Because of the Argentine government's attempt to restrict Uruguayan foreign trade and the mistreatment of French nationals, a French fleet blockaded Buenos Aires between 1838 and 1840. The dispute continued for some years; in 1844 William Gore Ouseley (Letter No. 4, n. 5) was sent as British minister to Buenos Aires, where he helped to arrange the removal of the Argentine fleet from Montevideo and its subsequent occupation by French and British troops.*

All day the Fog continued, dense as ever, the Vincennes firing Guns every half hour as a guide for her absent Boats. Captain Ringgold would not allow me to leave his Brig, for my Boat was not fit for a struggle and the distance was too great.[3] I acquiesced very readily, for I saw that by remaining my Boat's crew and myself would be spared a toilsome and anxious, if not hazardous time. My boat was hoisted in at Sundown, as the weather was threatening. By daylight the wind was blowing a Gale from the Seaward, a heavy swell was tumbling in on the beach, to which we lay *rather near* for comfort, and the Brig pitching *"bows under"* at every dive she took. This change had taken place suddenly and all hands were on deck without the customary call of the Boatswain because it was impossible to remain below. I turned out at once as soon as I felt the violent motion of the vessel, and from the appearance of things it was high time we should be under sail, clawing off the Land.[4] The atmosphere was still misty and the light had not yet become sufficient to see to any distance, so the Captain did not like to slip the cable until we could discern the other vessels. To weigh the anchor was impossible and every thing was gotten ready to put the Brig under canvass. I looked at the Shore and could not help wishing that we were a *little* farther from it.

At length we saw the Peacock looming through the mist with her Topsails set and the welcome order was given, "to Slip the Cable"; all the sail the Brig could bear was given her and aided with the set of the tide she soon increased her distance from the Shore. The sea was now running very high and breaking on the Land with tremendous

[3] *Lieutenant Cadwallader Ringgold (1802–1869), the son of prominent Maryland Democratic congressman Samuel Ringgold and grandson of revolutionary general John Cadwallader, who commanded Pennsylvania militia under Washington. Ringgold joined the navy in 1819 and had been a lieutenant since 1828. Subsequent to the Wilkes Expedition, he surveyed the California coast in 1849–1850 and led the North Pacific Exploring Expedition of 1853. Stopping in China to protect American interests there, he became ill and was relieved of his command and sent back to the United States in 1854. After being placed on the reserve list, he returned to active service with promotions to captain and commodore; he was promoted to rear admiral in 1867 on the retired list (ZB).*

[4] *"Clawing off" means to work a ship to windward, away from a lee shore.*

violence as if it would wash the sandy barrier away. All the vessels were likewise underweigh and by noon the Land was *not* in sight. At 3 the gale had blown itself out, and we telegraphed to the Vincennes that her "small Boat and officer was on board."

At Sundown, the water was smooth enough to permit a boat to pass between the vessels. The swell rolled heavily still, but did not break, and it is only the tops of the waves that are dangerous. "The small Boat" was tossed from the Brig's decks into the Ocean, was tossed on *its* breast for a few minutes, and then in a twinkling it was in its accustomed bed in the interior of the Vincennes. Oh! but I was glad to be on the *Old Ship's* planks again and I was welcomed back almost as one raised from the dead, for all hands had thought me cast away in the Fog. Two of the Whale Boats had reached the Peacock late in the previous evening, leaving 7 men of their crews on shore; they went a little ways from the Boats and could not find them again. The Captain said he had been very anxious for me, and all the while I was as safe as possible.[5]

The ships were now steering back for the Anchorage with a moderate breeze, and in the morning at 9 o'clock we were again in the berth we had quitted in such haste. This day was spent in getting the anchors and men. The Boats again had a narrow escape among the breakers. On the day following, which was Saturday February 2nd, we left the Rio Negro, I trust for ever, and steered to the Southward.

On the 14th we passed through the Straits "Le Maire" between Staten Island and Terra del Fuego, a place much dreaded by the old navigators; we experienced no difficulties. By this time, *more* news came out; we were to go into Orange Harbour lying near to Cape Horn, but for what purpose, or for how long, was not said. Well, to

---

[5] *Wilkes in his autobiography, written more than thirty years later, gives an account of this incident in complete variance with Reynolds's contemporary account. Wilkes wrote that those who rendezvoused in the* Porpoise *had "overlooked their duties and joined in a merrymaking" and that Captain Ringgold was absent, detached on other duties, hence "not to blame" (1978:40). Even in his Journal, Reynolds gives no hint of "merrymaking"; on the contrary, he "regretted much that Capt. W. could not know his boat & crew were safe" (1:87).*

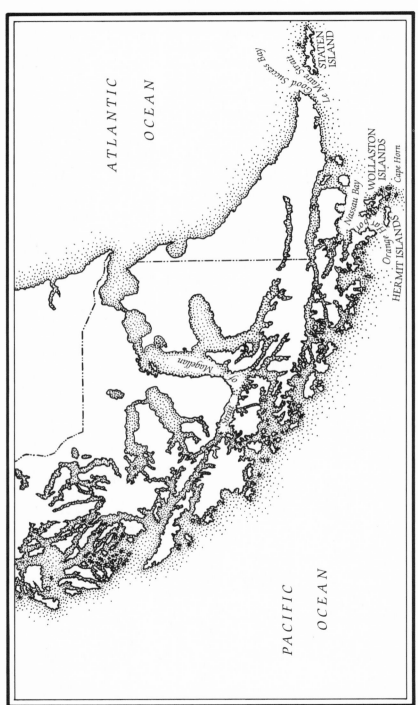

ATLANTIC

OCEAN

Le Maire Strait

Good Success Bay

STATEN
ISLAND

Nassau Bay

WOLLASTON
ISLANDS

Cape Horn

Orange H

HERMIT ISLANDS

Magellan

Strait

PACIFIC

OCEAN

Tierra del Fuego

be sure, on Saturday morning the 10th at daylight *we were close to Cape Horn,* with all studding sails set, a clear sky, and mild weather. I had the morning watch and I *watched* that celebrated promontory, the terror of all seamen (associated as it is in their minds with nothing but storms and Icebergs) with exceeding interest. There it was! thrusting its bold and rugged form far out into the Ocean, while the Sea was quiet as a sleeping child. Those indefinable sensations that set one's heart a throbbing while viewing new and striking scenes were dancing through my veins—but 11 miles from the termination of the Great Western Continent and that, the awful Cape Horn!! When night came, the Cape was still in sight and we were to the Southward and Westward of it. We had fairly *doubled it!* and for the first time I found myself in the Pacific Ocean—it looked very like the Atlantic![6]

During Sunday the wind was light and ahead; we beat against it toward the entrance of Orange Harbour, but without making much progress. A range of high and snow capped mountains made along in the distance, with summits tortured into a thousand fanciful shapes.

"All hands" were kept on deck through the night to work the Ship, for we were upon unknown Shores with nothing but watchful eyes and ready skill to guide us. At daylight we discovered the Relief at anchor and soon after were in a snug berth ourselves, when every one betook himself to sleep, seeking the rest he needed so much.

On the day before, I had written in my Journal, "after wooding and watering in Orange Bay, we shall *leave of course, but for where none of us knows!*" Now see what is written on *this* day: "No sooner had we cast anchor than the veil of mystery regarding our movements was withdrawn and all hands were set to work as if life and death depended on their exertions. The Peacock and Flying Fish were to go

[6] *By 1839 ships rounded Cape Horn increasingly frequently, but it still retained—as it does today—a reputation for severe and unpredictable weather conditions. The first American whalers traversed the Cape in 1789, but it was not until after 1800 that they began regularly to choose this route out of the Atlantic rather than the Cape of Good Hope. By 1819, there were 119 New England whalers operating in the Pacific; by 1840, there were some 500, not counting vessels engaged in other pursuits (Stackpole 1953:chaps. 11, 12, p. 303).*

South on one meridian, Captain Wilkes in the Porpoise with the Sea Gull to go South also but in a different Longitude. The Relief was to pass through the Straits of Malgahaens [*Magellan*]; this Ship to be laid up snug and to receive the invalids from the other vessels and supply their places with the strong and healthy of her crew.[7] Not only *this*, but many of the officers were to *change* their Ships and the whole *domestic* arrangement of the Squadron was to be overturned.[8] And of all this we had been in utter ignorance, we did not even dream of it, and yet were to be so much concerned in the change. We shall *not* get *our letters for months.* There, such are some of the annoyances of this accursed secrecy, just as if some terrible enemy was lying in wait to destroy us.

You may be sure all was bustle and hurry in the preparations, and in a few days they were gone; and the Vincennes dismantled, with but half her officers and men aboard, was alone in Orange Harbour.

---

[7] *The squadron's first Antarctic cruise took the* Peacock, Flying Fish, Porpoise, *and* Sea Gull *to the South Shetland Islands and Palmer Peninsula, to try to reach the farthest point south gained by Captain James Cook (1728–1779) in 1773–1774. The* Flying Fish, *in a remarkable voyage, penetrated as far as latitute 70° S. and 101° W. longitude. Meanwhile, the* Relief *was sent through the Straits of Magellan from the west to circumnavigate Tierra del Fuego; after losing two anchors in a fierce storm, however, the store ship proceeded instead to Valparaíso. E. W. Hunter Christie discusses this attempt at Antarctic exploration in relation to others (1951:chaps. 5–9).*

[8] *Wilkes assigned officers to duties based on his perception of their ability and merit, often disregarding the naval custom of basing assignment on seniority in grade. This practice caused some unrest among the officers, who also accused the commander of stifling independence and dissent. Although Wilkes certainly was given to suspicions, perhaps frequently unwarranted, about the motives of his officers, technically his action was justified by a general order issued by the secretary of the navy in June 1838 declaring the Exploring Expedition to be a nonmilitary enterprise free of the usual rules of seniority; the order, arranged through the efforts of Secretary of War Joel Poinsett, was intended to persuade William Hudson, slightly senior in rank to Wilkes, to take the position of second in command. (See exchange of correspondence between Wilkes and Hudson, 14 April, 19 May, and 5 June 1838; U.S. Navy Department 1838.)*

Orange Harbor, Tierra del Fuego, February 1839, by Lieutenant George Foster Emmons. This was the last time that the entire squadron would be together. From the right, they are the Porpoise, Relief, Vincennes, Peacock, Flying Fish, *and* Sea Gull. *Courtesy Yale Collection of Western Americana, Beinecke Rare Book and Manuscript Library.*

The Land around the anchorage is high and rugged, in some places well wooded, in others bare and rocky. As it was the *summer season,* the Forests were green and the patches of clear land were of the same hue, so that the rocky hills alone had a barren appearance; but there was a desolate absence of all things living, except ourselves.

The Observatory was erected on Shore, one or two officers and ten of the crew living there entirely. A gang of men were employed cutting wood and *burning charcoal* (I thought of Cornwall),[9] another

[9] *Charcoal was the fuel used in the great Cornwall iron furnace.*

USS Porpoise *and* Flying Fish *in Antarctic waters, 1839, by Titian Ramsay Peale. This drawing was made during the first Antarctic cruise, while Reynolds remained in Tierra del Fuego. Courtesy American Philosophical Society, Philadelphia.*

set were watering Ship, and the Carpenters were fitting out the Launch for a cruise among the Islands immediately adjacent to Cape Horn. A stove was set up in the forward Cabin for the officers, and one for the men, which answered also as an oven. Fresh bread for the crew was baked every day to save our hard biscuit for future consumption, so that on board we were made as comfortable as was possible.

Excursions on Shore were not much in vogue for the soil every where was spongy and marshy to such a degree as to render walking too fatigueing. Besides, there was nothing to be gained by pedestrianizing but exercise, and when we needed that we chose a fine day for a ramble. A short tour over the hills was sufficient and we never met with a *level place* in any part of the Islands of more *than 6 inches square.*

Besides March was setting in, the most stormy month in the year, and that in a region stormy at all times. Violent Gales rise suddenly and without warning, blowing with terrible fury for days without cessation, accompanied with heavy rain and the severest hail I ever saw. We had good reason to congratulate ourselves on the mild weather we had been favoured with while rounding the Cape, and were perfectly convinced that the dangers and terrors of Southern navigation had not been magnified by those who had experienced them. Good weather was a rare thing and more than once officers leaving the Ship on a morning that had dawned with a calm serenity of a summer day at home were caught ere night in one of these unexpected gales and unable to regain the Ship for 48 hours, passing the time in the rain without shelter from the blasts and without food, the violence of the wind preventing us from sending a Boat to bring them off. Once I went to hunt after May. By hard struggling, we got on Shore and built a fire; leaving some of the men to watch by it, the rest of us set out over the hills. The search was without success and, wearied to death and wet to the skin, after a tough pull we were glad to find ourselves by the *stove* again. In the afternoon the wind lulled and May was brought on board very much exhausted.

Heavens! *how* fearfully those gales blew! I never witnessed such angry gusts, and if they had been accompanied with thunder and lightning I think I should have turned coward and fled from the deck. In some night watches when I would be all alone on deck with the exception of the quartermaster, notwithstanding the Ship was securely moored, the blast would come down from the Hills with such tremendous fury that it seemed to me as if the Ship would be lifted out of the water and borne away.

And in the midst of *such* weather, the *Launch* was to be sent out upon the treacherous Sea. Captain Wilkes was pleased to call the Service which he ordered to be performed in her, *hazardous*—a *mild* term. When there is danger, there *may* be honor and there *is* excitement; therefore I was happy to be selected by the officer who was to command the Boat to accompany him. I was pleased, I was delighted—any thing to get clear of the monotony of life in Orange Harbour, even if [it] was to venture my personal safety in the Launch of a Sloop of war to the tender mercies of wind and wave.[10]

---

[10] *While the ships were dispatched on their missions, Lieutenant James Alden was to lead a survey of the southern portion of Tierra del Fuego in the* Vincennes's *launch.*

The said Launch *was* 33 feet long and of about 6 feet beam. She was to carry 12 male individuals, their provisions, bedding and clothes, a Gun, and various instruments. I cannot describe to you her accommodations in a manner that you can understand, but you may perhaps (if you try *very* hard) imagine the comforts and room so many persons could find in so small a space. While underweigh there was nothing to protect us from the weather. While at anchor the arrangements were such that we could keep *dry!*

All things being in readiness, we made a most propitious start on Monday March 11th, just after a Gale. The next day, however, we were caught in a heavy blow which came up with the quickness of thought and were near being lost. But as I have a long account of this cruise in my Journal and as it is impossible to give you the history in a letter, I shall cut the tale short and you must wait *my* return to learn all that befel us.[11]

We were 15 days in the Launch, passed near to Cape Horn, had in that time 4 mild days, lay at anchor in one place 8 days, a Gale of wind blowing all the while, with *snow, rain* and *hail* continually, narrowly escaped wreck again, almost thrown on the *rocks* at night, only comfort was that we could keep dry, felt the confinement to be irksome and tedious, not possible to survey, for which purpose we were sent out, obliged to keep close under the Land, and anchor before night in a snug berth and never leave it until the weather promised good, shot birds and caught fish in numbers, lived in a Gypsy style tolerably well, cooking on shore. Thermometer from 32° to 35°. Pleasant times.

---

[11] This "cruise," both dreary and dangerous, and disappointing as to surveying results, is described completely in the journals; the "Launch's Log" covers twenty-one pages in the Public Journal and fifty-five pages in Journal No. 1. On two pages inserted in the Public Journal at a later date, Reynolds did note one accomplishment: the discovery that Wollaston Island on the Beagle's chart was actually three. One island off the northwest end of the main island was named after Lieutenant Robert E. Johnson, who discovered it in the Sea Gull; the other, off the southeast end, was named Reynolds' Island because he was the first to see it. Another highlight of the cruise in the launch was Alden and Reynolds's celebration on 19 March of the "monthly-versary" of the former's marriage with a bottle of Madeira (Journal 1:142).

At last on the 26th of March, as we were trying to crawl back towards Orange Bay by slow and cautious movements, looking out for our safety as we despaired of accomplishing any survey, we met the Schooner Sea Gull just as day was breaking. Soon we were alongside her and when I stepped on board I thought *she* was as *large* as the *Pennsylvania*, that her masts *almost* reached the skies, and that her ropes were of *too* huge a size for men to handle. Such was the contrast to the insignificant Launch. I will honestly own that I felt I was safe from the moment I put my foot on her decks. Let all the Gales blow that pleased, now I was in a craft that could ride them out.

She had returned to Orange Bay from her cruise to the South a few days previously and was immediately sent in Search of us, and joyful was the meeting.[12]

The Launch's mast was struck, the crew removed from her and she taken in tow of the Schooner. With the utmost confidence and with a most happy feeling of conscious security, we kept away with a fair breeze for some Islands lying 60 miles from Orange Bay, where we had *not* intended to risk ourselves in the Launch alone. A Gale kept us at anchor all that night and the following day. After that we had good weather for five days and employed them to the best advantage. Then we met another and a severe Gale, in which we had to lie to; a tremendously heavy sea was running, the poor old Launch could scarcely keep afloat. Often we thought she would surely go and at length she *did* capsize; an awful Sea rolled *her* over bottom up and presently another broke over the Sea Gull and filled the Cabin with water. But the Sea Gull is a glorious craft, we could laugh at the waves and mock the roaring winds while in *her*; bouyant and lively, she rode over the billows with an ease that bid *them* defiance and gave to a Sailor's heart a charm, an extacy that cannot be told.

Mournfully we looked upon the old Launch, now a wreck, dragging helplessly in our wake. Snap! away went one of her fasts; then the other! The ill fated thing went adrift and we could not make

[12] *Because of the weather, Wilkes had ordered the* Sea Gull, *under Lieutenant Robert Johnson, to return at latitude 63° 10'S ahead of the other ships and hence she was back at Orange Harbor in time to set out in search of the launch.*

an effort to save her. There was an end of my first, first Lieutenancy. The craft was gone to Davy Jones' Locker where many a better one has gone before her.

Freed from the heavy tow of the Launch, the Sea Gull was a world more manageable; we could do with her as we pleased, now that her child was gone. So we turned her head Northward, made more sail on her and drove her along so as to make a harbour ere night. This memorable day was the 1st of April; by 8 P.M. we were under the Land, and at 9 safe and snug at anchor.

Here the Gale kept us two days. We then sailed and passed one day in looking for the Launch. Not finding her, we took advantage of a fine Easterly wind and stood for Orange Harbour. We were clear out into the Atlantic, with the Straits of Le Maire open, and it was 2 A.M. when we made sail, having then 80 good miles to run. It was my watch and I put the canvass on the Schooner until I had her going 10 $\frac{1}{2}$ knots the hour. The moon was bright, the Land showed plainly, and on we blew with the swiftness of a bird upon the wing.

The Straits were soon shut in, Island after Island passed, and at 8 o'clock we were near enough to Orange Bay to discern the Vincennes and Porpoise at anchor. A little while and we were riding quietly between them.

All hands on board both vessels were in a perfect fever of apprehension as we ran in—they could see *no* Launch; they thought the Sea Gull's search had been fruitless and that *we* had gone with the Launch, but they were certainly mistaken.

We were welcomed back most heartily, and they told us by way of consolation that they had been frightened for us several times and scarcely expected to see us again. They had had nothing but heavy gales with them and once the Ship dragged her anchors in the same blow which so nearly threw us on the rocks.

The Brig had been in 10 days. She had a narrow escape, was obliged to put to Sea in haste from Good Success Bay, leaving a Boat's crew and 3 officers on Shore who could not get off on account of the heavy surf raised by the blow, which came up as usual suddenly and unexpected. The Brig did not get back for 8 days. Those on shore lived on berries and muscles for 4 days, with no protection from the weather but that afforded by the Boat turned bottom up on the beach. On the 5th day they succeeded in reaching a Whale Boat left moored by the Brig with a long scope of line and containing provisions; this kept them from famishing. An attempt had been made to rescue them before the Brig slipped her cables, but the result was that the Boat was swamped and two persons were with great difficulty saved from drowning.

In a few days the Flying Fish came into Orange Harbour; on the 17 of April we left it, at last actually bound, fairly started for Valparaiso.

We saw some of the natives of Terra del Fuego and the adjoining Islands several times. They are the most hideously ugly race in the world, *go naked entirely, even in the snow storms,* smear themselves with filth and nastiness, eat revolting food, have scarcely the instinct of a brute and are certainly destitute of the human quality of reason, lead migratory lives, going in their canoes from hut to hut, having nothing but themselves to transport, no clothes, no implements beyond a spear, so miserably deficient are they of everything. Their habitations are small, formed of branches and covered with leaves, pervious alike to wind, rain and sunshine. In one of these huts, which has not the comfort of a wild beast's den, 15 or 20 of them crowd themselves round a scanty fire, sitting on their haunches, presenting a spectacle more abject and degrading than one can conceive of when he thinks that man is made "the image of his Maker."

They had nothing to offer us but a few otter skins, and we were wearied and disgusted with them at once. They afforded us some amusement, however, by the exercise of a wonderful talent and propensity they had to mimic our words, like so many mocking birds. The imitations were good and caused much merriment among us. The wretched creatures grinned horribly with silly idiotic leers that sickened one to behold, when they saw the effect their mockery produced. Except this, we could not elicit any thing from them either to amuse or interest us.[13]

[13] *The tribe he probably encountered was the Yamana, now extinct, but which then occupied the southernmost portion of Tierra del Fuego. Although written about as early as 1624, the tribes of the area did not attract Western academic attention until later in the nineteenth century; such studies have revealed relatively limited material cultures, not unlike what Reynolds describes, but ones nevertheless able to survive in very harsh climatic conditions. Reynolds, of course, had no insight into their oral traditions or other aspects of their culture (Wilbert 1977:1–3; Cooper 1946:81–106).*

Our passage hither was long and stormy, 26 or 27 days. We were driven as far as 59° South and had a continual succession of violent gales with much snow and hail. Ship very wet and strained almost to pieces; 30 men on the List with disease contracted by exposure. We were very uncomfortable. But I was fortunate enough to enjoy *Good health* and as long as I can have *that* and a *clear conscience*, why other matters are trifles.

N.B. You see I have commenced in the very [*illegible*]. The [*illegible*] midshipmen were torturing me at the time.

I am writing now at the Observatory on Shore; from the words "amusement however" on the other page, the previous part I wrote on board Ship in a haste.

I am not going to tell you much of Valparaiso, because I do not know sufficient of matters and things as yet. We have all been in a hurry and shall be while here. When I can find time for thought and leisure to arrange the stray ideas in order, I will *perhaps*.

But the Ladies are beautiful and their houses are open to us. I have been contented with looking, gazing at passers by, and have not made any visits, nor shall I.[14] But think of the contrast: Orange Harbour and the Fugeians, to a smiling sky, a mild climate, a Roadstead crowded with Ships of all nations, a busy town, and the lovely women. Oh! their very walk has an indescribable grace; even the common class of females have a bewitching gate that our *belles* would give the world to possess.

Lord Byron has showered his praises in many beautiful similes on the walk of the women of Spain. You will find them in the commencement of Childe Harold, I think, and when you read them you will wish that you could see for yourself. And supposing you will read them, I shall say no more, but my head is full of the thing now.

The Observatory is on a hill, from whence we have a fine view of the Town, the Bay and the Sea. I have this moment been looking at a snow capt mountain that is 160 miles distant, and 23,000 and odd feet high!

We have an elegant cottage with roses and honeysuckles twined over its front. Two or three others adjoin and have inmates who are young and lovely as my eyes can vouch for, and who make such

[14] *Reynolds refers to the Latin American custom of making social visits or attending evening salons at the homes of upper-class families.*

sweet music as glads my ear to harken to. Now *they* have gone to walk; they have bonnets and parasols, they remind me of Home. There goes a German lady, dashing by on a white horse. She has on a broad brimmed beaver hat, she rides as well as [Di Vernon?]. She is our nearest neighbor and we exchange bows. A servant follows her; he wears the poncho, the picturesque cloak of the Chilians. If I were an artist, I should have sketched them both, for the next souvenir.

I see a young girl looking forth from a bow window, around which creeping vines and flowers are trained. On either side of her are vases filled with flowers that were culled but just now, a canary is carrolling in his gilded prison over her head, and behind her are shelves of books. Well, what of all this, you will say? Nothing, but that it is a gladsome sight to me. There, she knows I am writing about her, she is gone.

This is the 6th letter I have written to you as you may observe by the no. on page the 1st. The last one from Rio was dated in January— that was No. 4. No. 5 was put on board the Whale Bark Leader at Sea. No. 6 goes in the "Philip Hone" of and for New York. May it have a speedy passage and find you all, as I heartily wish you, well.[15]

If I did not tell you where we were going and where we have been, what else could I write about? The thing is, I *must* violate the orders both of the Captain and of the Secretary of the Navy, and *trust to your discretion to save me from exposure.* Be cautious how you speak, or rather do not make my letters a topic to discuss *ever.* They are *for you at Home,* you who I am willing to believe have some small interest in me still, and for *no* one else. For third persons to know that I am well is sufficient and I beg and implore and entreat that you will not be imprudent. What you may mention casually may be repeated, "that the Expedition was here or there, that the Expedition had done this and not that," or any such expressions. They may be made public and the source traced at length to me, the offender against the Laws he should obey.[16]

---

[15] *Reynolds has forgotten the brief Letter No. 5, dispatched as he was leaving Rio. No. 6 was the note given to the* Leader *at sea. No. 7 is the one he was about to send via the brig named for the former New York mayor Philip Hone.*

[16] *The letters* were *read to the Coleman girls, who undoubtedly were considered part of the family.*

Rumour says we go from here to Callao, from thence to Sydney, New South Wales, touching at the *Islands* in the track and arriving at S. in October, there fit out to go South, then next April be at the Sandwich Islands where we shall meet the second Store Ship (and where I shall look for *such* a letter as this from you), then proceed to the Columbia River and make a survey, thence Westward for Japan, China etc. etc. etc., and the Cape of Good Hope. *Keep this quiet;* I believe it to be current, and *only imagine* the wrath of the Navy Department were such a paragraph to appear in the print emanating from me. I should be slain at once, so for mercy's sake do you be as close and mysterious to others as Captain Charles Wilkes is to us. I shall not suffer.

I think we shall *not* get home until 1842, but *most* say the fall of '41.

The most terrible contemplation to me is that I shall be an *old Beau*—26! horrible—that is providing I am not sent in any more *small Boats* or on future *Launch expeditions,* or I may meet "with an untimely fate and a watery grave," as the papers say.

You cannot conceive how wretchedly depressed and worn out we all became from tarrying so long in the cold, wet and stormy climate of Terra del Fuego. We were languid, good for nothing fellows and had we remained much longer there, we should have got the Scurvy from pure enui (have I spelled that French word right?). The change of clime and scene has brightened us up, and we anticipate much delight while cruising among the Islanders of the Pacific.

I trust all my letters have reached you safely and in good time. I sent an allotment of $40.00 a month, payable to Father's order at the Navy Agent, Philad, from Rio, with directions.

My red flannels were of excellent Service while we were in the bad weather and so were the woolen stockings of Grandmother's knitting, those she robbed Sam of to give to me.

Do you remember the brown handerchiefs I bought because I thought no one else would have any like them—a dozen others purchased some of the very same kind and for the like reason. The measures we take to secure success and guard against accidents often defeat our intentions. . . .

I wish you could have those three pictures of Ships framed, so that [they] will not be soiled, framed handsomely enough to hang up.

I intend they shall ornament my house when I get one, or else my *room* on board Ship and hope some of my money if Father draws it will be applied to this purpose.

Well it is now 6 o'clock. I have been here *alone* all day making the observations and now my relief has come. I will go down into the town and get something to eat.

The Brig sails in the morning and very likely I shall not be able to write any more; I shall leave it with some one to put in the Letter Bag, as I must return here for the night and cannot go down again until to morrow forenoon.

I'll take the whole page to bid you adieu and do you give to every one the kindest love and remembrance

of your affectionate Brother

Wm. Reynolds

Miss Lydia Moore Reynolds
   Cornwall
   May 22nd 1839

[*Outside wrapper:*] Brig Philip Hone

[*Postmark:*] New York, Aug. 24

Letter No. 8

U.S. Ship Vincennes
Valparaiso, June 2nd '39

My dear Sister Lydia,

We are still in this Port although, according to our custom, we have been sailing, sailing, and *to sail* every day, much to the annoyance of every one—the delay, when we were all ready for a start, causing a most vexatious disarrangement in every department. More money to be drawn from the Purser; more clothes to be washed; adieus to be made for the 2nd, 3d and 4th times; live stock running about the decks for a week too soon, which time they would have spent more profitably on the Shore; and just one million other disagreeable circumstances, each particular item being sufficient to put a Navy officer in a bad temper and all combined enough to drive him crazy. And so of course we have felt illnatured and cross, and at length have concluded that we are all perfectly miserable. We long to be on our way again. Our hearts are in the Islands, the charming Isles of the Pacific, and the speedier we are on our course, the happier we will be. Nearly 10 months have gone by and we have not been out of the old and beaten track that has been followed by vessels of all nations for an hundred years.

However, we shall sail, I believe tomorrow or the day after, and I will leave this scrawl (which is the production of an unquiet mind) to be sent by the first vessel bound home. A long letter of some 20 pages I put in the Letter bag by the *"Philip Hone"* and hope you will get it in good time.

I think it is to Father's care I am indebted for the news papers, though you do not mention who it was, so thoughtful and so kind. They were quite a blessing to me and I trust that next year I may receive a larger bundle with a *few* Lancaster papers in it. You say they have no news, but remember that *even* the *old* advertisements will be *new* to me and that the very sight of the old types, or rather of their impressions, will be to me as grateful as the glimpse of the running stream is to the traveller in the Desert.

Do not think me weak or childish in begging so earnestly and so repeatedly for long letters and every description of news from Home. Could *you* every become a wanderer, you would soon learn the intense and yearning force with which *our* hearts turn to the Home we have left. Again and again let me entreat that all of you will write me such a letter as I have asked you for in *my* long letter of a few days ago.

We have received papers of date to the 3rd of January. I see that Governor Ritner has been obliged to play "Oliver Cromwell, in *one* act,"[1] and I read of so many other disgraceful scenes happening all over the country that I had as leave own myself a Turk as an American every bit. All the satisfaction an honest American (and I believe such individuals are rather rare) can have now a days is in the reccollection of deeds done by his Fore Fathers, or in the contemplation of better times for the future, though this latter be but a precarious hope.

And now with all love to each and every one of you, with the kindest remembrance to all Friends, I bid you adieu

William

[1] *Joseph Ritner (1780–1869), Democratic governor of Pennsylvania, 1835–1839. The October 1838 elections saw Ritner lose his bid for reelection and resulted in a dispute over which of two political parties controlled the lower legislative house. This dispute was brought to a crisis when threatening crowds occupied the capitol, forcing Governor Ritner to call out the militia in what is known as the "Buckshot War." The state senate ultimately decided the issue in favor of the Democrats.*

Miss Lydia Moore Reynolds
    Cornwall

[*Postscript:*] John Mellen, Thomas, *Mary Ann,* nor any one else, not even James Thomas Gantt have been spoken of in any of your letters, just as if I did not care to hear about them.[2]

[*Postmark:*] New York, Nov. 19

---

[2] *Lydia answered this postscript in her letter of 1 December 1839. These were all employees at the Cornwall estate. John Mellen or Mellin was the carriage and wagon driver. Thomas McLane was the gardener. Lydia had reminded her brother before he left that "Thomas wishes foreign seeds that you think will grow in this country—do not forget" (1838a); William fulfilled this request, as he notes in Letter No. 19. Mary Ann had worked in the house but was then married to the Cornwall founder, John Shay. James Thomas Gant was a house servant, probably black, who had once worked at the Naval Observatory in Washington.*

Callao Bay, June 30th 1839

My dear Sister Lydia,

My letters from Valparaiso written in
the early part of this month contain information regarding our
movements until that time; they were put on board the Brig "Philip
Hone," bound for New York via Cape Horn. I trust you will receive
them at an early period, for this is the season most favorable for
homeward bound vessels to double the Cape and *every one* in this
Squadron has wished with all his heart that the passage of the "Philip
Hone" may be speedy and safe. There is a possibility that letters sent
from this port via "Panama" may reach the United States *before* the
Philip H. can arrive, and a certainty, that though dispatched a month
later, they cannot be much behind the Brig; so very likely you may
get both at the same moment.

We sailed from Valparaiso on the 6th of June. The next day a Gale
came on, bringing with it heavy Sea and weather such as we had
been suffering in for 3 months in more southern Latitudes. We were
in despair, we had looked for clear skies and the mild breezes of
the Pacific; we were weary of storms and worn down with long
struggling against their fury; we longed for a respite, and yet found
we were still pursued. Our toils began afresh; we had thought them
ended and for one day all of us were repining and made ourselves as

miserable as possible. The troublesome wind was *ahead,* and we could not steer our course; the rain fell in torrents and had we not been kept busily at work to get the Ship in condition for the Gale, I believe we should all have gone half crazy. The sailing away to the Southward and Westward again was *not* what we wished or expected; none of us had sufficient good temper to bear cheerfully with our fate, and so as the gale increased, we made ourselves the more wretched by giving way to numberless, bitter and unavailing murmurs of grief and vexation at what we deemed our hard lot. However, in two days the Gale ceased, the Sun shone brightly, the Sea became smooth, and we moved before a brisk breeze with Spirits as lively as they had before been depressed.

12 days of pleasant sailing in the trades under a crowd of canvass, with clear nights and a full moon, passed away delightfully and brought us to anchor under the Island of San Lorenzo 7 miles from Callao on the evening of the 20th.

The other vessels had preceded us and the Squadron were once more together, with the exception of the Sea Gull; we have not heard from her since we parted at Orange Bay in April and I am almost afraid to write it, but we are fearful she and the poor fellows in her are lost. God help them and keep them from *so terrible a death*! It requires but little effort of *my* imagination to picture all *its* horrors. We are delaying further movements, hoping almost against hope that we shall see them, reluctant to admit the belief that our associates and friends, with whom many of us have often gone through scenes of danger and peril, should so soon have found a Sailor's grave.

We have been extremely busy taking in provisions and stores, making many alterations in the Ship's interior arrangements, and changing the officers from Ship to Ship in such an extensive manner that I began to tremble for myself: but I shall remain undisturbed in my elegant and comfortable room, where I have already passed a tolerably happy twelvemonth almost. In a few days, I shall have been *one year* attached to the Expedition. Time, Time, how *it* flies! and yet *he* cannot wing his way *too* rapidly for the next coming years. When I am once more among *you,* he may rest his pinions! (I presume it is allowable to transfer the gender, particularly allegorically.)

I have been to Lima—the City of Kings, the Capital of Golden Peru, founded by the renowned Pizarro and now the resting place for

his ashes.[1] It lies 7 or 8 miles from Callao and from thence, as well as
from our anchorage, the whole City is in full view. The country
intervening is entirely level and bare, unbroken by a single thing to
offer any obstruction to the Eye. Immediately in the rear of Lima, the
Andes are piled up against the Sky, their snowy summits rising many
thousand feet. The Scenery is most singular; the wide extent of
country spread before you like a map, the grey City in the distance
and the stupendous wall of mountains towering above the clouds.

If you will turn to some history of Peru, you learn all about the
great Earthquake that capsized *old Callao* and buried it under the Sea,
rolling the waters and vessels for a mile inland, where a pillar and
cross mark the spot to this day.[2]

Callao is the Seaport of Lima, but has been battered down and is
almost desolated by the continual wars that have been raging for
many years past. There is nothing to interest one within its limits but
the two Castles that are strong fortifications and have withstood
memorable and cruel sieges in their day.[3] There is a Golgotha of
skulls and bones outside their walls, the remains of hundreds of
victims to the unrelenting severity of General Rodil; he slaughtered
men like Sheep.[4]

[1] *Founded in 1535 by Francisco Pizarro, who named it the City of Kings,
Lima was the chief city of Spanish colonial South America for most of three
centuries. At the time of the squadron's visit, the population was about
53,000 (Tschudi 1849:63).*

[2] *Callao, founded in 1537 by Pizarro and principal seaport in western
South America for two centuries, was devastated in 1746 by an earthquake
and tidal wave and was rebuilt nearby. Lima also suffered considerable
damage.*

[3] *Callao was rebuilt around the Castillo del Real Felipe, a fortification in
which a Spanish force held out against a Peruvian patriot siege for a year and
a half in 1824–1826—the final Spanish gesture in the Peruvian war for
independence.*

[4] *José Ramón Rodil (b. 1789), Spanish general who commanded troops
against revolutionary movements in Peru and Chile, known for his harshness
in dealing with all sympathizers of independence; he is said to have caused the
deaths of hundreds or even thousands of civilians. Rodil commanded the
diehard garrison in Castillo del Real Felipe until February 1826, when he
signed the Spanish surrender to the patriot armies.*

It was on Sunday the 23rd that our party mounted on the most wretched beasts I ever saw, sallied forth from Callao in slow array, armed to the teeth. The road, though much frequented by passengers and running so short a distance between two towns, is infested by Robbers who make their demands in open day without ceremony. As we could not by any means excite our charges into a Gallop, we prepared to fight in case of need. However, we were not attacked, but the excitement added interest and merriment to the ride. I believe honestly that most of us were actually disappointed.

The country was entirely waste and uncultivated; once it teemed with the rich luxuriance of Tropical productions, but the havoc of war, *civil war in a Republic,* has taken men from the Ploughshare to the Sword and the necessaries of life have to be procured elsewhere. It was melancholy to look on the barren fields, where there had been so much more blood spilled than seeds sown.

On this road, for the first time in my life, I saw the odd spectacle of a woman riding astride, which is the custom of the country.

An hour and a half at a snail's gallop carried us to the gates of Lima, where we passed a bevy of fair and smiling girls. Presently we alighted from the weary animals at the Hotel of Mad. Domenichoni, man and beast quite willing to part. I expected indeed the *Gallignacios* would seize on us as lawful prizes and fly away with both Horse and Rider, for they were running about the Streets and resting on the house tops as our Pigeons do at home. Gallignacioes are *Turkey Buzzards!* and delicate ornaments they are to the public thoroughfares.[5]

However, there was an attraction to draw our looks away from the Birds, and to turn our thoughts into a sweeter train than dwelling on the sorry appearance of our Skeleton Hacks: and that attraction was the Ladies tripping by, dressed in the lovely *"Saya y manto."* Of this presently!

The morrow, Monday, was the feast of St. John, the festival of the "Almankyse"—the greatest day in the year for all Lima—and every

---

[5] *Gallinazo. Reynolds probably saw the black vulture in Lima; both the black and turkey vultures are found in the region, though the former is more frequently in the interior and is a resident of urban areas (Tschudi 1849:37–38; Koepke 1983:38).*

one in Lima was afloat in the Streets in holiday attire, thronging the road leading to the wild and barren place where the festival was going on. St. John preached in the wilderness, and the Limanians in their devout observance of the memory of the Saint hold their rejoicings in a mountain gorge where there is not a blade of grass nor a leaf of foliage to be seen, only the bare earth and the black and gloomy rocks.[6]

The spot, however, commanded a superb view of Lima with its many domes and spires and the silvery Rimac winding by the walls, of the desert waste of country, of the crowded port of Callao, and of the blue Pacific sweeping far away until it met the Sky.

I cannot say that the festival was observed either in a devout or even a moral way. There were several rough booths on the ground, tippling shops, and dancing, drinking, *murdering*, profanity and obscenity in all varieties were going on in a miscellaneous manner, and just as if all that was done so publicly and on such an occasion was praiseworthy and highly creditable to the actors; and these actors were the descendants of the "Children of the Sun,"[7] of the *Incas* of Peru.

We soon were weary of looking on and turned towards Lima again in the midst of an hundred Horsemen, natives of almost *as many* climes. Most of them were gallantly mounted and bestrode their steeds with the grace of a cavalier. But the women's horses were as gay and fiery, and the women rode with the ease and security of a Centaur and with the recklessness of a devil may care Midshipman—though I must say, I do not wish to see their masculine habit of sitting astride ever adopted in North America.

[6] *Amancaes. The German scholar Johann Jakob von Tschudi, in his* Travels in Peru, during the Years 1838–1842 *(1849:95–96), writes that "one of the most popular recreations of the Limenos, especially the people of color, is the* Paseo de Amancaes. . . . *The Amancaes is a gently sloping plain, about half a mile north-west of Lima . . . bounded by . . . hills." Archibald Smith, in his* Peru as It Is *(1839), describes the festival as one of merriment and the mixing of social classes but without the violence Reynolds suggests.*

[7] *A reference to the belief in Incaic times that the ruler or Sapa Inca was descended from the god of the sun.*

Their riding dress *is short*; pantalettes all lace and embroidery *partly* cover the ancle and the tiny foot is shod with a silver spur of twice its own magnitude. For head gear, they wore broad brimmed straw hats decked with flaunting ribbons, and the graceful *poncho* fell across the shoulders, making their whole appearance exceedingly dashing and picturesque.

Many and various were the groups we passed, of all classes from the Grandee to the Negro, all going to and from the "Almankyse"; and moving, ever changing, living masses presented an infinite degree of interest and kept us wondering and admiring, so that Time flew by unheeded.

A row of Coaches were drawn up on either side of the "Almeda"—a shaded walk bordered with orange groves that were rich with their golden fruit and refreshed by the spray from many fountains.[8]

Slowly and leisurely, one by one, our Cavalcade rode by, peering with strained optics at the lovely ones who were the occupants of the "volantes";[9] three times did we turn and repass the line of beauties. I let the reins fall on my horse's neck and with my glass at my eye I inspected the charms of the fair Limanians with a much closer scrutiny than was consistent with home bred notions of decorum, politeness, or even decency; but the more we stared, the oftener we reviewed, the sweeter and more numerous were the smiles we were rewarded with. The dear creatures were, I believe, equally delighted, and I am sure I saw some faces the surpassing beauty of which I shall remember until my dying day, or at least until I can find a Mrs. Reynolds, whose greater charms shall drive the recollection of all other women out of my head for ever. Oh! these Limanians, they were lovely beyond belief and I could scarcely think I was gazing on flesh and blood. Sadly I rode away and I shall never see them again.

The side walks were thronged with females, all of them wearing that dress which is peculiar to Lima alone; for no where else in the world, not even in Callao which is but 6 miles distant, does the 'Saya

---

[8] *There were two* alamedas *or promenades in Lima at this time; Reynolds probably refers to the* alameda vieja *in the old San Lázaro section, near the Franciscan convent of Descalzos.*

[9] *Two-wheeled, light carriages driven by a rider on the horse.*

y manto' form the bewitching costume of the feminines. I know that I cannot describe its make or appearance so that you can have an idea of it, but I will bring Home some pictures that will.

The "Saya" is the lower portion of the dress and is of satin of any colour. It fits *taut* round the waist and is gathered or pleated very close, the narrow folds reaching to the skirts and taken in there also. Something rather larger than those "Bishops"[10] of yours which I used to cut to pieces in days of yore but answering the same purpose is attached below the girdle, and as far as improving the figure goes, which I dare swear is the only object *you* have in wearing the concern, I must say the Lima women have a much better taste than their North American Sisters. They render their forms perfect; in my humble and you may say ignorant, good for nothing opinion, you only spoil yours, but I must not write any more about this appurtenance for it *is none* of *my* business and I might perhaps get into a scrape. The skirts are short enough to display the ancle, and the circle of the dress is as contracted there as at the waist, preventing the wearers from taking long steps.

The upper part is of soft black silk, confined under the girdle behind and allowed to droop a little below it. It is carried up *over* the head and brought across the neck and bust by the hands, the right hand going to the left side and the left hand closing the parts over the face, leaving *only the right Eye* exposed, so that unless you can distinguish a woman by her feet and her right eye, the Saya y manto offers the most perfect masquerade habit. A better one could not be devised, the wearer being able to see every thing, but shrouded within the mysterious garment she is secure from identity, let the eyes *be* curious and prying as they may.

The position obliged to be assumed when the Saya y manto is adopted, even in infancy, has a great tendency to make the figure erect, graceful and stately, and consequently the Lima women are more majestic in their persons than any other in the world. Their walk is superb. Queen Victoria might envy them their step. Queen though she be, I doubt whether her foot has half the dignity and grace that I saw personified in hundreds of the Limanian women, the

---

[10] *The bishop was a type of bustle popular in eighteenth- and nineteenth-century North America.*

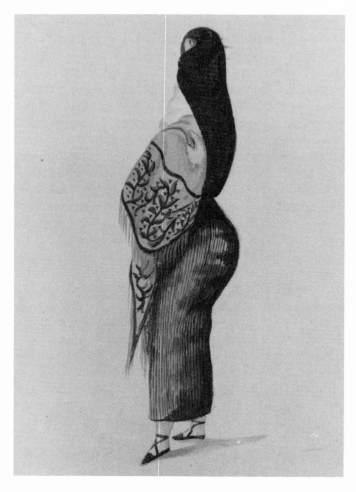

Woman of Lima wearing saya y manta, *by John Dale. It was this traditional attire of the* limeñas *which so intrigued William Reynolds. Naval officers of the period cultivated their sketching ability, as this drawing by Lieutenant Dale of the expedition testifies. Courtesy J. Welles Henderson Collection.*

veriest Peasant treads like a Juno. We were all in raptures and I thought I could wish to have a walking Saya y manto before my eyes forever.

The Lima women know how to use the only eye they expose, and many a glance was shot at us from those solitary orbs that wont

might to burn our very hearts up. Never tell me of a blue eye again,
but of those dark as the raven hair, bright and glowing as the
lightning flash and a cheek where the olive struggles with the rose.
Ay, of these *I* will tell *you* when I get Home once more.

The Lima women are not all hard hearted: *some* of them will
sometimes take away that left hand and let the impenetrable veil drop
for a moment, just long enough to make you wish the moment an
hour. It was amusing to see the dear creatures, *so* kind they were,
they *would* show their faces, blushing at their boldness yet smiling at
our wonderous looks. But it was only for an instant; the manto was
again adjusted and the fair one swept by in the crowd never to be
seen by us again, a melancholy fact that makes me wretched to think
of it.

The rulers of Lima have tried to abolish the Saya y manto, but
in vain. Man's authority could not in this instance do away with
woman's predujices. Wives, daughters, sisters rebelled, they regarded
not the mandates of the lawgivers and most stubbornly they persist
in wearing their favorite costume. So be it, may their descendants
imitate them until the end of time. That dress, which *as a street dress*
is the most unique, faultless and elegant attire that I can conceive of,
ought to endure for ever. How it originated, or why it is confined
exclusively to the City of Lima, I do not know and cannot imagine: *I*
wish it was in wider use.[11]

July 6th

We *are* to sail in a day or two. We *were* to have left some days *ago*,
but various causes are keeping us still. *No news from the Sea Gull* and
the most sanguine have given her up as lost. Poor, poor fellows,
what a terrible lot. The two officers were young men of my age, one,
if he be indeed gone, leaving a wife more youthful than himself and a
child that he has never seen.[12]

[11] *The family was less taken with Lima dress styles as interpreted by
William; Lydia responded, 1 December 1839: "None of us can understand the
description of the 'saya y manta.' We will be obliged to wait for your return."*
[12] *Passed midshipmen James W. E. Reid and Frederick A. Bacon were lost
with the* Sea Gull. *Reid was the son of Robert R. Reid (1789–1841),
congressman, judge, and later governor of Florida (1840–1841). Bacon,*

I have been to Lima once more and passed the 4th of July there without the least fuss or jollity. As I find that too many doubloons slip through one's fingers on such excursions, I shall not go again to the City of Kings. I bought a Gold chain such as are known as *Panama chains*, it will make an elegant guard for Mrs. Wm. Reynolds' watch; and one of Silver for Elly, the infant *"tween Victoria."*[13] I thought of her whenever I put on my red flannel shirts, and as I never was very comfortable at those times I used to wish myself looking at the "tween" in her snug crib, far far from all gales and mountainous Seas.

At this present writing it is 9 of the clock and I am in an open tent thrown up on the beach in the most cut throat spot of the most villianous portion of the globe. The others have gone for a time, I am alone, and the night is black enough. Simon Blunt has just been here rigged up as a countryman to borrow a pistol, as he is in search of Deserters. I lent him one; two similar weapons are touching the corner of this sheet and a huge sword lies across my knees, all to protect my self against the renegadoes who slit one's throat for a dollar with much less compunction than a Butcher feels in slaughtering a Lamb; it is a mere pastime with them and they have no scruples. It is exceedingly pleasant and cheerful, and I feel quite happy to be so comfortably situated; and yet it might be remedied by placing some Marines as sentries to protect us and the instruments, but the Captain does not seem to deem such a precaution necessary.[14]

---

appointed to the navy from Connecticut in 1832, had seen previous service in the Mediterranean before being warranted as passed midshipman and assigned to the expedition upon the eve of its departure in 1838 (ZB).

[13] *Eleanor (1835–1923), the last Reynolds baby, had been born while her brother was on his second cruise, aboard the* Potomac. *She had deposed as household favorite her sister Hal—Harriot Sumner Reynolds (1832–1898)—named after a Boston benefactor of her young midshipman brother, while William was on his first cruise aboard the* Peacock *in 1832. Lydia wrote, "Ellie talks a great deal about her silver chain and never forgets to pray for 'Brother Willie' " (1839b). Two years before, eighteen-year-old Victoria had become queen of Great Britain and Ireland.*

[14] *Between 1826 and 1865, the Peruvian government was presided over by no fewer than thirty-four chief executives, most of them military officers.*

I have only to say that the fewer nights I have in my life time such as those I pass here at this confounded observatory, the better for me and the more prospect that I shall reach an old age.

I have drawn my table across the entrance to the tent as a sort of barricade, but every footfall I hear thrills my nerves; and they are not generally very weak, but this fighting against odds and a Spanish knife in the dark is not to be without apprehension as to the issue. If we get to Sea with whole skins it will be more by good fortune than to any precautionary arrangements on the part of those who sent us here. There! I was sure some one was pulling at the canvass and that I heard stealthy steps. I could *not* sit still, but went out Lanthern in one hand, Pistols in the other— 'twas only the wind. I must say that my hand shook a little when I came in and I shall feel much relieved when my companions return.

I wrote a part of this letter last night during my watch when I felt just as I do now. I have been so continually busy that these midnight hours of terror offer the only time for such purposes. So you *must* excuse imperfections with a good grace and just remember the difficulties that are always in *my* way when you go to seal up a meagre letter to me. I worry and work and plot and take every advantage that offers to scratch you some miserable lines, and in return I want and I have begged *you,* who have every facility, to write to me often and more at length. If you get my last letters from Valparaiso, I do not think you will neglect me again.

I am getting old—that is in body. I know it, I feel it, I see it. Wrinkles are appearing under my eyes and *they* are rather worse from so much observing. Some mornings after a hard day and night's work reading the instruments and straining my eyes in the effort, till I get fair sick deprived of necessary rest and eating from hand to mouth, when even I can find a chance, I look like a man of 50 in the face and I feel more dead than alive. Three years without having a dozen nights sleep undisturbed and undergoing a constant exposure to the worst vicissitudes of weather will make a slight inroad into one's

---

This most tumultuous period in the nation's history was characterized by frequent civil wars and a resultant absence of security in the countryside. At the time of the squadron's visit, the Peru-Bolivian confederated government had just been overthrown by a Chilean army enlisted by Peruvian dissidents.

constitution, and I expect to find myself at the end of that time both looking and feeling a dozen years older than Sam.

I do hope Sam will have a wife when I return. It will be *so* nice to have *two real homes,* and I despair of setting up one myself. I shall be a good for nothing creature all my life, I am afraid, and Sam must look out for the family. John will not be much better than me and Jim will in all probability turn into a stupid sloth of a bookworm, or else a great philosopher.[15]

I had some glorious sport a few days ago, hunting Seal. Two or three of us went in a Boat to an Island 7 miles from here where they were abundant. The scene of activity was wild and savage, well suited for the haunts of the huge game we were in pursuit of.[16]

We were in a narrow pass between the large Island and a smaller one, with but little more room on either side than was requisite for our Boat, the Surf breaking around us in all directions. The Shores rose 5 and 600 feet, perpendicular as a wall though broken into innumerable small ledges, and many Islets and rocks that were exceedingly singular and striking in their outlines rose above the water to various heights and were alive with Birds. One of these Islets had an arch clear through it and altogether looked like a Fortress and a Bridge. Several of the rocks resembled antique turrets, the architecture of which might be a little irregular; they were tall and slender and looked as though they were the work of man. On some flat ledges of rocks that were but 5 or 6 feet above the water, Seals to the number of 3 and 4 hundred were lying basking in the Sunshine and stowed as close together and in some such manner as a drove of Hogs lie down to rest.

We were excited almost beyond bounds; we could hardly restrain our eagerness to blaze away at them. Slowly and cautiously we

[15] *Sam, only twenty months older than William, did not marry until his forty-third year. John and Jim never married.*

[16] *The Humboldt Current, which runs northward along the coast of northern Chile and Peru, is extremely rich in marine organisms, which in turn attract fish, sea birds by the millions, seals, and penguins. The islands along the coast—the so-called guano islands—are covered with these animals in great profusion; Reynolds was apparently at San Lorenzo and El Frontón islands.*

approached to within 15 yards of the herd and let drive with a fair aim right into a monster that looked like the Patriarch of the gang, but our fowling pieces were of no avail and nearly all of the Seals, awakened by the noise, arose and wollowed to the edge of the rocks and let themselves tumble clumsily into the Sea. Some remained and we loaded again. Looking up, the Sky was actually darkened with the millions of birds that our shots had startled on the wing; from off the small ledges on the hill side where they had been at rest on every spot that could give them foothold, from off the rocks and Islets, the swarm arose in countless numbers and were soaring about as if unable to understand why their solitary retreat had been invaded. I never saw so great a flight of birds, it was equal to the "Quails in Egypt,"and the effect of so many wheeling spots against the Sky was strange and startling. Highest of all were several *Condors*, out of reach. Next below them were flocks of *Pelicans*, but so shy they did not come within shot; I cracked away at two of them that were perched on a rocky point 150 yds. distant, just to have the satisfaction of saying I had shot at a Pelican, and actually I—frightened them off. The lower cloud was made up of Shags, Gulls, Pigeons and Ducks, and of these we shot a Boat load. We fired at the Seals until all our powder was gone, and though we wounded several, we could not slay one outright. They played round the Boat after they took to the water without any fear, but we did not shoot at them then, for if killed while swimming they sink instantly. The Surf was too high to allow us to land or we might have killed them with clubs, and though we had not the triumph of bearing a dead body away with us, I was highly pleased, charmed, delighted and almost contented. The sport was so novel—to be shooting at Sea Animals as large as the Boat that carried us—oh! it was grand. There was some adventure in it and I followed it with an ardour that would have done honour to the mighty Nimrod himself.[17]

I shot a beautiful Bird of the Heron kind—of white and delicate plumage, the only one of the kind that has been obtained. He makes a fine Specimen for the Naturalist and had not his species been

[17] *Nimrod was the son of Cush, described as a mighty hunter in Gen. 10:8 and 1 Chron. 1:10. He was a ruler in ancient Babylonia and founder of the Assyrian empire.*

already supplied with a name, I should have had him termed the
Rinalditus —— something else. Mercy! only think of the Capes and
Islands and Mountains that I shall call after the names of certain
individuals, having them all put in bold letters on that Chart that will
be a guide to all navigators for ever.

The Schooner Active, formerly one of the Exploring Expedition,
arrived here a few days ago, 125 days from New York.[18] She brought
dates to 8th of February. I received a package of newspapers up to
Dec. 19th, but no letters—*could* you have been *so thoughtless* and *cruel*
as to send me *printed papers* and *no written words? oh! no*, I will not
think so. I must believe that the letters were lost on the way and
bewail my ill fortune. I had rather they *were* lost, than that *you had
neglected me.*

And about writing—there is a possibility that we will run into
Valparaiso next Spring, as we return from the attempt South. All the
officers are directing their friends to send letters to that port until
about the 1st February 1840 by every opportunity, and I hope that
you will look out for notices in the papers of vessels bound for there
and forward letters and papers. As soon as you get this, write a
long, long letter and direct it to this Ship at Valparaiso through the
Lyceum, with a request that they will forward it according to its
direction. Send one every month to the same place until January or
Feb. Send a thousand by the Store Ship to the Sandwich Islands and
do not let me be always the worst off in the Ship, for it absolutely is
torture to see others poring over lines that were penned several
months after those from your own home. Most of the officers have
letters to February; none for me since November.[19]

I will keep this open as long as possible; this is the 9th and it is
not certain whether we sail to morrow or in two or three days.

The Observatory is broken up, much to my joy. I have not been
there since the night I have written about, but contrary to my

[18] *The* Active *was a 122-ton, 2-gun vessel bought by the navy in 1837
for the expedition; she proved unsuitable, however, and was sold to private
hands in 1838.*

[19] *In May, William had found three letters addressed to him in
Valparaíso, one of which was Lydia's of 18 November 1838, answering his
Letter No. 1 from Madeira.*

intentions I have been to Lima twice and shall go again very likely. Yesterday I was sent there to bring down a Deserter from the Ship and I made an excellent Constable.

I forgot to mention to you that I can *almost* say *I* was robbed on my first trip. I put a small Boy on my Horse to ride him back to his owner, while I went in the Coach; *he* was stopped and eased of a pair of spurs that *I* had borrowed, so you see that it is just the same as if the deed had been perpetrated on my own person. Two men were stripped on that day and several murders have been committed since; but none of the officers of the Expedition have been molested.

Two of the Falmouth's officers were severely hurt in an affray the other evening, and one of the Boat's crew run through the face by a bayonet.[20] The soldiers who were called to protect them sided with the mob and they made their escape with great difficulty. Oh! it's a charming country, pleasant in all its ways. The very first step I took on it, when I landed on the mole for the first time, was over a dead body half lashed up in filthy rags, and a dozen of us passing did not frighten way the Gallinaceos, who were waiting quietly for a meal. First impressions exceedingly favorable of course.

I *do long so much* to hear from you all, to know what you are doing, to hear how Bangor flourishes and of every little thing relating to any of you.[21] But you would not tell me in your letters and *I must wait another year*—poor, miserable me! . . .

[20] *The USS* Falmouth *was a sloop of war of about the same size as the* Vincennes. *Launched at the Boston Navy Yard in 1827, it was assigned to cruise Pacific waters protecting American citizens and commerce.*

[21] *In early 1836, John Reynolds purchased from Thomas Bird Coleman 507 acres and a forge named Bangor in York County. Samuel Reynolds, who had begun working at the age of sixteen as a clerk at Coleman's Castle Fin Forge, was given management of his father's venture. The forge was out of repair and the house was poor, but Sam was sure he could make money. Unfortunately, the construction of the Susquehanna and Tidewater Canal through the Reynolds's land did so much harm that by summer 1839 Bangor ceased to operate. Although John Reynolds was awarded $6,507.25 in damages at the time, the case was appealed and was still in the courts upon William's return in 1842. Lydia's 1 December letter told her brother that Sam was still at home in Cornwall and "uncertain of what he will do."*

I have written to a Mr. Johnson, Merchant, of New York for $500.00 worth of Sea Stores for my mess, to be sent out in the Store Ship that will leave the U. States in the fall of this year to meet the Squadron—my messmates of course being equally responsible with myself, which you may remember in case of accident. If you can think of any small thing to send me and have an opportunity to New York, Mr. J. will forward it with the Stores. *Try* and think of some thing, and whatever comes will be most acceptable, even if it were some nice white handkerchiefs, elegantly stiched and marked. Small donations from my friends of either Sex who would prove themselves to hold me in kind remembrance might be put in the same box, without the least detriment to the objects of this Expedition, and certainly would cause *me* to feel exceedingly grateful and obliged. I will hope and long for this, let me not be made wretched by disappointment.

There have been so many changes and promotions in the Squadron lately that I should now have had an acting appointment or have been at the head of the list ready for the next vacancy, *but,* and there is always a *but* to interfere with one's hopes and plans, Captain Wilkes has taken in this Ship an officer from the Falmouth as Master, thus overslaughing Baldwin, myself and a dozen others, contrary to his promise that he never would interfere with our rank in such a way.[22] There was no necessity for his so doing in this instance, and

[22] *This officer was Passed Midshipman Edwin J. De Haven (1816–1865), nephew of the* Falmouth's *commander, Isaac McKeever. McKeever took two passed midshipmen from the expedition in exchange. Born to a seventh-generation Pennsylvania family of Dutch descent, De Haven had been warranted passed midshipman in 1836. He served as acting master on the* Vincennes *until he transferred to the* Peacock *at the Fijis in 1840; the master was the chief warranted officer on a ship, responsible for navigation and ranking above the passed midshipmen. De Haven went on to command his own polar expedition in 1850–1851, when he was sent in search of Sir John Franklin and discovered Grinnell Island. After several years of Coast Survey duty, he was pronounced unfit for duty in 1861 and put on the retired list in 1862 (ZB). Augustus S. Baldwin was a passed midshipman who had been acting master of the* Porpoise *and was transferred to the* Peacock *at Callao; see Letter No. 15, n. 53.*

we all understand the motives that led to it too well to admire them and feel that we have been deprived of rights that were justly our due, obliged to remain in a subordinate grade when we had, by a year's service in the Expedition, become entitled to advancement when it offered. And to have the sweet cup dashed from our lips, when just anticipating the draught, by a stranger who himself may almost be accused of mercenary motives, is rather a bitter disappointment and has not the slightest tendency to increase our ardour in the Service, or to strengthen our faith in the justice of our Commander.

It is the heaviest blow *save one* that has fallen on me since I entered the Navy and the wound that has been inflicted will rankle all the cruise. The injustice of the affair and its cause and effect will be felt every day, because the different individuals will be continually in contact and made to know the line that is between them and one who should never have been among them.

However, it has to be borne with as an Evil without a remedy and though I should continue quiet, I feel as if my very life had been taken away.

I have not been ill a day and shall take as much care of my health as possible. I fear that another opportunity to write to you will not offer for some months, but whenever there is a chance I will not neglect it. We look for a pleasant time among the Islands and shall bring up at Sydney in the fall. The Relief is to go Home, touching at the Sandwich Islands and Sydney and discharging provisions for us. She is detached from the Ex. and will be so long on the way that we send no letters by her.[23]

The more, the longer I am away from you, the oftener my thoughts turn to Home and all that makes that Home so dear. If I had not seen an anchorage to run for and rest awhile, apart from the troublesome world and among those bound to me by closer ties than the rude companionship of acquaintance, I should feel that life had

---

[23] *Wilkes's decision to detach the* Relief *from the squadron at Callao made the expedition rely all the more on the arrival of supplies in the annual store ships and on obtaining provisions locally and led to reduced rations later in the voyage.*

lost its greatest charm, its first blessing; may it remain as a haven of Love, and I shall only be perfectly happy when I am once more an inmate of my own Home, though it be my fate to leave it soon again.

[*Inner wrapper*:] I must bid you farewell on this envelope, remember me to all friends and accept for yourselves all the love of

Your brother William

Miss L. M. Reynolds
    Cornwall

[*Outer wrapper*:] Via Panama

[*Postmark*:] New York, Oct. 7

Letter No. 10

U.S. Ship Vincennes
Point Venus, Matavai Bay
Island of Otaheite, or Tahita
September 12th 1839

My Dear Sister,

We anchored off this far famed and lovely
Island on the 10th after a 60 days cruise from Callao, 30 days of
which were passed in surveying and examining the clusters of Coral
Islands that were in our way.[1] As we were behind our time, this was
done in a hurried manner and we had but little chance or leisure to
enjoy ourselves by visiting the inhabitants or observing the curious
things that abounded in the Islands.

The formation of these Islands is one of nature's mysteries that
even in this enlightened age has defied a satisfactory explanation.
Theories have been started and much has been said and written in
support of them, but as no one of them agrees with the other, doubt
and uncertainty still follow in their train.[2] If you feel any interest

---

[1] *The squadron visited about ten islands in the Paumotu or Tuamotu
archipelago before Tahiti.*

[2] *Reynolds's curiosity about the origin of volcanic and coral islands was
shared by the expedition's geologist James Dwight Dana and conchologist
Joseph P. Couthouy, both of whom later developed theories about the
formation of such islands, based on the work of Charles Darwin. Essentially
the theories held that after the emergence of volcanic islands above the ocean
surface, coral reefs grow in the shallow water around their edges; with
subsequent subsiding of the ocean floor, the coral continues to grow, but a*

concerning them, by referring to the proper authorities you can pore over the scientific remarks of those who have visited and examined these Islands solely with a view to add to the Geographical [*overwritten:* Geological] history of the Earth. I think you ought to feel this interest because it behoves every one to be acquainted with all portions of the Globe we inhabit, to know of their peculiarities of soil, people etc., etc., etc.

These Islands are supposed to have arisen from the depths of the ocean by the almost incredible labours of the Lithophytes, or corralline worms. Think of this! of the feeble insects raising a strong wall out of the mighty sea. As well as I reccollect, there is some slight remark about coral reefs in my old Journal—place, Bencoolen.[3]

The Shores are low, just showing above the water's edge, the growth of trees and shrubbery forming the only elevation above the horizon. How soil came there and how the Trees came to grow is a question settled by conjecture alone!

In form the Islands are mostly oblong, but still there is much irregularity in their shape and extent. The Shores are narrow and in most places fringed with a dense growth of beautiful trees and shrubbery, but here and there occur waste and naked patches of reef partly under water. The centre of the Island is one immense Lagoon, a portion of the Ocean walled in, as it were, by the tiny worms; a labour that man shrinks from as he beholds it and which he is forced to credit as a more gigantic operation than any of his own. Excuse my attempt at illustration; though I do not make an elegant vignette, yet it may give you an idea of the singular conformation of these Gems of the Sea.

[*Sketch followed.*]

Do you see how the Trees show above the Land and how the Lagoon is environed by the shores? But I have to smile at the idea of my poor

---

lagoon forms between the reef and the island. Eventually the floor subsides to the point that the island disappears altogether, leaving only a reef and lagoon (Appleman 1985:91–95).

[3] *Reynolds visited Bengkulu, Sumatra, in January 1833 during his first cruise, on the* Boxer.

paper or my worse description being able to impart to you even a
faint picture of the lovely appearance of the Isles. The Surf breaks
furiously on the beach that makes next the Ocean, but the Lagoon
within is calm and unruffled as a summer lake and of a blue as
transparent as the azure vault of Heaven.

No soundings are to be had immediately after leaving the Beach
and we run the ships close aboard the Islands. The views as we
passed along the Shore were absolutely enchanting, though from the
Deck we were obliged to content ourselves with occasional glimpses
of the Lagoon, caught as we went by openings in the trees or the
naked patches of reef. "The trees were as a screen, a drop curtain,
and we could not see what was going on in the sylvan recesses of
their midst; but from aloft the blue extent of the Lagoon and its rich
green frame lay beneath the eye, looking as if it could have been
created for no impurer use than to yield up the Pearls that abound in
its depths: a fitting home it is for these precious things that possess
so much of poetry in their appearance and their use, a home that the
maiden might glance in for her mirror while she adorned her brow
with the treasures of its coral bed." So says my Journal and I spent
whole hours on the Royal Yard, entranced with the singular and
picturesque loveliness of the scene I was gazing upon.

The Groups of natives that were collected here and there on the
beach, following us as we sailed by, shouting, gesticulating and
dancing, added a peculiar life and freshness to the view and at times,
when we approached in Boats to land, from their behaviour and
appearance I was strongly reminded of the prints representing
Columbus stepping on the Shores of the new world—that is, of the
huddling together of the naked Indians and of the tropical
background in their rear.

One island that we passed was uninhabited; most probably it had
never known the presence of man the destroyer, for we could find no
traces to mark that such had been the case. It exhibited nature in her
Virgin State, free and pure from the desolating influence of the
human race: "The vegetation was rich and luxuriant, and the groves
of trees were beautiful as the leafy bowers of the fairies; the air was
darkened with clouds of sea birds on the wing and the whole Island
swarmed with myriads of all varieties of the feathered tribes. The

poor things had chosen this Isle as their resting places: mark their instinct! Surely they know that to avoid the haunts of men is their Safety, but yet they forgot to fly from men when they appeared, they were so innocent; that Isle had been an Eden to them, where they had lived and had all their little loves in undisturbed peace. It was a sweet scene to look upon, the mothers on the nests, the unfledged ones rustling among the grass, and the loving males flitting from tree to tree, all unconscious of harm, that ruthless harm which was so near to them. The scientific zeal of those who were the first invaders of their solitary retreats allowed them no mercy and the slaughter among them was immense. The poor birds were cruelly deceived; *they did not offer to fly or start, when approached* and, however much it may sound like a fable, *they actually suffered themselves* to be *plucked like fruit from the branches: bags full of young ones were brought off alive and any number of old ones, whose necks had been wrung as soon as they were gathered from the Trees"* [*Quotation from Reynolds Journal No. 1:208*].

There were no animals on this Island, but we procured some fine Turtle, which afforded us delicious meals. Sharks were thick as flies, thousands of them following the Boats: it was really fearful to see them!

Of the people of the other Islands I have nothing to say except that some of them were cannibals because they obligingly signified to us that if we came on Shore they would kill and eat us: and they showed their great white teeth and built a fire immediately as if to verify their words. We had interpreters with us and had no difficulty in sustaining a conversation. Gestures also were as significant in meaning as words and as they were evidently accomplished in pantominical (if there be such a word) representations of such an agreeable operation, we had no doubt that they had frequently been guilty of the hideous reality. This was at Clermont Tonnerre Island, and the talk was followed by showers of stones and clubs at our people; fortunately none were injured, as the boats were quickly pulled out of reach of their missiles.[4] A few discharges of small shot from three or four fowling pieces, which took effect in the legs of

[4] *Clermont de Tonnerre or Reao Island, in the Tuamotu archipelago, was the squadron's first landfall (13 August 1839) after leaving Peru.*

those who were the principal actors, sent them among the bushes and we landed without further molestation.[5]

Our intercourse with other Islanders was slight and to me extremely vexatious and unsatisfactory. Some half dozen came on board, wondering at all they saw; their likenesses were taken and they were dismissed with presents.[6]

I never fell in with them on shore and I was very happy when we dropped our anchor at this populous and charming Island. My happiness was increased to find that a Whale Ship was to sail in 10 days for the United States and that I could send letters to my own Home![7]

Since the days of Cook, this Island has been an object of interest to the world. It is identified with the name of that celebrated navigator from his frequent visits to it and from the wonderful interest his narratives possess.[8]

After Cook came the visit of Bligh in the Bounty, which terminated in the mutiny of his crew and their returning with the Ship to the Island, where they had formed attachments that they were loath to leave and where they hoped to pass a life of ease and indulgence free from labour or care, but they were sadly disappointed.[9]

[5] *One of the charges considered during Wilkes's court-martial in 1842 was the use of unnecessary and excessive violence against these islanders. The commander was acquitted of this charge.*

[6] *Expedition artist Alfred T. Agate frequently made sketches of islanders, often with the aid of a camera lucida, an instrument that projects a virtual image of an object by means of mirrors.*

[7] *Tahiti was a popular place for American whalers to rest their crews and reprovision during the 1830s, with some seventy-five ships visiting annually.*

[8] *During his first Pacific voyage (1768–1771), Lieutenant James Cook visited Tahiti to chart the transit of the planet Venus across the sun.*

[9] *Captain William Bligh (1754–1817), who had sailed on Cook's third Pacific voyage (1776–1779), visited Tahiti in the HMS Bounty in 1787; the famous mutiny occurred two years later. Bligh made a second voyage to Tahiti in 1792, accomplishing his original mission of transplanting breadfruit trees to the West Indies; he went on to become admiral and governor of New South Wales (1805–1808).*

The results of that mutiny were most singular and far more
important to the world than any of those who were engaged in it
could have had the least idea of. I allude to the colony that sprang
from those of the Mutineers who landed at Pitcairn's Island. This little
band, though they were the progeny of men who were deeply
stained with the blood of their fellow creatures, were without guile in
their lives: they were pure and innocent as angels and their history
has not a parrellel in the annals of the Human Race. As you read it,
you can scarcely believe that you are not perusing a pleasant fiction,
for it seems incredible that mortals *could be* so good. I have not time
to say more, but refer you to "Beechey's Voyage" in the English
Sloop of War Blossom; it has been published in the United States and
the account of his visit to Pitcairn's Island will repay you for the slight
trouble of procuring the work.[10] The "Mutiny of the Bounty" forms
the subject of a number of Harpers Family Library and will furnish
you with interesting reading. I forget whether it is mentioned in
either of these books that the retreat of the few mutineers to Pitcairn's
Island, and the fate of the Bounty herself, was an entire mystery
for many years. No one knew what had become of this remnant of
the crew and all search after them had been in vain. Long, long
afterwards, when the affair had been forgotten, the accidental visit of
an American Ship brought their history to light. Many and curious
are the reflections that come into one's mind while dwelling on the
singular circumstances of a people who had such a mixed and bloody
origin, whose habits were civilized if not refined, who used the

[10] *Frederick William Beechey*, Narrative of a Voyage to the Pacific
and Beering's Strait, to Co-operate with the Polar Expeditions;
Performed in His Majesty's Ship Blossom, under the Command of
Captain F. W. Beechey . . . in the Years 1825, 26, 27, 28 . . .
(Philadelphia: Carey & Lee, 1832). *After the twenty-five mutineers returned
to Tahiti, some nine of them and eighteen Polynesians took the* Bounty *to
Pitcairn Island in 1790; what followed, however, was not a history of purity
and innocence, and by 1800 only one Englishman remained there alive. The
next generation at Pitcairn was more peaceful, as Reynolds suggests. The
Pitcairn colony was first discovered in 1808 by the American ship* Topaz *and
not by Beechey until 1825 (Stackpole 1953:238–46, 252–53).*

English language and preserved the feeling that they were and ought be subjects to the Crown of England, being the inhabitants of an Island in the South Pacific and existing in a thriving state for so many years unknown to the busy world.

After Bligh, the Missionaries! the Christians leaving their homes to wean the Savage from his Idol Gods and from his human sacrifices and feasts.[11] The Missionaries have succeeded in this with a part of the Islanders, but some still reject their interference and hold no intercourse with them. However, I am not prepared to say any thing on this subject, as yet; but I shall endeavour to gain information and trust that at some future time I will be able to give you an impartial and faithful account of the influence the Missionaries have exerted among the Islanders and also of the individual characters of the Reverend Gentlemen! I am aware that this is a subject of earnest inquiry among many in the United States and that I am young and ignorant to speak on so grave a matter; but I will try all I can to inform myself correctly and what comes under my own eye, I shall endeavour to contemplate without prejudice and judge of it the best of my abilities.

The men who conduct an affair of such tremendous importance as the converting a savage race to the knowledge of the true God and directing them in all the windings of a new life should be wise and enlightened beyond ordinary mortals. Why, I am really about to perpetrate a prosy disquisition which I had better save you, particularly as my time is limited and I have been interrupted just about two dozen times while writing thus far, which must be my excuse for all inacuracies, and they are numerous.

This Island is high land and it was really refreshing to see the

---

[11] *The London Missionary Society (LMS) was organized in 1795 as an interdenominational Protestant effort to convert Pacific islanders. The society began its work in Tahiti and Tongataboo in 1797; by converting the chief Pomare, it was well established in Tahiti by 1819. In subsequent years, the LMS and other Protestant and Catholic missionary efforts made considerable headway in converting islanders and in gaining power over island governments and societies across the Pacific. The influence of the missionaries and the value of their work were the subject of some controversy in the West.*

sharp peaks above the clouds, after being a month among the low Islets of the dangerous Archipelago.[12]

All the rich beauties of Tropical Scenery are displayed here, and wherever the eye turns it finds something lovely to dwell upon. I only wish that some of you could be with me to enjoy the strange sights I meet with in these distant Lands, for tongue cannot tell of them, nor can the mind of man conceive of them unless he beholds them. Many, many a time has this feeling been uppermost in my heart, adding to my happiness from the very idea of the thing, although I knew it to be impossible.

If I should live to be an old man, I think I shall have exceeding pleasure in learning of the changes that have come over places visited in my youth. I feel such a curious degree of interest in them, as if I had a Home in each of them, *almost;* and it seems to me now as if I shall never rest satisfied until I go to each and every one of them once more. I am afraid I shall be a miserable, isolated wanderer, a vagrant roamer all my days and never know the comforts and blessings of a real *Home of my own* for my old age.

I have been thinking that when I return Mr. John will be a Lieutenant in the Army with a swab on each shoulder,[13] while I, notwithstanding my long, arduous and distinguished services on the briny element, may be still occupying the humble rank in which I stand at present. I shall be envious of his golden trappings, but it won't matter much, he is only a *Sojer* after all! God bless him! I hope he will do well.

What would I *not give* to know how you all are at this time? It is 10 months since your last letters. John has been home with you, Jim must have made great progress at the college, and Jane and Kate with their music, and Hal and Elly have grown, and Sam and Bangor; and

---

[12] *The Tuamotu (or Low) Islands, which consist of some eighty atolls spread along a 1,300-mile line. When Louis Antoine de Bougainville (1729–1811) visited the archipelago in 1768, he named it the Paumotu or Dangerous group, because most of the atolls consist of no more than a low coral reef surrounding a lagoon (n. 2 above).*

[13] *Epaulettes, one of the distinguishing features of a commissioned officer's uniform. At this time, William's brother John was still a cadet at West Point.*

I know nothing about you, though I pass all my watches in vain endeavours to conjecture and, by allowing for the difference in time, to imagine what you are about at that moment, for our night is your day. On Sundays this affords more satisfaction than at any other time because there is more certainty in my mind concerning your employment of that day. I am not alone in this, for it is a source of enjoyment that all hands of us turn to for consolation in our exile.

With Father and Mother there will be little change; I trust Time will lay his hand lightly upon them and that I may meet them and Grandmother and Aunt in the enjoyment of the best of health. I have not been ill a moment, though I have been much exposed in all kinds of weather. It will be a great blessing to me if I continue to be so healthy during the cruise of which, thank God! thirteen months have already passed away.

It will very likely be December when we get to Sydney; after leaving there our track will be the same as I have already mentioned, at least I have no reason to believe to the contrary. I will write to you from Sydney by way of England, for there may not be any direct opportunity. After that you will not hear of me for a long time, more than half a year, while in this first twelvemonth here is the 10th Letter, all in answer to *three little ones* from you![14] I hope you will

---

[14] *Letter No. 10 was received in Cornwall on 1 February 1840. Lydia and Aunt Lydia, their father's unmarried younger sister who was visiting them, answered the next day, a Sunday. The family had written "dear Willie" every month except January. This Sunday, Lydia wrote six pages in her extraordinarily fine hand, thirty-six lines on each 8 x 10 page: John is not doing as well as he might in his studies at West Point: "I am afraid he will not pass as well as you." Brother Jim (Letter No. 15, n. 48,) is a great talker: "We ought to make a lawyer of him; he is the greatest boy to argue I ever saw." Jane and Kate are not fond of their music at the Bordentown, New Jersey, school they are now attending, but speak French altogether now and have learned to waltz; they will leave "Spring Villa" this spring. Hal can read tolerably well: her favorite book is* Oliver Twist, *but she is mischievous and should be in school. Ellie is learning to spell and still continues to be a favorite with everyone. Sam will take the management of Cornwall, although he does not like it and would rather live any place else. Father is too busy to write. Mother has not been entirely well since her extended illness during her trip to Philadelphia last August. "We all collect*

attend to my suggestion in a previous letter of sending me a box *full* of *some thing* by the Store Ship. She will have sailed ere you get this and if you have neglected me, why you may consider yourself deserving of much reproach; but I am sure that you and all the rest will send me some trifle to make my heart glad while I am away.[15] I know it will give you pleasure to do so, *because I procure every thing that I can* in the happy thought that *you will all have an interest* and *delight in them when I return.*

September 21st 1839

In 10 days I have only been able to write this much—the fact will speak for itself. We have shifted our berth to the Harbour of Papieta, about 10 miles from Point Venus and the principal missionary station on the Island. This our Saturday is Sunday on Shore, owing to the well know[n] circumstance of those who originated a calendar here; coming by the way of the Cape of Good Hope, going East they gained a day.[16] We going West lose one.

---

in grandmother's room before we go to bed every night as we used to do when you were at home and laugh and talk. We miss you very much indeed. You often form the subject of our conversations, wondering what you are doing, where you are, how you are and I have often, often thought of you, dear Willie, this dreadful cold weather we have had. Here we have excellent fires and scarcely any occasion to leave them except for our own amusement and you so far from home must be exposed so much to cold, rain and all kind of weather. However, I sincerely hope and pray that you may be returned in safety to us at last. Eighteen months have passed since you sailed. To look back how short the time seems! but to look foreward to that length of time it seems an age." Aunt gave her nephew much Lancaster news, including the tidings that "Miss R[ebecca] K[rug] is still at home but she has admirers plenty." But William would not receive all this news until September 1840, in Honolulu.

[15] *The family had not sent a box to New York the previous autumn because of their uncertainty where to send it. Lydia wrote (1 February 1840), "I am afraid you will break out upon us when you find the box is not forthcoming, but do not scold me. I am willing to send you anything in the world . . . but Father said it was impossible." She did enclose for William a purse she had made for her grandmother, stuck among the newspapers sent to him, "for you dear Willie . . . poor as it is."*

[16] *Today, of course, this problem of relative time is resolved by the international date line, situated some 1,500 miles west of Tahiti.*

The ship is but a stone's throw from the Shore and from the port, abreast of which I am writing, I have a fair view of the lovely sweep of the bay with its groves of Trees, the beauty of which is unrivalled beyond the limits of the Tropics, of the dark clusters of the natives' huts and the white cottages of the missionaries and the consuls, lying sweetly in the shade of the glorious trees, and of the high mountains rising immediately in the rear of the Village, intersected by many rich valleys that terminate only at the water's edge. Thin columns of smoke are ascending here and there above the trees and add to the peaceful and holy calmness of the scene. Boats and canoes are fixed idly on the strand and I cannot see one living being in the range of my eye—they are all in church. I have been watching since daylight the crowds of people descending the hills and thronging the beach on their way to the house of prayer; the half clad natives going to offer their simple worship to the Christians' God. The Whale Ships are our neighbors, the Sea is glassy as a mirror, except the white line of breakers on the reef that defends the Coast. The lofty Island of Eimou[17] lies in deep shadow breaking the monotony of the distant horizon, while just astern of the Ship at the mouth of the harbour is a Circular Isle of perhaps an acre in extent and the most perfect picture in the view. It is thickly wooded, huts are peeping from under the trees and guns are planted around it, sheltered by sheds of thatch. The Isle and all that's on it seem so in miniature that the charm of its beauty is increased a thousand fold. I have no words to tell you of its loveliness.

Sunday is rigidly kept by these people, as to externals. Nothing is bought or sold during the day and divine service is held from Sun rise to Sun set. We cannot procure an orange even from a native and the day previous have to double our quantity.

The time has come; the Ship is going and I must sign and seal this letter, which I fear you will find tedious and unsatisfactory. However, as I have often told you before, my time is never my own and my mind has never rest enough to allow me to think over what I write. You have but little that is serious or grave, for praise be to the pigs, my mood *is generally* light. You have but little solid information about men and things, as I see them, because I cannot give it you without

[17] *Eimeo or Moorea, the second largest of the Society Islands, which reaches nearly 4,000 feet in height.*

preparation and reflection. Therefore you must take my letters as an evidence that I am continually thinking of you and that I never allow a chance to slip by without burthening you with the perusal of some silly lines, to let you know that your vagrant brother is living and that he still has that love for all of you which he hopes to preserve for ever. Remember me to all who inquire after me and do all of you write long letters to poor, worthless

William Reynolds

Miss Lydia M. Reynolds
    Cornwall

[*Inside wrapper:*] Since I finished May made the enclosed sketch of the appearance of a coral Isle.

[*Outside wrapper:*] Whale Ship Ulawinks

Eleven, to make sure: I do not use Roman Numerals

U.S. Ship *Peacock*!!!
Sydney, New South Wales,
near to Botany Bay,
December 1st 1839

My dear Sister Lydia,

I trust you will have received my letters
Nos. 7 and 8 from Valparaiso, No. 9 from Callao and No. 10 from
Otaheite long ere this reaches you; from the contents of which you
will be aware of our movements until the month of September.
Leaving Otaheite we proceeded Westward, making several Islands on
our way until we reached the Navigators Group.[1] We remained there
some weeks, of which I shall write presently; quitting this group, we
posted for this place in haste, so as to make an early start for the Icy
regions of the South Antartic. Two days ago we anchored here and I
was agreeably disappointed when I found a letter from Mother dated
February 13th. I had not hoped for one until our arriving at Sandwich
Islands in Spring, by Store Ship; this came by some fortunate accident
I suppose: for one from *you* should have accompanied it, which
nevertheless is lost for me.[2] I *know you wrote at* that time; *you would
not have directed Mother's letter, and be silent.* You have written and I
must bear with the disappointment and regret the loss; in the Spring I
trust to be happy.

[1] *Samoa.*
[2] *Lydia's letter of 17 February 1839 was not lost but was received by
William in the Sandwich Islands the following September.*

I am greatly indebted to Mother for her kind letter; it tells me that 3 *months* from the date of those received at Valparaiso you were all well, though alas, how time flies! that is now 9 months and more ago. Time does fly and rapidly with us—nearly 16 months out, one half the cruise gone and it seems as if it was but yesterday we weighed from Hampton Roads. The remainder will pass as rapidly and our toils ended. I shall look for a short, though a happy repose among you, whether you be at Cornwall, at Bangor, or "on the banks of the pleasant Ohio," as Father has often threatened. I feel that *I* must continue a vagrant wanderer—the more I see of our globe, the more do I regret that there remains so much to be viewed, and I believe I shall never rest until I have looked at the most of it with my own eyes. We shall see. I have no plans, but I am anxious for this Cruise to be ended. . . .

Dec. 9th

It *was* a mistake—Lt. Reynolds, alas! does not exist, and Lt. Ringgold commands the Porpoise.[3] I am flattered to hear that my Flowers have met with such conspicuous treatment. When we touch at Rio de Janeiro going Home I will buy enough to fill a dozen vases.

I shall expect a perfect journal of your visit to Philad. and of all other news. My budget by the Store Ship will I trust be immense, letters from every one of you great and small. John says "Time flies with him." That may serve as an excuse for not perpetrating long letters, but it is a poor one for total neglect; he must be a sad dog, worse than me and I am a poor, miserable good for nothing being and have lost all conceit of myself.

Poor Findley (I sympathize with my *own* sex), not married yet: Hope deferred etc., desperate case, terrible; what *will* the two unfortunate mortals do, I wish I could relieve them. I shall be melancholy unto death if I do not find them spliced upon my return. Verily the duration of their courtship will exceed that of Jacob of old.[4]

I cannot conceive how I omitted Kate's name in any of my letters,

[3] *Reynolds apparently refers to a newspaper story about the expedition which the family saw in the United States.*

[4] *Susan Ogilby, daughter of Lancaster banker Joseph Ogilby (1780–1840), finally married John King Findley in October 1840. They were friends of the Reynoldses.*

not because I have forgotten her; she must forgive me and to show that she does so write me by her own hand.[5]

Mother says that she will be *too old* to sing when I get *home*. Well, if I am not too much stricken in years and bent by toil and travel when that happy time shall come, I will tune my melodious voice as of yore; the effect will be irresistable and Mother will join in the song despite her increasing years.[6] And me, to morrow, if it shines upon me, I shall be 24—awful. Pity me, I am a victim of old age already. This cruise is making sharp work with every one's constitution: the continual change of climate, exposure to all kinds of weather, harrassing duty, want of proper food and a high degree of mental excitement, all tell with visible effect and there is not one of us who does not feel as if he were ten years older than when we sailed. The wrinkles about my eyes are as numerous as they are odious. The organs themselves are gradually retiring into my head, my skin is darker than John Mellen's, my beard has grown much, and altogether I am about as ugly a specimen of flesh as you would wish to see. When you do see me you will have to look twice to satisfy yourself that you indeed behold your brother, the man of 26 will be awfully different from the youth of 22.

Don't you think I have got to the most remote corner of the world—Botany Bay? Does not *that* sound afar off? If we go East or West now we will approach America! for not far from here is the Antipodes of your Home. It *is* curious! I never dreamed that in my wanderings I should bring up in this receptacle of criminals, the very last place in all the world for an American to find his way to, yet here I am.[7]

[5] *Catharine Ferree Reynolds (1825–1905), who was to marry Henry D. Landis (1824–1895) of Philadelphia in 1854 and have six children—one named William Reynolds Landis. At the death of their aunt in 1857 and the breakup of the Lancaster household, Kate and William's younger sisters Harriot and Eleanor, who never married, made their residence primarily with the Landis family, first on Spruce Street and then in a large house in Chestnut Hill, which became the gathering place for all the family.*

[6] *From her correspondence, it appears that music was the delight of Lydia Moore Reynolds's life, a delight she shared with her family—at the advanced age of forty-five! There was always a piano in the Reynolds households.*

[7] *Botany Bay was James Cook's first landfall in Australia in 1770 and the original destination of the first English settlement there. When the first fleet*

It is time to commence my yarn, however, so that you may know what we have been about for the last three months.

Leaving Otaheite, we steered Westerly until we made Manua, the Easternmost of the Navigator Group. Two or three days were occupied in surveying it, but as there were no Harbours on the Island we did not anchor. I was one of the party who were allowed to land. We were reminded of Tahita: the scenery we thought was even more enchanting; we were in raptures at the wonderful loveliness of the shores.[8]

There were no white missionaries on the Island, but the natives have embraced the Christian faith and are instructed by converts from Otaheite. We thought them of a much graver cast of character than the lively Tahitians and we did not witness among them any of the licenciousness which is such a characteristic of the latter people. The village was beautifully situated under shelter of groves of Bread fruit, cocoa nut and forest trees. I envied the people their quiet Home by the Sea Shore and I almost was tempted to live with them forever; 8 or 10 white men we found domesticated among them, care seemed to [be] banished from them entirely.

One day's sail carried us from Manua to Tutuila, one of the same group. We anchored in a fine harbour, shut in from the sea; the observatory was erected and we were to make a stay of 10 days.

---

of settlers arrived in 1788, they found Botany Bay unsuitable and established themselves instead at the next inlet to the north, Sydney Cove. Australia, of course, was intended to be a penal colony, after the American Revolution closed off that outlet for Britain's prison population. During the course of the next five decades, some 60,000 criminals, political dissidents, and other undesirables were transported to New South Wales, Van Diemen's Land (Tasmania), and western Australia. Many free settlers also came, however, and many convicts stayed after serving their terms, so that by 1840 nonconvicts outnumbered convicts in New South Wales, the total population of which was 130,000 (Fitzpatrick 1946:51).

[8] *Reynolds "rejoiced" to be in charge of a boat and to land on Tau, the largest of the Manua Islands in the Samoa group. His experiences in Samoa, with one notable exception, were probably the happiest of the cruise. The sixteen-page account in the Public Journal was the most vivid of any made while he was on board the* Vincennes. *The Samoan entries in his Journal No. 1, scattered between pages 230 and 314, were almost ecstatic.*

I was happy to be selected for a surveying expedition around the Island, to be performed in the Boats. Any thing to get clear of the irksome constraints of Ship board gives me positive delight, and then I knew I would mingle more with the people and see more of the Island than if I remained on board. So despite the comfortless condition of a Whale boat and the chances for accidents, the hard work, the sun and the rain, I was glad to have the duty assigned me. Two boats were to go, Lt. Underwood having the charge of the party, he being in the larger boat.[9] We were 6 days in making the circumnavigation, run some narrow chances for our lives and suffered bodily ills in many and various shapes; but on the whole we enjoyed the interest and zest which attends novelty and adventure to a great degree and we were satisfied. One cannot see the world and be all the while in his easy chair by the fire. A white man who had lived on the Island eleven years accompanied us as interpreter.[10]

We slept on shore every night, always putting into a village before sundown and were received by the people with great kindness and hospitality.[11] Life among them was so free—they made Gods of us almost, we were so wealthy in their eyes—that really I took a strange and strong fancy for them and I became almost as rude and primitive in my habits as the naked beings we were among. We carried no money with us; unlike the Tahitians, these people were utterly

[9] *Lieutenant Joseph A. Underwood (1809–1840), born in Maine but a citizen of New York, who had seen service with the Mediterranean Squadron after joining the navy in 1829 (ZB).*

[10] *William Grey, whose long sojourn on Tutuila had rendered his English rusty, even incoherent, nevertheless conveyed to Reynolds and Underwood much information about the traditions of the Samoans, their religion and hero tales, which Reynolds carefully recorded in his Public Journal (97–100).*

[11] *Reynolds wrote in his journals that his pride as a white man faded away: "These people have more claim to be called good, than me. . . . The simple honesty and kind and gentle demeanor of both sexes and all ages quite won our hearts" (Journal 1:269). He could not laud enough those who had been so kind to him. He promised Chief Tuetila of Leone that he would "clothe him like a Papalanga," or white man, if he would come to the ship on their return. The chief came, but Captain Wilkes refused to see him. Reynolds and Underwood did the best they could, giving him "many presents" (Public Journal 87).*

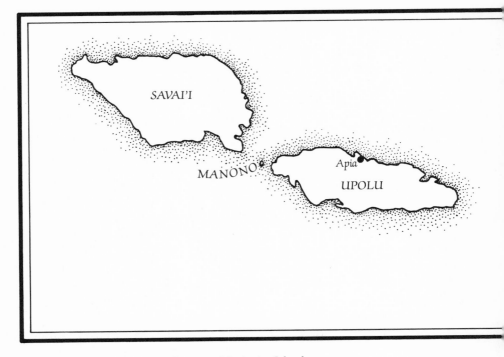

Samoa or Navigator Islands

ignorant of the colour and value of coin. Fishhooks were most valuable in their eyes—that is, of trifling articles. Hatchets were the diamonds of the *Samoans**; knives, scissors, needles, cotton cloth, etc. etc. were treasures to them, more than all the gold of the Indies. We carried a trading Stock with us to purchase provisions, make presents etc. etc. and it was consoling to me to know that *my* personal effects alone would constitute me a wealthy man in this portion of the world. I could have outvied in possessions the most influential chiefs in the Islands. At Home, how the scale would sink; with no other dependence than this, I should be in jail in a month.

* A term they apply to themselves as a people.

PACIFIC OCEAN

So you perceive there is a vast difference in the estimation of riches between the Samoa people and their white brethren. When I become reduced in the world's gear, I shall wend my way to the Samma [*Samoa*] Islands in the Pacific and live and die a rich chief.

Our Religion has been but lately introduced among this people; they have embraced it with much ardour and observe all its forms and precepts with the most scrupulous attention. Old and young attend the schools daily, and morning and evening you hear voices in prayer and the song of hymns ascending from every Hut. You cannot witness the least deviation from the strict code of morality and if you take the evidence of your senses you must believe you are among the very best people on the Earth. Weaned from their Heathenism they cling with fervour to the novel belief opened unto them. The savage and bloodthirsty traits of their original disposition have melted away;

Fiji parrots, Prosopeia. *Plate on right by Titian Ramsay Peale, from Cassin 1858, plate 20. Courtesy Smithsonian Institution Libraries and National Museum of Natural History, Smithsonian Institution.*

from Lions and serpents, they have become meek and humble as the Lamb or the Dove. As a people, you may almost say they are without guile, for their sole aim is to obey the commandments of God.

It is terrible to think that this good will not last long without its share of evil. The missionaries who have commenced this work already see that dissensions must ensue; they themselves have introduced the difference of Sects and neither party will give way.[12] The natives cannot understand this; it passes their simple comprehension, yet none of *them* either will *yield* or alter the forms

[12] *The first missionaries to Samoa were Tongan converts sent in 1828 by the Wesleyan Society, followed two years later by Rarotongan teachers planted by the London Missionary Society. The legendary John Williams of the LMS arrived in 1831; by the time Williams left Samoa in 1839 to open frontiers of*

they have been taught; each sect abides by the tenets of its Master. It is hardly to be supposed that in the end they will be more merciful to each other's creed than Queen Mary was to the Martyrs and there will be war and butchery for opinion's sake, as of old.

Nevertheless, the Soil was good to work upon, but the misfortune is and has been that the labourers employed have not been the right kind of men—uneducated, bigoted to their particular church, narrow minded and selfish in their judgement of their fellow creatures as the most of them are in my opinion. With the good they have actually done they have mingled much of harm: allow them to have been influenced by the purest motives, grant them the sacrifice of leaving their country and their friends, yet their policy towards the people they came to convert must be condemned and deplored. The observer can easily see that, had the missionaries really been (in the language of their beautiful hymn) those "whose souls are lighted with wisdom from on high," their efforts would have been better directed and have produced happier effects. They lack wisdom and they lack charity, the charity of their Master, who is the saviour of men.

However, I cannot discuss this in a letter; you must wait until I return for the *graphic* account of my adventures among the Islands. You will also have to trust to my Journal for really I have not time nor space to put them in a letter—and let me tell you, want of time is no idle excuse in this Squadron. The Government is having full use of every bodies' minutes, and amidst the whirl and change of scene and the continual duty, I can scarce find leisure to think of you and have to snatch the few chances that offer to put pen to paper. This is the 16th attempt I have made at this letter and this day is Saturday the 14th, two weeks since I commenced.

One day's sail from Tutuila carried us to Upola, where we anchored and remained more than a week. We had an interesting

---

conversion in the New Hebrides, there were eleven Western missionaries, including Wesleyan, in the group. The problem of sects was to continue, for though the Wesleyans withdrew from Samoa for a period in an agreement with the LMS, they were replaced in 1845 by French Roman Catholic missionaries; however, the LMS was always the most important influence (Masterman 1934:29, 35–37).

time at this place; it is the head quarters of the missionaries and is by far the most fertile and beautiful of the whole group. The Island is not so mountaninous as the others and there are large tracts of level land and rich valleys, while in the neighboring Isles all is mountain and forest, the only habitable sites being on the beach.

We formed for the people a code of laws for the government of their intercourse with white people, which was adopted in a solemn conclave of all the Chiefs and the officers of the Squadron.[13] The group in the immense hut were worthy of contemplation and the interest of the scene was intense.

After this was disposed of, Captain Wilkes acquainted them of his determination to make war upon the Chief of an Island but a few miles distant, who is notorious for his murders of the whites, and requested that they would aid him in his attempt. A long discussion ensued in which the Chiefs acquitted themselves well, but becoming excited and as the proposition was unexpected, they required time for an answer.[14] We met again and the result was that they would remain neutral, but they could not plunge into a war with their kindred because of one bad man who had injured our country men but never molested them. The Captain blustered and threatened rather too much and finding it was of no avail, the prospect of a war subsided in the offering of a reward for *Kocatoona*, alive or dead, to be delivered to any American ship. Previous to this a Secret Expedition under Command of Captain Hudson had been sent to the Island to capture him by stratagem, but failed.[15]

I was on a surveying tour along the shores of this Island for a short distance and afterwards *walked across it* to survey a harbour on

---

[13] *Lieutenant Wilkes negotiated a set of commercial regulations for Samoa intended to establish the rights of the islanders to receive fees for pilotage and provisions provided to ships, to control the behavior of sailors on shore, and to define the responsibility of islanders to return deserters and protect persons and ships wrecked on their shores.*

[14] *Reynolds observed in his Journal (1:281) the confusion of the natives, who were instructed by the missionaries to cease fighting but were now told by Wilkes to fight their neighbors.*

[15] *Kocatoona was also known as Opotuno. A subsequent attempt to capture him also failed.*

Commercial Regulations, made

by the principle chiefs of the Samoa Group of Islands, after full consideration in Council on the fifth day of November, 1839.

I.

All Consuls duly appointed, and received in Samoa, shall be protected both in their persons and property, and all foreigners obtaining the consent of the Government, and conforming to the laws, shall receive the protection of the Government.

II.

All foreign vessels shall be received into the ports and harbours of Samoa, for the purpose of obtaining supplies, and for commerce; and with their officers and crews, so long as they shall comply with these regulations, and behave themselves peaceably, shall receive the protection of the Government.

III.

The fullest protection shall be given to all foreign ships, and vessels, which may be wrecked; and any property saved shall be taken possession of by the Consul of the country to which the vessel belongs; who will allow a salvage, or portion of the property so saved, to those who may aid in saving, and protecting the same; and no embezzlement will be permitted under any circumsatnces whatever. The effects of all persons deceased shall be given up to the Consuls of the nation to which they may have belonged.

IV.

Any person guilty of the crime of murder, upon any foreigner, shall be given up without delay to the commander of any public vessel of the nation to which the deceased may have belonged, upon his demanding the same.

V.

Every vessel shall pay a port charge of five dollars, for anchorage and water, before she will be allowed to receive refreshments on board; and shall pay for pilotage in and out, the sum of seven dollars, before she leaves the harbour: and pilots shall be appointed subject to the approval of the Consuls.

VI.

No work shall be done on shore, nor shall any natives be employed on board vessels on the Sabbath Day, under a penalty of ten dollars, unless under circumstances of absolute necessity.

VII.

All trading in spirituous liquors, or landing the same is strictly forbidden. Any person offending shall pay a fine of twenty-five dollars; and the vessel to which he belongs shall receive no more refreshments. Any spirituous liquors found on shore will be seized and destroyed.

VIII.

All deserters from vessels will be apprehended, and a reward paid of five dollars to the person who apprehends him; and three dollars to the chief of the district in which he may be apprehended, shall be paid on his delivery to the proper officer of the vessel. No master shall refuse to receive such deserter under a penalty of twenty-five dollars. Deserters taken after the vessel has sailed, shall be delivered up to the Consul, to be dealt with as he may think fit. Any person who entices another to desert, or in any way assists him, shall be subject to a penalty of five dollars, or one month hard labor on the public roads.

IX.

No master shall land a passenger without permission of the Government, under a penalty of twenty-five dollars, and no individual shall be permitted to land or reside on the Samoa Group of Islands without the special permission of the Government. Any one so landing shall be compelled to leave by the first opportunity.

X.

If a sick person be left on shore from any vessel for the recovery of his health he shall be placed under charge of the Consul, who shall be responsible for his sick expenses and will send him away by the first opportunity after his recovery.

XI.

Any seaman remaining on shore after 9 o'clock at night shall be made a prisoner until the next morning when he shall be sent on board, and shall pay a penalty of five dollars.

XII.

All fines to be paid in specie or its equivalent, or be commuted by the Government at the rate of one months hard labor on the public road for five dollars.

XIII.

Should the master of any vessel refuse to comply with any of these regulations, a statement of the case shall be furnished to the nation or the Consul of the nation to which he belongs, and redress sought from thence.

XIV.

All Magistrates or chiefs of districts where vessels or boats may visit, shall enforce the rules and regulations relative to the landing of foreigners, and apprehension of deserters, or pay such a fine as the Malo shall impose.

XV.

For carrying into effect the foregoing rules and regulations the chiefs and tula fale of the respective districts shall meet and elect one of their number to act as Magistrate or Judge, to execute the laws.

XVI.

These regulations shall be printed, promulgated, and a copy furnished to the master of each vessel visiting these Islands.

The foregoing rules and regulations having been signed by the King and Chiefs in my presence, and submitted to me, I consider them just and proper, and shall forward to the American Government a Copy of the same for the information of all Masters of Vessels visiting the Samoa group of Islands.

CHARLES WILKES,
Commanding U. States
Exploring Expedition.

In presence of

WILLIAM L. HUDSON,
Commanding U. S. Ship Peacock.
CADR. RINGGOLD,
Commanding U. S. Brig Porpoise.
R. R. WALDRON, U. States' Navy.
B. VANDERFORD, Pilot.

Commercial Regulations drawn up at Samoa, 1839. As Reynolds describes, Lieutenant Wilkes had the original of this agreement signed with great fanfare, to impress upon the chiefs of Samoa their rights and obligations respecting Western merchant ships. This broadside was printed to make ship captains equally aware of theirs. Courtesy Yale Collection of Western Americana, Beinecke Rare Book and Manuscript Library.

the opposite side; 80 miles tramp across mountains where the paths were steep, narrow and rough, raining most of the time, was rather trying to us, who have done but little in the pedestrian way save walking on smooth planks for more than a year. However, I stood it manfully and did not suffer so much as I expected. We had 4 natives with us to carry our burthens and one white man as a guide. I took my Gun with me (for I rejoice in the possession of a double barrel) and though I was *sans* spectacles, I managed to shoot Pigeons enough for several meals. This expedition shall have particular mention in my Journal.[16]

We became acquainted with the family of the Rev. Mr. Williams who has been among the Island for 30 years and at this time was residing near our anchorage. He preached on board the Vincennes and his son was appointed Consul for the United States.[17] We saw a great deal of him and a few days before we sailed, he in company with several others left the Harbour in the Missionary Brig on a voyage to the New Hebrides to endeavour to introduce the Gospel among the People. We towed him out to Sea and we felt an interest

[16] *George Emmons and Reynolds started on the "80 mile tramp" along paths as "delicious as the entrance to Paradise." There were "monster trees," mountains, wilderness, and great beauty. Even "old Emmons," a most unexcitable temperament, "half echoes my frequent screams of delight." Horatio Hale, the expedition's philologist, was with them; they sat up late at night "learning the language from pretty lips." Reynolds thought the natives' own ways better than any the white man could impose upon them. "I could not help thinking of a life in this Eden" (Journal 1:295–306).*

[17] *John Williams (1796–1839) had come to the Pacific in 1816; arriving at Raiatea, he built a ship and sailed to Tonga and Samoa. He translated the New Testament into Rarotongan, and his best-selling* Narrative of Missionary Enterprise in the South Sea Islands *(1834) attracted many missionaries to the Pacific. Reynolds's four-day surveying cruise with Lieutenant Augustus L. Case, which preceded the trek across the mountains, had ended at the home of the Reverend Mr. Williams. Reynolds was embarrassed by his disheveled appearance at dinner, when he found three ladies present. "If Grandmother could only have seen me there . . . she would have been . . . lost in utter despair" (Journal 1:309). Wilkes appointed the reverend's son John C. Williams acting consul; Williams was to become a prominent merchant.*

in the Brig for we had met her at Tahita, at Eimeo, and at Tutuila; she followed in our wake as regularly as if she was one of the Squadron.

The day after we anchored here the Brig arrived also, but they had an awful tale to unfold; we could scarcely believe or realize the terrible story. We were all attending church on board the Vincennes and a minister from the Shore was addressing the same congregation that had listened to Mr. Williams but a few weeks before, when his associates came on board to tell us that he had been murdered and eaten by the Savages; and he who related it had barely escaped the same fate. It seems they landed on the Island of Erromango (one of the New H.) and were met by the natives with signs of peace; in a short time, however, Mr. Williams and a Mr. Harris were killed. The two others ran to the boat and just saved themselves. They had no arms for defence because they say the sacredness of their calling should be their only protection, and they seem to have a trust in the immediate interposition of Providence in their behalf—so much so, that they may almost be accused of fanaticism in such instances. A little more worldly knowledge and conduct would have saved the lives of two valuable men, as the Survivors now acknowledge themselves; yet they had many similar examples before them and heeded them not.

This intelligence was a shock to us. It will be a severe and heavy affliction to the families of the dead, who are yet in happy ignorance of the event.

Notwithstanding the superb and glorious Scenery of the Islands and the gentle nature of the people, we were right happy as the time drew near for us to leave them, with an English port in prospect. Our duty had been severe, we had lived upon Pigs for three months and however Pork may do as a rarity, I cannot recommend it as a continual diet in a sweltering clime, bah! I loathe the name of it. We could get nothing else on the Islands and a piece of Roast Beef to be enjoyed in Sydney was uppermost in our thoughts.[18] The crews of the vessels suffered also from exposure and other causes, several officers were afflicted with brain fever and strokes of the Sun, and we all felt the necessity of getting into another temperature. I have been

---

[18] *There were native pigs on many islands; in addition, Westerners had introduced other, larger varieties during the previous seventy-five years.*

so fortunate as to outbrave it all without the least feeling of illness. I have not been ill a moment since we left the U.S.

As I have said, my face, hands and neck were burned to a respectable bronze. I happened to be bathing one morning in a pool with a number of natives; on observing the line of demarcation around my throat and wrists, they were highly delighted, satisfied they had found the cause of the difference in our colour. They said, and they traced with their fingers the portions on their own persons, "that so much of me was Samoa, the rest Papalange" (white man), "that if I went wholly naked, I would soon be altogether Samoa." To this I assented and they were flattered and happy. I wish you could have seen me: I rarely had any thing on save a pair of sailor's trowsers and a collared shirt open at the neck. Barefooted also, I adop[t]ed my habits to the climate and the people and I was a great favorite wherever we went!

My old white hat that met with so much abuse at Home has been the greatest friend to me during the Summer. I have worn it on all occasions, rain or shine, and it has always been a comfort and protection, more serviceable than one of straw or tarpaulin; and now after the severe usage it has received, I have had it ironed and it is decent enough for me to wear on Shore and I do wear it. I have quite an affection for it, both for the sake of old times and for the service it will yet do me. It will be grand next Summer on the N.W. Coast— perhaps I may bring it Home and sport it again among the Hills.[19]

Just picture me in such a rig, with a knife belted around my waist, amidst a crowd of natives. Now I am dressed with exquisite care, mingling with those who are of my own customs and language; the change is miraculous and sudden, the enjoyment it affords beggars description. We are transported from place to place, from Nation to

---

[19] The "old white hat" so caught the fancy of his family that Mother, Lydia, and Jane composed a long poem, based on "The Old Arm Chair," and sent it off sometime before 17 June 1841. Lest the poem not arrive, Lydia copied it again in her letter of that date:

> I love it, I love it and what of that
> Who'll chide me for loving that old white hat—
> I've treasured it long as a useful prize
> And shall always love it, for shading my eyes. . . .

Nation, with magical celerity. We are with the new before the old is out of our thoughts and time glides away imperceptibly. A roving commision in a man of war is preferable to the possession of Aladdin's ring; of his lamp, perhaps not.

Sunday, December 22nd

We are here still, though the day fixed for sailing has passed. We will go on Wednesday, I think. I would have made this letter longer and more interesting, written more about the Islands and less about myself, if I had been able to find repose either in mind or body. But really we are all kept continually in the most feverish state of excitement, so that while we are not actually at work, we cannot enjoy or improve the moments of rest. I do not wish to give you the least uneasiness nor would I have troubled you with a tale of our griefs, had it not become necessary to account to you the cause of my transfer from the Vincennes, the Ship in which I have wore away the half of the cruise in happiness and peace with my fellows, and in which I had fondly hoped to terminate it. I commenced a letter at Otaheite with a relation of the state of affairs and of feeling in the Squadron, but loathe to make you aware of our difficulties, I tore the paper and commenced again.[20]

When we left the United States, there was felt by every single individual in the Squadron the most unbounded admiration for the Commander in Chief. Never was a set of men more enthusiastic in their praise or more devoted to the person of their Captain. He came with a high reputation as a Gentleman, all of us had the most entire confidence in him and we were perfectly happy in his selection as the Commander of the Expedition. It was treason to utter a breath against him. We would all have fought in defence of his character and, in short, he possessed the heart of every officer who was to sail under him. Well would it have been for him had he pursued a course of conduct which would have drawn us still closer to him and have kept the measure of his glory full, but by many acts which reason cannot sanction, nor honor, pride, or feeling bear with, he has become in the

---

[20] *Reynolds first broached the subject of his disaffection with Wilkes some four months earlier, in his Journal entry of 18 August 1839. "I had intended never to introduce such themes among these pages," he wrote on 22 August.*

eyes of the whole Squadron a false and malignant *villain*—no milder
term will do. I hope Father will not start when he reads this and say
it is all my youth and heedlessness that makes me write thus. He
must do me the justice to believe that in saying so, I am justifiable in
every respect. We have borne innumerable evils, the nature of the
man has become changed, he is as one possessed by a demon;
intoxicated with the power and rank of his situation, he forgets his
discretion and is guilty of the most wanton and outrageous attacks
upon every one who may chance to offend him. We have to suffer,
though of course we have taken the care to make respectful
remonstrances in writing whenever we could do so. We have
reported his conduct to the Secretary of the Navy who is our official
guardian and protector, but, as all such communications must go
through his own hands, he has refused to forward any. He thinks
time will destroy evidence; he will find himself grievously mistaken.[21]

I cannot recount all of the atrocities he has been guilty of, but they
have been of the deepest dye, deadly thrusts at the life blood of an
officer—his proffessional conduct. There are but three individuals in
the Squadron who are base and sycophantic enough to stand by
Captain Wilkes and his acts. All the others who were once so ardent
in his cause have now turned against him; there is the same
unanimity in this as there was when the tide was in his favor, and it
is this universal voice which is the strong proof of the justice of our
side: the Commander and his officers are at open variance. Whatever
advances he may make during the remnant of the cruise will be of no
avail—his sword has cut too deep already for the scars ever to be
effaced. If by a miracle he was to be changed from the fiend which he
now is to a God, he could not be worshipped; we would think the
old leaven was about him still. He may alter as the time comes for us
to return, but it will be in vain; we cannot forget the scenes we have
struggled through.

[21] *Reynolds details many of the complaints of Wilkes's capriciousness and
cruelty in his "Critique" of the commander's testimony at his court-martial,
brought about by the charges lodged against him by several of the officers,
including Guillou, May, and Lieutenant Robert Pinkney. The officers of the
expedition later published a* Memorial of Officers . . . *(1847) setting forth
additional aspects of their position and petitioning Congress for redress.*

It is as singular to look back upon the ill judged and violent measures pursued by Captain Wilkes in his conduct of affairs, as it was to notice them as they occurred. We find ourselves entirely at a loss to account for his motives or to imagine how any man in a sane mind could be guilty of such wrong headed measures. One by one, the chords that bound us to him personally were snapped asunder and our love has been changed to hate. He might have done with us what he listed, we would have given ourselves to him entirely, but he [did] not [know] how to use the men who were so much attached to him and by his own doings he has turned his warmest friends into deathly foes. While there is the same martyr like devotion to the cause in which we are embarked as there was when we sailed, the healthy feeling that was so strong and pure is now destroyed, the sap of the Expedition has been frosted in the bud, the happy hopes and prospects of every one have been blasted and we lead a life of torment and strife, feeling that every thing we do will be taken at an unfair advantage. Confidence in the Commander is destroyed; there is none where there should be all. Every man does his duty, but he keeps aloof from Captain Wilkes as if he were an adder and never trusts himself with him save in an official manner; thus you may see that the state of things is terrible indeed. Imagine a family where all are at variance with the father and you will know our state. But our consolation is that there is but one voice and one feeling among us; we have suffered together and together we have resisted. There are no dissentions among us and we have the happiness to know in our own heart that we did not cast the first stone; we bore with circumstances until forbearance ceased to be a virtue and then we should have been stones not to have made ourselves heard.[22]

[22] *They made themselves heard on 20 August, in answer to an order of that date from the commander. Noting that navy regulations assigned separate quarters to officers according to their grade "to secure good order, discipline, proper respect and efficiency," Wilkes complained that the junior officers of the* Vincennes *had converted the apartments of the deck officers into a "lounge," thereby producing a "familiarity" tending to thwart regulations; he ordered this practice stopped (Wilkes 1839). Reynolds, Dr. John S. Whittle, William May, and Simon Blunt, all steerage officers, replied that they understood and had not disregarded the designs of the government,*

I beg you will not be alarmed for the consequences as far as my standing is concerned: deeply do I regret the turn affairs have taken, but I am proud of every thing that has been done by those with whom I have acted. Though some have been sent Home in the Relief and others are now under suspension, the evidence must all go with them. It will crush the prosecutor with a truth and force that he cannot resist. United as we are, in that consists our strength and our security; what affects one affects the whole, and the mass are ever too much for the individual. Fear not for me nor think the objects of the Expedition will suffer because of the unfortunate dissentions I have referred to. We work with all our might and all our strength, only we can no longer have the least respect for him who heads us, save in his official capacity.

By way of variety, I will just tell you one of the mildest instances of the manner in which he dispenses justice. To tell you how I incurred his displeasure would involve me in a long yarn; suffice to say that I was so unfortunate. He sought opportunities to oppress me, but he sought long in vain. At length he thought he might take advantage of me and by a slight straining of the truth submit me to a severe and mortifying punishment. He suspended me from duty and confined me to my apartment below decks for 6 or 7 days in the heat of a sweltering clime, put me on Penitentiary limits for an offense which I had no knowledge of, as it is his avowed creed to *punish first and inquire afterwards*. Six days I remained in durance vile and the

---

but that the "harmony of feeling" between them and certain senior officers of the ship was a highly commendable state of affairs, making "a Ship really a Home." They added that they were all jealous of their rank and zealous in their duties—and also in their "social enjoyment" (Reynolds et al. 1839). In his Journal (1:204), Reynolds noted: "Conscious of our own innocence, we could not brook the foul nature of his charges."

Dr. John L. Fox, the other steerage officer, refused to sign their letter. On his copy of the exchange, Reynolds noted: "From this time forward there was 'war to the knife' between Captain Wilkes and most of his officers—and there commenced on his part a series of persecutions which have not ended yet. He took Dr. Fox to his Bosom and thus secured a partisan in the Steerage—this was an immense advantage to him and has led to monstrous results."

confinement was irksome to me, as you may suppose. Take from me
air and liberty and what else is there? I would have rotted there, ere I
would have opened my lips to complain; but at length he saw fit to
send for me to let me know the cause of my suspension. The charge
he had to bring against me was false and scandalous in the extreme,
without the least foundation. I defied him to prove it, for I was
indignant that I should have been persecuted for malice alone. I had
the authority of all the witnesses to contradict the Captain's Statement
and I did so, but what was the use? he had gained his end. I had
been punished and he, reckless of truth or consequences, cared not
how his conduct was viewed.[23]

The next scrape I had was as outrageous as this one and I was
ordered out of the Ship at Sea.[24] A very few moments sufficed to

[23] *The account of this incident in Reynolds's Journal (1:274–76) describes
the near wreck of the* Vincennes *on surf-dashed rock as they departed Pago
Pago. During the crisis, the captain stood "on the weather gangway, leaning
on the booms, with his face hidden in his hands"; the ship's deliverance was
owing only to the pilot's efforts. Once the vessel was clear, Reynolds was
below dressing "some hurts" on his feet when "All hands" was called. He
did not get to his station for a few minutes and was immediately ordered
suspended, with no explanation. After six days in "an apartment 12 feet
square, devoid of daylight," 80° temperature, he was called to the captain's
cabin. There he was told the punishment had not been because of the delay but
"because I had come on deck in an improper and disrespectful manner and set
a bad example for the crew." Lieutenants Augustus Case and Samuel Knox,
standing considerably closer to Reynolds at the time, had seen nothing amiss;
they credited it to Wilkes's nearsightedness.*

[24] *The squadron sailed from Apia Bay in Upolu on 10 November.
Reynolds's transfer to the* Peacock *on the following day was the result, on
the surface, of a picayune incident. While he was on a surveying assignment,
someone had worn an "India rubber frock" or waterproof jacket issued to
Reynolds and left it on deck. It had been found and, although identified as
Reynolds's by First Lieutenant Overton Carr, stowed in the "lucky bag,"
where objects left by the crew were deposited and eventually auctioned off.
It was not the custom to put officers' clothing in the bag, and Reynolds
protested, first to the lieutenant and then to the captain. Ten minutes later he
was ordered to report to Captain Hudson on the* Peacock. *"There was great
hubbub in the Ship—and God knows, I fairly cried to leave those whom I had*

transfer ~~Caesar~~ Ceasar and his fortunes to this Ship and here I am, situated very pleasantly! That is, I have the good will and the kindly feelings of every soul in the Squadron, *save two*; they are not in this Ship and I am happy to be rid of them. Do not distress yourselves by imagining that I have acted wrong; my heart, my head and my conscience have prompted me, and in whatever I have done I have been supported by all. I have no enemies, save two, and though I tell it to you myself, I have made many and warm friends who care for me more than I deserve. Good for nothing as I am, it is a blessing I have always enjoyed to make friends, and every one almost who has entered the least in life has experienced the want and the value of a true friend. Honest intentions and quiet, firm behaviour have hitherto borne me on in a manner flattering to myself. It may savour strongly of vanity (but I know how prone you will be to think that I have been much to blame) in me to say this, but I must tell you that in every occurrence of this cruise I am perfectly satisfied with whatever I have done and I am happy to add that my friends one and all go with me, heart and hand. I will write no more on this; I shall have the longest yarn to spin when I return and the history of all the transactions of this cruise will be lengthy, wonderful and entertaining.

Sydney is the funniest place I ever was in, this penal settlement, this population of individuals who, to say the least of them, have at one period of their lives been unfortunate. You may talk of Convicts at Home, but it [is] delicate ground to venture upon in Sydney. You see a man driving a Tandem, his *term* you will be told has just expired. Pass an elegant house, a convict's daughter is the possessor of it. The richest people here were convicts and the state of society is singular in the extreme. One man has built himself a house on the

---

learned to love so well. M[ay] and I made perfect babies of ourselves, 'twas like the parting of man and wife. [Jim] Gibson came to me, in not much better plight than I was myself and helped me to pack up, poor fellow, I was sorry to leave him, too. . . . . I never felt leaving Home with half the forces of grief, that oppressed me, at being thus torn from my happy mess!" May accosted the captain with accusations of treating his "friend, Mr. Reynolds, with the greatest injustice" and was forthwith ordered to the Flying Fish *(Journal 1:314–18).*

very spot where stood the gallows, to which gallows he had been taken three times with the Rope around his neck! Curious place this you may be sure, a country peopled with criminals!

Botany Bay is seven miles from here. There are no houses there, as the settlement was abandoned just after its discovery for the more eligible site offered where Sydney stands. The French have erected a monument there in memory of La Perouse, as it was the last place from whence they received direct tidings of that most unfortunate navigator.[25]

While I write this, the Ship is under weigh and it is Christmas morning; but we anchor again and I suppose we will not actually go until to morrow. If I find leisure, I will fill this sheet; if not, you must believe that I have written whenever a moment offered. I do not know where you must direct your letters hereafter, but send thro' the Lyceum and any opportunity that you come aware of. I hope you received my letters from Callao, via Panama, ere the Store Ship sailed and that you attended to the request therein—a Box of trifles from Home would make me happy above all things.

And now the time has come when I must say, or write, adieu. This is the day after Christmas and we are actually under weigh going out to Sea. We shall have a dreary time among the Ice, and God send us safe out of it. When this is over, the rest of the cruise

---

[25] *Jean-François de Galaup de la Pérouse (1741–1788), French navigator, who in 1785 led an expedition across the Pacific. The squadron disappeared in 1788 with no indication of the circumstances until a British merchantman came across the wreck near Vanikolo Island in the Solomon group in 1826. La Pérouse's cruise is described in the book* A Voyage Round the World Performed in the Years 1785, 1786, 1787, and 1788 by the Boussole and Astrolabe . . . *[1799].*

During Reynolds's surveying expedition in Tutuila, he and Underwood had attempted a landing at Massacre Bay, where La Pérouse had lost a number of his crew in 1787 (Public Journal:92). Throughout the Pacific, the exploits and mishaps of earlier explorers going back three-quarters of a century were fresh and lively in the minds of expedition members. For example, the scientific Charles Pickering described in detail and with utmost interest what he learned of La Pérouse's Tutuila incident in his journal entry for 29 October 1839.

will go more easily and every move we make will be bringing us nearer Home.

If we should fail to come back! I cannot write more, my heart is full; Good bye and may God bless you all

Wm. Reynolds

Lydia M. Reynolds
    Cornwall Furnace

William Reynolds's Letter No. 12 is lost. According to the careful list he kept of his letters on the last page of Journal No. 2, Letter No. 12 was sent from Sydney on the American barque *Shepherdess*, Boston. Although this letter may have been written in December, as he mentions in No. 13, it apparently only "Sailed 18th February 1840." In any case, the letter was never received.

As neither the town nor the countryside had the appeal for Reynolds of a tropical island, his coverage of Sydney and New South Wales is brief in the Journal—five pages for his first visit (1:319–24) and eight for the next (1:331–39). The quotations below are taken from the Journal.

The squadron made a spectacular entrance into Sydney harbor. On 29 November they sighted "the high land of New Holland;[1] Sydney was near at last." Reynolds at first thought they would not make the anchorage until the next morning, but "undertaking rather a critical chance, Captain Wilkes run his Ship clear up into the Harbour. We

---

[1] *Australia was known as New Holland from the early seventeenth century because it was the explorations of Dutch East India merchants after 1606 which first brought the continent into general knowledge. Even after eastern Australia gradually became known as New South Wales subsequent to the founding of Sydney in 1788, for some years the western portion retained the old name.*

followed, anchoring off the town at 11." In the morning, "greatly were [*the inhabitants of Sydney*] astonished, never having had such a thing been heard of. . . . The papers were full of jokes about it and we had notoriety at once, highly flattering to our nautical skill and daring." The first visit of an American squadron to this place gave us "so much eclat!" He noted that in time of war such an undetected entry could have given real advantage.

The officers of the Fiftieth Regiment, the Queen's Own, gave a dinner. "We returned it soon after with all the display we could muster on board the Vincennes! again on the Brig, and again on the Schooner." Reynolds enjoyed dining with the British exceedingly:

> They began with stately ceremony and progressed with all courtesy, but when the veterans withdrew, the scene was most hilarious. . . . The Regiment had been in a thousand battles, had fought through the Peninsular War and every where else. . . . The Colonel, the Major had been through it all and tales that had been history to us were now narrated by the Actors themselves! . . . They were fine fellows, these Sojers . . . I dined and supped and lunched and breakfasted in their mess hall and slept in the barracks and rode with them to Botany Bay and the Red Coats made our time pass very pleasantly. . . . What a life these men have in peaceful times! 18 years they are kept from their Home and in Climes that kill them like sheep. . . . I did not go into any other Society save that of the Military there. The social circles in Sydney are rather peculiar. . . . There are a few, a very few, honest persons there. . . . The Soldiers gave us a Pic Nic [*in Botany Bay*], which was charming! No ladies, of course—the Red Coats do not mix with the fashionables of Sydney and few of them are married.

The Journal records mainly these military contacts. Obviously, Reynolds adopted the attitude of the British officers toward the local population.

Sydney, February 25th 1840

My dear Mother:

We came in here on the 22nd, just 6 weeks after we left. We got jammed among the Ice away down South and were very near paying a visit to "*Davy Jones*," from which none of us would have been likely to have returned. We came within an ace of being lost: I have no time for particulars and I have not much confidence in the opportunity, but nevertheless I do not neglect it, merely in the hope that this will reach you some time—if not *early*, why it will not be my fault. I will write at length by the way of England before we leave, sending a drawing of our situation among the Ice.

I did a draft for Fifty Pounds, or two hundred and fifty dollars; the return here will increase my expenses so as to render this necessary. Things are dear here beyond telling, *Eggs 75 cts. a dozen and scarce at that, and every thing else in proportion.* I hope Father will honor it off the money I have left at Home. This will go by New Zealand; perhaps you may not get it for a year and you may perhaps in 3 months.

I have not time to say more. Good bye, my love to all, and as there are no more Ice bergs to be encountered I hope to see you all once more.

Good bye my dear mother, God bless you all.

Your affectionate Son

William

We will be here 6 or 8 weeks, hard at work repairing the damage we sustained and which it is a miracle we survived.

W. R.

I wrote you twice when here in December, once by England, once direct to America.

[*Postmark:*] Philad. July 7[1]

[1] *Lydia answered on 15 July; her letter reached William the following year on 20 July at the Columbia River. "I need not tell you how distressed we all were to hear of the dangers you had encountered, nor how thankful that you escaped. I rejoice to think it is the last of the kind you may meet with, my dear Brother. . . . I send you a paper containing a letter from Sydney giving an account of the new continent said to be discovered. . . . How does it happen that these officers write home and extracts from their letters are published, while we are not allowed to read yours to your friends. . . . It is passing strange."*

$$\mathscr{Letter\ No.\ 14}$$

U.S. Ship Peacock
Sydney, March 4th 1840

My dear Mother,

A few days ago I sent you a very short letter
by way of New Zealand merely mentioning that we were obliged to
return here to repair damages received among the Ice, etc. etc. I think
it likely you may get this first and as I have now a little leisure, I will
endeavour to spin you the whole yarn.

We left Sydney the day after Christmas and after rather a rough
time for more than two weeks, we reached the barrier of Ice, having
made *Maquarie Island* on our way.[1] *Ice bergs* we met with in Lat. 61° S.
and passed them daily until we arrived at the *field of Ice*, which
prevented our farther progress South and sent us along its edge to
the Westward. We separated from the Squadron while in the clear
sea, but fell in with the Vincennes and Brigs soon after we made the
barrier. We did not continue together, however, but parted, each to
do our best, alone.

When we crossed the 60th degree of Latitude, we seemed to leave
the stormy region behind us entirely. The weather was fair and
mild and the Sea smooth; fog and sleet disappeared, and we had
sunshine instead, which was gladly welcomed. Our hopes were high;
appearances were so flattering, that we were sanguine of penetrating

[1] *Macquarie Island, the first rendezvous of the squadron after leaving New
South Wales, is situated 2,100 miles south and east of Sydney.*

to a high parrelel without encountering danger or obstruction, confident that we should have the fame and the honor of finding *Land* where none had ever sought for it before;[2] full of joy that we should accomplish this and so gain a name for us and for our country.

On, on we sailed for days with a fair breeze over almost a summer Sea and meeting with no signs of a *barrier* to cloud our fair expectations. At 12 o'clock on the 16th January, there *was not a particle of Ice to be seen from the mast head* and *we were nearly as far South as the Ship had gone last year*: the weather was quite clear and the excitement on board was intense.[3] We were confident that we should eclipse all

[2] *In the eighteenth century, many persons had theorized the existence of a large, temperate body of land in the southern Pacific as necessary for the balance and symmetry of Earth. Cook's voyage to Australia and his failure to find other land to the south, however, had largely dispelled the notion that there was more to be discovered. Before the Exploring Expedition, only a few isolated points of Antarctica such as Palmer Land and Enderby Land had been discovered.*

[3] *The previous March the* Peacock *had reached 69° 08'S., 97° 58'W. On 16 January, Reynolds's Public Journal recorded Lat. 65° 55'S. and Long. 157° 34'E.*

There are discrepancies between this letter and Reynolds's day-by-day account in his Public Journal (pp. 113–30). The major discrepancy, done for reasons of secrecy as he explains further on, was that he sighted land that day. He recorded (p. 119): "clearing up during the morning watch . . . at 8 no ice in sight . . . about 10 we were close in with a barrier of Ice . . . beating up, Porpoise to windward. At times weather thick with snow! Saw Land from the Mast head at 10 A.M." (This last sentence may have been entered at a later date.)

There is a page inserted in the Public Journal between pages 120 and 121, written "April 1840," after leaving Sydney: "January 16th a little before noon Mr. Eld and myself went to the mast head to obtain a good view over the barrier of Ice . . . the weather was clear and breeze moderate. . . . Simultaneously, we observed the appearance of Land, at a great distance over the barrier; there were several peaks showing very distinctly, and other summits were hidden by clouds—they were of immense height." Reynolds reported to Lieutenant Thomas A. Budd, officer of the deck, and Eld to Captain Hudson. "No one else was sent to the mast head, nor was the appearance of Land mentioned in the Log Book . . . Cap. Hudson

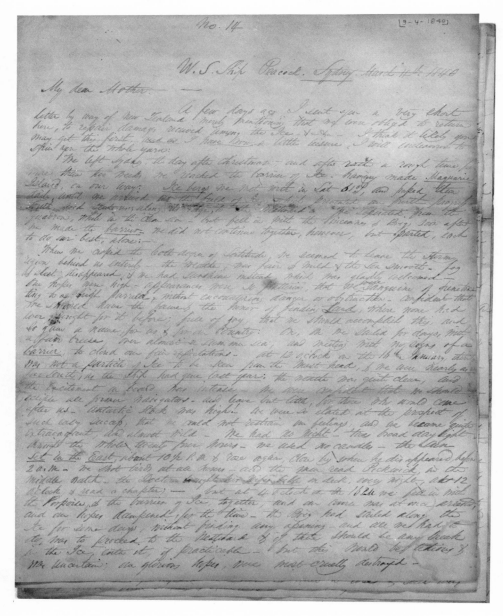

*Facsimile of Letter No. 14. Written from Sydney in March 1840, this
letter describes the historic Antarctic cruise and Reynolds's own role in
sighting land. Courtesy Franklin and Marshall College Archives,
Lancaster, Pennsylvania.*

former navigators and leave but little for those who would come after us. Antartic Stock was high! We were so elated at the prospect of such easy success that we could not restrain our feelings and we became quite extravagant, and almost wild.

We had no night—'twas broad daylight through the whole twenty four hours. We used no candles. The Sun *set in the East* about 10 ½ P.M. and rose again, close by where he disappeared, before 2 A.M. We shot birds at all hours and the *men read Pickwick* in the middle watch; the Doctor brought *his wife's bible* on deck every night at 12 o'clock and *read a chapter.*[4]

But at 4 o'clock on the 16th we fell in with the Porpoise and the barrier of Ice together, and our course was at once arrested and our hopes dampened for the time. The Brig had sailed along the Ice for some days without finding any opening, and all we had to do was to proceed to the Westward and if there should be any break in the Ice, enter it, if practicable—but this would be tedious and was uncertain; our glorious hopes were most cruelly destroyed.

A few days after turning to the Westward, we came to an opening in the Ice, which we entered though we scarcely thought it extended far to the Southward: we sailed along 30 miles ere we came to the head of it and were then enclosed on all sides, save the one small passage to the North, by immense fields of Ice. The long swell of the Ocean was shut off altogether, the water was smooth and motionless as an Inland Lake and lay like a vast mirror in its frosted frame. It was as a Bay making far into the Land, but the boundaries *were not the green of Earth.* As we approached the end of the Bay, we fell in with innumerable pieces of floating Ice, broken off from the mass and

---

remarked to Mr. Eld that we would very likely see more in a day or two!" Reynolds was "under the belief" that he had mentioned this in his Journal at the time, but he had neglected it, while Eld had not. He hoped the sighting would be accorded them and "thereby give us three days advance of Capt. D'Urville, instead of a part of one day" (n. 13 below).

[4] *The assistant surgeon on the* Peacock *then was Charles F. B. Guillou, who became an intimate of Reynolds during the ensuing months. Guillou had joined the navy in 1837 from Philadelphia and volunteered immediately for the expedition (ZB). See Letter of Introduction for Dr. Guillou, n. 1.*

drifting out into the Sea. Though the temperature was 21°, I spent more than one hour at the mast head for the sight from thence was grand, wild, strange beyond description: far as the eye could see, the Icy plains extended until they met the sky; the sligtness of their elevation above the water, relieved in many places by towering Ice bergs of every form and hue and by immense Islands that arose like mountains from amidst the Desert of Ice; the whiteness of all this was dazzling and intense; unbroken, save by the glistening sheet of water where the Ship floated, idle, quiet and at rest.

I was alone on my airy perch; the hum of voices from the deck did not reach my ear for the tones of all were subdued and there was naught to disturb the solemn and almost awful stillness that hung over the frozen plains: the Ship ceased her groaning and the very sea birds had gone from us; all that there was of life in the picture was beneath my feet, and *that* I heeded not. I thought there was no one but God near me and as I looked upon the mighty scene around which was neither Earth nor Sea, I was more impressed with the idea of His creative power and of the insignificance of man, than by any prospect that ever Earth afforded, or Sea assumed. *My feelings were new* and I enjoyed the hour far more than I can tell.

Once we thought we saw Land and as it happened I had been the first to discern the appearance, from the mast head: we neared it, and its high and broken sides and summit confirmed our conjectures. We were sure it was a portion of the Southern Continent and were elated beyond measure. We gave names to Points and Peaks and I stipulated for two, which were to be *Lancaster* and *Cornwall*, besides a *Cape Reynolds*. Alas! we could not land upon it but it seemed to be an Island 1000 feet high or more. So it was frequently, though we were more than once deceived. Many circumstances prevented a close approach and the snowy mantle deceived us and kept us long in doubt and suspence.[5]

[5] *Public Journal, 19 January (p. 120): In an immense bay, "at 3.50 discovered appearance of land bearing W by S; tacked and stood for it." In small handwriting, possibly inserted later: "it was of great height, of rugged broken and rounded summit, and rough sides; I thought it over 1000 feet; it was entirely covered with snow, but on a nearer approach, I could not give*

On Thursday evening January 24th we were in another Bay and were strongly impressed with the belief that we were near Land and that some ridges that we saw were not all Ice, but Earth beneath. Two boats were sent away from the Ship for different purposes and the Lead line was put over the side. It was watched going down by eager eyes and when it brought up suddenly, there was almost a scream of delight: we had found the bottom at 350 fathoms—*mud* and *pebbles* came up on the lead and line and *then* we got a first sight of the Southern Land. Great was the joy and excitement throughout the Ship, for this was a certain indication that our belief was correct *this time*. We had "terra firma" in our grasp, as we thought, and the prize would be our own, poor, short sighted fools that we were! The boats were returning about this time and the crew were sent into the rigging to give three cheers for our luck; they did this with such a hearty good will that the old Ice rang out with the sound.

All was bustle about the decks; below, some were playing shuffle board; on the Gun deck, we were *rolling nine pins* (the Ship was so perfectly at rest) and on the Spar deck, the men were running away cheerily with the lead line to the music of the fiddle, occasionally bursting into the songs and hurrahs common among them when at any exciting work. When this was finished, all hands were called *to splice the main brace* and we were a merry Ship. Little did any one think of the change that a few short hours would bring about! I shall

---

up my belief that it was land, actually Terra Firma. Lat. 66 31 S., Long. 153 40 E."

Again, sheets were inserted (between pages 124 and 125), written in April: "On the 19th Mr. [Midshipman George W.] Clark and myself were at the Fore Top Gallant Mast head about 3 o'clock P.M. I pointed out to him the resemblance of land to the West, which he assented to!" Reynolds reported it to Lieutenant Emmons, deck officer, who concurred; it was visible from below, also. Reynolds turned in, but upon returning to deck, was told it was only an "Ice Island, for it was all white." *Reynolds clung to his belief: it was too high and he did not* "expect to see *much earth* in this region." *His belief was corroborated on their return to Sydney, when he found that the* Vincennes's *log and charts also showed land at that spot; the flagship had crossed the mouth of the same bay in which the* Peacock *lay on the nineteenth.*

never give way to high wrought hopes again! When I have done so, disappointment was sure to come with a mountain's weight!

One of the Boats brought on board a mammoth penguin. A beautiful and kingly bird he was, but it was a bad day for him that the Peacock came to his haunts; he was cruelly put to death that his skin might be preserved for the satisfaction of those who are content to see the curious things of the world second hand.

The Sun set at 10 with all the splendor of a warmer clime, leaving a ruddy glow in the Horizon which vanished not, but chamelion like changed its hues from bright to brighter. 'Twas my middle watch and when I came on deck at 12, there was a deep peace all around; but a breath of air was stirring and the Ship was quiet and motionless as she would have been in *Speedwell dam.*[6] The Moon was bright in the Heavens, but she threw no light abroad: this eternal day puts her to shame and blots out the Stars altogether. The East was illuminated with those soft and blended tints that form the glory of an Italian sky at Eve and the reflection of these colours upon the Ice produced an effect, splendid, dazzling, grand beyond conception; the eye quailed at the sight and the imagination was utterly confounded. I felt that I was looking upon the painting of God! To heighten the scene, in the North and West the clouds were black and hung in gloomy contrast over the stainless field of Ice beneath them. Tell me no more of Earth! I have seen its fairest portions, but never have I looked upon so much vast, sublime and wondrous beauty as this rising and setting of the Sun presented in the midst of the Icy Sea.

The Captain[7] came on deck in the greatest glee—35 large pebbles had been taken from the maw of the Penguin, another sympton that

[6] *The dam at Speedwell Forge, seven miles south of Cornwall, was part of the Coleman estate.*

[7] *William Levereth Hudson (1794–1862), of New York. In the navy since 1816, Hudson was commissioned as lieutenant in 1826, slightly before Wilkes. In 1843, he was promoted to commander and commanded the* Vincennes *for a period before promotion to captain in 1855. A year later, he was involved in laying the first Atlantic submarine telegraph cable and, in 1860–1861 commanded the Boston Navy Yard. Hudson was a loyal supporter of Wilkes throughout the voyage and its aftermath (ZB).*

William L. Hudson, by Alfred Agate. Hudson was the faithful second in command to Charles Wilkes. Popular with the younger officers, he had a reputation as a better sailor than the temperamental commander, despite the loss of the Peacock *under his command in 1841. Courtesy Naval Historical Foundation, Washington, D.C.*

there was *Land* about. Poor man! he was nearly beside himself with joy.

At 4 o'clock I turned in, dreading no evil and confident that we would succeed in finding the desired Land ere we were many days older—true! even in a few hours we came near to finding it, *but at the bottom of the Sea*!

At 8 o'clock, I found the Ship entered among the pieces of drift

Ice; the Captain was trying to get near the barrier to determine whether the appearances of Land were real or false. At 8.40 it was evident we could go no farther with safety and that we had best get back into the clear water as speedily as possible. We were entirely surrounded by loose Ice; some pieces were much larger than the Ship and they were packed so closely together that we had no room to proceed or to manoeuvre in. Here and there small clear patches occurred, but these filled up and changed continually. In endeavouring to tack, the Ship got Sternboard and went Stern on to a huge lump of ice, splitting the rudder head and carrying away the wheel ropes.[8] This shock sent her ahead, against all her sails, and it brought all hands on deck; but in another moment she gathered sternway once more and this time coming in contact with the same mass, the rudder was shattered and the head of it carried away entirely.

This was a terrible disaster alone: the Ship, with all her spars standing, her hull entire, her crew safe, was helpless as an infant— her *guiding power* was gone—but this was *merely* the *commencement* of our troubles. Our situation was evident at a glance; we must get clear of the Ice at once, *if we could?* repair the rudder, *if we could?* and get back to Sydney, *if we could?* All, or either of which, was problematical in the highest degree. We failed in the first attempt, *to get out!* Our own efforts could not succeed and we were most reluctantly obliged to run her farther into the Ice to reach a clear place that we noticed near a large Island of Ice.

We were obliged to steer the Ship by the Sails and of course her movements were awkward and slow: we could not avoid the Ice in our way and thumped heavily many times, carrying away part of the Fore foot and doing other damage.[9] This was becoming too serious, the Ship could *not bear such shocks long.* It was really terrible to see her bearing down upon these masses and then feel her bring up, arrested at once by the mighty obstacles in her way; her whole frame quivered

[8] *With the loss of the rudder head, or upper portion of the rudder shaft, and the ropes leading to it from the steering wheel went the ability to control movement of the vessel.*

[9] *The fore foot is that part of a ship where the stem or bow is joined to the keel.*

and shook and the poor craft groaned in her distress. *How we watched her as she freed herself and more than once we thought spars and all would come down about our heads: the danger was thickening fast.*

We now lowered the Boats and carried out Ice Anchors to the largest pieces, hoping to ride by them until we could hoist in the rudder: the sails were furled, but, vain hopes, the anchors would not hold; the wind freshened a little and, notwithstanding the exertions of the men to keep the Iron flues in their bed, we broke adrift and ere we could raise a hand to save ourselves, the Ship *went on to the Ice Island with a tremendous crash.* This Island was many miles in extent: from the mast head, I could see over its flat top a long, long distance, but could not discern its termination. It rose from the Water, bluff as the sides of a house, the uper edge projecting like the eaves and when we were under it, it towered above the mast head. It was the weakest part of the Ship's frame that came in contact with this mass, and the shock and crash and splintering of the riven spars and upper works was any thing but agreeable.

For *an instant, I thought that* the whole stern frame *must* be stove in and that a few moments would send us to the bottom. I thought any struggle for life would be in vain: to reach a piece of Ice would only be to linger in agony and suffer a more horrible death, and I settled in my mind with startling quickness *that it would be best to go down with the Ship.* With this thought came neither terror nor dismay, though it was the thought of going to my eternal sleep. (One does not know what the mind is capable of bearing in such situations until experience has learned us; I was astonished to find myself *reasoning* in such a moment as this.) An hour before we had been in safety: *now* we were a wreck at the mercy of the elements and the Ice. I may safely say I felt neither fear nor dread, though there was that quickening rush of blood towards the heart and those creeping thrilling sensations, indescribable, but such as must come over every one at the startling approach of sudden death. Of course no one felt at ease, but there were no shrieks, no exhibitions of bewilderment; and from what I know of my own feelings and from what others have told me of theirs, I verily believe that *had* the old Ship *settled* in the water, she would have gone down to her grave with three as hearty cheers as ever came from an hundred throats. God knows what it is that should prompt a man to send out his last breath in a hurrah! I do not! I thought my feelings strange and perhaps unnatural, but I was mistaken: the burst would have been spontaneous and universal, curious as it may seem. I know now as well as I know that I am sitting here, I can *see* the very *one* who would have been the first to say, "*let's give her a cheer my lads as she goes!*" and it would have been done!

The action was prompt, there was no time to lose, and sail was made with as much celerity and steadiness as if we were leaving a Harbour. The Ship moved, her head paid off from the danger,[10] slowly but surely she reached ahead and *we were clear of the Island*, where to have struck again would have ensured our destruction. *Scarcely* had we got from under the pile, when *down came the overhanging ledge of snow*, flinging the foam it raised in the Sea upon our decks. *Mercy! a moment longer and it had crushed us.* I cannot tell you *how* I looked upon that Island as we were leaving it, by inches; there were the marks of the Ship's form and paint, and there, at its foot, were the tumbled heaps of snow that had so nearly overwhelmed us.

I had been almost immediately relieved from the apprehension of the Ship's sinking. The destruction had been great, but it was *only* the *upper* part of the Ship's frame, that was carried away, and *she was saved*! I shall never forget the look of the old craft as she lay beneath that ridge of Ice, trembling from the blow, and Ice, Ice piled around her, so that we could see nothing else from the deck. The dark figures of the men and boats were the only relief to the dreary whiteness.

Now that we were freed from this peril, it was determined to struggle again for the clear Sea: 'twas about 11 A.M. We thumped, thumped until 3 in the afternoon, making but little progress and drifting to leeward all the while, with the Ice and the distance between us and the open Sea increased every moment from the quantity of floating pieces brought down by the wind. The men were kept incessantly at work, but all our efforts to get into places where the Ice was thinnest were of no avail; we were so jammed and the

---

[10] *That is, the bow of the ship turned to leeward.*

Ship so unmanageable that we missed every chance and became
more and more involved. An hundred times we thought we should
surely succeed, but the Ice crowded upon us the more and the Ship
continued to strike as if she would knock herself to pieces. Labour
was not slackened, however unfavorable appearances were: all the
resources that ingenuity suggested were tried and the men did
their duty, as sailors always do when working for their lives: calm,
obedient and untiring, they pursued their exertions with a steadiness
that could not be overthrown.

At 3 the wind died away and it came up *thick* and *blinding with
snow*. We made fast again with Ice anchors and hoisted the rudder in.
All of us were relieved to see *it* inboard, for oh! *how much depended on
its being repaired*! The Carpenters went immediately to work upon it.
Soon after, the breeze sprang up again, the anchors would not hold,
and we made sail once more to try and force her out. It was the same
thing over, with the same ill success; we became more and more shut
in and the chances for *getting out* seemed more remote than ever. To
dwell at all upon our situation, while in a measure free from instant
risk, afforded but little consolation: the Ship was so helpless without
her rudder and it seemed as if we were striving against fate and
would *never get clear*: allowing that we did escape the Ice, until we
could get command of the Ship once more we could not choose our
course; and after that *would* be accomplished, in the imperfect manner
that was alone practicable, we had a long tract of stormy Sea to pass
over ere we could reach our port. I did not allow these anticipations
to occupy my mind, but I could not help their intruding at times: how
wearily the time wore by and how vexatious, killing, torturing it was
to miss chance after chance for escape, when we had struggled for
dear life to obtain them. *You good people* in your *quiet Home* can know
but little of men's feelings in situations such as this and sure am I
that I can tell you mine but very faintly.

We toiled, toiled on: *"never say die"* was the word. Even the Boys
worked with all the ardour of Hercules, if not with his strength.
Officers and all, there was no one idle, no one thought of rest. We
used the Boats to plant the anchors for warping by[11] and when we

---

[11] *That is, hauling the ship forward by pulling on lines secured by
anchors.*

could use them no longer, the men went upon the Ice and crossing from piece to piece by planks laid over the chasms, transported the anchors to different positions; we had spars over the bows also, pushing with might and main. In this way, by 6 o'clock our exertions had brought us to within 100 yards of the open Sea, but we were wedged immoveable: we could neither advance nor recede and we had the cruel mortification of seeing the place of *comparative safety* so close at hand, and yet be in as much and more peril than we had experienced through the day. We *could all have walked* to the edge of the Ice, but the masses surrounding the Ship were so huge that all our thumping only did *her* injury, while it did not budge them an inch. *Now* was the time when the anxiety became *almost terrible!* Hitherto the weather, though thick, had not threatened. The wind had been moderate and there was but little swell; consequently the Ice had but little motion, not sufficient to throw *it* with any force against us: the *Ship* had been forced upon *it!* Now it seemed the tables were to be turned: Black clouds were gathering in the West; they were rolled and curled together in windy looking wreaths and they had all the appearance of *a coming storm.* I went up aloft and I fixed my gaze upon that portentous sky; I watched until I *saw its shadow coming over the water* and then I thought in sad earnest, *our time has come at last!*

While I was in the rigging descending to the deck, when as I thought the last grand scene in the drama of Life was so soon to be enacted, there was *something spoke at my heart* and with a few words I recommended my Soul to the mercy and keeping of God! *I gave up all hope of Life!* The approach of the squall seemed so evident and certain that I saw no prospect of escape and I thought that in less than an hour there would not be a vestige left of the Peacock or her crew! I know of no feelings more terrible than those that are likely to be called up in moments such as these: here were *two hundred of us* in the full vigour of health and strength and in a few moments *not one* would be left to tell the tale of our destruction: *all must go,* without *even the hope of a struggle for life:* there could be *no resistance;* when the crash came, *we* should be swept away like the spars and timbers of the Ship!

Every one was watching those clouds: men and boys knew that in their shape hung our fate and *they were coming on like the angel of death.*

Every rag was taken in and now, as we could do no more, we *silently awaited our chance.* The little breeze which had been blowing from another quarter died away entirely and that sort of breathless calm succeeded which is generally ominous of the wrath and tempest about to follow. *Now* you might see eye turn to eye, seeking for Hope or a glance of consolation; but even during this dreadful crisis, which thank God! was brief, there was no feeling *betrayed* that any one should be ashamed of. *With nothing to do,* you could read anxiety in many a face; you could tell of the trouble within by the quivering lips and the unsettled eye, but there was neither the voice of murmur or of fright; there was naught that could cast a stigma upon the manhood of the crew. Those who were timid kept their fears to themselves; if they needed the example of restraint and composure, it was set to them by the many who were made of firmer stuff.

I am not going to say that while we were in this harrowing suspense, I or any one else felt unconcerned or at ease. On the contrary, my feelings were *almost* overpowering in their force: the sense of the dreadful fate impending over us was suffocating and all the tumult of thoughts likely to crowd upon a man with *such a death* before his eyes pressed with a *stunning* weight upon my poor heart. So it was with others, so *they* tell *me since.*

Nearer and nearer came the funeral cloud; but suddenly its appearance changed! It spread wide and broke away! It lost its stormy aspect; the windy looking wreaths were dissolved in mist and thick snow! With *that change,* our sense of *present* danger passed away. We were relieved from the *fear of instant destruction!* It was evident to the eyes that had watched the progress of that cloud with so much anxiety that there need no longer be any apprehension of a storm. With the keenness of judgement common to seamen, every one knew *that the crisis had gone by* and that we might once more deem ourselves in comparative safety. The spell was broken! we breathed freely! the deep and joyful feelings of *that moment cannot be told!*

Heavens! What a hideous death we escaped: the poor old Ship was lying with her whole broadside exposed to the Ice, pressed, strained, groaning in every part of her frame. Her strong build alone enabled her to hold together; the Vincennes could not have borne it so long. The least increase of either breeze or swell would have brought the Ice down upon us in a thousand *avalanches!* We could not fly, we could not stay the advancing Ice; Ship and men would have gone down beneath the frozen piles and our fate would have been forever sealed in the mystery which enshrouds the Polar Sea!

Cold and weary, some of us went below to solace ourselves with some hot compound and something more substantial. We enjoyed the lunch with a keen relish and returned on deck to participate in the toil that was renewed.

Instead of a storm of wind from the cloud, we had a thick snow squall that almost blinded us and shut both Ice and Sea from our view. Presently a light breeze sprang up and sail was made once more. The Ice still came drifting down and, as before, when we had got the Ship nearly in a channel, it would close up and we had to try another and be again disappointed. In this way the time wore heavily and wearily away.

At 1 in the morning, we had all been up 17 hours hard at work and as it was *labour in vain,* one watch's hammocks were piped down and the officers and crew, save the watch on deck, went below to sleep—if they could. I turned into my cot at once to make the best of a short *three* hours, for I had the morning watch to keep. I suffered horrible tortures during my troubled Sleep; all the feelings I had mastered during the day haunted me in dreams. I died an hundred deaths, I was buried crushed under the Ice and the whole terrible catastrophe of a wreck, from the first moment of the Ice striking the Ship to the last drowning gasp, occurred with a vividness that I shall never forget. God keep me from ever feeling so, when awake! At every jar of the Ship or when any one touched my cot, I started up in agony with the idea that we were sinking and with the suffocating sense of strangling in my throat (a cold in the head was nearly choking me from the accumulation of phlegm). Those 3 hours in my cot were worse a thousand times than all the time on deck with real danger to look upon. I was glad when they were passed and got up very willingly to renew my watch. Just at this time, aided by a light breeze and a fortunate opening of the Ice, the Ship of her own accord slid into the clear water, free from the rough and cold embrace that had held her so long.

The weather was thick and chill and the wind light, but we managed to steer our disabled craft tolerably well, and without further accident reached the middle of the Bay we had entered with so much confidence and where our hopes had been raised so high. Towards 8 the mist cleared and all around as far as we could see the Icy barrier extended, save one little corner left for us to creep out of.

My eyes were red and smarting from the loss of rest and I was fairly done over, half dead from anxiety and exertion. The Carpenters had worked all night upon the rudder and at 10 A.M. it was ready to be shipped. This was too important an operation not to be witnessed by every one on board and so, foregoing the chance for sleep, we all assembled to see it completed. The precarious manoeuvre was accomplished with a seaman's ready skill and by 11 we were once more on our way, heading for the only passage that lead to the ocean.

I lay me down until dinner time, but it was not until after this meal that I could get any refreshing rest. But from 3 to 6, I slept like one of the dead and when I had to rise to my watch again, I felt fresh as ever: the change was blessed indeed.

The evening was clear and mild, the sky rosy, the Ice no longer dangerous but reflecting a thousand tints, the Ship was manageable once more, and *all was different* from the same hour of the previous night.

The Dr. was the only one who had exhibited visible signs of perturbation—poor man, every one noticed his nervous anxiety. He was in every body's way and asking questions which had better not been breathed. I spoke to him once when he followed me aloft. He said he had never lived through *such* a day before, his alarm had been dreadful and he was almost crazy; but 'twas not for himself! his mind was with his *wife* and the *child* he has *never seen*.

Our passage to Sydney was long, stormy and anxious. We were not, could not be certain of the rudder amidst such tremendous Seas, but luckily it held on and we made it safely. We had much thick weather while passing Ice bergs, so that we could not see two yards ahead of the Ship. Many a four hours did I stand with my eyes fixed on the mist before us and my heart in my mouth; for to have come upon an Ice berg would have been fatal and we could scarcely see them in time to avoid them, snow coming down all the while, too, in a manner such as would delight one when anticipating a sleigh ride, but rather disagreeable in a mid watch when you consider that the Season was Summer. Pleasant times, I assure you.

Sketch of the USS Peacock *in Antarctica, 1840, by Charles F. B.
Guillou. Courtesy Anne Hoffman Cleaver.*

I send enclosed a sketch made by Dr. Guillou, but it will give you,
of course, merely such an idea as three inches of paper may be
capable of conveying. I do not mind the bulk and you must not
complain of the Postage, because—very nearly—you might never
have been troubled with this tale.[12]

Sydney we found the same as before. To accomplish our repairs,
we moved the Ship into a retired cove that runs far into the shore,
hemmed in by high hills and not much larger than *your dam at
Cornwall* (that is the upper part of it), which takes a sudden bend, so
that on approaching it you do not perceive the Ship until you come

[12] *In February 1841 Lydia wrote, "We have the drawing of the Peacock
among the ice framed and hung up in the parlour."*

right on top of her. We hauled in by the wharf, stripped the Ship, got every[thing] out of her and have been hard at work ever since. By the way, this is now the 20th and our repairs are nearly completed. Much to our surprise, the Vincennes came in here the other day and as they have made public in the papers the results of the cruise to the South, why I shall be more explicit than I could have been otherwise: I cut a piece from the Sydney papers and enclose it—the Latitudes and Longitudes are incorrect. The Vincennes ran some terrible risks and was more than once within an ace of destruction. They merely came in here to refresh and had no idea of finding us.

You will see that the French made the Land on the same day as the Vincennes, but in different Long. Now as it happens, *we* in this Ship discovered *it two days* before, on the 17th, *and Mr Eld* and *myself* who were by accident at the mast head were the *first* and only persons *to put eyes on it.*[13] So on *us two* devolves the credit of the discovery and, modest man that I am to write it, the hopes of the

[13] *A French expedition under Captain Jules Sébastien César Dumont d'Urville (1790–1842) had embarked in 1837 with two ships. Dumont d'Urville announced that he had sighted land on 19 January and landed two days later on an island off Antarctica, claiming the territory for the French crown. As J. E. Pillsbury (1910) points out, these dates were actually 20 and 22 January because the French did not correct their time with the longitude.*

Passed Midshipman Henry Eld (1814–1850) had joined the navy from Connecticut in 1832. He had worked under Charles Wilkes doing survey work in 1837 and, after commissioning as a lieutenant in 1842, assisted Wilkes between 1843 and 1846 in publishing the expedition Narrative. *Eld died of yellow fever en route to Rio de Janeiro in 1850 (ZB).*

Unfortunately, Hudson was uncertain enough of the sightings that they were not entered into the log of the Peacock *at the time; however, the word "Land" was obviously overwritten later in the passages for those days. This situation caused some controversy about the primacy of the American discovery.*

Reynolds's reference to the seventeenth here is probably a memory lapse and conflicts with his Public Journal for 16–19 January and the later April entry which give 16 January as the day of discovery and refer to "three days advance" on Dumont d'Urville; see n. 3 above. In the Public Journal, there is no mention at all of land in the entry for the seventeenth; but again, on the nineteenth, "appearance of Land" is recorded.

country and the honor of the Expedition, as far as regards the rights of priority. *We also saw the Land on the* 19th *and, fortunate me, I was again at the Mast head, spectacles on, and was the first to descry it. I made my report,* as before, and this was the Land I have mentioned as receiving so many names in prospecto.[14] I could not have told you so plainly as I do now, but for the printed publicity authorized by Captain Wilkes!

The French kept their intentions quiet as the grave—we knew nothing of their intentions until our return here. They are very jealous rivals to *this* Expedition, though they were fitted out to compete with the *old one under Commodore Jones.* Louis Phillippe, in an audience with the Commanders, promised them any thing, should *they get the farthest South.* They sailed a year before we did, were in such a hurry that they would not stop at Rio Janeiro, but sent a boat in to see if *the Americans were there!* They went on South, got not so far by 6° as we did, afterwards, and were obliged to turn back with half the crew dying of the scurvy. Some of the officers published a cock and bull story about the discovery of a Continent, which merely referred to Palmers Land and was utterly untrue; some of the inferior officers must have written this account, it was so glaringly incorrect.

The next year, that is, the winter of 1838 and 39, while our Ships were South, the French took a holiday and this year when we thought them all on their way home, lo and behold! they were close at us! Mortified, perhaps, at the difference between their former attempt and ours, they tried it again; but in their eagerness, they spoiled all—they only ran 150 miles along the Ice and then put back. They could not wait longer, when to have persevered might have enabled them at least to say *that "they had done all they could"* and *"accomplished all that was practicable or necessary"*; but no! Frenchmen like, they must run away to *tell* of their success and that has ruined them! Their 150 miles will show *but small* alongside of the 1600 and odd miles made by the Vincennes along Land. So much for the Antartic Continent! I thank God that the honor rests with us, both as

[14] *The names Reynolds assigned on 19 January (Lancaster and Cornwall peaks and Cape Reynolds) did not enter the geographies. Wilkes, however, did name two peaks after Eld and Reynolds in recognition of their sightings on the sixteenth; they are situated in longitude 157° 36′ E.*

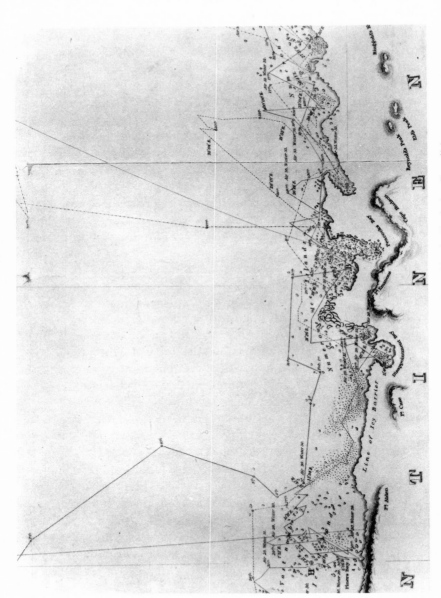

Portion of the Coast of Antarctica, as charted by the Exploring Expedition

to its discovery and as to the great length of the run along its Shores. The Vincennes had several weeks of summer weather after the time we turned back. They met the land at 8 points; of course they did not have it in sight all the time, but nevertheless, there were no doubts about its being a Continent and *not so many Islands.*[15] Never before had Land been discovered *so far to the Southward.*

If Father would buy in Philadelphia or New York (at Blunts) the last London Edition of [*blank*] general chart of the World, on Mercater's principle (*large size,* such as were bought for this Expedition and used by all navigators), you will find all former tracks laid down on it; furthermore you can trace our progress among the Islands with more satisfaction, *and when I come home,* I will cover it with the marks of all my cruises. I hope he will get it![16]

So much for our Southern cruise, at present! *More,* when I get *Home.*

The Vincennes has gone to New Zealand. The English have taken possession of the Island and they will soon crowd to it as they have done here. They are establishing a *Bank* there already! a paper money affair, in wild New Zealand! The world is turning upside down, sure enough. The inhabitants do not seem to like the measures in progression since the Governor's arrival among them! They say *"he* may *govern his own people* and it is very well for the *Queen,* in *her* regard for *them* and *her* love for *justice,* to send a Governor to look after *her* subjects and keep them straight—but then, *he must not govern them! they are in their own country!"* Poor souls, they will soon find out

[15] *Sir James Clark Ross (1800–1862), the English explorer who followed the Americans and French to these same Antarctic waters within a matter of months, belittled Wilkes's claim of having found a continent by claiming that the Americans had discovered only a chain of islands. Should it prove to be a continent, Ross said credit for its discovery should go to the English whaling captain John Biscoe for having sighted Enderby Land in 1831. In this regard, Ross ignored the discovery some years earlier of Palmer Land by the American Nathaniel Brown Palmer.*

[16] *Reynolds undoubtedly refers to Aaron Arrowsmith's chart of the Pacific Ocean first published in London in 1798. Arrowsmith's chart went through several other editions through 1832 and was the principal map of the Pacific during the period. The chart was drawn on a scale of 1:9,000,000 and was printed in nine sections.*

to their cost what it is to admit the white men to their Shores! And yet you hear these English with the utmost self complacency and assurance cry aloud about our Indians—they cannot see the mote in their own eye. While the policy of our Government is confined to our own Land, the English go over the Sea and settle, and then burn, slay and destroy![17]

The natives have all disappeared from about the Sea Shore in this Colony, save a few miserable drunken beasts that wallow about the streets. In the interior, when they raise any disturbance the Dragoons are after them, sword in hand! An officer told me of a butchering match he had a hand in and 'twas as murderous a tale as I ever heard! *They call them brutes* and then turn to weep for the savages of North America because the Americans force them to leave their Homes and make war upon them when they rise in arms—rare consistency!

The French Government, I perceive, are somewhat touched at this quiet occupation of New Zealand by the English; and really one cannot help smiling to read the most gracious proclamation of Her Majesty, Victoria, announcing the addition of the Island to *My* Dominions! Whew! The country is extremely rich and abounds with Timber for Ships, Water, and every thing of which South Wales is deficient.

The last page I scribbled at Paramatta, a small country Town 13 miles from Sydney whither I went for a change of air and to get out of sight of the Ocean for a few days.[18] I was glad to find myself

[17] *After several unsuccessful attempts to colonize New Zealand from New South Wales beginning in 1792, the English crown did succeed in negotiating the Treaty of Waitangi with the Maori and sending a governor to North Island in 1840. By the treaty, the Maori acknowledged British sovereignty yet were to retain possession of the land. The British soon afterward annexed the entire territory, leading to war with the Maori until 1845. In 1840, the Bay of Islands area of New Zealand was a great trading and provisioning center for whalers but had a reputation for lawlessness (Dodge 1976:143–49).*

[18] *The second British settlement in Australia was Rose Hill, which shortly after its founding in 1790 came to be known by the aboriginal word Parramatta. Located inland from Sydney on the banks of the Parramatta River, the town was one of the principal population centers of the early New South Wales colony.*

among the fields and I would have given the world could I have opened my eyes and found myself in Cornwall. As I walked about I endeavoured to persuade myself that I *was* near Home, but it would not do! It was too sure that I was in Australia! I met several in Paramatta whom I knew, English officers etc., and had quite a pleasant time. I visited the Female Convict Factory, wherein were confined 1,000 women, *every one of whom* had been transported for crime. They were differently employed in needlework and light out of door labour, and work about the House! There is a sort of "man of war" discipline preserved among them and the Superintendent told me he had not much trouble, but that he persevered with his severe system and always kept them busy. Some were in the cells in solitary confinement and many were in the *Straw;*[19] the women were dressed in mob caps, short gowns and petticoats, and altogether the assemblage and their condition were very curious to see!

This is now the 25th of March and I am writing in a very strange place: in the quarters of Lt. Murray of the 50th Regiment. I slept here last night after dining with the mess and, as Murray is on guard all day and night, I have taken quiet possession for the night and absented myself from the dinner, though the temptation was great and the band is now playing close by, on purpose that I might bring this letter to an end, for I am so occupied with duty and other things that I have to manoeuvre and take chances as they offer to say my say to you. I am often in almost despair, but I do not think you can accuse me of neglect. I always manage to write some thing, bad as it may be! But it *is* funny that I should be writing away here in her Majesty's barracks to you my dear Mother, who are so removed from any thing appertaining to the said Victoria! unless it might be the "rival Queen" in her 'red night gown.' Poor Elly, how does she come on? Has she grown, can she read yet and all about her?

These Soldiers are all very attentive to us, and I am and have been much among them. This Murray is a young Lieutenant, rich, of a good Scotch family; his cousin, same name, has lately traveled in America and has published. Buy his book for curiosity's sake, for I like this Murray very much and hope I may meet him again—than

[19] *That is, in childbed. Transportation of criminals to New South Wales was discontinued in 1840.*

which nothing is more likely, for I expect to continue a vagrant all my days.[20]

I shall be glad when this cruise is out: I have *so much* to tell you about; but *then* I cannot stay long with you, for if any vessel is sent to look after the Schooner that we lost off Cape Horn, and I trust that it will be ordered as soon as we get back, why *I must* be the first to volunteer and to go! Poor fellows! I am afraid we shall never see them again, but they came after me when I was in distress in the old Launch and I shall go with all readiness to search for them! If they escaped the wreck, they fell into the hands of a merciless race of beings and in a clime the very worst in the world! Poor, poor boys! they had a hard fate, indeed.

Well, when I return from this, which I think most certainly *will* be done by the Government, I *must* go to France and become a Frenchman as far as the Tongue goes: I am determined on spending one year there at least and after that I have no plans, only to keep moving as I despair of a wife to anchor me fast in any one place. Indeed, if I got one, I should endeavour to give her the mania for Travel and we could cruise in company. However, this year I am 25—30 will soon come. I have some arrears of misspent time to buy up and I intend to make the year in France one of much study and mental improvement. I have it all arranged, companions and all, and *it is to be done* as soon as we can leave Home when we shall have once more reached there safely. So you cannot keep me long, you see. As I live on, I begrudge every moment that passes and I am

---

[20] *When the ships sailed for the last time from Sydney, many of the officers and crew were waved off by female admirers who crowded the piers. Reynolds, Eld, and Passed Midshipman James B. Lewis, the three who spent the week at Parramatta, were cheered by three "Red Coats" who rowed out, came aboard, and shared a last glass of hock and "ice from Boston." Reynolds noted that "for [Hood] Murray, I had the love of a brother . . . a very gentlemanly man of my years and I hope to meet him again" (Journal 1:334). Reynolds did so when his ship the* Allegheny *paused at Gibraltar in December 1849: "Capt. Murray, late of the 50th Regiment, now of the 117th," was stationed there with his wife, two boys, and two sisters (Reynolds 1847–1849). His cousin Ballou Maturin Murray (1820–1895) wrote many books of fiction, biography, and travel under the name "Lt. Murray."*

selfish about my years: I find they are becoming too valuable and that they slip by much too rapidly. 'Tis never too late to do good and I have much to learn ere I can take a responsible station in the world! So to Europe I go; I should never study at Home!

I am very anxious to hear from you; it is more than a year since the date of your last short letter and 17 months since those before! . . . And after this fall, write by every chance to Rio de Janeiro. This letter will go by way of London by Dr. Gilchrist, who leaves the Squadron here very much to the regret of all of us: Captain Wilkes is sending him Home on a very frivolous charge.[21]

I shall not draw any bills here as I mentioned in Letter No. 13, but at the Sandwich Islands *I shall*. Drafts cannot be procured here and our expenses have been so great that I must draw on my *reserves* which I had hoped to leave untouched. However, I shall not make a large hole in it. I do not think I shall touch more than $200.00, which I must trouble Father to pay whenever he may receive my note!

An American Whaler came in last night 5 months from home and brought a few papers up to October, the latest dates we have had. I read a *Keystone* much to my surprise, but there was nothing in it. We heard of the Bank failure by way of England; what do people think of Nick Biddle now?[22]

On account of our long delay here, we will not visit New Zealand,

[21] *Edward Gilchrist, assistant surgeon on the* Vincennes. *Appointed to the navy in 1832, he had served on the* Boxer *and* Peacock *during the period of Reynolds's first cruise. A passed assistant surgeon since 1836, Gilchrist requested appointment as fleet surgeon when that position became vacant during the cruise. Wilkes refused because he did not consider the doctor qualified and because the commander considered him one of the officers leading a "cabal" against his authority. Despite Wilkes's action, Gilchrist was immediately promoted to surgeon upon his return home. Gilchrist went on to be a fleet surgeon during the 1850s and was appointed inspector of hospitals shortly before his death in 1869 (ZB).*

[22] *The* Keystone *was a weekly newspaper of Democratic leanings published in Harrisburg between 1836 and 1843.*

Nicholas Biddle (1786–1844), former president of the Bank of the United States, continued to operate the bank as a private corporation in Philadelphia after the Jacksonians refused to recharter it in 1832. Biddle's corporation failed as a consequence of the Panic of 1837.

so will be deprived of great pleasure and interest. I wanted very much to go there, but it can't be helped. We meet the others at Tonga Taboo and then proceed to survey the Fegees; then on to Sandwich Islands by June, July; then North West Coast, Caroline Islands, Sandwich again, Japan, Canton, Singapore, Cape of Good Hope etc. etc. etc. There, I believe this is the third time I have perpetrated a sketch of the cruise: we have much to do yet and much water to go over before we get Home, but 19 months and more have already passed quite fast and the rest will go before we know it. I am quite well and comfortable on board the Peacock and have now no wish to rejoin the Vincennes. All her officers would leave if they could; all ours are contented. Captain Wilkes is as unpopular as he well could be! I have scarcely seen him since I left his Ship and have no wish to see him until the cruise is over! When perhaps I can say something to the purpose! I shall never forget Him.

I cannot give you the scandal of Sydney. I must keep that in my head for you when I get back. The social condition of the place is so singular and so utterly different from any other part of the world that one meets with incidents every day that may well be called curious; and certainly Sydney and its inhabitants shall ever be remembered by me. The man who kept the Inn at Paramatta was once a convict and is now as rich as a Jew. The most beautiful girl here was transported for a slight theft when young; to look at her delicate form and bewitching face, you would not credit it. The *daughters* of convicts are married to *respectable* men and now lead the *Town*. An American who took his wife from such a source entertains the officers, and his children are educating for the best society. All those convicts managed to get rich and the *honest* men have no scruples as to taking their daughters—queer, queer, very.

I went on board the Buffalo when she came in with the *Canada rebels* and saw all she had on board. I thought there were several Yankee faces among them—poor devils! This is a change of climate for them, indeed.[23]

[23] *Reynolds refers to the members of the Reform parties of Lower and Upper Canada who rebelled against British colonial government in 1837 and were transported to New South Wales. In April 1841, Navy Secretary George Badger wrote to Wilkes, addressed to Singapore, that U.S. citizens imprisoned in the rebellion were at liberty to return and that the squadron*

Now I must bring my yarn to a close! I have inflicted on you a long tale of the Ice and hope you will bear with it patiently—I never wish to have occasion to tell another! As to the rest, why written at snatches, you must excuse dullness and all other faults—I cannot always be entertaining, you know! And when I get among you you may scold me as much as you please, but don't now! I hope you will mind my oft repeated requests for long letters and if Father has time I shall be most happy to have a letter from him. Good Bye! My love to every one and do you all write, from Grandmother to Elly. Your most loving and worshipful son,

William Reynolds

Mrs. L. M. Reynolds[24]

[*Inside wrapper:*] Good bye once more. We are under weigh and glad to go. We hope to be at Sandwich Islands by June and then, happy, happy thought, we shall get our Letters from *Home!* Good bye, Good bye,

William

Remembrance to all friends and a mountain of love to you.

[*Outside wrapper:*] Via England

[*Postmark:*] New York, Oct. 2

---

was authorized to offer free passage to any encountered; by that time, of course, it was too late for the expedition (Badger 1841).

[24] *On 5–6 November, Lydia wrote: "We received your letter giving an account of your escape from the ice islands. What an awful, horrible situation you must have been in. How could you have cheered the ship as she was going down? . . . We could scarcely read your letter aloud. Everyone in the family is so anxious to hear your letters that we are obliged to read them aloud, but that one was too trying."*

Peacock, at Sea, Saturday Evening
September 21st 1840
Lat. 14° oo′ North
Long. 150° 45′ West

To Father, Mother, Grandmother,
Aunt, Sam, Lydia, John, James,
Kate, Jane, Hal, and Elly—
each and every one,

After much hesitation I have determined
to commence a letter before we get in to Oahu, so that I may give
you a history of our doings since we left Sydney six months ago. I am
not much in the mood for this, however, for I am so anxious about
the letters which I hope to get in a few days that I have scarcely the
patience to sit still for any purpose whatsoever; added to this, we are
suffering afflictions in divers ways that are very trying to one's
temper. We are in utter ignorance of what is to be done with us for
the next six months and to cap the climax, we *do* know that we are to
remain out the *fourth* year from Home, which is consoling in the
extreme. So I had intended to wait until I had read *all* my letters and
learned how *you* all were, and picked up some information regarding
our future movements, by which time also, having *had something to
eat*, I hoped to be in a more amiable humor and able to write with
some satisfaction. However, I must go back to April and come along
regularly, if I can.

I wrote twice from Sydney during our last stay there—Nos. 13 and
14, both of which I trust have found their destination ere this. The
first went by New Zealand, and the latter by Dr. Gilchrist (of the
Vincennes) to England. Since then, there has been no opportunity.

We sailed from Sydney on the 30th of March for Tonga Taboo, one of the Friendly Islands,[1] where we were to meet the Vincennes and other vessels preparatory to commencing operations among the Fegees. We were just a month in the passage, which was longer than we expected and without the occurrence of any thing unusual or interesting. On the 1st May we anchored in the Harbour, but some distance from the Shore; the Vin., Porpoise and Schooner were all waiting for us and as soon as we hove in sight they got underweigh and took their berths farther out. As we were running in, we saw them making sail much to our disappointment, for we knew that we should have no chance of seeing the Island, but be off in a trice for Fegee. We had hoped to find the Harbour empty, thinking that Cap. Wilkes would not delay for us, and anticipated with much pleasure a stay of several days. The Island is celebrated on several accounts, is very beautiful and richly cultivated by the natives, who are amongst the finest of all the people in the South Pacific.

It is hard to bear with such a cruel misfortune and we were vexed beyond measure at our situation. In all likelihood none of us will every see the Island again and here we were, close to its shores, and yet debarred from treading on them: obliged to content ourselves with a spy glass view, which only increased the desire to have a nearer survey. It was useless to repine and we bore the deprivation with all the philosophy we could muster; nevertheless, it was a severe trial to our patience.[2]

We had not seen the Brig or Schooner since we were among the Ice and now had the pleasure to meet with our friends and to spin

[1] *Today, Tongatapu Island in the kingdom of Tonga.*

[2] *During the voyage from Sydney, Reynolds exulted, "We are bound for Tonga Taboo!" Ever since he had read "the romantic tale of the celebrated cave in the Tonga Islands" fifteen years before, he had wished "so much" to see it, and later Byron "cast his web of enchanting poetry over the spot, and now we are going there, and I shall see it at last!" Reynolds was referring to the underwater cavern described by William Mariner (1791–1853) on the island of Nuapapu, an account elaborated on by Lord Byron in his 1823 poem "The Island." Reynolds got as close as he could: before they sailed on, he went with "Old Emmons to a small island, merely to say that I had landed on the Tonga Group" (Journal 1:349, 346; Mariner 1820).*

yarns of our mutual adventures. Bob Johnson,[3] and May, and Blunt, all sent us some fresh provisions, which were very acceptable after a month on salt fare at Sea: live stock was so exhorbitantly high in Sydney that we could not afford to carry even a chicken with us, and tho' we had plenty of Sea Stores, a continuance on such food gives one a keen relish for a change to the sweet viands of the Land.

We had expected to hear of more changes in the Squadron and of fresh troubles, and we were not mistaken. Lieut. Pinkney was suspended from his command of the Flying Fish and sent on board this Ship as a passenger after having suffered the grossest ill treatment from Cap. Wilkes; so that he is to leave the Squadron also, the sixth officer that has been sent Home under scandalous and frivolous pretences.[4] There were many other disturbances but I will not trouble you with the recital of them. I am living in peace myself and as well contented as circumstances permit.

On May 3rd we sailed from Tonga Taboo for the Fegees. It was understood that we would stay among the group about 6 weeks and then push on for the Sandwich Islands so as to get there in the latter part of July, then hurry to the North West Coast, work there as long as the weather would permit, and then return to the Sandwich Islands and take a fair start towards *Home*, but touching at many places on our way, and this would have occupied the three years.

The Fegee Islands had never been surveyed and there was a great deal of work to be done there in a short time; besides the Islands, there are innumerable reefs and shoals round and between them on

---

[3] *Lieutenant Robert E. Johnson, from North Carolina, had commanded the* Sea Gull *during the first Antarctic cruise in 1839 but had relinquished the schooner to Midshipman Reid upon returning to Orange Harbor. Detached from the expedition during the second stop at Honolulu in 1841, he was one of the four officers Wilkes had court-martialed on various charges in 1842.*

[4] *Robert F. Pinkney, from one of Maryland's leading families, had been a victim of the commander's sometimes capricious behavior for at least a year before this. When the expedition reached Honolulu, he prepared formal charges against Wilkes, in return for which the commander had him arrested and ultimately court-martialed. Pinkney went on to become a commander in 1855, resigning in 1861 to serve at the same rank in the Confederate navy (ZB).*

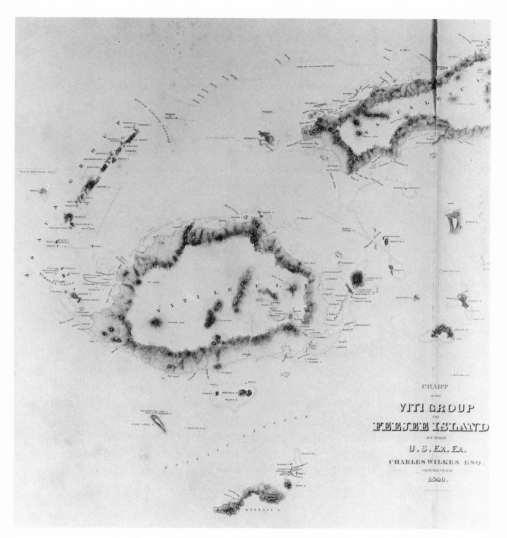

Portion of the Fiji Islands, as charted by the Exploring Expedition

which many vessels have been wrecked, and, as we understood, the inhabitants were generally fierce cannibals who murdered every white man that came in their way; so that added to the perils of the navigation we would have to guard against the treacherous nature of the people. We were very busy in making preparations, fitting out the boats etc. etc. and we scarcely expected to accomplish the duty without meeting with some loss of life. Captain Wilkes was silly enough to say "that *he* expected to lose two *of his vessels*," but that was all fudge and uttered for effect. However, as we knew that we would be very much exposed in boat service, we were settled in the conviction that some of our number would meet with their fate and although it was no jesting matter, it was somewhat amusing to see the dispostions that each one made in case he should be the victim.

The Vincennes had a Pilot on board whom they procured at Tonga. He was an Englishman who lived on Ovelow, one of the Fegee group and where it was intended to anchor.[5] The weather was thick and rainy when we entered among the Islands and had we been left to our own guidance, we might have ornamented a reef without any delay at all, for no one knew where to steer and we could not see well in the day, much less in the night. The Pilot was perfectly acquainted with all the dangers, and by keeping close to the Vincennes, after several anxious days and nights we got safe to Ovelow on the 8th. The Brig had been left to survey the first Islands we made and the Schooner parted company one very dark night and had not rejoined.

We anchored close to the Shore and immediately in front of the Village which stood on the beach, sheltered by groves of cocoa nut and Bread fruit trees. The Island was high and clothed in the most luxuriant verdure, with many bold points of rock and immense forests; and here and there shining waterfalls glanced amid the

[5] *Ovalau Island. In the* Narrative, *Wilkes gives the name of the Englishman as Tom Granby. Reynolds records in his Journal (1:346) that "Captain Wilkes said to him [Granby], with his usual assumption of superior knowledge, 'you will find when we get to the Island [Fiji], that I know as much about them as you do. . . . This was just like old Killbiscuit."*

foliage, so that the finest contrasts in scenery were mingled together and formed a picture that was beautiful indeed. After the Ice and the barren shores of New Holland, we hailed with joy our return to the ever green Isles of the Tropics.

We saw only two or three persons moving among the Huts and the canoes were hauled up high and dry, so that there were no signs of life or bustle on the Shore for some little time after we had anchored.

We were all looking with our glasses at the hills and scanning them from base to summit with all the interest that men feel when viewing something new for the first time, when a loud cry of rapture from one of the Midshipmen startled me and he called out, "look, Reynolds, look! there is *a Cow* up there among the bushes as sure as I'm alive!" This was a domestic and barn yard feature that we had not expected to find in Fegee. I looked and sure enough there *was* a red cow, half way up the lower hills, whisking her tail and chewing the cud with much the same quiet air of satisfaction and enjoyment that marks the demeanour of our Cows at Home; the being in a cannibal country did not seem to affect her in the least, but what we wondered at, was, how the devil did she get here?

We saw many little villages peeping from amidst the trees and scattered huts clinging to the projecting ridges of rocks, clear up to the highest parts of the Island, and we fancied we could see the people like so many dark specks moving to and fro.

Presently crowds of the Islanders collected on the beach in groups, some sitting under the trees and gazing on the strange Ships that had thus suddenly appeared before their very doors, and others were launching their canoes and preparing to visit us themselves. We could see that they were very dark skinned and were naked, save a narrow girdle of white tappa around the loins; some wore turbans of the same on their heads and others had their hair frizzed out to the size of a bushel measure and dyed of various colours—red, yellow, and blue.

In a little while the canoes came alongside and our curiosity was gratified in obtaining a near view of a Fegee man. We inspected them with curious scrutiny and they returned us the compliment. These were tall and powerful men, with a strong dash of the Negro in colour and feature; but well made and models of symmetry and strength.[6] The superabundant profusion of their wool, which was dressed in such fantastic forms and hues, was quite a novelty to our eyes and it was evident that the chief pride and ornament of an exquisite among this people was precisely the same part of the person that receives so much attention, and the adornment of which is so highly estimated by the opposite sex among us—no offense, ladies, if you please.

The portions of wool that were of different colours were carefully seperated from each other and trained to grow apart; and the various tastes displayed were so whimsical, that the effect of this bushy head gear produced much laughter on our part. The flowing wigs that were fashionable in the olden times will not bear comparison with these curls of nature's growing on her own children, and a group of Fegees might shame the English lawyers of the present day into wearing their own hair after the manner of other Christian men. This custom is not universal however. Many of the Islanders wear their wool short or of the moderate growth which a gentleman of colour, in high life, indulges in with us. Those who are given to the extravagant mode have a peculiar pillow which they place under *the neck* at night to preserve the arrangement undisturbed. All the females cut their hair short when they marry.

The faces of our visitors were naturally fierce enough in expression, and this was heightened by the red and black paint which was most liberally bestowed over all the portions of the countenance. Their bodies were not tattoed nor tended with any colouring, and their only covering was the white girdle which decency required. Some had necklaces and armlets of polished shell, and breast ornaments of mother of pearl, but to which they did not attach much

---

[6] *Heretofore the squadron had been among the islands of Polynesia, the portion of Oceania which ranges over the vast area of the southern Pacific between Hawaii, Easter Island, and New Zealand. Fiji can be considered as part of Melanesia, which includes the southwestern Pacific south of the Equator and east of Australia, where lie the Admiralty and Solomon islands, New Hebrides, and New Caledonia. Polynesian societies generally were more stratified and subject to central authority; in Fiji, by contrast, there was no king or chief with comparable authority.*

value. We permitted only a few of them to come on board at a time and very soon there were many canoes alongside thronged with people, all clamourous and noisy, and importuning us to let them come aboard. They had bows, arrows, clubs, spears, shells, cocoa nuts, yams, tarro for sale.

We found there were 5 or 6 white men living in this village under the protection of the chief and that the most free communication could be held with the Shore without any risk whatsoever. Accordingly the Vincennes made signal "that Officers could go on Shore, armed, but not to pass beyond the limits of the Chief *Lebooka.*"[7] This Chief was already on board the Vincennes; unlike the majority of his people, Lebooca had early in life evinced a favourable disposition to white men. Shrewder than others, and perhaps with a little more of the milk of human kindness in his composition, he saw how much it would be to his interest to preserve an amicable intercourse with the Papalangies, who brought things of such value to his Shores. And with wonderful honesty and forebearance, he was content with what came to his share by all fair means and never resorted to treachery and murder to secure the riches of his visitors, although by so doing he could have made himself the envy of all Fegee. His character was without a stain and these white men felt themselves perfectly safe, so long as they were within the range of his authority.

They were all married to native women and were leading an idle life, following only the bent of their own inclination and rarely leaving the shade of their own bread fruits. We thought it strange that they should have domesticated themselves among a people who had so little in their appearance to reccommend them and whose general character had such a dubious reputation, but the vagrant principle is very strong in the breasts of some men and there is no accounting for the caprices of human kind. They said that their lot had thrown them among these Islands, the people were very good,

---

[7] *Wilkes's orthography for the chief of Ovalau is Tui Levuka. White men brought prestige and power to the chiefs of the islands where they settled. Not only did they act as translators and pilots with visiting ships, but their knowledge of modern warfare and other aspects of Western technology was much desired.*

and they were content to live with them for a time and take their
ease, and such were all the reasons they could give. At Tahiti, or the
Navigator Islands, where there is every thing to attract, I would be
almost willing to sling my own hammock, but in Fegee, no, the
people are too ugly, they are not cleanly in their persons, food is not
so plent[iful] with them, they are almost continually engaged in wars
with each other, and life is altogether too unsafe.

The white men told us that there were several other places among
the Islands where some confidence might be reposed in the friendly
nature of the people, but that they would not trust themselves any
where with the same freedom as they did here. At two different
Islands some English Missionaries were established, but they had not
met with any success in their attempts at conversion. At intervening
portions of the same Islands, and generally throughout the group,
the people were hostile and treacherous as ever, fighting among
themselves and butchering without mercy any stragglers, white or
black, that came in their way. There is no such thing as journeying by
Land; the rugged nature of the country is an obstacle and a man may
have enemies on both sides of him, through whose land he could not
pass with safety, so that every one is careful not to venture over his
own boundaries and on all occasions they carry their arms with them,
so fearful are they of being attacked and surprised. They never know
the indolent repose of a peaceful people and in their wars are so
convinced of their own natural deceit that they put no trust in their
enemy, but kill, kill, to the last man. They are prone to lying, or
rather are yet ignorant of the moral force and virtue of truth, and
they know themselves too well to have any faith in a promise, so that
their international intercourse is not to be envied by those who are
fond of a peaceful and honest existence. Nevertheless, at this time I
can give it as my opinion that such habits are the best suited to
themselves. The sooner they are exterminated as a race, the better,
and if they do this goodly work themselves, it will be a great saving
and a general blessing to mankind at large.

Agreeably to the permission extended by the signal, several of us
left the Ship for a stroll on shore. The village stood at the outlet of a
valley that swept down from the nearest range of hills to the beach
and on the banks of the stream which having followed the gorge·over
its rocky bed, here emptied into the Sea. The huts were singular

structures, having low sides and high peaked roofs and gables. The *walls* were made of cane work covered with mats and the roofs were of thatch several feet in thickness. One or two small doors were the only openings for air and light and the inmates, so that to us they seemed to be close and uncomfortable. They had not the airy and cleanly appearance of the houses in sweet Samoa and the open spaces in the village were far from exhibiting the order and neatness which was so apparent in the Towns of the Navigator people.

The people crowded around us and attended us wherever we went; they invited us to enter their houses and we made no scruple about going wherever our curiosity prompted us. They do not deem white people as intruders and there is so little secrecy practised in their domestic economy that their doors are open at all times, to all comers. We were always offered food, according to their custom, for like all other Savages they possess the virtue of Hospitality and in return we purchased some trifles of their own manufacture. The women were monstrous ugly; instead of the tappa round the loins, they wore a girdle of grass wove into a belt about three inches in width, from which fell a fringe of the same. This was of various Colours, very neatly made, and the only covering in vogue among the dames of Fegee. They were very good natured, however, and were very curious in examining us from top to toe.

When we had amused ourselves sufficiently, we left the town and walked along the stream to find a place to bathe. The path was shaded and wound through a beautiful country amid plantations of tarro, bread fruit trees, with bold and striking scenery encompassing the lovely valley through which it led. It had a gentle ascent and the miniature rivulet fell as a succession of cascades over rocky falls that added an indescribable freshness to the scene. Many birds were fluttering about us, singing their songs of gladness in notes that equalled the melody of our own sweet choirister, the lark, and others of more brilliant plumage were glancing to and fro, with their gaudy colours rendered yet more dazzling by the play of the Sunlight on their rapid flight. A group of natives were following us with stealthy steps and whispering among themselves at whatever seemed strange to them in our demeanour. We were shut out from the Ships and the Sea, and, amid sights and sounds so new and strange with no one to control us and with unlimited space so different from the crowded

decks, we gave loose to joyous feeling of freedom. With all the wild
and reckless gaiety of boys just let out of school, dignity went to the
dogs and we scampered about as if there was no such thing as care in
the world.

After a most refreshing and luxurious bath, we returned to the
village feeling like new men and with a glorious appetite for the
dinner that was waiting for us on board.

The natives were now permitted to come alongside to trade; they
brought but few pigs to dispose of, much to our regret, but of the
other things that I have mentioned, they had abundance. For bottles,
we could get cocoa nuts, yams, bows and arrows, and other trifles.
Red paint was highly valued, and hachets, plane Irons, knives,
razors, scissors, fishhooks, looking glasses, calico, beads were a stock
with which you could buy any thing in Fegee. Muskets, powder,
lead, *whales' teeth*, and chests with locks were the things most valued,
but these are only used as presents, or given in payment for Tortoise
Shell or for the hire of those engaged in gathering *bich le mer*.[8]

It was an everlasting source of amusement to witness the traffic
that was continually going on: every man and boy in the Ship was
busy from morn till night in procuring edible things, as well as such
articles as would be deemed curious at Home, and the Ship was a
Babel of tongues to the infinite confusion of all those whose ears were
not proof against harsh sounds. We were as eager to buy as our sable

[8] *Trading from the ships of the squadron was strictly regulated. The
islanders were invited to come only at a certain time of day, when a white
signal flag was raised. The purser or other officer on each vessel was
designated as trade master, and all transactions were to be made through
him and exchange rates set by him. Food was acquired by trading small
manufactured items, as were many ethnographic specimens collected by the
scientifics (Wilkes 1845, 2:419). Chiefs were invited aboard to receive more
valuable objects as gifts. Wilkes's predecessor Thomas ap C. Jones had
requested these trade items in a memorandum to the secretary of the navy
(1837), which included a list of goods desired at Pacific islands prepared by a
merchant Captain Egleston.*

*American merchant ships, which formerly came to Fiji for sandalwood, at
this time came in search of tortoise shell and bêche de mer for the China trade.
The bêche de mer or sea cucumber (Holothuria) were collected in shallow
water and cured on shore before being shipped to Canton, where they were a
favorite item in the cuisine.*

friends were to sell, and they had such strong fancies for our goods that they readily parted with every thing in their canoes; but they could not understand what we wanted with them. Museums and Lyceums not being established among this people, they are not touched with the passion of collecting curiosities, and we tried in vain to explain to them the reason of our carrying their spears etc. to America. They said, "we had plenty of muskets and every thing wonderful, and what *could* we want with such simple articles as they could manufacture?" By this time we had a Pilot on board who served as interpreter and he was kept busy enough; he was an American and had been among the Islands eleven years.

Several days passed and the Schooner did not appear; we became very anxious about her and several of us volunteered to go out in boats and look for her. On the 12th she came in and our fears had not been groundless; she had run on a reef in the night and had great risk in getting clear.

On this day *"Snuff,"* the most powerful chief in Fegee, was received on board the Vincennes with all the honours and ceremonies befitting the distinguished occasion.[9] The Ship was dressed with flags, the Marines paraded, and all the officers from both vessels assembled to make as imposing an appearance as possible. Snuff was complimented by a passage in the Gig and his train followed in an immense double canoe that was ornamented with a profusion of white shells.

The drums rolled, the marines presented arms, and the officers bared their heads when this mighty despot stepped over the gangway. His Majesty was naked as his subjects and bore no external marks of authority or rank, save that his girdle of tappa was of such a length that the ends trailed on the deck. He was old, tall and gaunt, with a moderate quantity of wool and a grisly beard that reached to his middle, and he looked as much like a superanuated ourangoutang as an individual of the human species. He was met with the utmost respect by the two Captains and conducted aft to a seat, where

[9] *Reynolds refers to Chief Tanoa of Ambau, from an island to the west of Ovalau, who was recognized as* primus inter pares *among Fijian chiefs. In the* Narrative *(3:56), Wilkes describes him as about sixty-five years of age, five feet ten inches tall, and with a countenance "indicative of intelligence and shrewdness."*

*Tanoa of Ambau, by Alfred Agate. Wilkes felt King Tanoa's support
of his proposed commercial regulations was essential to their
acceptance elsewhere in Fiji, hence the elaborate ritual conducted on the
Vincennes described by Reynolds in Letter No. 15. From Wilkes 1845, 3:
facing p. 56.*

mutual compliments were interchanged between the high parties, and the others were lookers on.

Then Snuff was conducted over the Ship and all her wonders displayed to his admiring eyes. He was in astonishment at all he saw and he said, "that the man of war was very different from the trading vessels that he had been on board of before." He was delighted to see the blacksmith at work and the operations of the turning lathe set the whole crowd in extacies; they counted the muskets that were shining in the racks and looked at the array of Pistols and cutlasses with an admiration that could not be suppressed; they cried out at the immense room between decks and were amazed to find the Ship *so hollow.* The number of men, the size of the great guns, the weight of the shot, and an hundred other things attracted their attention, and they whooped their surprise and pleasure aloud to the infinite amusement of all hands. The marines marched and counter marched and went through their exercises with great *eclat;* they fired volleys and the air to which they kept time was *"the King of the Cannibal Islands."* This part of the show was very much relished by the natives and they thought that such *fighting men* must be invincible. The guns were loaded with grape and round shot and discharged in succession; the noise deafened them, and when they saw the water dashed up in jets of foam at a distance of a mile by the shot as they skimmed along, they were fairly confounded and shouted, *"Venaca! Venaca!"* louder than ever.

Finally when all these Theatricals were ended, Snuff and his principal counsellors were seated in the Cabin and the same regulations read to them which were adopted by the Navigator people for the government of vessels visiting the Islands and guarranteeing the protection of the Chiefs towards Ship and crew.[10]

---

[10] *The commercial regulations adopted by Tanoa and, subsequently, other Fiji chiefs were similar to the Samoan ones of 1839, although slightly simpler. Their purpose, as before, was both to guarantee the rights of merchant vessels to get help in rounding up deserters and to protect their crews from violence, and to guarantee the rights of the islanders to be compensated for pilotage and other services and goods provided and to be protected, in their turn, from abuse from ships' crews. (A copy of the Fiji regulations can be found in Wilkes 1840a.)*

His Majesty made his mark to these and promised to observe them, and then regaled himself with a glass of whiskey of which he is remarkably fond.[11] Presents were then made to Snuff and his Chiefs, the most valuable of which was a patent rifle that loaded at the breech and the like of which had never been seen in Fegee.[12] Blankets, shawls, axes, copper kettles etc. were liberally distributed, and they left the Ship impressed with the idea that the power of a man of war was too dreadful to be resisted and that here riches were inexhaustible.

"Snuff" was the title most irreverantly bestowed upon this potent monarch by the white men; his native name is too much for my orthography. Snuff did not dwell on Ovelow, but lived on a small Island close by. Like "Lebooca" he had always been friendly to the whites and had often protected them when in distress. Captain Vanderford, the trading master on board the Vincennes, was once wrecked off old Snuff's town and was hospitably entertained until a vessel arrived and took him away, so that Snuff deserved a welcome reception and his merits met with their reward.[13] He had been a great warrior in his youth and had carried his victorious arms to many parts of the group, so that now in his old age he was possessed of more power and riches than any other chief in Fegee. Lebooca was under his sway and he was generally termed "the King of the Fegees," though this was only in compliment, for there is no

---

[11] *"Snuff did me the favour to hug me in his arms and call me his son, but this was after he had taken his second glass of whiskey—the idea that those arms had slain so many men made me feel quite strange" (Journal 1:360).*

[12] *The Hall patent rifle was the first breech-loaded firearm in the U.S. military. One in the collections of the National Museum of American History at the Smithsonian (accession no. 54537), a model 1819 manufactured at Harpers Ferry, Virginia, in 1838, is caliber .54 with barrel length 32.5 inches and overall length 52.5 inches.*

[13] *Benjamin Vanderford, a former Salem merchant captain, who in 1821 had been the first American to harvest and export bêche de mer from Fiji (Dodge 1972:16). His long experience in the Pacific was of considerable assistance to the expedition in piloting, interpreting, and so forth. Vanderford died in March 1842 while the squadron was homeward bound through the Indian Ocean.*

monarchy. The people are governed by independent chiefs whose rank is hereditary and power absolute in their own dominions. Many like Snuff extend their possessions and authority by conquest, and to gain this end there is everlasting rivalry and war.[14]

The observatory was erected on shore in a convenient position and operations commenced there forthwith.[15] Two boats from the Vincennes and two from our Ship were dispatched on a surveying expedition. The Schooner was to be actively employed, and on the 15th we sailed on a cruise, leaving the Vincennes only half manned.

Next after noon we anchored in Rewah Harbour, on the largest Island in the group and close to Snuff's abode.[16] We commenced to survey this place at once, and boats were dispatched to the Town, which was several miles distant up the river, to bring a chief who was brother to the King of the place, and who from having been much on board American Ships, could speak tolerable English. The officer who went was accompanied by the Pilot and part of his mission was to invite the King himself to come on board. The young Chief, who went by the name of "Phillips" (after the owner of the vessel in which he went to Tahita), returned in our boat and readily agreed to pilot a surveying expedition, which was to trace the river to its source. As we could communicate with him directly without the aid of a third person, he was pestered with innumerable questions, asked as much with a view to listen to a Fegee talking our vernacular as for any other purpose whatsoever.

[14] *Tanoa came to power some thirty years before with the help of a crew of wrecked sandalwood cutters, who brought firearms (and rum) to Fiji (Dodge 1976:64).*

[15] *Reynolds dined with Lieutenants Oliver H. Perry and Henry Eld in the observatory tent that first night, and they were pleased to drink Rudesheimer wine so far from the Rhine. He had "no fancy for work which is so hard on my eyes." "I went off surveying, a duty which, though arduous in the extreme, always interests me in the performance" (Journal 1:356, 362). Perry (1815–1878) was the son of War of 1812 hero Oliver Hazard Perry (1785–1819); he was to leave the navy in 1848 (ZB).*

[16] *Rewah is today the location of Suva, capital of Fiji. Viti Levu Island, on which it is located, lies some twenty miles west of Ovalau; Ambau or Bau Island (Tanoa's home) lies just east of Viti Levu.*

Two English Missionaries were settled here, and the next day being Sunday they came on board and had service.[17] Most of us were absent surveying and the congregation was very thin. Monday morning we were detained on board to receive 'Tuindrecate,'[18] the Sovereign of this place, who came in a double canoe with several others following in his wake, and who was received after the same fashion in which Snuff was greeted on board the Vincennes.

This Chief was in the prime of life; his features were good, but there was a settled scowl upon his face which was rarely removed; he was over 6 feet in height and of a very commanding figure; his hair was cut short and he wore neither beard nor paint; altogether, he was as fine a specimen of a man as you need wish to see. He was enriched with presents and treated with all kindness and respect. The Captain and several others accompanied him to his Town and spent the night in his house, and the most amicable intercourse was established [between] his people and ourselves. He sent us a large present of yams, which were very acceptable, and Snuff sent him a message to the effect that he was to do every thing we wished. Mr. Agate had painted Snuff's likeness at Ovelow and was now busy in getting those of the *big bugs* here.[19] This delighted them exceedingly, they sat with much patience and composure, and were overjoyed to find that their friends knew them *on the paper.*

When the boats returned from the river and the survey of the harbour was nearly completed, Tuindrecate brought his wife and all his household on board to see the Ship and her wonders, and the fore part of the day was spent in great hilarity, the natives being delighted with all they saw. The Queen was a comely woman and some gaudy feathers that were given her pleased her beyond measure. She put them in her hair and sat for her picture with them nodding over her brows; her childish vanity was gratified and she

[17] *"Mr. [David] Cargill and Mr. Jaguaar" (Journal 1:362), Wesleyan missionaries.*

[18] *Also spelled as Tui Ndraketi by Wilkes (1845, 3:111).*

[19] *Alfred T. Agate (1812–1846), a miniature painter from New York, who served as one of two artists on the expedition. Agate did numerous portraits such as Tanoa's, as well as botanical illustrations.*

*Club dance, Fiji, drawing by Joseph Drayton. From Wilkes 1845, 3:
facing p. 198.*

was all joy and smiles. While this happiness was at its height, the
scene suddenly changed: the drum beat to quarters, the men went to
their guns, the decks were cleared of the natives, who were bundled
into their canoes and obliged to haul under the stern, the marines
were paraded before the cabin door, and the Royal party from the
condition of illustrious guests were made prisoners without a blow.

Some years ago, a brother of Tuindrecate had planned and
executed a massacre of the crew of a Boston Brig. It was a part of our
errand here to take him, but he had kept aloof, although his name
had never been mentioned, nor any inquiries made concerning him in
order to avoid suspicion. Captain Hudson thought that very likely he
would come on board in his brother's train, but his guilty fears would
not allow him to venture among us, even when presents were so
lavishly bestowed on his relatives. Disappointed in this, the Captain

determined upon confining the King and holding him as a hostage until *Vendobi* should be brought on board.[20]

When Tuindrecate found himself thus a captive, his nature took fire at once and his wrath broke out into angry reproaches and complaints. He had a mighty struggle with his passions, and I suspect he longed for his club and a clear field. He upbraided the Captain for his treachery in seizing him by surprise and was too indignant to listen to reason or to the proposals the Captain had to offer. "At first," said he, "you treated me well, you gave me presents and good words, and I thought you a good man. If you had demanded my brother, I would have given him up, but now how can I take him? You will not let me go." When he was able to listen calmly, the Captain after much discourse persuaded him "that he had only adopted a necessary course, that he had expected Vendobi on board and then should have made him a prisoner without troubling any one else, and that the matter might now be accomplished without much difficulty and the blame would rest entirely on the man of war. If the King would send his brother Garraningia[21] to the town with orders to bring Vendobi on board, there would be an end to the business and on the morrow all the rest should go free and unharmed." There was much farther discussion. The King and both the brothers who were with him, Phillips and Garraningia, said "that Vendobi had done wrong in murdering our countrymen and that it was right we should punish him, that they had often told him to treat the white people well, but he would have his own way and now he must suffer for being so bad!"

[20] *The incident involved the* Charles Doggett *of Salem, whose crew was engaged in processing bêche de mer on nearby Kantaku Island in 1834. Ten of them were killed by surprise and their bodies eaten at the instigation of Tuidrecate's brother Vendovi. This event was among those cited in a memorial from the East India Marine Society of Salem (1834) petitioning Congress to mount an expedition "of discovery and survey to the South Seas." The memorial mentions that some thirteen ships were engaged in the Fiji trade from Salem alone and that both lack of charts and hostile natives had led to serious losses.*

[21] *Spelled Ngaraningiou by Wilkes in the* Narrative *(1845, 3:111) and Ngganraniuggis by William Hudson in his journal (1838–1842, 1:501).*

Finally Garraningia shoved off in his canoe about 4 in the
afternoon, with the explicit orders of the King to take Vendobi and
bring him to the Ship—"alive, if he could, but to kill him and bring
the body if he resisted." Tuindrecate showed in this a desire to do *us*
justice, although at the expense of his fraternal feelings, as well as to
gain his own liberty; but his spirits were gone, and the gayety of
the Royal party had vanished altogether.[22] They were quiet and
reconciled to their situation, even more than we had hoped for, but
they were in such evident distress that none of us cared to interrupt
them and they remained together in the cabin, a sad contrast to the
lively group they had formed in the morning. The canoes were still
kept astern, but as the night was rainy and cold, the natives were
allowed to come on board and were stowed upon a sail on the gun
deck, with sentries over them, for the night. They were 70 in number
and before Garraningia left they had by far exceeded the force of our
crew, but they were unsuspecting of any danger, unarmed and the
surprise was too complete and instantaneous to admit of any
resistance. They were also separated from their Chiefs, but even
under other circumstances they would not have had the courage to
offer battle to us, on our own decks. So they remained perfectly still
and the Ship was quiet until morning.[23]

Garraningia was of a fierce and sanguinary disposition and had a
brotherly dislike to Vendobi, with whom he had had many jealous
quarrels, so that there was no fear of his having any compunctions in
executing to the very letter the somewhat unnatural office which he
had so willingly undertaken. His return was looked for with the

[22] *Hudson reported in his journal (1838–1842, 1:500) that at this point
Tuindrecate admitted that Vendovi was also guilty of having shot his eldest
brother.*

[23] *Hudson writes that he "endeavoured through the Evening to entertain
them with various amusements of the men, such as singing, dancing,
jumping Jim Crow, the Bellowing Donkey and his sister, etc., with all which
they appeared quite delighted. . . . The King had cava made two or three
times in one of my dish covers, accompanied with all his own ceremonies;
with his Queen and Chiefs smoked any number of segars, ate, drank tea, and
expressed himself when he turned in as having passed the evening very
pleasantly" (1838–1842, 1:500).*

utmost confidence and the only problem was whether our victim would be living or dead.

I had the morning watch and soon after day light I saw the canoe coming out of the river, with as many streamers flying as a Royal barge; at 7 she was alongside and in a very few minutes Vendobi was in double Irons, with a body guard to look out for him. He had surrendered himself to his brother without resistance, for he knew the other's character too well to have the slightest hope.

A council was held in the cabin. Vendobi acknowledged the murder, and we had a white man on board who had witnessed the whole affair.[24] The King again acknowledged that it was but just for us to avenge the death of our countrymen, and he gave Vendobi a lecture concerning the evil course he had followed and reccommended him to conduct himself peaceably while he was away and never to forget that he was a chief of Fegee. They could hardly be persuaded that it was not our intention to put Vendobi to death ourselves, and despite of many appearances to the contrary, they were sure the "big chief" would have him killed as soon as he got to America. Captain Hudson told them that Vendobi would be shown every thing in America, that he might see what a *great people we* were and the vast difference there was between our country and Fegee, he would be learned to speak our language and then returned to his Home, in the hope that during the remainder of his life he might by his good offices repay in some measure the evil he had done. He would then know that to kill a white man was the very worst thing a Fegee man could do. All this they could not comprehend; it was altogether contrary to their notions and they seemed to have but little hope of ever seeing Vendobi again. The King promised to keep his wives and slaves and all his property for him, and reccommended him very earnestly to the Captain, begging that he would take care of him and not have him killed, if he could help it. After a very affectionate and sorrowful farewell, during which we saw the curious

[24] *An Irishman, Patrick or Paddy Connel, who had been serving the* Charles Doggett *as interpreter. Hudson also had the deposition of another survivor of the attack, James Magoun, a resident of Fiji who had been hired to help with curing the bêche de mer. Magoun's deposition was included with Wilkes's Despatch 68 (1840c) to the secretary of the navy.*

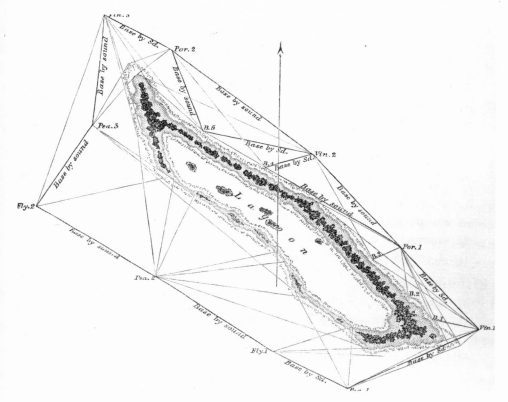

Diagram of surveying method for islands. Wilkes prepared a manual to instruct junior officers in his methodology for surveying. The ships were positioned around an island and, where possible, boats and men placed near or on shore. By measuring angles between landmarks and calculating distance by sound from guns fired from the vessels, data for an entire island could be collected and later assembled into a chart. From Wilkes 1845, 1:431.

spectacle of a group of naked savages in tears, the King and all his train shoved off for their homes, having previously received more presents to compensate them for their confinement.

While we were surveying, the natives always followed us along the Shore and crowded round us, so that we could scarcely make the observations. They were full of wonder at the sight of the various instruments and they could not conceive what we were doing with the Sun; a peep through the spy glass was an indulgence that set them in rapture, and they thought the watch must be a spirit, for it was moving and talking to us though no one touched it. Simple and ignorant as they were, I found a strange and pleasing interest in gratifying their curiosity and they looked up to us as beings of a mysterious order, and infinitely superior to themselves. One of the boat's crew had *four false teeth in front* and when he unshipped these before them they were absolutely confounded and cried out that he must be the Devil.

The day after this grand row, we sailed from Rewah and continued our progress along the shores of this Island, surveying as we proceeded. The navigation was very intricate and tedious; we were obliged to anchor every night and the work during the day was constant and fatigueing. We picked up our two boats on the way and the same day the Launch sunk as she was towing astern. We swept for her, without success, and were obliged to proceed without her. She was a serious loss just at this time and one that could not be replaced.[25]

We got hard and fast on coral shoals three or four times, but the water was smooth and we hauled off without much trouble or damage. These shoals were a fathom or so under water and we run upon them in broad daylight, as we could not see them to steer clear of them.

On the 5th June we left this Island and crossed over to the next larger Island, where we anchored the same evening in Sandal Wood Bay.[26]

A Boat from the Vincennes was waiting for us here and she brought news and rumours that were far from being agreeable. Just after we sailed from Rewah, Captain Belcher of the English Navy arrived there in the Sulphur with the loss of his rudder.[27] He had

---

[25] *Each ship carried several boats used for surveying and the like, the largest of which was a launch.*

[26] *Sandalwood (now Mbua) Bay is at the western extremity of Vanua Levu Island, which lies north and east of Ovalau.*

[27] *Sir Edward Belcher (1799–1877), R.N., a hydrographer who had accompanied Beechey to the Bering Strait and the Pacific in 1825 and done subsequent surveying of the African coast. Although Wilkes provided him*

completed a survey of the NorthWest Coast and was now on his way home by way of Sydney and C. of Good Hope. A Schooner that he had with him stopped at Ovelow, and Captain Wilkes immediately went to Rewah in the Flying Fish. Belcher said that it was impossible to work about the Columbia River in the fall and unsafe to remain there after the summer, with the Ships. This knocked in the head our scheme of going there this season, and it was the general belief that we would continue among these Islands for at least three months and make a more complete survey than had originally been intended, that we go to the N.W. Coast early in the Spring of '41 and not leave there until August, after which we would be 10 months in getting Home—so that our stay would be prolonged to *four* years, instead of *three*.

This was not relished much by any of us, but we could see no other prospect, and thus far our anticipations have proved true. We did stay more than 3 months among the Feegees and as to the rest, we know of nothing to give us more favourable hopes. I do not care very much about this, yet I had rather get Home next year for several reasons. I had rather go to Europe in my 27th year, than in my 28th, and I never bargained to be absent more than 3 twelvemonths, but I have no *particularly* strong ties to draw me Home. I may be just as well off where I am and shall not suffer near so much as many of my friends, who married just before we sailed. At all events, it was none of my fault and if the *Expedition is delayed* why it is a moral certainty that I will stay with *it,* nolens, volens. So it is according to my philosophy, to put the best face on the matter and reconcile myself to the disappointment as cheerfully as I can; *you all* will be the losers, in my humble opinion, because you will be for so long deprived of my most delightful society. I hope that you will bear this cruel misfortune with the like fortitude and resignation which has characterized me in this crisis, and that you will be ready to welcome me, when I *do* come, with the same joy that I shall feel myself on finding myself once more at Home.

Sandal Wood Bay was surveyed and on the 11th we left it to

---

the rudder pintles needed to repair the HMS Sulphur, *Belcher was not forthcoming in providing the Americans with details of his survey work on the West Coast (Blair [1846]:10, 13, 16, 18, 20–21.)*

cruise on along the Island. Close by its entrance is a tract of wooded country, which has never known the footsteps of man and has never been defiled by fire or the axe. It is the Elysium of the Fegees, "*the Spirit Land,*" and is held sacred as being the abode of the dead. They believe that when a man dies, he becomes an invisible Spirit and is obliged at once to appear before a 'great Spirit,' who dwells on an Island near Ovelow. 'A black giant' is in the way, however, armed with an axe and he strikes at every one who passes him; if the blow can be avoided, the Spirit passes on without further hindrance, and after a visit to the great Spirit returns to this woody region and remains there ever after. They suppose that the giant wounds those who have been bad in their lives, or with whom he may be displeased. Those who are badly hurt must wander about for a time and try again.

The priests alone can hold converse with these phantoms and, on all occasions, they appeal to them and are governed by the answers they receive. In every village, there are one or more houses of a different structure than the dwellings and dedicated to the Spirits. In these, the priests retire to pray and the departed souls are so complaisant as to leave the blessed fields for a time, and by virtue of their immortality, command and advise the holy men concerning the welfare of their friends who are still subject to the troubles and ills of this earthly existence. These 'Spirit houses' are ornamented with white shells, spears are struck through them in every direction, and clubs, miniature canoes, streamers of tappa, the feathers of the Tropic bird, fans, and a variety of other things are hung up inside and out, the whimsical offerings of the superstitious people.

The priests, of course, have enough to do, as they are resorted to on the most trivial as well as the more important occasions. In cases of sickness, they imagine their Spirit is angry with them and has hit them. The priest singles out the particular spirit of the afflicted person and endeavours to appease its wrath, and regulates his own conduct according to the nature of the interview with which he is favoured by the airy Sprite. He directs so many yams, pigs, or tarro, or so much cloth, or a musket, or whatever it may be, to be brought for 'the Spirit has demanded it'; or else, the little toes or fingers of the applicant must be cut off; or if his or hers are already gone, then those of the children or relations. This singular practice is so often followed that you scarcely see any one, man, woman, or child, with their digits complete. I saw babies of under a month old who had suffered this mutilation, and certainly the Spirit must be a cruel one that could demand more [of] this. The operation is performed with a shell. Sometimes the Spirit is so vexed as not to answer the call of the priest, in event of which the offerings must be increased and a more favorable period awaited. If all be in vain, and the evil of sickness or any other distress still continues, the Spirit is considered as implacable and the unfortunate individual submits with perfect resignation to the ill will of his invisible tormentor.

The Spirits of Warriors and Chiefs are consulted when a war is in contemplation; a propitious time is kindly named and success foretold. If a reverse and defeat should unfortunately happen, it is only a proof that the Spirit became angry for some reason or other and punished them by allowing them to be vanquished, or else that the Spirits of their enemies were more powerful than their own; which is doubtless a very comfortable reflection, as it saves them the mortification of attributing any inferiority or bad management to themselves. They are true to their creed and in every situation repose the most confident reliance in the Supernatural agency of their Spirits and in the inspiration of the Priests. This sacred office is hereditary and descends from Father to Son; those who fill it are necessarily of the utmost importance among the people and are the chosen confidants of the Chiefs. They take especially good care to provide for themselves when they demand offerings in the name of the Spirits and always have plenty of every thing, without the trouble of lifting a hand.

Though they impose upon the multitude the idea of their miraculous power, they are not themselves believers in the extraordinary faith which they proffess, but like some of their Christian brethren take advantage of the blind ignorance of the people and gull them with a worship which secures their own consequence and supports the authority of the Chiefs. The mysteries of their order remain with themselves and they exercise all the functions of their calling with the most perfect impunity, as the failure of their prognostics is burthened on the Spirits, who are supreme.

Cunningham, our Pilot,[28] asked the old priest at Ovelow "if he believed all the Stuff that he told the people?" The hoary hypocrite answered that he did not suppose white men would, nor did he care for *them*, but that he *could* make *his people* believe it, and that was all he wanted.

They have no wooden idols; their whole religion consists in the trust they put in these Spirits of the Dead.

It was in the first of the morning that our Ship swept slowly by this Sacred Shore, within a stone's throw of the rocky beach. The land on either side of it was entirely destitute of trees, so that the extent was distinctly marked. A thousand curious fancies were thronging in my imagination, called up by the singular character of the place and were I a poet, I should tell you them; but as I am one of the stupid kind, they must be lost to every body, save myself.

We saw no Spirits, but there were many birds, who had undisturbed possession of the Forest, and *their* matin hymns were certainly more agreeable than a sight of all the Fegees that ever assumed an immortality.

I landed here afterwards and for a little while was in the Heaven of these people, without experiencing any unusual felicity. Their Hell, which must certainly be in the vicinity of the 'black giant,' we did not see!

However, I find that I am spinning my yarn to an intolerable extent for a letter and must be more concise, so that I must leave much untold at present, with which I will regale you hereafter.

We continued cruising about in the Ship, always busy from morn till night; two of our boats were again sent off to survey some distant Islands and those that remained were never idle.

When we left Sandal Wood Bay, we stopped next at a Harbour where an American Ship was procuring *Bich le mar*.[29] She was the only vessel among the Islands at this time, besides our Squadron, and had sailed from the U. States just a year after our departure. The

[28] *Jacob Cunningham of Nantucket, who had been wrecked at Fiji eleven years before with Benjamin Vanderford.*
[29] *This was the* Leonidas *under Captain J. H. Egleston, presumably the same person who had earlier helped Captain Jones (n. 8 above).*

Captain had offered to bring out the Stores for the Squadron and had some correspondence with the Department, but they could not agree upon the terms. She brought *one letter* and we were very much vexed and disappointed that the opportunity had not been known and embraced by all our friends. A *letter* in *Fegee* would have been welcomed with that intense rapture which stirs all wanderers on such joyous occasions, but there were none and we were miserable for 5 minutes at least.

Soon after this, it fell to my turn to be sent away on boat service and I was amused with a cruise of 20 days in a whale boat 27 feet long, 4 feet wide amidships, and 2 feet 6 ins. deep. In this immense vessel were 5 men and myself, with our food, clothes and other lumber, so that we had infinite space for our accommodation and personal comfort. I never had my clothes off and it was a matter of great contrivance and ingenuity to stow ourselves away for the night. My bed beggars description and as to the rest I had on it, I cannot say much for that; 'twas most uneasy, and altogether opposite to the luxury of repose and sleep, such as is commonly enjoyed upon pillows of down. I was always ready and glad to turn out with the peep of day; my bones were as sore as if I had been well beaten with a bunch of clubs and then shoved under a pump, and if it had not been for the sovereign virtues of my red flannels which I wore next my skin, and rather more than a thimble full of raw whiskey which I made it a point to swallow as soon as I opened my eyes, I verily believe I should have become a premature victim to the Rheumatics, which is an infliction that I have every desire to avoid. The nights were very chilly and we had no more room for exercise than a chicken in the shell. My toilette was easily made, after the fashion of Dogs, by two or three good shakes and the vigour of these was a faint aid to the more powerful stimulus of the whiskey in dissipating the nervous tremor, which was the natural consequence of such exposed lodgings. A salt water wash was neither freshening to the feelings, or to the complexion, and though sometimes we took our breakfast before we went to work, we were often obliged to commence operations with the dawn, to save the tide, and wait with hungry impatience until noon for a meal. There was a larger boat in company and in her we had a barrel arranged so that we could boil a pot very readily. Some days we fared sumptuously on such stews as

Sailors excel in making—salt pork and yams, fresh ditto and yams, with fried ribs and liver, fish chowders and clam soup, seasoned well and sprinkled with the juice of lemons, and hot chocolate that was rich and good. We had not much of an equipage and all the spoons went into one dish, in pretty much of 'a hand to mouth' fashion, but that was not minded. We had ravenous appetites, kept up a flow of Spirits, accommodated our humours to each other, and made ourselves as agreeable and contented as we could. We were 3 officers, and of course we messed by ourselves, but with the exception of the chocolate we fared on the same food with the men.[30] At times, however, when we could not 'fire up,' we were reduced to raw pork, which, though not unpalatable, affords any thing but a wholesome or hearty meal.

The work was excruciating and unceasing. Surveying keeps the mind on the utmost stretch of attention and a moment given to relaxation might spoil or injure the whole. There are a thousand things to be noticed, both near at hand and at a distance, and the employment of all the faculties is necessary to an almost painful degree. There is a responsibility attached to the duty that forces one to be keen, watchful, and correct; if a Ship trusting to *your* chart gets into danger, *who* is to blame? We had much to do, knew nothing of the hidden shoals and the intricate passages that were to be found and laid down, and were limited to weeks to perform that which required months. We did as well as we could, but sometimes I was so perplexed that my brain was all in a whirl.

We were expressly ordered not to land except in uninhabited places, but we transgressed nevertheless, taking every precaution to guard against attack or surprise. Thus we managed to buy pigs and keep up our stock of yams, which were so necessary in our stews. At night we anchored and kept a regular watch, with the arms ready, for the natives have an ugly habit of swimming off and capturing small craft if they can get alongside unnoticed. Twice they came near us

[30] *Lieutenant Thomas A. Budd, Reynolds, and Midshipman William H. Hudson (Journal 2:69). Budd resigned from the navy as a lieutenant in 1853 because of the unlikelihood of promotion but served at that rank during the Civil War. Hudson was Captain Hudson's son and later served as U.S. consul in Buenos Aires (ZB).*

with murderous intent, but finding they were seen, they did not venture. The large boat had two blunderbusses mounted on pivots on her gunnels and we loaded these to the muzzles with *even a little sticking out*, as the men said, and we had a musket, cutlass and pistol for each man, so that we were well provided for defence. I had a patent rifle that loaded at the breech without ramming and could be fired, I don't know how often in a minute, besides having a long bayonet that rigged out full 3 feet.[31]

I displayed the virtues of this whenever we went among the natives and they thought it a weapon of wonderful advantages and the most curious they had ever seen. They have many muskets among themselves and are connoiseurs in every thing that is useful in war.

Being so continually in the Sun and wind, and receiving frequent baptisms of brine from the spray full in my face, I was bronzed to the dark hue of James Thomas Gauntt, and my once delicate skin became as rough in texture as the hide of an old saddle. During the days I went as thinly clad as possible, sans jacket, sans drawers, and sans stockings, with my neck open and bare, and a pair of monstrous wide trowsers for the convenience of rolling up when it was necessary to step overboard and wade to places where we could not take the boat. Often have I been up to my middle, screwing away with my sextant upon objects perhaps twenty miles off, with a foothold that I could scarcely preserve from the depth I was in and the swash of the Seas, and surrounded by the men who were holding books, pencils, spy glass, and watch, all of which were used in turn. This was highly amusing and is but a slight specimen of the many comforts and delights which attend one on such duty as this. Nevertheless, there is a strange interest and excitement in its performance, despite of the dangers and privations that are incurred, and one is tempted to persevere and to surmount obstacles with a resolution that will not be baulked. It is a manly pursuit and calls into activity all the resources that a man can well command.

[31] *Reynolds is describing the Hall rifle mentioned in n. 12 above. The principal firearms carried on the expedition were the standard Model 1816/22 flintlock musket, caliber .69, and the standard 1826 or 1836 flintlock navy pistols, caliber .54.*

My *old white Hat*, that you all abused so much, has served me faithfully on these excursions and is still good for future use; it is as light as a feather, is impervious to rain, it never forsakes my head in the hardest squall, but holds on like an old friend and the more it is worn the better it becomes. I ironed it yesterday myself and I cherish it with all the affection which its worth deserves.

We had several heavy blows, in one of which I carried away my mast, which risk I ran in the hope of getting to the Ship, but we were obliged to put back for shelter and trying again next day could make no way against the Seas. The third time, after a long and tough struggle we got on board, the men having been at the oars from 6 A.M. until 11 in the forenoon, pulling in a Sea way that tumbled us about in the most unnerving manner and wet every thing fore and aft. Our food and whiskey had just given out the night before, so that we were quite ready for a breakfast which we had immediately prepared.

I felt very curious when I first stepped on board and could not stand steady, but staggered like a drunken man, which was owing to the quick and sharp motions of the boat that still affected my attitudes. I enjoyed the luxury of a shave and abluted in a *basin* of *fresh* water, and dressed myself from top to toe, so that I felt like a new man and again knew the *real comfort* of *being clean*. I prepared some chocolate myself, for I was loath to trust such an important affair to the cook at this crisis, and fell to on my breakfast with a relish that you, who always live well, can have but a very faint idea of. Want teaches us the true value of possessions, and this was not the first time I had experienced this, nor was it to be the last.

At this time, the Ship was again at Sandal Wood Bay and the Vincennes had also arrived there from Ovelow July 12th. The very next day the Launch of the Vincennes came in alone and reported that the Cutter had been taken by the natives, at a place 20 miles distant only, and the officers and crew barely permitted to escape with their lives. An Expedition of 11 boats and the Schooner was instantly fitted out to retake the Cutter and started before dark. I was not permitted to go, but ordered to remain on some duty which I very heartily wished at the Devil.

They pulled all night and appeared off the Town early in the morning, where they landed and commenced operations at once. A parley was held and the natives, intimidated by seeing such a force of white men arrayed against them on their own ground and ready for fight, were disposed to be peaceful and delivered the stolen Boat at once. They had such a dread of the superiority of whites in warfare that this sudden and bold invasion was too much for their nerves, and there had never been any thing of the kind even tried among the Islands. Our men went to dinner and then landed again to burn the towns and property after the approved method of punishing this kind of people on such occasions. The natives did not offer to resist, but retreated to the hills, and two villages, a quantity of yams, and a double canoe were soon in flames. After this was done, the boats left to return and the natives then came down among the mangroves and fired away with their muskets. Some bullets whistled over our men's heads, but none were touched and they reached the ships that night, where we were awaiting them with much anxiety to learn the result.[32]

We had frequently made inquiries of the white men and of the natives themselves concerning the custom said to be prevalent among the Islands of eating "*Human flesh.*" The white men gave explicit and unequivocal testimony in regard to it and according to them, there were but few, if any, who were not fond of such meals and who made no scruple in indulging their hideous tastes. The white men had seen them at their banquets, although the natives generally preserved secrecy about them, knowing the prejudice of the whites against the practise. Not that they took any shame to themselves, for when they were observed, they readily conversed about the matter. In reply to our questions, the natives generally denied that they ever were guilty of touching men for food, but this was false and they said so merely because they thought we would be disgusted with them and neither give them presents nor trade with them.

However, one day several of us were ashore on a beautiful Island and were standing by the Spirit house, when a native pointed to an oven on the ground and said that they had baked a man there a few weeks before, and that a part of him had been boiled in a pot which

---

[32] *The loss of the cutter occurred at Solevu, on the southern coast of Vanua Levu. Wilkes relates (1845, 3:240–44) that because the cutter was returned stripped of its contents, the attack was ordered on the town of Tye.*

was now gracing the sacred edifice as an offering to the Spirits. There
was a Robinson Crusoe horror crept over me as we listened to him
and found ourselves so near the spot where such infernal orgies
had so recently been conducted. The embers were still there and I
gathered some of them and also a few of the stones, which I carefully
wrapped in paper to the great surprise of our informant, who himself
had shared in the feast. The Victim had been taken prisoner while he
was taking a walk by himself and his capture was made into an affair
of triumph and rejoicing.

The Chief of this place and myself had become great friends; he
was quite young and I made him many presents. He *dined* with *me*
twice on board and he showed me his riches and consequence on
Shore. His Village was clean and was so lovely a spot, that I was
enchanted with its charms and only saw one other that could equal it
in all Fegee. It did not suffer in a comparison with the scenes of
sweet and never to be forgotten Samoa. But one morning, he and his
wife and many of his people came alongside in Canoes and they
brought with them a *part of the body* of a man which they had just
cooked, and partly *eaten*. The wife, who was a mild and delicate
creature in appearance, first told the story of the transaction: "that
her husband had captured 3 of his enemies and had cooked them all
by the Spirit house on Shore; two were sent to another Island where
there was to be a grand feast held and the other, or rather what
was left of him, was in their Canoe. The Shin bone and the Skull
were brought on board by the natives and the flesh that adhered to
them was torn in strips and marked by the traces of the teeth. One
fellow was gnawing away on the bloody muscles of the Eye with
evident relish and calling out good, good! to assure us that he was
experiencing the height of Epicurean delight. This eye and skull and
bone were purchased and are now on board. My friend the Chief had
his chops all greasy from the part he had borne in the repast, and all
hands of them seemed to be of the opinion that they had been
engaged in the most praiseworthy and glorious occupation and that
they had celebrated their triumph to the utmost advantage. Every
one on the Ship was affected with a nervous and terrible feeling of
mingled horror and disgust, and the natives were turned out of the
Ship with all possible dispatch—my friend too, who had drunk of my
wine and eaten of my food. My feelings were indescribable, but I can

never forget them. Oh! to look at that rugged skull and think that a day before it had contained a cunning brain. I have been used to rude and uncouth sights, but this one was too rude and discomposed me more than I can tell.

They do not confine themselves to eating prisoners only; the Chiefs kill their women and slaves to gratify their appetites, and *Phillips* was never *allowed* to *eat any thing else* until he was a *man* grown. His father kept him on this diet *to make him a warrior*, for it is their belief that such food has the effect of gifting a man with the courage and ferocity that are requisite for a fighting chief. The nursing of Phillips must have been expensive and pursued to the inconvenience of his Father's subjects, but it answered the purpose intended, for he is known to be one of the most sanguinary and terrible men in his wars that ever was renowned among the Islands. Snuff's cannibal propensities were strong and so were Tuindrecate's, and we were well convinced that the abominable and revolting custom was universal among the people and that they found in its indulgence the chief pleasure of their existence.

All this while we had on board one of the most singular characters that I ever had the fortune to fall in with: an Irishman who had lived for *Forty years* among the Islands and was at this time over 70 years of age, came to the Ship at Rewah and had remained with us ever since. His beard reached to his knees, but he gathered up the ends and tied them in a knot about his waist; both it and his hair were grey and he was the very picture of a Patriarch of the ancient times.

He came to the Islands in 1800 and had never left them for a single day, so that he was perfectly familiar with the nature of the inhabitants, and had gone through so many adventures that I was never tired of listening to his yarns. As his tongue had had a long holiday so far as talking English was concerned, he was disposed to be very communicative and in his speech he mingled much of the humour of his own countrymen with the flowery style of expression common with the people he had lived amidst so long. Many a watch did I pass away with old Pat Connel at my post and we became great cronies. He told me that he could make more free to talk with me than with the others, "for *who* should he know better than *Ould Squire Reynolds* of the County Cavan and his daughters? and there was that in the *name's sake* that made him bold to speak with me." Whether this "ould squire" was of the stock of my ancestors I do not know, but owing to this I acquired Pat's confidence and he told me all the marvels of his life.[33]

"He had had 150 wives and 50 *children* and had been in more battles than he could remember; and according to his account, he had a high reputation as a fighting man, among the people of the Islands." And he said "that if all he had seen and heard and thought and gone through with could be printed in a book, that it would be wonderful" and so it would; but Pat was above learning at school and his memory could not preserve the events with which his life had been most strangely checkered. He regretted his inability to write, for he had much time and would like to have the 'old man's' history be known to all the white men. He was still hale and hearty, and his eye was as bright and his teeth as fresh as ever. He was so childlike and simple in some things as to belie the whiteness of his hairs, and his discussion would betray so much innocence that I almost thought I was conversing with a youth who had been entirely secluded from the society of men; but again, he was sharp enough and he knew the wiles of the natives as well as his own beard. He wants to live to the age of an hundred years, to have a few more children, to kill a few more Fegees, for long habit had so accustomed him to this that it was his ruling passion, and he thought it was the best thing he could do.

When he died, he hoped there would be some one to read a little of *the book* over his grave. He would not think of going away from the Islands, for he had no kindred or ties and it was better for him to remain where he was known and honored than to starve in insignificance among whites, and he was sure that his habits had totally unfitted him for any thing else but the life that had ever been so free. He was good humoured and inoffensive on board, and was of great use as an Interpreter. Every one felt a degree of regard for him and we all have an interest in his future fate. I have given you a very slight notion of him, but two months association with him laid open to me the history of his life, which was replete with *real*

---

[33] *Reynolds's grandfather William Reynolds (1743/4–1801) emigrated from Kilraughts in the parish of Loughgale, County Antrim, about 1765. Connel had been transported to New South Wales for his part in the Irish rebellion of 1798 and subsequently escaped to Fiji.*

romance, and I certainly shall never forget 'Pat Connel,' "the old man of the Islands."

Up to the 24th of July we continued at the Boat work with the same unceasing labour and as yet had only met with the accident of losing the Vincennes' Cutter. We began to hope that notwithstanding the exposure to the dangers of navigation in such great concerns, and the treacherous and hostile nature of the people in many parts where we were obliged to go, we might finish the Survey without the loss of a life on our side. We trusted greatly to the dread which the natives generally entertained of the power of our Ships and almost persuaded ourselves that they would never dare to make an attack, even when they might have an opportunity. Still we never relaxed any precautions, but were ever on our guard.

At last, we were fatally undeceived and two of the best and most loved among us all were butchered, in the presence of their comrades, who could only get ashore in time to save the bodies. They had landed to buy a Pig and some yams, and had sent off to the boats the Son of the Chief as a Hostage. For the sake of the paltry trade, and the clothes and arms of the two officers and the few men who were with them, the Savages commenced the work of death; there was such a crowd and confusion, and the natives swarmed so thick, that those in the boats could not see what was going on until the shots that were fired warned them that there was bloody work. All hands hurried to the Shore and one of the boats commenced a fire from her blunderbusses and small arms upon the natives with effect. The two officers had been clubbed, but they had each killed two of the Fegees before they fell; they were stripped and the natives, finding that they were suffering severely, retreated at once taking with them all their dead but two and the clothes, arms, and trading stock of the victims. One of the boats' crews was badly wounded in the head and another had a narrow escape. The natives directed their attack principally upon the two officers, and they, seeing that escape was hopeless, directed the men to save themselves and commenced the goodly work of avenging their own sad fate.

When the crews of the other boats got to the beach, there was not a living native to be seen, they had all disappeared among the bushes. But the mangled bodies of those poor fellows who had been so awfully destroyed, who had been thus suddenly martyred in the very ripeness of their youth, were lying upon the sand with the last gasp of life just quivering on their lips. By their sides lay the dead Fegees and the contrast was hideous. There was no time for delay, the natives were near at hand and too numerous to risk an attack. The bodies were carried to the boats, and they hurried to leave the horrid place which they did without experiencing any molestation. The Flying Fish with Cap. Wilkes on board was near at hand, and the Porpoise came soon after; to the Schooner the boats proceeded with their melancholy burden, where the remains were prepared for burial. Lt. Underwood and Midshipman Henry were the ones who thus met with a cruel death and they were the two, above all others, who had the most enviable reputation in the Squadron. The former had married only a few weeks before leaving home, and the latter was almost the only child of a widowed mother and the nephew of Captain Wilkes.[34]

The Boats were sent back to row guard around the Island while the Schooner proceeded to a group of small Islets 5 or 6 miles distant, where the two bodies were buried side by side in one grave. The canvass in which they were sewed up was crimsoned with their blood

[34] *Writing of the incident to his father, William May stated that Underwood "had not his superior, if equal, in the Navy—he was very talented, spoke fluently French, Spanish, Italian, was a profound mathematician and surveyor—and possessed many other accomplishments, such as drawing, engraving, and music" (1840). Underwood had taken leave of his ship in the Mediterranean to travel in France in 1832–1833 and had risen fairly rapidly to a lieutenancy in about nine years' service (ZB).*

Wilkes Henry, who had been appointed to the navy only in late 1837 at the age of sixteen or seventeen (ZB), was the only son of Wilkes's sister Eliza, who lived in New York. In a letter to his wife a few days later (1840b), the commander wrote that during the cruise his nephew "had very much improved and was beloved by all the officers and men of the Squadron and is regretted."

Wilkes felt the blame for the incident lay in Underwood's overconfidence but that there was nothing to be gained from an investigation then. As for his own feelings, Wilkes wrote that "all, however, has caused me great regret and tended in a great measure my dear Jeannie to unfit me for further duty at present." The attack occurred on Malolo Island, west of Viti Levu on the periphery of the Fiji group.

which poured from them like rain and the sand in which they were laid was deeply tinged ere the earth covered them forever. The grave was in the heart of a shady grove and, for the first time since creation, the Silence was broken by the volleys which pealed the requiem of the early dead. The same hands which consigned them to their last resting place on the morrow avenged their deaths, and but few of the murderers were left to tell of their own treachery or of the prompt and terrible vengeance with which it was repaid.

Eighty men were landed to attack the Town wherein the actors of the tragedy had entrenched themselves to await the assault; it was fortified completely after their fashion and had long been deemed impregnable in their mode of warfare.[35] It had withstood many attempts, for the inhabitants were a gang of pirates who owned no authority save that of their own Chief and who were the terror of all their neighbours on the main Shore. Their situation commanded a much frequented passage in the navigation of the group, and these villians made no scruple in murdering and plundering all whom they could surprise, then retreating to their own fastnesses they were secure. They taunted our men to come ashore and fight, and to encourage them said that *they* would have a supper of all who were killed. They fired at the Boats and cut up all sorts of capers, thinking that they were invincible. The town was surrounded at Pistol Shot distance, our men being sheltered by some cocoa nut trees and houses that were outside the pallisades. A fire was kept up whenever chances offered as the natives presented themselves at the loop holes, and with sure effect they returned this with showers of arrows and with musquetry, but there were no serious wounds received on our side. Rockets were sent into the Town and caught the combustible thatch of the houses, so that the whole was soon in a blaze and the natives found themselves in a trap from which there seemed no escape.[36] They were losing lives on all sides and as yet had not killed

[35] *Sualib, fortified by a palisade surrounded on both sides by a moat.*

[36] *The expedition carried the Congreve rocket, developed by the British during the War of 1812 and consisting of a carcass or casing propelled by niter, charcoal, and sulfur surmounted by a warhead filled with a combustible mixture which ignited upon impact. The rockets were mounted on ships or in boats for use as a shock weapon or carried ashore for use such as at Malolo in*

any of the besiegers. They were confounded at the mysterious effect of the rockets and bewildered at seeing fire communicated from such a distance, and though some continued to resist with the same determination as at first, the most were disheartened and turned to flee. Several ascended the houses to attempt to extinguish the flames, but they were shot down at once. The interpreters were now ordered to call out, that the women and children should be taken away, and a passage was left for them to escape to the hills. Many of the warriors went with these fugitives and some were killed in their flight. The town was now entered and the dead bodies of the natives were found lying in the ditch with bullet holes right through the head, which was the only part exposed. During the firing, the women were seen dragging away the bodies of the men as they fell, so that the number of killed could not be fixed. The flames were raging with such fury that it was impossible to penetrate into the place or to remain long. Two children were seen burned to death, and the Cap of Underwood was picked up.

This so successfully accomplished, the party marched over the Island towards a town at the opposite end.[37] Two natives were met who were shot by a dozen; no others were seen, they were stowed away in their secret hiding places. Three boats had gone to destroy this Town; they found it deserted. Every body had gone to the strong hold and removed all their property with them in the belief that they would be victorious, and so this village, which was also well fortified, was burned without any hindrance and before the Shore party got there it was nearly to the ground.

The boats also attacked a number of canoes, and 30 of the natives were killed outright and 8 or 10 made prisoners. One of these latter had a narrow escape; several were swimming, having jumped overboard from the canoe, and Lt. Alden who was after them in his boat was desirous to take them alive and ordered his men not to touch them.[38] But the sailors all were bloody minded and were

---

setting roofs afire. The rocket was guided in flight by a long wooden stick attached to the carcass. See Congreve (1970) on the rocket's various uses, sizes, warheads, and range.

[37] *The town of Arro.*

[38] *James Alden (1810–1877) of a long-established Maine shipowning and seafaring family, who had been appointed as a midshipman in 1828; he was in*

worked up to the highest pitch of excitement in their eagerness for revenge. Kill, kill, was their cry and they had no idea of sparing any one, and indeed the orders were to kill every man that was seen. So on coming up with these swimmers, one of the boat's crew caught the first by the hair and raised his cutlass to strike; Alden had just time to snatch a Pistol and threaten to shoot him if he did not let go his hold. So the blow was stayed in its descent and as the struggling creature turned round, every one saw with surprise the breasts of a woman. She was taken into the boat and the rest were also secured.

So ended this day's bloody work, and the only injury sustained by our men were several arrow wounds. The trees were sticking full of these missiles and if it had not been for the protection they afforded, we should have suffered a severe loss. Bad powder, bad muskets, and overloading them caused bad aim and none of their shots told, although the distance was so small. Eld saw a fellow fire three times at him as he lay behind a tree; when the scamp came for the fourth trial, Eld shot him through the head and got his musket, which had a load of *eight fingers,* or as the natives say, *a load for a big man.*

The destruction had been complete and not a native was seen during the night. Early in the morning they sent a *woman* down to the beach to say "that they could fight no longer; they were nearly all killed, and they begged for peace and mercy." Captain Wilkes sent her away to tell her people that "we warred not with women and would have nothing to do with any but men." Soon after, two of the prisoners were dispatched on shore to direct the natives to come to a certain Hill at noon, where Captn. Wilkes would be to hear them; if

---

command of the surveying boats at Malolo when Underwood and Henry were massacred. Alden went on to serve in the Mexican War and the Civil War and was appointed chief of the Bureau of Navigation in 1869. He was commissioned a rear admiral in 1871.

Reynolds gives a touching report of how he learned of the Malolo incident from Alden (Journal 2:90–100). He, May, and Blunt had been drawing up surveys on the Peacock—May was working on the very one which Underwood and Reynolds had made of the harbors of Samoa—when Alden came to the ship. Joining him in the wardroom, they heard how Alden and his boat crew had jumped into the water to save the bodies of the two officers. Alden lifted Underwood's bloody head upon his arm and "said aloud, almost unconsciously, 'Your poor, poor wife, Joe, little is she thinking of this.'"

they did not appear, he would kill every one he could find on the Island.

Accordingly, the men were landed and posted on the hill to await the coming of the natives who were still alive and after much hesitation and delay, and by the persuasion of the white interpreters who went among them, a body of them came to the foot of the hill and then crawled up to the summit on their hands and knees and knocking their heads on the ground. The Chief was in advance and they kept up a doleful wail, lamenting the losses they had sustained; they begged for mercy and peace and said they were aware of the power of the white man, and that they could not resist any longer and that most of those concerned in the murder had been killed. They had a long palaver and were lectured on the atrocity of their conduct. Captain Wilkes promised them peace on condition that every man, woman and child should on the morrow bring such provisions as they could find: yams, pigs etc. for the vessels, and to fill them up with water; and to this they agreed, overjoyed that their lives were spared. They acknowledged the crime they had been guilty of and the justness of its punishment, and they seemed to the last moment in doubt whether they were all to be massacred or not: they did not believe that we would be satisfied with the slaughter that had been made already, but that like their own country men would fall upon them now as they were unarmed and not let one escape.

The next day, they were busy from morn till eve. Our men were hard task masters and showed them no mercy. They worked unceasingly until their task was completed and then boats, Schooner, and Brig left the Island where for the last three days they had been engaged in Scenes of such thrilling interest and which we all have such a sad cause to remember.

The place of the murder was called "Massacre Bay"; the Islet on which the bodies were buried, "Henry's Island"; and the group that surrounds it, "Underwood's Group." And in this lonely place, in the midst of Savage Cannibals and far from their Homes, they must moulder into dust without a stone to mark the spots wherein they lay. The traces of the grave and the footsteps of the living were all carefully removed, so that there might be no sign to guide the natives should they search after their victims for the hideous purpose which they practice of devouring their enemies. Such was the end of two noble souls. A few days before, I had parted with them in a merry mood, when they were as full of life and health and hope as myself, and now! oh, it was horrible to think of such a death! yet it was one to which we had all been exposed.

The natives said they had lost 56 killed in the Town and more were badly wounded; 30 were killed in the Canoes, and 8 or ten at the time of the murder, so that their loss was indeed severe; their property was all gone and they had no shelter for their heads. The Pirate's nest was broken up and they, who had been so long the dread of the Islands, were now without the means of defence. The Porpoise had detained a Canoe belonging to a Chief of the Main Land, who with his family happened to be passing by. This Chief had often suffered from the depredations of the *Mololo* people and when he was permitted to depart after the fight was ended, he said that in a very few days he would return with his men and kill all who were left, as they were in no condition to resist, so that the work begun by us has been completed long ere this and hereafter the passage may be accomplished without the risk which always attended it before.

That this will be a salutary lesson there can be no doubt, but it cannot be hoped that it will entirely suppress murder and treachery among this people. Even at this *very time,* an American Whale Ship was wrecked at an Island not far distant and some of her crew massacred as soon as they got ashore.[39] Altogether, the number of Americans and other whites that have been destroyed by the Fegees is so great, that if the Islands were to be depopulated entirely the retribution would not be enough to repay the loss of life and property; I have no idea that the nature of the people will ever change. Once a Fegee, always a Fegee. They seem to be one of the races of men that are afflicted with the curse of God—"their hand against every one, and every one's hand against them"—and the sooner they are extinct upon the earth, the better, which event I heartily pray for.

[39] *Lieutenant Ringgold was sent to Turtle or Vatoa Island to investigate the wreck of the American whaler* Shylock *in June 1840. The* Porpoise *found no crew members there, the eight survivors having already been picked up by another whaler and some of them deposited at Vavao Island, where, later, the* Porpoise *did take on three of them.*

When the news of the murder of our friends reached us, we were oppressed with such a degree of horror as men feel when the ties of the heart are rent asunder and there were many wept who rarely shed a tear. We knew the worth of those we had lost and I can tell you that Death *among us* is as severe an affliction as when it enters a household of those connected by blood. It is no common feeling which unites those who have often been companions in danger and who have depended on the good offices of each other for safety and mutual support; and it has been our great happiness to have lived together in the enjoyment of a friendship that has been uninterrupted by any thing like discord among ourselves. The loss of *any* of our little band would be a source of sincere sorrow and the deepest regret, but to have *two* of the very best and the most loved, butchered by these hellish Cannibals, to whom mercy is unknown! It was terrible to us! and alas! *what! how! will* it be to the widowed mother and the widowed wife, who have yet to learn of the bloody and violent death which deprived them of their all in all on earth?

The *officers all* met together, before we left the group, and we have subscribed *$2000.00* to erect a monument to our departed brothers at Mount Auburn cemetery, near Boston, as a testimonial of the esteem in which they were held by us, and that their names, and the fate that befel them, may be preserved in the Land to which they were not permitted to return.[40]

We were now all hands in the Squadron put upon short allowance of provisions, in order to make the quantity on hand hold out until the 1st October, and this was far from being agreeable, as we were still on active duty. I was again sent away for 6 days in a boat cruise, was hungry all the while, and never slept until I got back to the Ship.

There was much that occured which I cannot possibly write you of. And as to the customs etc. of the people, the very imperfect and slight mention I have made of them must suffice until I can show you my notes and talk with you myself; and when this happy time shall come, I will tell you of marvels more wonderful than those related

[40] *The monument memorializes all the officers lost on the expedition, including Bacon and Reid from the* Sea Gull. *See Eyde (1986) for a description of Mount Auburn, in Cambridge.*

by the veracious Sinbad of old. I hope you will excuse the defects and errors which I am afraid are numerous in this letter. I have smuggled opportunities to write and have always been in the midst of disturbance and noise. I have had no time to think, first, or to revise afterwards; so you must take this, as well as those written before, as hasty effusions and with all their imperfections receive them as evidence that I do not neglect you and that I have no disposition to forget the duty which I owe to you all.[41]

August came, and we were all longing to quit the Islands. We *hated* the looks of the people and we were tired with the harassing work. We were *crazy* to *get our Letters* from which we had been detained so long and to learn what was going on at Home. At last on the 11th August we fairly sailed from the Fegees, and *I trust never* to see *them again*. The Brig was left behind to go to the rescue of the survivors of the Whale Ship, and though those on board her were thus delayed, they went on their errand of mercy with willing hearts and with the hope they might not be too late to save.

We were overjoyed to find ourselves clear of Islands and reefs and natives and once more upon the wide deep with no land against the Sky, but the passage was tedious in the extreme and in some respects exceedingly disagreeable. We had nothing to eat, or at least we had not enough to satisfy even a common appetite, and ours were ravenous. Flour, Butter, Coffee, Sugar, Tea, Mollasses, Bread etc. etc. all gave out and we were hungry all the while. Nothing but water and bread crumbs for breakfast was all that we had for more than once, and supper was not spoken of, by mutual consent. Once in a while, we raised enough to fill us up, but with stuff that was destitute of nutriment and any thing but wholesome.

I thought often of the plenty on your table at Home: of the vegetables and fruits of the summer and the fresh and juicy meats upon which you daily regaled, and which are served before you as regularly as the days pass. You are never on reduced rations and every thing you have is healthy and good for the inner man; you

---

[41] *Reynolds's day-by-day account of the three-month stay in the Fijis covered 16 pages in his Public Journal; his private account of the same period was written on some 152 pages in Journals 1 and 2.*

keep no watch; your rest is secure and undisturbed; your house is always on its legs and never capsized—you ought to be happy and contented.

No wonder Sailors are short lived: the exposure and deprivations which they are almost constantly undergoing makes bad work with their constitutions and they are worn out when they ought to be in their prime. Sam Weller never saw "an old Post Boy, or an old Jackass."[42] I have never seen but one *old* Sailor in all my cruising. They disappear in the Autumn of their existence, though with all the marks of Winter on their frame. Nevertheless, with all its dangers and ills, I am quite satisfied with the Sea and expect to follow it for the rest of my life. I do not regret having chosen it and am very firmly in the opinion that I was fit for nothing else: 9 years of rough servitude is a pretty fair trial, and as each day rolls on I am the more and more convinced that I am just where I ought to be. There is a joy in roaming which all the luxuries and comforts of Home can never purchase, and there is much in my memory which the incidents of a quiet life could never supply and which I would not have missed, or part with, for worlds.[43]

As to bodily inconveniences, they are easily endured, and as long as the extreme of endurance is not called for, all are disposed to make light of the present and trust to better luck in future. Sailors are your true philosophers in these cases and never employ themselves in fancying their situation worse than it is. The curse of the Life is that we are seperated so long from our homes and often removed from a knowledge of what is going on in the busy world of civilization.

I have enjoyed the most glorious health and with the exception of one day's headache in Sydney have never troubled the Doctor for a moment. With health and a clear conscience, a man ought to be happy any where and I am not disposed to complain when I see

[42] *Sam Weller was Mr. Pickwick's faithful attendant in Charles Dickens's* Pickwick Papers *(1938).*

[43] *"How often in this cruise have I thought of Robinson Crusoe and his man Friday and remarked the singular fascination that book always possessed me with. I once knew it by heart, but little did I think in those days that I would ever realize some of the Scenes myself. I think that it [was] chiefly instrumental in determining me for the Sea, to which element I grew up a complete stranger and never saw a Ship until I was Sixteen"* (*Journal 1:353*).

those around me who are not so fortunate in the former respect as myself.[44] I am thankful that I am so blessed, but this is being very prosy and dwelling entirely too much upon myself. I dare say you are tired of reading already and I will oblige you by cutting my yarn short.

We saw no land on the passage, nor did any thing occur to break the monotony of the low and wearying navigation against the trade winds. We thought we should never get in and our Philosophy received a very rude trial; nevertheless, we kept our spirits up wonderfully for hungry men with letters in prospecto and at length, on the last day of September, we made the Land and on the same evening we were anchored in Oahu and reading the precious lines with an interest that cannot be described.

It was just sundown when we came to and none of us could quit our stations until all the work was done; never was this accomplished more speedily, yet never did time seem *so long*. At last we *could* leave the deck and I hurried to the Cabin, where I got such a pile of letters and papers as I could scarcely carry—my arms were full. I was completely puzzled, I did not know which seal to crack first, and after much inspecting and turning and tossing I found it was no use to select and so picked them up as I could; but I had not read through them before I was called for duty on deck again. This was cruel, but I had to go. In a moment I heard someone cursing his ill luck and wondering where *his* letters *were?* With the most happy presence of mind, I took advantage of this unfortunate individual's situation and pressed him in my place, which he made no objections to taking, and down I ran once more to read my letters from Home. Fresh food and tempting fruits were already spread upon the table, sent to us by the kind attention of the Vincennes, who had arrived a week before us, but on my word I could not eat. I heeded them not, but stuck to my budget until I finished them all. As I took up the letters so irregularly, I was several times at a loss: "the girls are still at Bordentown"—what girls? thought I. Presently I found out the grand change in regard

[44] *"Thank God, I am naturally lighthearted and everyday troubles disturb me but little. If there is anything to call up gayety, my laugh is among the first and loudest. . . . This cruise would kill a melancholy man" (Journal 1:255).*

to Jane and Kate, at which I rejoiced and hope they will become accomplished ladies. Then "Sam is still here and undecided as to his future employment." This I could not comprehend, but I soon came to the melancholy story of the ruins of Bangor; "farewell, a long farewell, to all its greatness!" I had the highest hopes that Bangor would flourish in spite of the canal and was grievously disappointed to learn that its value was gone for ever.

Reading on in this way for several hours, I finished the whole and so learned how you were situated 10 months ago and all that had occurred during the previous year. I was happy to find my dates as late as any that were received, and was rejoiced that you were all well and happy and had not forgotten or neglected me. . . .

Lydia's letters were not any too lengthy and when she writes again she need not fear of trying my patience; but fill up as many sheets as she can scribble with all sorts of intelligence, domestic or otherwise, and embracing every thing or person. . . . There is nothing about Home too trifling to be overlooked, and I hope that you will all remember this whenever you are writing to me.[45]

James is an amusing boy; he writes to me with the utmost sang froid, on condition that I bring him a pointer dog of a breed whose virtues he celebrates by a long quotation, but which unfortunately is confined to a country that I have never visited. I have not gathered many specimens of rock, for I have no judgement or taste in the matter, and every thing curious is sacred to the Scientifics themselves. *But* I *have some stones* from the *Southern Continent,* where *man had never been before us,* and if these will please him, I shall be happy to enrich him. . . .

I found no letters from Father, nor any mention of the receipt of an allotment of $40. a month which I sent Home from Rio de Janeiro and which was payable to Father's order at the Navy agent's, Philadelphia. As I sent duplicates, this allotment must certainly have

[45] *Lydia did in fact supply her brother with the mundane details of daily life at Cornwall and Lancaster which he requests here. In her eight-page answer (17 June 1841) to this letter, Lydia meekly writes, "I hope you will not complain of my letters, dear Will, for I try my best to give you all sorts of news that I can think of. If I was only gifted with one fourth part of your talent for writing, I should be very thankful, but as this cannot be, I must be content and bear with all the scoldings I get."*

reached you and I suppose that the acknowledgement was made, but that the letter containing it was lost.

On arriving here, we learned that the extra pay which we have been receiving by the written order of the Secretary of the Navy, whatever *he may say to the contrary,* would not be allowed us and so we are reduced to the common pay of the Navy, though subject to most extraordinary expenses. I have no doubt that the extra compensation will be granted us when we return; we have earned it and I do not know how Mr. Paulding will extricate himself from the dilemna in which he is placed by denying that he ever authorised an increase in our pay. If it is withheld, the most of us will be bankrupt to a certainty. I have ordered that this allotment be stopped from the day which I shall name; if Father can draw the amount due until then, I hope he will do so and there will be no more trouble about it until I get Home. My trip to Europe is robbed of all its glory, but if I do not get there, notwithstanding the loss of my little fortune, I shall wonder. *I will go* if I have to work my passage over and beg my way on foot afterwards. I do not care for the money; but to have been promised it by the highest authority, inveigled into the purchase of expensive instruments, and obliged to pay heavy bills *or starve!,* and then to have the Honorable Secretary come out and affirm that *he never* gave such an order and very cooly take from us money already spent in the belief that it was our own—why, to say the least, it is very disagreeable and places us all in the most awkward situation that can be conceived of. I confess I do not see the particular justice or honesty of cutting down our means in this way and am entirely at a loss to understand Mr. Paulding's motives, when Captain Wilkes has his written order which says in direct terms, "The officers of the Exploring Expedition will be allowed the Extra Compensation granted to the officers on the Coast Survey, to enable them to purchase instruments and on condition that they are employed in Scientific duty." We shall all be in debt and I wish the Government joy in recovering the amount we have been overpaid; it will be *so* highly honourable to the head of the Navy Department.[46]

[46] *Navy Secretary Paulding wrote Wilkes 12 July 1838 assuring him that the officers "will be allowed extra pay equal to that received by those engaged in the service of the Coast Survey, on condition that they are employed in*

I mentioned in a letter from Sydney that I should draw on the fund which I congratulated myself on possessing at Home, for $200. Now, however, I will not do so, but endeavour to pay this debt, if I can, before the Government sends the Sheriff after me. The amount which I allotted exceeded the 'extra' by $9 or $10 a month, but then there were 6 or 9 months elapsed before it commenced for which I drew the full pay, so that the balance is against me.

I hope Sam will be successful in any undertaking he may embark in, though for the sake of having him at Home I should be glad if he would accept of the berth at Cornwall: it would be so much

---

scientific duties" (Paulding 1838). The officers of the U.S. Coast Survey received extra pay to compensate them for instruments they were expected to purchase for their work. A navy midshipman at that time earned $750 per annum. Paulding rather shamefacedly had to withdraw his pledge in March 1839, writing Wilkes that he had made it "only twelve days after I came into the Depmt." and, as he subsequently learned, without authority to do so. The issue was to be presented to Congress, "and there is every reason to anticipate its favorable decision" (Paulding 1839).

Lydia wrote William (17 February 1839), "Every paper that has anything relating to the navy or Navy officers we lay by to send to you—a resolution has passed the lower house of Congress directing the Secretary to inform the House what pay and imoluments are allowed Lieut. Wilkes and his officers and if any assurances have been given that the acting appointments now held by them will be confirmed, and whether the expedition is considered of a Naval Character or not."

James Kirk Paulding (1778–1860), despite his disclaimers of inexperience and ignorance, had played important roles in the navy for many years. He began as secretary to the Board of Navy Commissioners (when he was approached by John Wilkes [J. Wilkes 1816] seeking an appointment in the navy for his son Charles), then became navy agent in New York in 1824, where he remained until President Van Buren named him secretary of the navy in July 1838. A prolific and prominent writer, Paulding attempted to impose discipline on both officers and men of the naval service, trying to reduce meddling in politics by the former and drunkenness among the latter, to little effect; he also opposed experiments with steam-powered vessels (Coletta 1980, 1:165–71).

The issue was not finally resolved until an act of Congress of March 1843, although Wilkes apparently delayed past that date certifying some officers with whom he had had disagreements (for example, Smith 1843).

pleasanter than having a Stranger. But, as he says, he wants to get a start in life and be concerned in business of his own and it is very natural, and I think creditable, in him to try. . . .[47] What is James destined to? which of the learned proffessions is he to become an ornament of? I am at a loss to conjecture, yet the young gentleman must certainly have some bias of his own. . . .[48]

I am not in the least disposed to any sort of misanthrophy nor am I oppressed with any particular or general dislike to the daughters of Eve, either at Home or abroad, but as there has never been any very fascinating inducements among the female circles at places we have

---

[47] *William Reynolds felt a special relationship with his nearest sibling, always noting his birthday in his Journal. Samuel Moore Reynolds (1814–1888) apparently had none of William's eloquence and imagination, John's strength of character, or James's scholarship and uneven brilliance. He sought to prove himself to his father—and to himself—but he was a plodder and somewhat of a loner. He took over the management of Cornwall Furnace in 1840, but that same year journeyed to Clarion County in northwestern Pennsylvania to inspect Lucinda Furnace, worked by a bankrupt Lancaster man; his father and James Buchanan subsequently bought Lucinda and 4,351 acres of timber land and put Sam in charge. Thus, on William's return in 1842, Sam was once again managing an "out of repair" property with a "poor house" and talking of future success. Nathan Evans (1813–1893) had assumed management of Cornwall until, in 1846, Evans married Lydia and they went to run Lucinda for some twelve years.*

[48] *James Lefevre Reynolds (1822–1880), who was only nine when William left for a life at sea in 1831, graduated from Marshall College in Mercersburg, Pennsylvania, in 1841 with honors. (This college was later joined to Franklin College to become Franklin and Marshall.) Admitted to the bar in 1844 after studying with John R. Montgomery of Lancaster and John Weidman of Lebanon, he was in active practice only ten years. In 1854, he refused a position on the Pennsylvania Supreme Court, apparently devoting his time to study and politics. An ardent Democrat, he was Buchanan's lawyer and chief political aide until the Civil War, when he became an ardent Republican and quartermaster general of the Pennsylvania militia on Governor Andrew Curtin's staff. He was a member of the Pennsylvania Constitutional Convention of 1872, but, rather typically, refused to sign the resulting document because he objected to a portion. His 1880 obituaries stress his scholarship, vast library, powers as a conversationalist, and warm circle of friends. Like his father, he was "tall, portly and commanding."*

visited, I have contented myself with other modes of enjoyment and found myself a gainer. It will be strange if I pass this cruise after this fashion—I, who never was so happy as when in the midst of girls. The first fair face or intelligent countenance will certainly tempt me, and this is all that has been wanting heretofore. There are none here in *Oahu*, and where or when I will be so blessed is a matter of extreme doubt; at Sincapore or the Cape of Good Hope a year hence, perhaps. Until then, we shall be among the dark skinned people of the Islands in the North Pacific and the Indians on the North West Coast of America.

You will have to redeem me from the state of rude barbarism into which I have fallen and in which I will most certainly remain as long as this cruise lasts. I must be polished up anew and accustomed to the forms and ceremonies of polite society, which are totally neglected in our mode of life; and I am afraid I shall be so uncouth and frightful that it will be impossible for me to find a wife. I must trust to the grand tour to qualify myself for a conquest. After that, I certainly ought to be able to persuade some poor girl that I am a much more important character than I shall be in reality. Sam says he may be married before I return; I hope he will precede me, as he has the right of seniority, and I suspect will made a better Benedict than his vagrant brother. If I *should* get command of a fine Frigate, in the matrimonial way, Captain and craft must sail together, for I shall never be contented to live in one place as long as I am young enough to enjoy the supreme luxury of travel in foreign lands. Mrs. William Reynolds must prepare herself to cross the Seas at once, or she will be no wife for me. Sam will marry, let go the big anchor and ride out his life without ever changing his berth, according to the fashion of Shore people and which, doubtless, is very much to be preferred; but I feel as if I *must* keep moving, and I should want my wi—I can't write it—to see the world and all its glories as well as myself. I had better stop here: it is *very amusing* for a *wretched Navy officer, on poor pay,* to talk of *travel* and a *wife*—pshaw!

I see by the papers that the Navy is before the Public on several accounts, some of which do no credit to the proffession; but that it is necessary that the condition of the Navy be bettered, there is no doubt. Every body reccommends a reform, and why is it not accomplished? The interests of the Country require an efficient Navy and ours has been going to the Devil as rapidly as it could. It is not now the Service which gained so much reputation in the last war, but the mere ghost or shadow of what it was then. It has been mismanaged and neglected so, that the officers have no hope of promotion until they are passed the time of life when they should have enjoyed it; and they must have had more than mortal pride to have kept alive the feelings of zeal and devotion for their calling, which it is so necessary for every one to cherish. With their energies kept back and confined to the same series of subordinate duties for a long term of years, without the least hope of advancement, it is a miracle that the officers have done their duty at all. At 35, a man *may* be President of the Country. At 45, after 30 years of service, a Lieutenant *may* be promoted and get a command. Those who entered life with him but who followed civil pursuits have outstripped him, and long ere this are in the highest offices in the State. The poor, worn out Naval Hack, who has been dragged from his family and sent to climates that do no benefit to his constitution, without being allowed the least choice in the matter, is at last, when he is gray haired and worn out, ornamented with a *pair of swabs*[49] and allowed the smallest Command in the Navy.

As to the lower grade, here am I myself—25 years old—have been 9 years in the Service and *still a Midshipman, living among boys,* and doing the *same trifling duties* that have been *my every day's task since 1831.* Promotion is still *so far* from *me,* that I cannot look for it until I shall be *30 years of age* when, by the present method of filling the vacancies occasioned by *deaths* and resignations, I *may* be made a Lieutenant and *trusted* with the performance of responsible duties. *What* a prospect *is this!* it is enough to drive one crazy. I have been often tempted to quit in disgust and try the Merchant Service, where I could soon get the *command* of a Ship and have a chance to try my own energies while I am young enough to exert them all. In the Navy, if I should survive the exposures that *must* be met in the course of Service and live to be 55, with the constitution of 65, I may possibly be fortunate enough to be called a Captain and live in the Cabin of a Sloop of War. This is cheering and well calculated to keep alive ardour and to fill me with love for the proffession, which *does*

[49] *That is, promoted to the rank of captain.*

so much for me. What a rule to govern it by! no advancement except by the *Death* of its members! I do love the Navy in spite of all its imperfections, but I scarcely *dare* to look forward to my future career in it, for I can see nothing but a life of continual disappointments and heart burning jealousies such as kill the very soul.

What makes this so bitter to be borne with is, that it is only the ignorance and timidity of those who govern us that keeps us back. With an immense commerce in every sea, *they will not increase the Navy* to a force sufficient for its protection, which is all we ask. Increase the Navy, keep ships afloat and busy, employ the officers in their *proper* stations, and there would be none to complain or resign. The necessity of promotion is notorious—half the Ships have been manned by *acting* appointments for the time being; but these are taken away again instead of being confirmed and the poor aspirants, after having tasted of the sweets of rank, reduced to their original nothingness and despair.

The older officers of the Navy, the Captains that are now, had all of the glory in the war and none of them ever served more than two or three years as Lieuts. Commod. Patterson was 1st Lieut. of a Frigate when he was 21 and so it is with the others.[50] They have been Captains ever since, no one can remember them as any thing else. They have had commands 5 times over and again and again, until at last every one thought, and the opinion was universal, that no one but these old Captains was fit to be trusted with a Ship! How absurd, that a man at 35 with the experience of 20 years was not qualified to conduct a Ship or a Squadron. Make these men Admirals, for sooner or later we *must* have that grade, though it has an ominous name to

[50] *Daniel Todd Patterson (1786–1839), a New Yorker and descendant of Robert Livingston, had been appointed to the navy in 1800, served in the Tripolitan wars, and covered himself with laurels in the Louisiana campaign during the War of 1812. Promoted to captain in 1815, he remained in the navy for the following twenty-four years, serving as one of the three navy commissioners, commander of the Mediterranean Squadron, and commander of the Washington Navy Yard until his death the previous August. Reynolds knew Patterson and his family both during his 1834–1836 Mediterranean cruise and in Washington in 1838, when he was a frequent visitor in the Patterson home. In May 1838, he had led off the Regatta Ball as aide-de-camp to the "Lady Patroness," Miss Georgy Patterson, the commodore's daughter.*

the democratic republicans who tremble for the Union if the title of Admiral should be admitted, fools that they are! Let the commands descend a little lower on the list, and give the men who were Midshipmen during the hard fought war and have been Lieutenants ever since, give them, in mercy to their services and their gray hairs, give them a command before they have one foot in the grave and are ready to follow it with the other.[51]

Murder! how I have been carried away. You are not Secretary of the Navy, nor have any of you interest at Court, can do nothing for *poor me* and I must struggle on, a miserable discontented Midshipman, until I am too old to experience any of the rapture or pride which would attend *promotion now*. I shall receive it with a curse that it did not come before.

Well, I must take breath and turn with better feelings to something else; it makes me fairly sick to think of future prospects and it cannot delight you much to read of their melancholy state. I have a light heart yet and expect to be *equal* to *any fortune that awaits me, good or bad.* I can still laugh as loud as ever and care will have a hard bargain if it ever kills me. So, never mind, and I'll jog along and take every thing that happens for the best! There are many persons in the world worse off than me. . . .

I should like to have in old age the same friends who were my associates in early youth, but this rarely happens to any man and I do not see that it will be my case, if I should live. I have had the fortune, however, to make friends since I have been in the Navy, whose intimacy I should be loath to lose and of whose affection I am as certain as I am proud. It shall be my *endeavour* never to lose one by any act of mine and if any of them should find their way to Cornwall,

[51] *The paralysis in navy officer ranks at this time meant that a midshipman appointed in 1839 might have to expect to wait more than twenty-five years to rise above the rank of lieutenant. This situation was caused in part by the large group of 1812-era senior officers remaining at the top and in part by the irresponsible dispensing of midshipmen's warrants by members of Congress. Many people, like Reynolds, felt that the absence of the rank of admiral (not introduced until 1862) further contributed to the paralysis. The issues of promotion, officer training, and navy readiness were addressed during the 1840s with the reform of the navy and the establishment of the academy at Annapolis.*

or wherever else may be our home, I am sure that you would all be happy in my choice. The great comfort of my life now is that I have associates who never misunderstand me and between whom and myself there is the utmost *harmony* and almost love, if that be not too strong a term between men. They are the very best fellows in the world. Although you may never know them, I will write you their names, for accident might throw some of them in your way and with them there need be no reserve: *Dr. Gilchrist, Lt. Alden, Johnson (Bob), W. L. Maury, R. F. Pinckney, Dr. Whittle, Dr. Guillou; May, Simon Blunt, Eld* of my own grade; *Clarke and Elliot,* Midshipmen.[52] I almost forgot *Baldwin:* Father saw him at Chester.[53] In the event of any accident to me, I refer you to any of these and you may write *to them* as you would to a brother.

I am very much obliged to Lieut. Marston for his very flattering

[52] *William L. Maury, a passed midshipman who had served with Reynolds on the* Vincennes *but at this time was on the* Porpoise; *he was commissioned a lieutenant in 1841 and resigned from the navy in that rank in 1861. Dr. John S. Whittle, the assistant surgeon on the* Vincennes, *who bore a strong dislike for Wilkes and was transferred to the* Peacock *at Honolulu when Reynolds was moved to the* Flying Fish. *He had been appointed an assistant surgeon only two months before the squadron sailed from Norfolk and was to die in 1850. Midshipman George W. Clarke had also begun the voyage on the* Vincennes; *warranted a passed midshipman in 1844, he resigned from the navy in 1846. Samuel B. Elliott was another young midshipman who remained with the* Vincennes *during the entire cruise; he became a passed midshipman in 1846 and resigned in 1852. Many of these "very best fellows" were also on Wilkes's blacklist. Johnson, Pinkney, Guillou, and May were all court-martialed upon return in 1842; like Reynolds, Maury was once suspended from duty; Alden and Whittle were heartily disliked by the commander. Elliott, however, was better regarded by Wilkes, who wrote a letter at the end of the expedition certifying to his performance (ZB).*

[53] *Commissioned a lieutenant with Reynolds in September 1841, Augustus Baldwin finished the expedition as second lieutenant on the* Oregon *(Letter No. 19, n. 11). Retiring in 1855, he rejoined the navy as a commander in 1861, was made captain on the retired list in 1867, and died in 1876. Baldwin had served with Reynolds on the* Boxer *and the* Pennsylvania. *John Reynolds would have met him when he visited the latter ship in Chester in December 1837.*

reccollection of me and shall be glad if any of you can assure him so personally, or through our cousins.[54]

I did promise to write to Newton Lightner, but I am afraid I will not fulfill it. I wish some of you to remember me to him, and I suspect he is the only young man in Lancaster with whom I could desire to keep up an intimacy. I hope he has practise and is doing well; if you will mention me to the Judge and to his sisters, and to Isaac Lightner and his Father and Mother, I shall be obliged to you, for I owe them this courtesy and have every desire it should be paid. I have made so many pleasant visits to their houses, that I am greatly in their debt and shall never forget the kind reception I always met with, nor the happy days I spent among them.[55]

I have not forgotten Aunt and I was delighted to get her letter. She has a share in this and I hope she will always write with the rest of you, to assure me that she is comfortable and contented. I suppose she has deserted Mr. Buckwheat altogether.[56]

I think that if we all get together once more, I shall be so happy that this long cruise will seem to be a dream. I have been so lonely at times, particularly when away in the boats, and have been for so

---

[54] *Presumably John Marston, then one of the senior lieutenants in the navy, having been commissioned in 1825. Marston went on to become a captain before retiring in 1861, subsequently being appointed commodore and then rear admiral on the retired list. On a visit to Philadelphia to her father's cousin Hannah Lefevre Witmer and her grocer husband, Jacob, Lydia had met Lieutenant Marston, who, as she wrote William (1839a), "told me I had great reason to be proud of my brother, that he was a great favorite with all the officers on board the Pennsylvania and desired to be particularly remembered to you when I wrote and not, as is generally done, at the bottom of a letter, but to mention him particularly."*

[55] *Isaac Newton Lightner (1813–1889) did become a successful lawyer. In June 1841, Lydia recorded her astonishment that he had married his cousin Anne Hopkins (1809–1886), who was the aunt of her good friend Emily Hopkins. The Lightners were an old Lancaster County family.*

[56] *Lydia Reynolds (1792–1857) was the unmarried sister of John Reynolds, who took charge of the East King Street house and of the permanent Duke Street house in which all of the family remaining in Lancaster lived from 1848 to 1857. "Mr. Buckwheat" was the nickname of the Reynolds children for then Senator James Buchanan. The reference to his relationship to Aunt Lydia is unclear.*

many months cut off from all communication with the world, that I have often felt as if I had no ties to bind me to any one, nor a Home to cheer me with its affection and its smiles. If I could only have lost sight of those accursed cannibals and looked upon Cornwall and all of you, I would have given my very head. But my mind was so full of what was before me that in spite of all my efforts, I could not bring it to dwell on any thing else and I grew fairly sick of Fegee and all its people. However, as I have said before, my spirits are buoyant and I am as gay and lighthearted as ever; if gloomy feelings will cast their shadow over me at times, they never last long. I drive them off and I never yield to any thing but mirth, which I like to indulge in without restraint. Don't have any fears for me, I am enjoying myself as well as can be expected, and you may be sure I put the best face on matters as they turn up. I am far from being miserable, and now that I have had some good food, am in a very proper bodily condition. I hope to weather the rest of the cruise without damage and then I will talk to you as long as you will listen; I have such a character among my shipmates for yarning that I think you will be bored first. We shall see.

This is the 12th October and this very tedious letter must go the day after tomorrow by the Whale Ship Elizabeth, Captain Wood, for New Bedford. I shall have no time to write after to night and I think that you ought to rejoice at the prospect of a termination. It has been such a great while, though, since I have had the pleasure of conversing with you after this fashion, that I have not been able to stay my pen, but have gossiped on with all the tiresome garrullity of a stupid person, exceedingly loath to stop, and yet well aware that I have neither been interesting nor amusing. You must excuse me, my fault has been on the right side and if you should read this wearisome thing to the end, do not abuse me but remember that I have always been hurried, yet never tired myself, for I could write away to you forever and a day after.

We expect to be here a month yet with our Ship and then be employed surveying the Kingsmill group of Islands, near the line,[57] until it will be time to start for the Columbia River; the Vincennes will

---

[57] *The Kingsmill group, better known as the Gilbert Islands, now the republic of Kiribati.*

not leave, it is thought, as the Pendulum is to be swung on the top of a mountain 14,000 feet high, boats built, and many other things to be done.[58] This is all conjecture, however, for we are never told where we are going or what we have to do, but driven around blindfolded like a horse in a mill; which is, has been, and will be highly agreeable and satisfactory.[59] However, *we expect* to be in *Sincapore* in December and January of '41 and '42, or perhaps in November of the former year. The passage from the U. States to that port or to Batavia is from 3 to 4 months and never less than 90 days. We shall get no letters until then. You must write by every chance to the Cape of Good Hope, and to Batavia or Sincapore, up to October of 1841. Boston and Salem vessels are most numerous in the East India trade, and if you see none advertised, why be sure and send a package to the Navy Department and to the Lyceum at Brooklyn *every month*, and I cannot help getting some of them. There will be a third Store Ship. She will have sailed before you get this; I hope you will not have missed that chance. After October write to Rio de Janeiro every week if you can. Vessels are continually sailing from Baltimore and New York for that port. In March or April you may cease, for we are promised to be home the last of May. The men have been reentered to serve until then[60] and Captain Wilkes wants to arrive before the Congress

[58] *Wilkes took the* Vincennes *to the island of Hawaii, where a large party made an arduous ascent of Mauna Loa. They encamped on the summit for about a month in December and January, taking measurements of the volcano, the boiling point of water, the dew point, and so forth, as well as continuing the usual studies of magnetism. Traces of the encampment are still extant.*

[59] *Reynolds was less flip about this issue in his Journal, where he wrote that the close mystery about the movements of the squadron cause "vexation, distress, discontent and disappointment. . . . Why treat us who are to contribute so largely to the success of the cruise with so little confidence? . . . We certainly have the deepest possible interest in the fate of the Expedition in which we are embarked" (1:340).*

[60] *After some persuasion, most of the crew reenlisted for another eighteen months at Hawaii. Wilkes indicates that some sailors instead "took passage in vessels that were bound to the United States" (1845, 3:385). Some fifty islanders were signed on as replacements for the voyage to the Northwest Coast and back.*

adjourns. Only think, your *last dates* are *now ten months old* and it will be *more than a year before* I can think of *another letter from Home; do write and send many papers.*

We have no more cruising to do among *such people* as the Fegees, so you need not be apprehensive of any more danger. The Fegees were always a bugbear, and none of us ever thought to get clear of them without loss. *Now,* we *have a fair chance* once more and we do not dream of risk, so far as men are concerned. Belcher was two summers on the N.W. coast and never was molested nor did he meet with a single accident to his officers or crew. So you see that the worst is over and there is no occasion to worry yourselves with unnecessary alarms. I have a confident feeling, which never forsakes me, that I shall surely be preserved. I have been in so many risks already and always escaped, that I have no idea luck is going to quit me yet: I certainly have the lives of a Cat. It is astonishing how near a man may be to destruction and be saved; I have seen this an hundred times, and wondered.

I hope you will be still at Cornwall when I return. I want to live for a while in the quiet of the Country, and with healthy diet and exercise repair the damages of the cruise. I always liked the place and it must be much improved in appearance now from the alterations that have been made. I will be contented to seclude myself there for a month or two and I shall be as happy as the day is long.[61] Time has never seemed long to me yet, and the remainder of the period we are yet to be absent will fly. We will be Home before we know it: continual occupation and change of scene make the days go rapidly, and on some accounts I am almost glad that we will be detained; but I must say that I would prefer to have all over by next August, as was originally intended. It can't be so and I am content: the longer we are kept out, the *more leave* I can *claim* as a recompense. It will be curious

---

[61] *In 1847, the year before the Reynolds family left Cornwall, a visitor wrote of it: "Stopping at the Mansion we were welcomed and entertained in the old fashioned gentlemanly style of true hospitality. To look through the Mansion with its garden, arbors, fish pond, and summer houses, is calculated to create in the minds of those aspiring to splendor, a feeling of discontent with their lot" (Miller 1950).*

if they get *me to Sea before* I am perfectly ready. *"The tour" must and shall be made.* After that, what will come I know not—a wife, I hope.

I cannot write to Rebecca Myers and I am grieved that I have broke a promise to a Lady, but it can't be helped. Remember me to her and to all her house, and to every body who does me the honour to inquire after my humble self. One of the newspapers containing Com. Elliott's trial has Mr. Montgomery's name on it; if I am indebted to his care and kindness for furnishing me with it, I beg you will give him my most particular thanks, for I can tell you that even such an attention reaches the very heart.[62]

Lydia mentions that Father wrote to me and I am very sorry that his letters have gone astray. If John *did* write I can only regret that I did not receive his effusions, while I am thankful to him for the effort he made. Let Grandmother and Hal and Elly write *their names* in some of your letters, if they can do no more, and as I addressed you all at

---

[62] *Commodore Jesse Duncan Elliott (1782–1845) was tried and found guilty of cruelty to subordinates and other charges while in command of the* Constitution *in the Mediterranean. Elliott had had a distinguished career, displaying great valor and competence during the War of 1812 and subsequently seeing service against the Barbary states and as commander of the West Indies station and the Boston Navy Yard. Reynolds may have served with Elliott in the Mediterranean; in any case, the commodore was known to the family, if not uniformly held in high esteem by them. Writing to William about the "great fuss with Commodore Elliott" caused by a petition presented to Congress by a disgruntled junior officer, Lydia added, "I am afraid he [Elliott] will come off with flying colours" (1839a). On 10 May 1840, she added: "We had a visit from Commodore Elliott; he stopped for dinner on his way to Churchtown . . . he is a amusing person to talk to, but I cannot say I admired his manners at table much." On 15 July: "I send you a paper containing Com. Elliott's defense. It is said to be a very able and elegant speech. I merely looked over it. The impression made by the Com. was not quite so favourable as to induce me to read such a lengthy affair." Suspended for four years, he was reinstated by President John Tyler in 1844 and appointed commander of the Philadelphia Navy Yard.*

Mr. Montgomery was John R. Montgomery (d. 1854), good friend of John Reynolds and able lawyer, in whose office James Reynolds first studied law.

the commencement, so now at the end I will bid you good bye, and with all, every bit, of love to you, once more, farewell

William

There will be other opportunities of writing before we leave here. I shall not miss any of them.

U.S. Ship Peacock
Honolulu Harbour, Sandwich Islands
October 19th 1840

To Father, Mother, Grandmother,
Aunt and all the Household
great and small,

Mother, Lydia and Sam have requested me to direct to them; as the wisest course, I address you all in the inside and put the Commandante's name[1] on the outside. I hope this will satisfy all.

We anchored here on the last day of September after a very tedious and disagreeable passage of 52 days from the Fegee Islands, and just 6 months from the time we left Sydney.[2] I had a letter partly finished then, and after extending it to the unwarrantable length of ten or eleven sheets, I sent it off some days ago in the Ship "Elizabeth," bound *Home,* direct for New Bedford. If you will have the patience to read it, you will learn how we have been employed since I last wrote from Sydney, in March.

[1] *A marginal note. By "commandante," William refers to his father.*
[2] *Both the* Peacock *and the* Vincennes *had dropped anchor in Honolulu harbor before. Lieutenant Thomas ap Catesby Jones had arrived in the* Peacock *in 1826, when he negotiated the first treaty of friendship and commerce between Hawaii and a Western nation and defused the continuing feud between the missionaries and the merchants. The visit of the* Vincennes, *Captain William C. B. Finch commanding, in 1829 resulted in a renegotiation of long-standing debts between the king and chiefs and the American sandalwood merchants.*

I wish I had detained this long letter, for *now* an opportunity offers, by which *this* will reach you in 70 or 75 days: about the 1st of January. The Elizabeth will not see America before March or April; slow but sure. This goes from here, day after to morrow, to *Mazatlan*, on the Coast of California or Mexico, and thence by Land.[3] Referring you to the long letter for particulars, I must be brief in this one. We touched at Tonga Taboo the 1st of May and then entered the Fegee Group, where we were hard at work surveying until the 11th of August, a little more than 3 months. The original idea had been to remain there but 6 weeks and then to hurry on here for provisions, so that we could get to the Columbia River in August or September, work there for two months, and then think about turning Homeward. But Captain Belcher of an English Surveying Ship came in to the Fegees and gave such accounts of the weather on the N. West Coast as broke up this plan altogether; he had been there two seasons and it was impossible to remain there after October set in. So, much to our dismay, it was resolved to stay where we were until a tolerably accurate survey could be finished and not go to the Columbia River until the Spring of 1841. *This arrangement will keep us out until May 1842*, or later, and you may be sure it was not relished much, but there was no help for it and we have put the best face on the matter that we can. I am not very much distressed, myself, as I have no *particularly strong ties* to draw *me* Home; but the young married men, and several who are relying on the faith of engagements, are in a state of utter sorrow and despair, poor fellows. It is very bad for them indeed and I esteem it as peculiar good fortune that I am so free and that there is nobody who cares *so* much for me as to feel in the least pathetical on account of this delay in *my* return; but there are many bright eyes that will be dimmed and tearful when the news is known, for my case is an exception, and almost every one else has a wife, or a lady, in waiting. Four years! it is an awful period to such folks: they ought to have known better.

True, I had much rather be among you all next August, but I am

---

[3] *Mazatlán is situated in Sinaloa state at the mouth of the Gulf of California, due east of the Hawaiian Islands. Its importance as a shipping and transfer point warranted the presence of a U.S. consul there in the 1830s and 1840s.*

reconciled and make light of it because those about me are so much worse off than myself. I can't sport with their misery, but I try to persuade them that the cruise will be over before they know it, and I am sure it will. Time has never hung heavy yet, and continual employment and change of scene banishes any thing like ennui. Two years and two months have passed already since we sailed and the rest will fly. When the time *does come,* there will be as happy a set of mortals let loose as the world ever saw. We shall be crazy with joy; you will see, I shall be so good and peaceful that I know you will be glad to keep me for a little while.

The Fegee people were mostly treacherous cannibals and we were obliged to be always cautious and on the defensive, either in our intercourse with them or whenever we left the Ship. The duty was very severe: we were away in open boats for 20, 30 and 40 days at a time, never daring to sleep on Shore or trust in any wise to the natives, exposed to the weather, cramped up in the small boats like shad in a barrel; with little sleep, most irregular meals and constant and harassing toil, this Boat duty yielded but little comfort or delight, yet it was performed cheerfully and all of us enjoyed excellent health. I never was more hearty in my life. We met with no accidents or losses, save the capture of one of the Vincennes' boats by the natives, which was recovered afterwards by an Expedition despatched for the purpose, until the work was nearly finished and we *began* to hope that we *might* leave the Islands without losing a life on our side. There were so many risks to run that we had always dreaded something fatal, to some one. It seemed to be hoping against hope to indulge the thought that we should all escape; but when more than two months had elapsed and all of us alive still, we congratulated ourselves on the prospect of leaving none of our number behind. But we were horribly disappointed: on the 24th July, Lt. Underwood and Midshipman Henry were murdered by the natives, under circumstances of the utmost treachery. While they were engaged in trading for Eatables among a crowd, they were beaten to death with clubs; several of the men had narrow escapes. Their bodies were recovered by the Boats that were near the scene of the Massacre, but that came *just too late to save.* Ten of the murderers were killed at this time, and two days afterwards they were attacked in their fortified town and in Canoes, and were beaten, with a loss of 90 men on their side, the Town and Canoes burnt, and much of their property destroyed. On our side, only a few were wounded with arrows. They begged for mercy and were completely humbled. The bodies of our poor martyred comrades were buried in one grave on an uninhabited Island not far from the place of their death. It was a melancholy satisfaction to know that the remains were saved from the hideous feast which the murderers would otherwise have made. Though such a violent and bloody end had been in the minds of us all, when it at last did fall upon the two whom we most loved, we were not the better prepared to bear with the affliction, but, as it might have been our own case, we felt it more acutely. It was terrible to know that *those two were gone* in such a place and by such a death! They were the very best among us: the one was married only 6 weeks before we sailed and the other contributed a part of his scanty pay to support a Widowed Mother. Their letters are *here* for them now and they *cold* in their lonely grave: the writers of these unread lines have yet to learn that they have lost those who were the dearest to them on Earth. Our grief, deep and sincere as it is, must be but light when we think of the Widowed Mother and the Widowed Wife; and when *they* learn of their bereavement, time, the chastener of all sorrow, will have softened, though it may never remove, our feelings of regret.

I need not say that when the day came for us to quit the group and its horrible people, it was a day of rejoicing; we were heartily tired and sick of them and we were almost crying for our letters, from which we had been so long delayed. Provisions were almost out and we were on a very scanty allowance of very indifferent food until we came here. Not quite so bad as the time of Starvation in the Schooner Boxer, but next door to it. I could not bear such deprivation now as well as when I was a boy. I found it a much more serious matter, but never mind, it's all over and suffering is nothing after it is passed.[4]

---

[4] *At the age of sixteen, Reynolds experienced fifty-three days of very short rations on the* Boxer. *On the short passage from Belém to Recife, Brazil, head winds and squalls sent the schooner almost back to Africa. Officers and men were put on an allowance of seven persons per three rations. "Our pork which seemed pretty large before it was cooked, when it was boiled was reduced to a terrible small size, so we eat it raw frequently to have more"* (Reynolds 1832).

I found a whole budget of letters, from February to Dec. of '39, and many papers; *you* were *all well* and I was glad that my dates were as late as any one's else. I am obliged to you all for having attended to me so well and I am quite sure, that if you get all the letters I have sent, you will be convinced that I have no disposition to neglect my part of the correspondence. I am afraid that you will not be able to get through with the half of what I have written, but you must try, and excuse all faults.[5] I did not find any letters from Father, John or *Cate.* Lydia mentioned that Father had written and I am very sorry that his should have gone astray; the other two, I am quite certain, did not write from the account you all give of their laziness.

Father's letters contained an acknowledgement of the receipt of an allotment of $40.00 a month, I suppose, for no one else mentions any thing about it. I sent this from Rio Janeiro and it was payable to Father, at the Navy agent's Philad.

Our extra pay has been stopped by the Secretary of the Navy and in my 'long letter' I mentioned that I would have this allotment discontinued; but on reflection I have determined not to do so, but to let it run on. I shall have to pay it back to the Department and there is no use taking any trouble about the thing now; my little fortune is gone and my trip to Europe must be performed in a more humble Style, that's all. I am determined not to give it up.

In the long letter, I said that there would [be] no opportunity to write to us except to Sincapore, but *this chance* appears a speedier way: in March 1841, a trading caravan will leave Montreal for the Columbia River; write to me under an envelope which direct to "D. McLaughuin, Agent of the Hudson's Bay Co., Columbia River; *Care* of the Agent of the Hudson's Bay Co., Montreal," paying the postage to Montreal. About the same time, a company will leave St. Louis, Missouri, to cross the Rocky Mountains; direct "to the Care of Jno. F. A. Sandford Esq., St. Louis," with a request to him to forward to Columbia River. These letters we will get before we quit the River and they will be a treat indeed. There is still a third way, by New Orleans and Mexico and Mazatlan, the direction of which I will add

---

[5] *Lydia's answer of 26 February 1841 assured him "I have told you not to be afraid of tiring us by long letters. We read every word; even Samuel, who has such an aversion to long letters, reads yours twice."*

as soon as I can procure it. I trust you will not let any of these slip by, for to wait a year, and then only trust to a most uncertain chance at Sincapore, is a thing not to be thought of.[6]

If it had not been for the unexpected offer of a vessel direct to Mazatlan, the Elizabeth would have conveyed you the first news of your wandering Son; it would be too late for you then to write by either of the routes I have named. Now, however, you have a fair and certain time to avail of and I am sure, when you remember that even the letters you then send will embrace a period of from 14 to 15 months since your last dates that we have received, you will all write me at length and make up a large package. I do not place much reliance on hearing from you at Sincapore; I fear you will not see vessels advertised, but you can send *monthly* through the Department and the Lyceum—this last is a very sure method. We expect to be in Sincapore in December of '41, or thereabouts, and will afterwards touch at the Cape of Good Hope and Rio de Janeiro. Up to September and October, letters sent would find us at the two first mentioned places and after that, until March, you will surely write every month to Rio Janeiro. Boston vessels are the most numerous around the C. of G. H.; from Baltimore and New York there is frequent communication with Rio Janeiro. Do not fail to write as I have requested, for if any letters go astray the loss will be on my side and the trouble but slight upon you.

I am still in excellent health: I have only been on the sick list one day, in Sydney. I could not be in better condition and you may be sure that I am thankful for this blessing, which I have learned by experience is the very greatest enjoyment that can be allowed us. With Health no one ought to complain.

There is nothing certain known regarding our destination during the winter months. We suppose that we will leave here in two or three weeks on a surveying cruise, but whether to the Kingsmill

---

[6] *In the same letter of 26 February, Lydia noted that they had tried all these avenues: "Kate Reynolds made such a wonderful effort and wrote you. They all wrote and sent their letters to Missouri, and Sam's went also. Father's went to Montreal and mine to Matzatlan." None of these letters is extant, except this one of Lydia's, which was received in January 1842 in Manila.*

Group or in another direction is all conjecture. Thank God, there are no more people like the Fegees to be visited; let us go where we will, we will not be so exposed again and there is much comfort in that thought. The Fegees have been a bugbear to all navigators ever since their discovery. We shall return here early next year to take on provisions and then proceed to the N. W. Coast, where we will remain, it is supposed, at least 4 or 5 months. We look forward to our stay there with much delight: the climate will be fine, there is abundance of Game, Ducks and Deer, and Salmon, so that we shall fare sumptuously and have rare sport in hunting. The settlers on the River are kind and hospitable, the country is interesting on many accounts, and I am sure we will enjoy ourselves highly—most certainly if we get the letters from Home. It will be so strange, will it not? *We* will be in America, in our own land, yet more than 3000 miles from our Homes and when we leave, we will have 21,000 miles to traverse, if we went direct, ere we can touch its opposite Shore.

The English are surely having an eye to the occupancy of that River: they have a fort there, they have surveyed it, they have vessels trading there from these Islands, and have an Agent residing here to regulate the trade. If they are allowed to put one foot in, they will soon follow with the other. Whoever fortifies the mouth of the River will have the Command of the whole Coast and of all our Territory: if our Government neglects this much longer, they will have another dispute to settle, of as much difficulty and importance as the Maine boundary is at present.[7] The Officers of Belcher's vessels, like true Englishmen, heard with surprise that we intended to Survey that Coast. They seemed to think it belonged to them and that we had no concern there at all. You may be sure that when Belcher reaches

---

[7] *The Northwest Coast—present-day British Columbia, Washington, Oregon, and Idaho—was occupied jointly by Britain and the United States under the terms of treaties of 1818 and 1827. The boundary between New Brunswick and Maine (then part of Massachusetts) was one of the ambiguities of the Treaty of Paris in 1783. After Maine achieved statehood in 1820, local resentment gradually increased until, in 1839, the national government felt compelled to intervene to prevent border warfare. General Winfield Scott was able to negotiate a temporary settlement, finally resolved in the Webster-Ashburton Treaty of 1842 (Clark 1977:82–86).*

England his Government will do something towards increasing the Colony they have there already. The English are too jealous of us. With Colonies all over the world, acquired by all sorts of means fair and foul, they will not hear of our possessing one. They raised a hue and cry about Texas and when I was in the Mediteranean, they were in agony at the rumour of our establishing a fort on the Coast of Morocco. They are jealous of the influence of our Missionaries here; though their Missionaries are spread over the richest Islands in these Seas, they say the American interest has been exerted here long enough and must be put down. They want a large slice of Maine and if we do not take care, they will be in the Columbia River before us, and we may get them out, if we can.

I have just been up in the Topmast Cross Trees[8] with my spy glass to see two natives hung on the walls of the Fort, almost immediately beneath my eye. The execution is over, the criminals are dead, and the crowd dispersed. It was conducted with much decorum and ceremony, and all the Military and Militia were paraded within the Fort. Their crime was murder; they poisoned a woman and now they have gone from the Earth, before their victim has grown cold in her grave.[9] There have been but one or two examples of this kind before and none very recently, so that the affair has caused great excitement. One of the murderers was a Chief and the intimate friend of the King,[10] and it was thought he would be saved—but justice had its course. The other was a common man; a son of his, the image of the

[8] *The topmast was the second section of the mast above the deck, which in turn supported the topgallant mast. The crosstrees were short timbers attached to the masthead which supported a small platform and to which were secured the shrouds for the upper mast section.*

[9] *According to Reynolds, this murder was the result of a recent law forbidding the dissolution of marriages. A chief of middling rank employed a commoner well versed in the art of poison to remove a wife he no longer desired. Reynolds deemed this law an injudicious reform on the part of the missionaries (Journal 2:163).*

[10] *Kauikeaouli (1814–1854), who had assumed the throne as Kamehameha III in 1824. He promulgated Hawaii's first constitution during the squadron's visit in 1840 and secured recognition of the kingdom's independence from the major Western powers in the Pacific (the United States, Great Britain, and France) in 1842 and 1843.*

"Fat Boy" in Pickwick, attends on us with his Boat and is a great favorite on account of his good nature and his readiness to work; he is not so lazy as his great original.[11] I asked him last night if he would see his Father hung? He said, he no like to see that! Did he expect ever to see his Father again? "Yes, suppose me die, me see him up there!" He was far from being sad, however, and I suspect he never knew what care was.

I am living quite comfortably here, have part of a fine airy house on Shore where I make myself perfectly at Home;[12] a bath house is attached to it, where I almost drown myself by showers of fresh water both morning and evening. The virtues of this I think are beyond all praise. I feel as if I had added a year to my life every time I quit the bath; it is a pity it is so much neglected among us. If I ever live ashore, I will not suffer a day to pass without deluging myself from head to foot—'tis better than all the physic in the world, try it and you will say so. A momentary laziness is all that is to be overcome; after the suspense attending the first shower, you are in a perfect glow of rapture.

I ride two evenings out of four, always with three or four in Company; the gallop of 5 or 6 miles is exhilerating and it is only necessary to remember Fegee to increase the excitement to absolute hilarity and joy. The Horses here, as in most other places, are trained to go at the gallop, and bound and leap like so many greyhounds. We never ride at the jog trot, peaceable gait practised at Home, but rush along against the wind, and prance and jump and carry on like mad. I wish you could see us: at Home we would be called crazy and pelted in the streets, but 'tis not so abroad. A Sailor on Horseback

[11] *The fat boy is Joe, Mr. Wardle's indolent servant at Dingley Dell in Kent, where the members of the Pickwick Club visited on an outing and later spent Christmas (Dickens 1938:chaps. 6–8, 28).*

[12] *Reynolds and some of his friends were frequent visitors in the pleasant home of "Halileo." This was undoubtedly Timothy Haalilio, private secretary to Kamehameha III, who in 1842 would travel with William Richards, the king's adviser and translator, to the United States, Britain, and France to obtain treaties of recognition and died on the return trip. Several of the officers rented two small houses within Haalilio's very pretty garden. They rode with him, played billiards and ten pins, and altogether felt very much at home (Journal 2:144).*

Hawaiian Island, by Alfred Agate. Reynolds long felt the attraction of the Pacific islands, returning to Hawaii during the 1850s after he left the navy for reasons of health. Courtesy Naval Historical Foundation, Washington, D.C.

and he rides—the old proverb is almost true. I am about hiring a Splendid Horse from the King's Secretary for my own use, only $15.00 a month, which will be a saving. The House is the same and among 7 of us costs nothing. After Fegee, this is grand and I have learned to enjoy moments as they pass. When we leave this port, we leave all such diversions behind, not to be renewed in a long, long time. . . .

Jane[13] and Kate will be so elegant and accomplished as to throw all the rest of us in the Shade. I am very happy that they were removed from Lancaster and shall waltz with them to their hearts' content. I have not spoken to a Lady since I left Home and I am as rude and uncouth as a Bear; you will have to civilize me when this 4 years of rough servitude are over. There are few who have retained their good manners; we are all alike, perfect monsters and very vulgar. . . .[14]

I have written *so* much in the long letter, that I am confused here; I do not like to make repetitions. You will find in it all that is unsaid in this hasty affair, for I have scarcely had an hour to give to you. The chance was so unexpected and the time so short, that I could do no better; you must excuse errors. I will try and write a long letter

---

[13] *Mary Jane Reynolds (1824–1901) married George Gildersleeve (1822–1900) of Baltimore in 1849 and had one son, William Reynolds Gildersleeve (1851–1869). The news of the death of his first namesake greeted Captain Reynolds on his return from the* Lackawanna *and Hawaii.*

[14] *Lydia answered (1841a), "Kate* [age fifteen] *is very much altered. Her person particularly is improved. You were afraid she would not have any figure at all, but hers will be better than Jane's I think. . . . Kate seldom writes to anyone. She was out here* [from Lancaster] *for a day or two and did nothing but laugh and sleigh all the time. She is the greatest laugher I ever heard." On 26 February she added, "Jane will be home the latter part of next month . . . I hope to spend a pleasant summer with her to ride and walk with. . . . Since you left, I have had no companion to roam through the woods with at all, except when the* [Coleman] *girls are here." Jane (age seventeen) wrote on 17 June: "Lydia is more lively than ever and they all say I have made her as wild and bad as myself, but don't believe it. I am getting quite a sober girl—all my wild oats are sown." She consoled her elder brother, "We will revive the ancient days of chivalry, when the ladies polished the manners of the more rude sex. You say you are all so unpolished."*

by the Lausanne, to sail about the 1st November. She carried 19 missionaries to the Columbia River from the U.S. 9 months ago. I send a great deal of love to you all, from Grandmother to Elly. Remember me to all who inquire for me and believe me yours most affectionately,

William R.

The "Brig Harlequin" has been delayed in her sailing and I have taken a moment that offers to scribble a little more. I think this is the first time I have *crossed* a letter for it is a practise that is reprobate in the extreme; the only redeeming thing is the use of a different ink. Do not follow my example, however, and I will not use it again. . . .[15]

When the young ladies visit you, I have not the slightest objection to their reading any or all my letters, but shall feel very much flattered if they find the least interest in the perusal of my indifferent attempts.[16] I am quite confident they will be too merciful to criticize that which is written in the careless security which every one practices when addressing those of whose affection he is sure.

I only wish you to guard against making public any information from me that will find its way in the papers. Several letters purporting to be from officers have been published and there has been much difficulty here among us about this which is not settled yet. I disobey positive orders when I write to you concerning our movements, but the injunction is so unnatural that I cannot respect it. What else should I write about? The idea is so absurd. I will tell you all I know, but I do not care to be drawn into trouble. Not to publish is all very proper, but not to write Home—I will not yield that privilege. Captain Wilkes is making a great to do about a letter in the Philad. Papers which termed him "delirious," etc. etc. I would *whisper*

---

[15] *The last four pages of Letter No. 16—beginning with this paragraph—are overwritten at 90 degrees, often illegibly. Problematical passages are bracketed.*

[16] *Reynolds refers to Anne, Margaret, Sarah, and Isabel Coleman.*

to you that in charity to *him,* we have thought him crazy more than once.

Since I quit his Ship, I have been unmolested and quiet on board here and I expect to remain where I am until the cruise is over. I have not the same elegant and comfortable quarters that we had in the Vincennes, and this Ship is far from being in as good order as the order on board her in which I took so much pride. Things are most lamentably changed there also—the rooms that we occupied have been knocked away in a peak of petulant spite by Captain Wilkes and all *hands* live in Common as in the Steerage of a man of war.[17] May and I spent $100.00 in Norfolk and Rio in decorating our apartment and making it comfortable. We made it a little palace and it was far more tasteful than any room I ever saw on board a Ship, thanks to May's [work]. We were very happy in it and it really was the pride of the Ship. When visitors came on board, they were always shown it that they might see how well we were accommodated. Wilkes tore it away without the shadow of a reason, and all its expensive fixtures were rendered useless and went to the dogs. I owe him a heavy debt for a million [wrongs, but] I am one of his lightest creditors.[18] However, this is a subject which I have forbidden myself to trouble you about. I beg you will be contented to know that I am in no difficulty myself and that I have no wish to quit this Ship.

May has been ordered back to the Vincennes so that [we are] only together when in port.

I have tried my new Horse: he would eclipse Jim's actions even on his best days.[19] [*Illegible*] all the rides here are superb, through and up valleys [with raging] streams and waterfalls hemmed in by magnificent hills and affording views of Land and Ocean that are really Sublime. Every time I mount, I consider that I am doing more

[17] *In a man of war, the steerage was the common quarters of junior officers.*

[18] *Reynolds reported in his Journal (1:344) that he and May had spent $150 on the embellishment of their "room" and added that Lieutenant Alden had been turned out of his cabin for Dr. Fox—all "to gratify the malignant spite of Mr. Wilkes."*

[19] *Jim was brother Sam's horse.*

for my health and spirits than any other kind of recreation could afford. I am always [heady] with delight when in the midst of fine Scenery and every one knows the excitement in the gallop of a generous horse.

This place is a great resort for Whalers to refresh their crews. Several days ago we saw an American Whaling Ship heading for the anchorage with her colours at half mast and went out to render assistance and found "all hands" from the Captain to the Cook afflicted with the Scurvy and in a very bad way. They could not work the Ship; he had buried 4 men and had been afraid that they should not get here in time to save the rest. I never saw a man more grateful than he was to find his country men alongside and tendering them aid. He fairly hugged me, was not content with [setting] Brandy and [asked] for tea to drink. He wanted to break[fast first and then] had some Brandy. He was very happy to find himself in a Port. I looked at his men's limbs and they were really a horrible sight. They were sent on Shore and are recovering. We have only had one scurvy case in the Squadron and none since we left Cape Horn.

The time has come; the "Harlequin" is going out and I [must end and] say farewell. I shall surely mind Grandmother's [third] caution to take care of myself, and with remembrances to friends and the greatest Love to you all. Good bye,

Wm. Reynolds

. . . I have not collected many curiosities; the Government is so selfish as to require *all Specimens* for the [Public] Stock. Some that [I] have, [the] chance [furnished]. In the English Expedition when two Specimens of each article were procured the officers were at liberty to collect for themselves. The policy adopted with us has not been attended with good effect and I suspect will be remonstrated against when we get Home. It is too unfair to submit to.

I think you all must be very happy at Cornwall and sometimes almost envy the quiet life you lead there. How different it is from this [strange] life of mine, but there are joys attending even the wildest hazards of the Seas that all the luxuries and comforts of the Shore could never purchase and I would not give the last 9 years of my existence for an hundred passed on the [Shore].

[*Inside wrapper:*]

I note the directions here to avoid mistakes

"Under cover to Dr. D. McLaughuin, Fort Vancouver, Columbia River. Care of Agent, Hudson's Bay Co. Montreal." Post paid with request to be forwarded immediately, and written in February next.

To me, Ex. Expedition, Fort Vancouver, Columbia River: Care of Jno. F. A. Sandford, St. Louis, Miss. Post paid to St. Louis and request to be forwarded. Also in February.

Again, to be sent *at once*. Under cover "Via New Orleans, to Parrot Scarborough and Co., *Mazatlan,*" post paid to New Orleans.

Do not fail to try these three.

W.R.

Jno. Reynolds etc. etc.
Care of Pierce, Brewer
Oahu, Sandwich Islands

[*Outside wrapper:*] John Reynolds, Esq.
Lebanon, Pennsylvania
United States of America

By Brig Harlequin
for Matzatlan

Came to hand February 11th, 1841

[*Postmark:*] New Orleans, La.
Jan. 27

Peacock, Honolulu, Nov. 16th 1840

My dear Father, Mother,
Grandmother, Aunt, Sam,
Lydia, and "all hands,"

A Ship will sail for New York in a few days and I will send by her this letter, and perhaps something else.

I have written to you twice from this port, once by way of Mexico and again by a Whaler bound Home by Cape Horn, both of which you will certainly have received before *this* makes its appearance and so be apprised of our doings up to this time.

We have been making some repairs to the different vessels and building two fine Launches for Vincennes and Peacock; the observatory is in full swing; the Scientifics have gone on different tours;[1] the men have had their 'liberty' and as their times were out, some of them have refused to serve any longer and have been discharged. Natives have been taken to supply their places, but these make but a poor fist on board Ship. We have 17 of them on board and to get them to work properly is the most worrying task I ever undertook. We shall miss our lost Seamen very much, but nothing would induce them to re-enter.[2]

[1] *The scientifics visited several of the other Hawaiian islands on collecting trips in the* Flying Fish.

[2] *By law, if seamen whose terms of enlistment expired while abroad chose not to reenlist, their commanders were obliged to return them to the United States by public or private vessel; sailors who reenlisted were entitled to a bonus of one-fourth of their annual pay (Langley 1967:88–89).*

The Porpoise is to sail in a day or two for the Marquesas Islands and Tahita as is conjectured, no one knows with any certainty.[3] The Peacock, it is supposed, will go in ten days, but whither we know not and, of course, feel quite satisfied and comfortable in our ignorance. We do not know how long we will be gone or whether we will come back here at all before we proceed to the Columbia River, so that in this, which concerns us so much, we are no wiser than you are at Home. The general idea of the remainder of the cruise I have sketched in the former letters and have nothing new to add.

I have been enjoying myself in every way during the past 45 days and find life here to be much more delightful than it was in the Feegee: I have ridden almost every evening on a fine Horse of my own, for the time being; I have rolled ten pins on an excellent alley and felt the good effects of the healthy exercise; I have sluiced myself with torrents of cool fresh water and thus refreshed myself beyond measure, and I have broken the Ice, at last, and figured away at several parties with a zest that was not at all diminished by long deprivation.[4]

Dancing assemblies are of very rare occurrence at these Islands, but we have been able to muster a few among the families of the foreign residents and I could not resist the temptation to shake a foot once more. Nevertheless, I must own that the attraction so far as the Ladies were concerned was not very fascinating, there being only one single *woman* in the place and she a *girl* of sixteen—pretty to gaze on but without animation, and with conversational powers only equal to the occasional ejaculations of yes and no. Miss Fanny was the solitary bud amidst the fading flowers of the elders of her sex and as such she received the most universal attention, but she made no conquests and my Heart is safe as ever. Still, it was so new and strange to find

[3] *Between November 1840 and March 1841, during the expedition's stopover at Hawaii, the* Porpoise *under Cadwallader Ringgold cruised over a large area of the southeastern Pacific, through the Line Islands and back to the Tuamotu archipelago and the Society Islands, searching for reported islands, correcting their own earlier surveys, and core drilling in coral.*

[4] *"I thought you would not come home without being at some party or other. Fate always throws some ladies in your way" was Jane's teasing reply to this passage (1841).*

myself, once more, actually in a room full of women (not so *very* full either) and engaging in the mazes of the dance, that when I thought of Feegee, it seemed as if I was subject to changes bordering on the Supernatural and as wonderful as those we read of in the Fairy tales. Several of the married dames had some beauty to reccommend them and to my eyes all were fair enough, but there were none who could interest me as a companion and I was confined to nonsense and small talk, much to my regret. There is nothing that would afford me so much delight as the occasional society of women, such as I *have* known. I have such an abundance of thoughts stored up that I have no chance to utter, but which I should glory in sharing with those who would feel their influence alike with myself. I am aweary of the converse of men; they are too rude and unsympathizing, and I do long for the day of our return, that I may seek the presence of the Softer Sex and repay myself for this never ending Quarantine.

We also have given a party in return, procuring for that purpose a House in the Country, which we decorated in the most tasteful manner after a Sailor's fashion by arranging National flags and gay colored signals, and various other nautical ornaments, so that the effect was very splendid and far exceeded any thing of the kind ever attempted at the Islands. The interior had the appearance of a gorgeous pavillion fit for the reception of a monarch and our guests were both astonished and delighted to witness so grand a display. It has been the talk and wonder of the Town ever since, and all agree that we have been the first to show these people *how* such things can be done. We spared no expense and we succeeded to our hearts' content.

The King was not present, as He is living on another Island, but the Governor and His Majesty's Secretary[5] honored us and they were

---

[5] *The king was in Maui. The governor of Oahu was Kekuanaoa, whom Reynolds describes as "graceful, looking the well bred gentleman," well liked and a judicious manager of island affairs (Journal 2:144). Kekuanaoa was married to Kinau, the king's sister and premier of the government; their son Alexander Liholiho (1834–1863) succeeded to the throne in 1854 as Kamehameha IV. Some twenty-five years later, in June 1867, Captain Reynolds was to receive Mateo Kekuanaoa for a visit on board his command the* Lackawanna *in Honolulu harbor. Timothy Haalilio was the king's secretary (Letter No. 16, n. 12).*

nearly dumb with surprise: the long array of tables, the quantity of eatables and drinkables, the gaudy drapery, and the well dressed crowd, all formed a spectacle which they declared they had never witnessed the like of, and which they regretted the King was not here to see. English, French and Russians have been before us, but we outdid them all, and our Countrymen here are quite enthusiastic in their praise and happy that this result was produced by the first great National Expedition of our free and enlightened people. Amen.

I have ventured myself at a Ladies' tea table once or twice, and really, I found the beverage much more palatable coming from a delicate hand than that with which I have been nightly served during the cruise by our dark visaged imp of the Steerage. Indeed, I feel the influence of the Sex so keenly after the slight intercourse I have indulged in here, that I am actually a *little* homesick for the first time this cruise. It is well that I have never been strongly tempted, for I should certainly have made a fool of myself; but, really, I have not met with, or heard of, any lady with charms sufficient to fascinate even a miserable Sailor. I suspect there are plenty at Home, however, and I long for the day when I shall get *there* to see: once more, amen! This is all very foolish! but I am in a very curious humor and you must bear with it.

After the starvation passage from the Fegees, and the very limited variety of food that fell to our lot while among that accursed group, the living here is really luxurious. The tables are turned and *we* have the advantage of even *you*, now. The climate is Heavenly—I know what November is at Home—and vegetables and fruits are in profusion. While there are scarcely any of the tropical fruits to be found on the Island, some of our own are in the greatest abundance and of a flavour not at all inferior to the productions of a colder clime—particularly water and musk melons. I live on them almost entirely and drink almost as much milk as in the never to be forgotten days of old Peggy and the auld black cow; the latter certainly was a mother to me, and I regard her memory to this day with as much veneration as I felt regret for the unceremonious manner in which she was disposed of. Well, we live famously, and have made up for past suffering; indeed, we have even anticipated somewhat and provided for privations yet to come: *Sea Stores* are very scarce here and of those sent out from New York many were spoiled, so that we will be on poor fare until next Spring when we expect to live upon game and

every thing that's good during our stay about the Columbia River.[6]
The crew of a Ship lately from the C.R. grew *tired* of feeding on
venison. That is better than becoming disgusted with nothing at all, as
has been our case so recently.

I would very gladly give Grandmother some account of the Islands
if I could do so to any extent, or with any fairness, but in the very
short intervals that I have to devote to letter writing I can not find the
leisure necessary for such an attempt. As yet, I have had no time to
think. I have seen much and heard more, but until one can reflect
upon these things and arrange his impressions, it is idle to record
them; so I will not venture to say a word now, but I shall be too
happy to run my tongue for a whole month, or as long as I can find
interested listeners, when I am once more among you all. I can
venture the assertion that you will be tired first. I want a chance to
talk and you will find me possessed of all a traveller's garrulity about
things, "all or most of which I saw and part of which I was"; to
extend the matter, I have had to modify the quotation.

As for writing, I have troubled you with two monstrous epistles
already and it will be wise for me, and no doubt gratifying to you, if I
make this brief and not weary you with my absurdities. I hope you
obeyed implicitly the directions for sending letters contained most
particularly in the letter by Mexico. If you have, I shall surely hear
from you before we leave the Pacific; and this will be the most joyful,
because it was so unexpected. It will repay me in a measure for
our protracted absence from Home, itself. I wonder whether you will

---

[6] *Reynolds was a caterer on the* Peacock *again, and by the end of the
month he could write in Journal No. 2 that he was very pleased to have been
able to procure a liberal share of the $500 worth of supplies which he had
ordered in Callao for the* Vincennes. *He had "every stow hole full [of
supplies for his mess] when on the last day of November, I was thrown
into despair by receiving orders to the* Flying Fish *and she to sail the next
morning. . . . Bundled my traps aboard and found myself in a mess utterly
destitute of any stock whatsoever. . . . Luckily the schooner needed repairs
and I had a part of two days to transfer a few things from the* Peacock *and
to purchase some other on shore, but I regarded with a sad stomach the very
scanty supply upon which I was to depend while others were feasting on the
bountiful store which I had taken so much trouble to procure."*

feel as much regret, mingled with your astonishment, when you first learn of the prolonging of the cruise, as I did when it was announced? I scarcely think you did, but I am quite sure all of you will recover from the dreadful shock as easily as I have and that you will be as glad to see me at the end of four years as you would have been a twelvemonth earlier.[7] Mean while, I shall have a chance to visit places which must have been neglected otherwise, and my curiosity is not abated yet, but rather strengthened by the wonders I have seen; my love for adventure is also as keen as ever.

We have just received papers of June 10th by a Brig from New York. Several were so fortunate as to get letters, but as the opportunity was scarcely known, even at that port, I readily acquit you of any neglect. My expectations were not raised at her arrival, I indulged in no hopes of being blessed with a line from Home, but I envied the few whose dates were so very recent and who had friends on the spot to give timely warning and to take advantage of the chance. My trust lies strong in the answers to my letter by Mazatlan—I am sure I shall get *them*. You will not fail to write, as I requested, and *then* I shall be contented and almost happy.

The papers have parts of Elliott's trial, and the little that we have seen has made us the more anxious to know the result, which at this time is an old song with you. I suppose his sentence was severe. Flogging is abolished, the Pensions cut off, and Promotion slower than ever—three things not at all calculated to benefit the Service.

As to the latter, I look forward to being a Lieut. when I get to be past 30, and in regard to a Captaincy, I consider *that* as distant as the day of judgement. About 20 years after the term of my natural life

---

[7] *Lydia wrote back on 14 February: "Your delay in returning is a great disappointment to us indeed, for I was expecting we should all be together again once more this summer. John will graduate* [from West Point] *this summer and have three months leave perhaps and Samuel will probably be here this year and James' vacation* [is] *in the fall, so we might have passed a delightful time, but that is all over now, and we must wait another whole year for your return. Really it is too bad." His sister also noted (1841d) "that you, dear brother, have not spent a Christmas with us for 10 or 11 years." Lydia's expression of regret was received in New York the month after his return—in August 1842.*

shall have expired will come "my turn to be Captain." To look forward is dreadful; prospects could not be worse and I do not know what to do, unless they mend. However, I am fixed safe enough until the cruise is over. I *must* see *it out*, and then will be time enough to think of what's to be done next. I must try something, I cannot be a Midshipman until the prime of life is over. I am crazy when I think of this. I seldom allow it to trouble me, but when I do, every thing else is driven from my mind and I am miserable. I want to be something better, my pride is dying fast. All that I want, and all that the rest of us ask, is for the Government to fit out the vessels we have instead of letting them rot, promote us who are dying for promotion, and send us to Sea in the rank we ought to occupy. Lieuts. over 50 and Midshipmen from 25 to 30—it is horrible, a sweep in the streets is better off.

I notice the arrival of an Arabian Ship from Muscat. I should like to see her and her officers; I dare say I knew some of them. That Sultan *is a Sultan*: he is one of the remarkable men of the age, though his history is but little known and he is certainly about 500 years in advance of any of his neighbours. It was just like him to send that Ship to America, and I think her voyage as wonderful, almost, as the first one of Columbus, an unheard of and miraculous affair without a parrellel in History.[8]

I would inflict a chapter on you concerning this same Sultan had I time, but I am hard pushed, which must account for the very wretched and abrupt style of this letter. What a pity that the presents had to be sold! Congress must have a very tender conscience in such matters. I think the things might have been kept as national property without endangering the liberties of the republic, but to sell them by Auction! Better have thrown them in the Sea, but we *are* a great

---

[8] *Reynolds refers to the arrival of the Omani ship* Sultanah *in New York in April 1840, perhaps the first trading mission from the Middle East to arrive in the United States. The ship, a twenty-gun corvette, was sent by Sayyid Sa'id bin Sultan Al Bu Sa'id (1788–1854) in furtherance of the treaty of friendship and commerce of 1834 between his kingdom—which ranged from Oman south to Zanzibar—and the United States. Some seven years earlier, Reynolds in the* Peacock *had visited Muscat as part of Edmund Roberts's mission to negotiate the treaty (Oman-U.S.A. 1983:5–13; Phillips 1967:105–11).*

people and like the King can do no wrong. I see new proof of this every day. Why cannot men do away with prejudices that are a disgrace to the age we live in and to the enlightened wisdom that is so generally proffesed? Oh! what a paltry return to the magnificent and noble generosity of the Sultan! Why *we* gave *him* presents twice, but they were such that a private individual would not have owned, much less offered to another; yet *His* costly ones must be refused and sold.[9] We *are* a great nation! beyond any doubt, and deserve all the praise we covet so much as the most liberal people under the Sun.

I send you several sermons delivered by the Chaplain of the Expedition on the occasion of the murder of Underwood and Henry among the Fegees. I have more of them, and you may dispose of them as you like. I also send one newspaper, the Polynesian, printed at this place.[10] I have bought a file of papers for 3 years back on purpose for Grandmother to read; these I cannot send, however, but will bring them when I come myself.

November 29th

Yesterday a vessel came in from Mazatlan, bringing news from the U.S. up to September 13th, less than 80 days old. Several of the

[9] *When Edmund Roberts returned to exchange ratifications of the treaty in 1835, he brought with him a complete proof set of U.S. coins in a crimson leather-covered box; other gifts included an American flag and map of the United States, a book of poems, and several cut-glass lamps (Newman 1962:62–65; Phillips 1967:107).*

The gifts presented by the sultan's representative on the Sultanah *in 1840 caused a stir during that election year. To avoid political liability, President Van Buren had two Arabian stallions sold at auction; the other gifts, including a presentation sword and a carpet, were accepted in behalf of the people of the United States. In return, the United States presented a barge built by the navy, Colt firearms, mirrors, and a chandelier (Oman-U.S.A. 1983:12–13; Eilts 1962).*

Reynolds presumably was deprecating the gifts presented during the Roberts missions. The set of coins is no longer extant; however, a second set struck at the same time for presentation by Roberts to the king of Siam is now in a private collection in this country.

[10] *The* Polynesian *was a weekly published in Honolulu beginning in 1840; it ceased operations in 1863.*

officers got letters by her and they are the envied of all the Squadron. This proves how sure and speedy is the conveyance by which I requested you to write to me and by which I am sure I shall be favoured, ere we quit the Pacific. We hear that Paulding has retired from office and that Poinsett is Secretary, and hope for better things and promotion.[11] If I am not made a Lieut. soon, I shall die of pure shame and grief, and dispair and disgust, and this will, of course, be a loss to the Service and the Country which will be severely felt. We learn that the Expedition is becoming popular and that the news of the Southern Continent was received with great Enthusiasm, that Harrison is sure of his Election,[12] that the Maine Boundary is settled, that the French and English are going to war at once etc. etc.—half of which I do not believe.

The Lausanne sails in the morning for New York, it is now past

[11] *Joel Roberts Poinsett (1779–1851), a South Carolinian who had served as a special commissioner in Latin America during the wars for independence, member of Congress, and minister to Mexico. As secretary of war under Van Buren, he had pushed Navy Secretary Mahlon Dickerson to launch the expedition, taking an active role in the selection of Wilkes as commander and in its organization. Active in the cultural arena, Poinsett was influential in the later disposition of the expedition's collections to the care of the National Institute, a forerunner of the Smithsonian Institution and which he had founded in Washington.*

[12] *At just about this same date, Lydia was describing the political commotion in Lancaster. 5–6 November: "The Whigs had a convention here [18 September]. The children were coming in to school and I came in to see the fun also . . . it poured all day, yet the town was crowded; every place was full. I never saw such a concourse of people in my life . . . as was in the procession. . . . A great many of the banners were beautiful, they had several log cabins on wheels drawn by horses, and Fort Meigs, and a boat with rails manned by boys dressed as sailors, drawn by horses also, and the different trades, blacksmith's shop with the celebrated Buckeye blacksmith at work . . . a printing office and several others. . . . James I suppose has told you about the election. Such a state of excitement as the people are in never was heard of. If Van Buren is elected, it will [be] pretty tight work." Jane added, "Ladies have caught the mania. . . . They ride about with Tippecanoe flags and sing nothing but Harrison songs. . . . The ladies are almost as warm as the gentlemen."*

midnight, and I have left my cot to bid you good bye; I must close this so that it will be ready. I have to beg that you will excuse the wretched style of this letter. I have had no leisure and I have never been able to quiet my mind down to sober thinking since our arrival here. The only excuse I have for sending it is that I *must* write something and have nothing better to offer.

We sail certainly in two or three days; it is conjectured that we are going among the Caroline Islands and that we are to have a delightful cruise, all by ourselves, but in reality we do not know where we are going. We think we will not return here until we have finished the N.W. Coast, perhaps not then even. There is no telling; all that is given out is that we are to be Home in May 1842, as Wilkes most profanely said to his crew, "God willing, or not." That day will be one of rejoicing when it comes, and I think time will fly with us: 18 months will very soon be over and I shall be too happy to be once more at Home. So good bye to you all. I send Elly some kisses and would give *all* my money for a sight of her sweet little face.

Next time I go to Sea, I shall take somebody's child with me to keep alive the milk of human kindness in my breast. I am so tired of men as rude as myself. . . . If I could only have had a letter of September! . . . It's hard to see a few so happy and smiling, and I tried *to buy* a letter to day in vain—the odour of Home was too recent upon them and the most liberal offers were refused. . . .

God's blessing be with you all and may he keep us, so that all shall meet and none be missed. Once more, good bye.

Wm. Reynolds

[*Outside wrapper*:] Ship Lausanne
New York

[*Postmark*:] New York, Apr. 15

Honolulu
June 1841

William Reynolds's list of letters includes a fourth letter from Honolulu, dated 25 June 1841. Because this letter was presumably lost, his family had no word from him after Letter No. 17 of November 1840 until Letter No. 19, which closed exactly twelve months later. Hence they had no knowledge of his transfer to the schooner *Flying Fish* in November 1840 or of the subsequent six-month surveying expedition. This period is covered in both the Public Journal (155–208) and the Journal (2:169–264), each in its particular fashion.

Public Journal (155): "On 30th November, I joined the Flying Fish agreeably to orders Received that day from Captain Wilkes."

Journal (2:169): "Old Knox was again in command of the schooner and I knew we should agree much better than 3 in a bed, but two men form a poor society and, despite of some disagreeable duties aboard ship, I felt I would prefer the Peacock with her comforts and the companionship of 20 fellows to the tiny schooner and a solitary associate, amiable as he might be."[1]

[1] *Passed Midshipman Samuel R. Knox commanded the* Flying Fish *during most of the cruise, until the schooner was sold in Singapore. The descendant of Boston pilot boat captains, he had served in the navy some ten years before the expedition sailed, with both Mediterranean and Pacific service. Promoted to lieutenant in 1841, Knox was placed on the reserved list in 1855. During the Civil War, he volunteered for duty and served as first*

The *Flying Fish* sailed from Honolulu in company with the *Peacock* on 2 December. Orders from Captain Hudson told her two officers, to their considerable astonishment, that they were headed once more for Samoa, with "some islands and shoals on the way." (This and the following quotations are from Journal 2:169–264.) Wilkes had learned from Captain Belcher of HMS *Sulphur* that the weather in the Oregon territory would preclude their going there before spring, so the commander conceived of a number of items of unfinished business—cruises for the *Porpoise, Peacock,* and *Flying Fish* and his own ascent of Mauna Loa—to occupy the intervening time. On the *Flying Fish*, this meant long stretches of time with "nothing to do from morning til night, but to stare at each other and to talk about any and every thing."

> My Birthday! [*10 December*] passed quietly, but I drank a bumper of Champaign to all hands at home. 25 years old—over 9 years in Service and a miserable midshipman still. . . . And this is Christmas! but alas! how unlike the merry, many headed Christmas such as I remember in days of yore . . . Christmas, joyous, hearty, old Christmas. . . . Ten times hast thou rolled by and found me among strangers. . . . I see one old and sea worn mortal as my only companion . . . Old Sam Knox . . . seated 2 $\frac{1}{2}$ feet across the table . . . Sam Knox is one of the very best old fellows in the world and he has a heap of shrewd common sense. . . . An excellent sailor . . . worth his weight in gold . . . has a good and a kind heart. . . . Been at sea almost his whole life, as have his father, grandfather and all his brothers . . . Sam Knox and I never became cross at each other.

But the voyage was dull and uncomfortable. There were no books; Reynolds had just supplied the *Peacock* with new ones at Oahu. The

---

lieutenant and executive officer on the USS South Carolina *under fellow expedition officer James Alden (Letter No. 15, n. 38). Alden wrote on 20 December 1861 to the commander of the Gulf Blockading Squadron that, although Knox had "done good and efficient service" during the previous half year, nevertheless (and here Alden was influenced possibly by two instances of Knox's drunkenness), "he is too old and broken for the position, not enough perhaps to be condemned by survey; but a man of more than fifty is, you will admit, very likely to become of less and less use the longer he is kept in a subordinate position, and particularly when he sees his juniors constantly placed above him in the same squadron" (ZB). Despite Alden's recommendation that Knox be returned home, the latter apparently served at least until becoming a captain in 1867.*

Sailor at ease, by Alfred Agate. This drawing shows the typical daily dress of seamen of the period. Courtesy Naval Historical Foundation, Washington, D.C.

hatch acted like a shower bath; in the least sea, the table was useless. They could not walk or even stand in their tiny quarters unless there was something to hold on to, "and there was nothing to hold on to." No exercise: "I am pining for a run among the woods. . . . Never in my life have I been so idle." There were two poor meals a day, no supper, because the schooner did not carry wood enough for a fire after 4 P.M.

After surveying small islands in the Phoenix Group, on 25 January they made Duke of York (Atafu in the Tokelau Group), some two thousand miles south of Oahu. The *Peacock*'s boat went ashore, but not the *Flying Fish:* "55 days have I been confined to this diminutive craft and never ashore to stretch my limbs." "Old Knox" got tired of listening to him: "Well, you shall go ashore if the boat will float." With a bailer, the leaking boat was not too bad. "I felt like a bird let out its cage!" The island had been marked as uninhabited by the *Pandora* on her search for the mutineers of the *Bounty* in 1791. Now there were people, natives who appeared delighted to see them. "It was with a curious interest that I wandered about with the Chief, his arms thrown around me, his tongue going as if I understood all he said. I have been all over the world. . . . He had never left his shores. We were a strong contrast."

They found a previously uncharted island. Reynolds regretted very much he could not go ashore because it was evident the people there knew less of the white race than any other. Captain Hudson, who was treated like a god, named their discovery Bowditch Island.[2]

Finally, on 6 February, they made the Navigator Group. The *Peacock* hove to off Upolu. "Not to go into Port at all! but to commence a survey of the Island at even. and carry it all around. . . . 66 days at Sea! right off the Harbour, full of the idea of entering. . . . Was it not *too* bad? besides this, the Island had been perfectly surveyed when we were here before—this same Schooner had circumnavigated it; the Peacock's boats had worked all around it and Judge, Chase and my miserable self were fried to death for 4 or 5 days in 'fixing in' the reefs and shores for 20 miles to the west of Apia."[3] He asked Captain Hudson for permission to anchor; it was granted.

The natives welcomed them exuberantly. Reynolds walked toward the village, came across the grave marker for the murdered missionaries Mr. Williams and Mr. Harris, saw the new church and missionary Mr.

---

[2] *Named for Nathaniel Bowditch (1773–1838), under whom Charles Wilkes had studied in 1837; see Introduction, n. 3.*

[3] *"Judge" refers to George Foster Emmons (1811–1884), who was promoted to lieutenant at the very time of Reynolds's entry. A Vermonter, whose family had emigrated from England in 1718, he had seen service in the West Indies and the Mediterranean. Emmons went on to serve in California during the Mexican War and the Brazil station twice and published a history of the navy in 1850. After the Civil War, he commanded the USS* Ossippe *which took U.S. representatives to assume claim to Alaska and commanded the Hydrographic Office and the Philadelphia Navy Yard before retiring in 1873 as a rear admiral (ZB).*

"Chase" must refer to New Yorker Lieutenant Augustus L. Case (1813– 1893). He had been assigned to the expedition in 1837 when it was under the command of Thomas ap C. Jones and served on the Relief *until it was detached from the squadron and subsequently on the* Vincennes. *During the Civil War, Case was attached to the North Atlantic Blockading Squadron and went on to a distinguished career as commodore and rear admiral, commanding the European Squadron, before retiring in 1875 (C. Reynolds 1978:63–64).*

Mills, the consul and the old chief, who met him "in friendly recognition." He was carried to the Big House, where a "whole village" was gathered.

They sailed with fresh food and water, spoke the American whaler *John Howland*, boarded it, and found it exceedingly strange to look at huge strips of blubber and blood. Between squalls, they commenced the survey but, hating the work, were "as cross as men ought ever to be. . . . Our instructions were a perfect curiosity; it was impossible to fulfill them at all. . . . We concluded to do as our own reason told us and to let the orders go to the dogs."

Anchoring beside the *Peacock* in the port of Saluafata, they learned there was to be an attack the next morning to avenge the death of an American seaman murdered soon after the squadron left a year before.[4] Reynolds tried to squeeze into the *Peacock*'s landing party but was sent back. Three towns were burned.

The following morning the *Peacock*'s boat with Emmons and Passed Midshipman George W. Harrison came alongside. Reynolds was to go on a "Secret Mission" to the small island of Manono, to take prisoner the old chief Pare, uncle of Opotuno, so that the latter would be delivered up to answer to charges of murder against him.[5] For the first time he was not greeted openly but was asked why he had come. "Emmons made a show of observations and proceeded in the Boat." Reynolds started his walk around the island, "to gather information," but the natives knew he had been at Saluafata and kept their distance. Even Mr. Heath, the missionary, had heard he had come to take Pare. Reynolds was dumbfounded; his destination had been so secret that even the other officers on the *Peacock* did not know about it. "Pump Mr. Heath indeed!" Reynolds told him "a complicated mass of falsehoods . . . I nearly choked . . . altogether it was very unpleasant to tell so many lies. I thought the whole idea absurd. Taking Pare would not procure Potuno. . . . But I deceived Mr. Heath . . . as my sense of duty would not allow me to mar [*my superior's*] plans by any scruples of my own."

---

[4] *Sailor Gideon Welles had deserted from an American whaler in May 1840 and was killed over an incident of theft of his belongings. The towns of Saluafata, Fusi, and Salelese on Upolo Island were burned without opposition (Wilkes 1845, 4:103–5, 5:25–31).*

[5] *See Letter No. 11, at n. 15.*

He did not find Pare, but back at the landing place the natives, now appeased, offered him cava. "The natives were much pleased to see me quaff their favorite beverage with an apparent relish, and I set down the fact of my having done so as pretty strong evidence of a readiness to accommodate myself to circumstances. . . . Thus ended a stay of one month in these Islands. I had anticipated much pleasure from the second visit; how little I found may be gathered here." Especially galling was the knowledge that the *Peacock*'s officers had spent most of that month agreeably among the populace.

Sailing northwest, the ships reached the Ellice Islands on 13 March. Reynolds felt the natives were of a "new race." "It is curious to me that we spend months among people who have been visited for centuries and when we come amid those who know so little of white men as to think they come from the clouds, we cannot spare a day."[6]

After four days a survey of DePeyster Island was finally completed. The *Flying Fish* was "so low in the water that a single stop from a boat or canoe will place a man on the decks. She has no bulwarks to afford the least protection to the crew," which then numbered eight. Reynolds declared her "tabooed," and the swarms of canoes pushed off toward the *Peacock*.

Another new people, distinct from those of DePeyster and Ellice, very good looking and bearded, populated Drummond Island (Tabiteuea) in the Kingsmill or Gilbert Group.[7] "My beard at this time has attained a darker hue than it had when I left home and I have suffered it to grow under my chin to a peak of some length. About all the natives that came alongside, young and old, noticed it most smilingly, stroking their faces and pointing to mine in a way to signify their admiration of my taste." He was happy to go surveying with "Old Emmons" and De Haven—"right sociable." On their return, they found one of the *Peacock*'s party ashore had been killed, so on the morrow the town was to be burned. "More war! it seems to me our path through the Pacific is

[6] *The Ellice Islands, today the nation of Tuvalu, were inhabited by Melanesians until invaded by Samoans (Polynesians) in the sixteenth century. The group was reached by the English Captain John Byron in 1764.*

[7] *The Gilbert Islands (today Kiribati) fall into the third great subdivision of Oceania, Micronesia, which incorporates the western Pacific north of the equator.*

to be marked in blood." Hudson, with some officers and men, had landed without marines and without fear. But as the visit proceeded, women attached themselves to the party while men swarmed about and picked pockets. They had decided to retreat to the boats when they discovered seaman John Anderson was missing. Shrieks were heard. Two officers went to search, called, but were stoned.

Thus the next morning, 9 April, the *Peacock*'s boats with a large party pulled for the beach. Through Mr. Hale a parley was attempted to learn Anderson's fate, to no avail. "Mr. Peale shot 2 fellows with his rifle at a distance of some 200 yards," a feat the natives could not believe.[8] Others were shot; the village was burned.

Reynolds had purchased two suits of cocoa fiber armor from an old man the previous day. "I sent one piece of Armour to Mr. Peale for the Public Collection and hope to present the other to the 'Lancaster Museum,' an establishment which afforded me so much entertainment during years which *I shall never forget.*" He had taken "especial care" to demonstrate that the armor could be penetrated by bullets, but the natives apparently did not believe him.

After more days of surveying islands and atolls, Reynolds confessed to nearly running up on a beach. He had the middle watch, but he was thinking of home. "I think of [home] too much, but I can't help it, and it gives me positive pleasure. . . . I believe I have thought over every little event of my childhood, and I have often wondered at the extent that my recollections have gone."

Many more islands later, on 24 April Reynolds decided that "as during the last five months I have been on shore exactly 12 hours and a quarter . . . I might as well take the opportunity to stretch my limbs and to have it to say that I had landed among the Kingsmill Group. Knox has only been 15 *minutes* on shore . . . his curiosity is not nearly as alive as mine!" Emmons gave him passage to narrow Matthew's Island (Marakei), only two to three hundred yards long. He came upon Alfred Agate sketching one of the island gods, the houses, and the people—"and me peering out of the gable of a hut—with my White Hat!" The schooner did not arrive, so he went with the boats to the *Peacock*. There he learned the *Flying Fish* was "ashore, hard and fast." If Captain Wilkes had been present, he felt he would have been suspended, but "I knew Captain

---

[8] *Titian Peale; see Letter upon Departure, n. 4.*

Hudson would view the affair in a reasonable light." The *Peacock*'s cutter and crew were with the schooner, so Reynolds "dined with the fellows" and turned in on the *Peacock*—which "now seemed of monstrous size." The next morning the schooner approached. Knox reported a most unpleasant night; they had had to fire on the natives to keep them off.

> 28 April: Pitts Island (Butaritari), the last of the group—"to my infinite joy and satisfaction, after 25 days cruising that was just as dangerous as it was disagreeable. . . . Eternity seemed nearer to me than all else and the gloomy passage of those long hours was to me whole years in duration. . . . I felt how much we needed aid and more than once, during those [*night*] watches, did I pray to God that he would preserve us from the Perils. . . . Here where 'the Heathen in their blindness bow down to Gods of Stone,'⁹ the truth and beauty of the Christian belief steals over our hearts with a holy charm."

The last of April, Knox and Reynolds were told that Ascension (Ponape) and the Carolines to the west were to be given up for lack of time. They were ordered to go on half a gallon of water a day and a three-quarter meat allowance to retain a sixty-day supply, with the surplus going to the *Peacock*.

After surveying the Pescadores, the ships parted company on 8 May, the *Peacock* steering toward Oahu. "Right glad were we to be rid of the ship with her signals and humbugging." The schooner was to search for a white man detained long since and then "to proceed to Honolulu with all dispatch."¹⁰ Convinced there was no settled population and no white man, the *Flying Fish* stood to the north on 10 May.

> 24 May: "Our long indulged suspicions have been verified! The water casks are full of dead mice. . . . Visions of a domestic life with a loving wife have intruded themselves in my imagination lately with a peculiarly vivid force. . . . The Schooner kills me . . . it wearies my very soul . . . 1500 miles from our port and wood enough for 2 days.

⁹ *Reynolds paraphrases the last lines of stanza two of the* Missionary Hymn *by Reginald Heber (1783–1826):*

> *The heathen in his blindness*
> *Bows down to wood and stone.*

¹⁰ *An American captain named Dowsett disappeared in the Pescadores while on a shelling voyage; the American consul in Honolulu had requested the squadron's assistance (Wilkes 1845, 4:105).*

We will either have to burn the spars or eat the horrible meat raw. . . . The mice, the mice—the mice—and the cockroaches that are like so many Turkey bussards . . . never a single night of sweet or refreshing rest for 6 months."

6 June: "15 hours in 186 days have I had the use of my limbs. . . . The schooner has dived and pitched and rolled, is in poor shape." Now, close to Oahu, with good wind, they "never took a rag off . . . tore and pitched through the foaming sea . . . no one could stand up . . . it was a cheering excitement to *feel* her *go.*"

At four in the morning of 13 June 1841, Knox and Reynolds pointed the *Flying Fish* for Honolulu harbor. They did not even wait for a pilot.

Letter No. 19

Flying Fish: at Sea
Monday November 7th 1841
Lat 33° 00′ North, Long 136° 00′ West

My dear Sister Lydia,

We have *all* got *safely away* from the Columbia River, for which I thank God! We are bound for Oahu again, where we expect to join the rest of the Squadron next week, and then for Home!

I wrote to you in June last from Oahu and I may as well go back to that date and bring my yarn up to the present. It was a delightful week that we spent there, and we recruited wonderfully upon fresh beef and pure water mixed up with the wild exercise of gallopping over the hills. The place was like a second Home to us, for we had friends there who were only *too* kind, and to *my* great happiness I found Simon Blunt there also, who is one of the dearest naval associates I have. Perhaps you will have seen him before you get this letter, as he was going Home on a sick ticket and promised me to visit Cornwall, if possible[1] It was a joyous change, though so brief,

---

[1] *Blunt's farewell letter to Reynolds, dated April, from Honolulu, came to Reynolds in August via James Alden in Oregon (Blunt 1841). William May meanwhile wrote to Reynolds from the* Vincennes *in Puget Sound that Blunt, who was suffering from an unidentified testicular ailment, promised "he is yet good for our contemplated tour" of Europe (May 1841). Blunt himself assured Reynolds in Honolulu that his health was restored and that "Captain Hudson offered him passage in his Cabin to the [Columbia] River,*

from the harassing cruíse we had just completed and we made the most of it, for we had a good idea of *what was in store for us yet.*

I had the curiosity to be weighed then and was very much shocked though not surprised to find that I had lost 12 pounds of flesh—enough to have satisfied a dozen Shylocks—during that miserable six months' cruise.[2] Now, I never was in a condition to spare even one pound and it was quite alarming to consider, that if things did not change for the better, by the end of the cruise I would rival Calvin Edson himself. I am sorry to say that up to this time *no improvement* has taken place, but I have hopes.

We sailed from Oahu on the 21st June in company with the Peacock and on the 18th of July were off the mouth of the Columbia. We knew the entrance to be very dangerous and the only directions we had were very imperfect and obscure. Capt. Hudson had intended to try the passage in *the Schooner* before he ventured his Ship and had been very careful not to part from us, on this account. Accordingly, on this day we made all ready to receive him and were disappointed to find him wearing the Ship in shore,[3] without waiting for us, as we happened to be four or five miles leeward of him.

Very soon, however, we made her out to be *hard and fast among the breakers,* and as we neared her we could see that she thumped and lurched heavily, and that the Seas were striking her with a fury that must soon break her to pieces. We gave her up for lost from that moment. Here was a change, indeed, and all in less time, that it

---

but he would not put himself again under Capt. W.," preferring to ship home instead. "With one of the kindest hearts, with a simplicity of character that rarely survives boyhood in anyone, with a soul of honour and truth, Simon Blunt is liked by all who know of him and it is my happiness that he calls me friend, or brother!" (Journal 2:267). After returning to the United States, Blunt was assigned to the Depot of Charts and a series of other brief duties until his death in 1854 as a lieutenant (ZB).

[2] Reynolds noted that the combination of "temperature at 156°, Fear and Food that ruin the digestive organs" had reduced his weight from 149 to 135 pounds (Journal 2:164). The only available measure of his height is found in a letter home from his first cruise of 1832–1834, when he had reached five feet ten and a half inches; his brother John was six feet.

[3] "Wearing" means to have a ship go about by turning the stern, rather than the bow, to the wind.

would take to tell of it. We could approach quite close to her, but not to be of any service, for there was a barrier of boiling foam between us that was impassible. They hoisted out a large boat for the purpose of carrying an anchor into deep water, but she was stove immediately and the tide brought her planks right alongside of the Schooner. They succeeded in lowering a small Whale Boat and sent an officer to sound about the Ship, but after swamping once and running the most iminent risks, he was obliged to return. We looked for the entrance in vain: the breakers seemed to extend from shore to shore and all we could do was to keep as near to the Ship *as was safe.* The tide was running strong out to sea, night was fast coming on, and they must all remain in the Ship until morning, *provided they held together so long.*

Signal was made to us "to stand off shore for the night," and with sad hearts we obeyed. We *hoped* to find the Ship standing in the morning, but the night was long and anxious to *us.* The feelings of *those on board her* cannot be told: the bottom of the Ship stove in, the water flowed in at the ports, the breakers washed away the bulwarks, the poor old Ship thumped and struck and rolled in a way that was frightful, and all of the poor fellows on board had just to stand and take it, waiting for daylight, when they *might* be able *to get the Boats out* and reach the Shore, which was only two miles distant.

At 4 in the morning we stood in shore and in half an hour we had the satisfaction to see the Ship with her masts and yards still standing, the upper ones being sent down to ease her. At 6 we were close to her again, when she made signal to us "not to approach nearer" and immediately afterwards she hoisted her Ensign *Union down,* the melancholy mark of extreme distress and which to every sailor's eyes is, of all signals, the most forlorn. It really was the saddest sight I ever saw. So many friends cooped up in the poor, helpless Ship, and she at the mercy of the wild breakers that were rolling on to her in awful force, and surging her on to the sandy bottom, worse than ever she went on to the Ice. All without the breakers was quiet, the Sea was stilled and the Shore was like a Desert without a sign of life, but around the Ship the uproar was terrible: I really cannot tell you what my feelings were—it was soul sickening to look on.

By and by, the Ship lurched so badly that every time it seemed as if she could not recover herself, but was about to lay herself on her

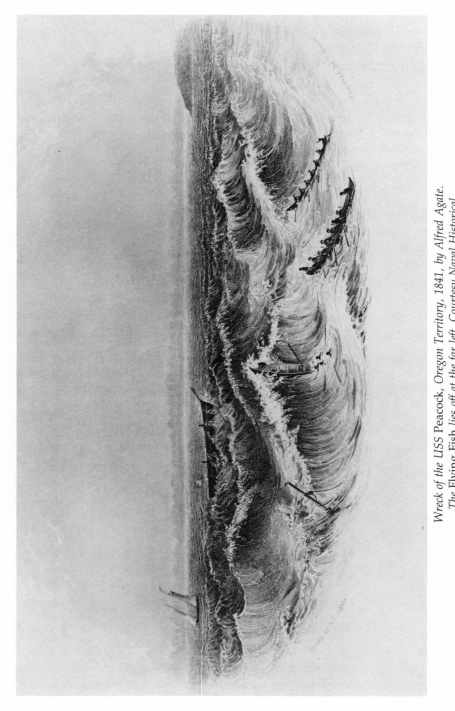

Wreck of the USS Peacock, Oregon Territory, 1841, by Alfred Agate. The Flying Fish lies off at the far left. Courtesy Naval Historical Foundation, Washington, D.C.

side; the motion, the other way, would be equally as violent and as quick as thought. At last, *the masts went* by the board and nothing was left but the naked hull. They had succeeded in getting the boats out and a portion of the crew were already landed. Whether the remnant would escape was until the very last moment a matter of great doubt. By sundown *every one was safe on shore,* but not a thing was saved from the wreck except the Ship's papers, the Purser's books and a few instruments and fowling pieces. The order had been passed for "every one to leave, in the clothes he had on" and it was God's mercy that they all landed without loss of life.[4] This was not done without infinite toil and risk—one boat was swamped and the crew picked up by another, and the *landing* was as perilous as their situation had been *on board* the night before.

The Missionaries and some of the Hudson's Bay Co. officers from Astoria were on the beach and had brought with them tents, blankets and food.[5] The men and officers built themselves huts with the branches of the Pine tree and all the hands bivouacked comfortably enough. While *they slept* that night, *the Ship sunk* and in the morning only her Bowsprit was to be seen above the water. An Indian pilot was sent out to us, who brought us safely in, and we anchored in the

[4] *Journal 2:277: "The Captain saved his journals and the surveys, the Master his Chronometer, the Artist a few of his sketches, and all else was left a prey to the Sea." One man cut the portrait of his wife from its frame and carried it off rolled up "in his bosom." "Of all the store of Curious things collected in the last 8 months, how little was left." An interesting postscript is revealed in Reynolds's later letter to Henry Eld (1843a) reporting he had just seen George Emmons married in Baltimore in his full dress uniform "preserved with so much cunning and forethought from the wreck of the Peacock."*

[5] *Astoria had been established in 1811 as a trading post near the mouth of the Columbia by the partners of American entrepreneur John Jacob Astor. The first permanent settlement on the Pacific Coast, the fort passed into British hands between 1813 and 1818, and its trading activities—along with those of the entire Oregon Territory—were dominated by the British Hudson's Bay Company until the 1840s. Astoria was also known to the British as Fort George (Simpson 1847, 1:256). The principal American presence in Oregon in 1841 was several American Missionary Society settlements, mainly south of the river.*

quiet and beautiful cove where the shipwrecked ones had found a refuge, overjoyed to take our brothers by the hand and happy to find for ourselves a peaceful resting place, after the nervous and harrowing excitement of the past days.

Now, we had always entertained a wholesome fear of the dangers of the Columbia River and had looked forward to the time when we should be employed there with a presentiment of the risks we should incur. The Ice, the Feegee Islands and the Columbia River had ever been the bugbears of the cruise. We escaped the two first, *narrowly* enough; the third, we dreaded more than we cared to admit. So fatal a commencement did not cheer us a bit, and it was very evident that we had not magnified the dangers that would attend our work. Thus, before we commenced, the prospect had sickened us, and as we went on, matters certainly got worse with us and reached their climax *at the very last.* I should any day have considered it *a kind* of consolation, could I have known that I was born to *be hung.* I should then have been relieved from a very unpleasant prospect *of drowning* which generally offered a dozen times a day.

We learned that the Vincennes and Porpoise were employed to the North, that they had not entered the River yet, and that *they* had given *us* up for lost among those low Islands where we so narrowly escaped from wreck. Three months behind our time as we were, 'twas no wonder they thought the worst had happened to us, and it was a settled thing that they were to search for us on *their* way Home. Both vessels were expected at the River daily and we were to wait their arrival, an express being sent overland to inform Cap. Wilkes of what had happened.

The officers and crew of the (late) Peacock went up to Astoria, 10 miles from the mouth of the River, to establish themselves there, and we remained in the Cove near the entrance to look out for the Vincennes and Brig. Much to my delight, I found a letter from Lydia (July 1840) which had come by way of Oahu and was as welcome as unexpected.[6] It drove shipwreck and drowning out of my head for a while, and I was the envy of the others who were not so fortunate:

---

[6] *Lydia's letter (15 July 1840) was passed on to Reynolds by William May in his letter of 9 May 1841 from Puget Sound. In it, she complained that "I shall be 22 this month—I shall be an old maid by the time you come home."*

you must know that among us, those who get letters are always important personages for a day or two at least and are looked up to accordingly as being supremely happy. So they are.

I must not forget to say that the men of the Peacock behaved like *men* during the whole of the danger and that order and discipline were preserved to a degree that reflects credit upon them all. Mr. Birnie, the Company's Agent, supplied each individual with a blanket, and shanties and huts were constructed at Astoria for the shelter of all hands.[7] The Purser sent to Fort Vancouver for clothing etc., and the ration was served out the same as on board ship from the provisions belonging to the squadron, which had been brought from Oahu by a store vessel hired for that purpose—so that all hands were doing quite well.[8]

[7] *Hudson's Bay Company agent in Astoria James Birnie (ca. 1799–1864) was described by the company's governor, George Simpson, in 1832 as "14 years in the Service. Useful in the Columbia as he can make himself understood among several of the Tribes and knows the country well; but not particularly active, nor has he much firmness: deficient in point of Education; a loose talking fellow who seldom considers it necessary to confine himself to the truth. He has not pretension to look forward to advancement indeed is very well paid for his Services at 100 p Annum" (Simpson 1975:202). Reynolds wrote (Journal 2:291) that Birnie "is a tall, portly, hale looking Scotchman, has an Indian wife and a houseful of children and was exceedingly kind and hospitable to us all. The Peacock's officers were messing in common at his home, but almost every individual had his own little hut to sleep in."*

In August, when the two officers "under arrest"—Lieutenant Robert Johnson and Dr. Guillou—were left behind by Wilkes in the little settlement (called "Bobville") while the Columbia was being surveyed, "Guillou was Schoolmaster to the tribe of young Birnies." In the evening, the young men told nursery tales and played games with the adoring children.

[8] *The purser of the Peacock was William Speiden, who had served as purser's steward for some twenty-two years at the Washington Navy Yard before his appointment as purser in 1837. Subsequent to the expedition, he was to return to the Pacific—during the Mexican War, with Commodore Perry on his visit to Japan, and finally with the East India Squadron. He was sent home in ill health in 1860, and died at Washington, D.C., in 1861.*

Fort Vancouver was the headquarters of Hudson's Bay Company operations in the Northwest; established in 1825 some one hundred miles up

As the loss of the Ship would necessarily have a great effect upon the after operations of the cruise, all kinds of surmises were started among us as to what would be the result, but we worried ourselves to no purpose, for none of us could agree except on one point and that was, that until Captain Wilkes came, nothing of the kind could even be guessed at.

Until the 6th of August, we were daily employed in running out to sea and back again and examining the channel, so as to be of service to the Vincennes and Brig.[9] On that day, they both appeared off the River; we joined them outside and had the great pleasure to meet our friends well, after a seperation from them of 8 months. The Vincennes was *not* to be trusted in the River. Captain Ringgold (*not* Reynolds) of the Porpoise took charge of her, to proceed to San Francisco in Mexico,[10] while Captain Wilkes took the Brig in to carry on the survey. Knox was installed as Pilot of the Porpoise and *I* was trusted to look out for the Schooner. We got safely inside of the Cape and anchored for the night. The next morning, the *Indian* pilot of the Brig run her aground; neither Knox or I knew anything about the *up* river. My pilot carried the Schooner by without touching and as the Brig stuck fast for an hour, I got to Astoria before her and had the honor to anchor the first public vessel of the U.S. off that famous settlement.

---

the Columbia near present-day Vancouver, it was equipped with warehouses, forges, hospital, and sawmill. The fort is now a national historic site.

The merchant vessel Wave had been hired to ship supplies and provisions for the expedition from Hawaii to Oregon, arriving in May 1841 (McLoughlin 1943:34–35).

[9] Captain Hudson had ordered Knox and Reynolds "to get under weigh and make ourselves acquainted with the passage of the River." For this task they had two Indian brothers, Ramsey and George, who had served as pilots on commercial "Boston Ships" (American) and "King George Ships" (British). But Reynolds fretted that because Hudson had no competency in surveying, precious time was being wasted (Journal 2:283–89).

[10] San Francisco, then generally known as Yerba Buena, was a small town that had grown up near the mission and presidio of that name in the Mexican province of Alta California.

"Captain Ringgold, not Reynolds" refers to an error in a newspaper article about the expedition which had excited the family.

An American merchant Brig was laying there, and being a good servicable vessel, Captain Wilkes bought her to replace the Peacock. Her Captain asked $1000 pr. month to charter her, so that to buy her was the cheapest proceeding.[11] She was christened the "Oregon" and sailed up the River to Fort Vancouver with the Porpoise, while we were left alone in the Schooner to survey the entrance.

For more than two months we were at work whenever the weather permitted, running all kinds of risks, just getting clear with nothing to spare, and continually expecting to lose the Schooner and all hands. Frequent fogs and fresh winds, but above all the rapidity of the tides, retarded us very much and when the two Brigs came down again, with their survey of over 100 miles of the River, we had not

[11] *This was the ship* Thomas Perkins, *Captain Varney. John McLoughlin, chief factor of the Hudson's Bay Company at Fort Vancouver, reported to the company's governors (McLoughlin 1943:96–97) that Purser Waldron had intimated to him that Wilkes was considering discharging the* Peacock's *crew in Oregon at their request and to avoid paying the asking price on the new ship. McLoughlin wrote that he told Waldron that Wilkes would have to "leave some one to keep order among them and prevent their getting into quarrels, with the natives," and that the sale was thereafter immediately concluded. Mindful of the American settlers' growing disaffection with British control in Oregon, McLoughlin was also concerned that the idle sailors would be "ready to join the first that came to oppose us." Governor George Simpson, then visiting Oregon, reported that he had been told the sale price was $9,000, an amount considered high for that vessel (Simpson 1973:84n).*

Although relations between the company and the expedition were outwardly cordial, a subtle tension underlay all of their interactions, revolving around the issue of control of the Oregon Territory. Both McLoughlin and Simpson reported cooperative relations with the Americans, but Simpson wrote to the company's governors in England that Wilkes "was by no means communicative on the object of [the expedition's] surveys and examinations; but I collected from a very intelligent and confidential member of the expedition, that it was the intention of Captain Wilkes to recommend strongly to his Government, to claim the whole of the territory on the shores of the Northern Pacific, from the Mexican northern boundary in Latitude 42°, to the Russian southern boundary in Latitude 54° 40'" (Simpson 1973:145). In fact, Wilkes's report to the secretary in June 1842 did recommend that the United States take over Oregon, but not California.

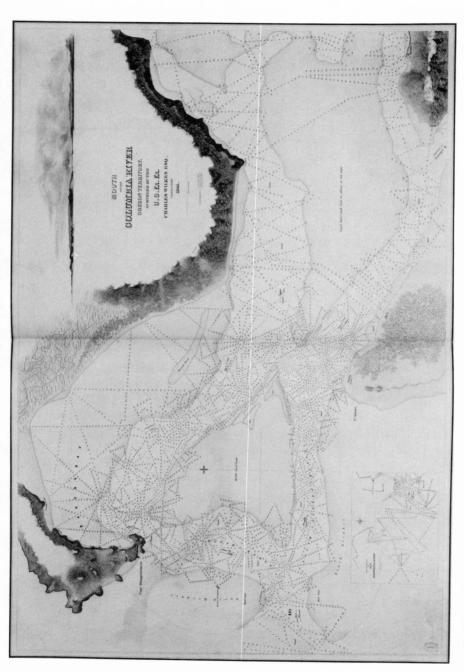

The mouth of the Columbia, 1841. This chart depicts perhaps most clearly just what engaged William Reynolds during his stay in Oregon. One of seven charts of the river published in the expedition's Atlas, it shows the painstaking labor of depth-soundings and surveying involved in the navy's efforts during the cruise. The site of the wreck of the Peacock is at the far left; Astoria is at the lower right corner. Wilkes 1850, 2:68.

completed all that had been assigned to us and the *outer* part, or the *very worst*, was still undone.[12]

It was now October and the Season was at hand when all work is stopped for the winter and the chances of getting in or out of the River very uncertain and unsafe. So the Brigs were to be got to Sea at once, and again Knox and I were made Pilots, he of the Porpoise and I of the Oregon, to carry them out. Three days we were detained waiting for a chance; on the 5th, the wind served and we were soon beyond all danger, the Schooner following us out.[13] Two Boats were still in the River at work and Captain Wilkes came on board the Schooner to go in with us and drive on, while the Brigs stood "off and on" the Land. Next morning we had a favorable wind and ran in, were busily at sounding until the 10th, when all *inside* was finished and we got to sea again the same evening. The Brigs joined us and Captain Wilkes, leaving us to complete the bar and the *outside work*, made sail to the South for San Francisco.

The surveying *in* the River had been bad enough during the summer months, and apart from its dangers, had been so disagreeable and solitary that we were sick to death of it. We never saw any one for weeks, save a few Indians now and then who brought us Salmon and Deer and who were welcome enough, but as to Society, after a hard day's labour, we might as well have been in the great desert.[14] We did long with all our hearts to see the face of some *human* creature. Once in a great while we *did* manage to run

[12] *Passed Midshipman James Blair (see Letter No. 3, n. 10), who had been master on the* Peacock, *was now aboard the schooner, and they were furnished with two good boats. Dr. Guillou joined them also, on the departure of the rest of the squadron. Captain Wilkes had apparently contemplated leaving the doctor to find his way home as best he could but at the last moment ordered him first to the* Oregon *and then to the* Flying Fish *(Journal 2:308, 317).*

[13] *During Samuel Knox's duty as pilot, Lieutenant George T. Sinclair had temporary charge of the* Flying Fish *(Journal 2:317). Command of the* Oregon *for the return voyage devolved upon Lieutenant Overton Carr when William Hudson preferred to sail on the* Vincennes *without command.*

[14] *Reynolds described the first salmon the Indians brought as being four or five feet long and big enough to feed everyone on the schooner (Journal 2:279).*

up to Astoria and have a chat with the folks there, and sometimes we saw the young wives of the missionaries, pretty, rosy cheeked women, the very sight of whom gave us the heart ache. I am disgusted with all naked Indians and primitive people whatever, and shall be too happy (and partly insane, I fear) when I can associate again with the more intelligent and attractive portion of the human family, who carry ideas in their heads, wear clothes on their bodies and are fair to look upon.

After the Brigs left us, the weather proved so bad that for some days we could do nothing, and as the Schooner was all to pieces, we already experienced the inconvenience of splitting our sails and being hardly able to repair them. She needed refitting so much that Knox had asked Capt. Wilkes to allow him a few days in the River for that purpose. "No, you must do it at Sea!" This was about as practicable as it would be for a half drowned man to mend his clothes in the water. Finally, after 10 days delay, after once nearly losing the boats and once running a frightful risk with the Schooner near the same breakers that destroyed the Peacock, we did all we could on the bar and took our departure from the Cape Disappointment, which had been so prominent an object in our sight for more than three months.[15]

We commenced to survey the Coast Shore, but as we had expected the weather proved so bad that we could do nothing and we had already been delayed too long. We anticipated a stormy commencement to our passage and knew that we should meet with disaster in some shape or another, but we certainly did not think we should suffer so severely as we have. In the very first gale, while lying to, the Forestay, on which *both* of the masts *depend* for support, *parted smack in two.* By the greatest good luck, *we saved the masts* and

[15] *Cape Disappointment lies at the northern mouth of the Columbia River. The issue of the danger of the river to navigation flared for many months in 1846, when James Blair, Samuel Knox, Reynolds, and some of the other expedition officers engaged in a letter-writing dispute with Wilkes in the* Washington Union. *The junior officers were supporting the position of Missouri Senator Thomas Hart Benton that the Columbia was a safe harbor and that American control of Oregon promised many commercial benefits. The letters are reprinted in Blair [1846]. (See Epilogue.)*

got the stay *temporarily* secured, but there were some moments when we looked for the very worst to happen.

Next we were jammed in with the Land during another gale and the wind howling *brought the shore dead under our lee,* from which it was *claw off, if we could.* Even had we been well found in sails and rigging, we should have felt uneasy there, for the wind fairly *howled* and the seas were big enough to frighten Paul Jones[16]—but we had *nothing to depend on!* If *one* of our miserable ropes, blocks, or sails went, we were almost entirely disabled. All day *long* and the ugly looking land was coming closer and closer and amid rain, hail and lightning and whirl winds the time was very *disagreeable* and the prospect worse. Towards dark, *one sail split.* With much risk to the men, we got it in and commenced to repair it. Then *our main hope went: the Foresail tore across* and we lowered it *to try* and mend it: meanwhile the Schooner lay at the mercy of the Seas. We could *set nothing* to steady her and with the water coming on board on all sides she rolled and tumbled enough to drive one crazy, and all the while *was drifting right on to the Shore*: this was at 9 at night.[17]

I can tell you that no *charitable* wishes were expressed towards him who had said with the utmost indifference "you must refit at Sea." We *were* refitting at Sea, with a vengeance. It was 11 before we got ready to show any sail *and those two hours* were any thing but pleasant: they were terrible. *We all knew it would be a chance if we got clear.* The poor Schooner did all she could, but she had not fair play. Under the sail we were able to give her, she exceeded our hopes and behaved nobly, and it was cheering to know that our confidence in *her* qualities was not misplaced.

Knox was so sleepy that at midnight he fell asleep on the lockers and I had to keep the watch until 4 o'clock. I had no desire to close my eyes, though I had been on deck from 4 in the morning and like

[16] *Revolutionary naval hero John Paul Jones (1747–1792) was known for bold offensive action in British waters and against superior enemy forces.*

[17] *The* Flying Fish *normally carried three sails: a mainsail, a foresail, and a jib. In the rough weather and poor visibility then prevailing, and the poor condition of their equipment, the schooner may have been carrying only two sails—foresail and jib—so that they found themselves without any canvas up at this time.*

the others had had no rest on the night before. It was necessary to carry sail to the last moment and drive the Schooner off shore by inches. The wind now favoured us, so that we made a tolerable course from the Land, if our canvass would only hold until we gained an offing. This was what we had cause to doubt, as the sails, threadbare at first, had only been half repaired.

I never was more excited in my life; to some of the squalls I was obliged to shorten sail, but I carried through others in a way that should have frightened me at any other time. I scarcely felt the rain and hail and more than once I was surprised to find that I had bitten my teeth so hard that they ached, though I was not aware of it until the stir of the moment had passed. Every mile that she gained made us all breathe easier and when I doubted whether to hold on to the Mainsail or to take it in, as the clouds threatened, I had only to remember the looks of the Land during the day and my nerves were strung to the necessary pitch. I had no desire to see that shore again and, as far as lay with me, I was determined it should be looked for at day light, *in Vain.* Oh! but it was good to watch the Schooner as she made her way through the Seas and *never faltered once:* how can I help loving her, when she carries us safely through such scrapes as this?

I staid up until day break. We had run more than 30 miles and there was *no Land* to be seen. *Soon after*, every sail we had split and tore, so that again the Schooner was left to be tumbled by the Seas while all hands were employed in repairing the damages. The Log book is a very matter of fact concern and *its* leaves savour *nothing* of romance. This day it reads, "we are now entirely at the mercy of the weather, having neither sails nor standing rigging to trust to." We really were in a very bad pickle—spare sails we had none and the Forestay was not at all safe. More gales we certainly should meet with and there was no Port for us to run to in any direction. We were puzzled to think *what would* become of us and we heartily wished ourselves safe in Oahu. I was scarcely more distressed when we were breaking Ice bergs to pieces in the poor old Peacock, and it seemed to me now as extremely problematical whether we should ever again see any body, or any body else ever see us.

No sooner did we get the sails patched up, than another gale came over, which, however, moderated the same day after blowing hard enough to have answered for a week and left such a huge swell that we had to lower all the sails, at once, to save them from splitting. The Schooner rolled so that she would soon have flapped them to rags. *Two days* we lay this way with the masts bare, of course making no progress, while the motion of the vessel and the quantity of water that rolled over her decks kept us as uncomfortable as we could wish. We began to wonder when our troubles would cease or what new disaster would happen next, but *this calm* was our *last* and on the 3rd Nov., 13 days after sailing from the River, we at last got a fair and fresh wind which carried us out of the stormy Latitudes and has now, on the 9th, brought us fairly into the trades and about 1000 miles from Oahu, without any more damage to the sails and without distressing us by being in the least unsteady.[18]

I have said before, "thank God, we are all safe away from the Columbia River," and this relieves us from a world of fear.

I believe I have generally tried in my letters to you to speak lightly of anticipated dangers, so as not to frighten you beforehand, and then *after all was over* to give you a full dose of it all. I hope I have succeeded in this and I suppose you can bear to be told of such things when their consequence has ceased. I am naturally sanguine enough as to my own personal good fortune and despair is a companion that seldom troubles me, but I must confess that I have been, with the others, exposed to so many risks during this everlasting cruize, as on more than one occasion to have this sort of confidence very rudely smashed and my composure very much disturbed. Since the wreck of the Peacock, the days have been so crowded with the excitement of being in all sorts of dangers and of getting clear of it, and such strong feelings have been continually in play, that it actually seems to me, as if I had lived a year, instead of three of the *longest* months I ever knew.

Now, however, I need no longer practice any concealment, or endeavor to delude you again. In perfect truth, the hazardous portion of the cruise *is over* and we have but a beaten track to follow Home:

[18] *Convinced all were doomed should they continue down the coast to the Umpiqua River as charged, they had opened the sealed orders and were directed to Oahu to sell the schooner. "This was good News" (Journal 2:340).*

my apprehensions have taken unto themselves wings, and with a heart brimfull of the most buoyant hope, I look forward with as much certainty *as man can,* to the happiness of being with you ere *this letter* will have grown cold. Look out for us *next June!*

But it is high time I should tell you of the most pleasant event that has occurred [to] me this whole cruize. Never were letters more welcome than those four *of July last* by the way of *St. Louis* which found me at Astoria on the 23rd of September. We had run up there to land two sick men[19] and that same day the letters came down the River in the Oregon, so that I got them at once. You may be sure I was very happy to have such late news from you coming to me at a time too, when I was in a fever of disgust with almost every thing in the world: they were from Mother, Sam and Jane, Cate, Hal, and Aunt.

We had given up the hope of receiving letters overland, as the Express had arrived from Montreal without bringing them, on account of the extraordinary route it was to take—the Governor of the Company on this side of the water, Sir George Simpson, travelling with it and visiting the out of the way posts. He brought the intelligence of the President's death.[20] The letters were to come by the next Express which was expected about the middle of October; they will be forwarded Home, via Oahu. I was too glad that you had written by *all* the channels I pointed out, and I shall receive your letters by Mazatlan when we arrive at Oahu.

[19] *During this period of surveying the Columbia, Dr. James C. Palmer (1811–1883) had been left in Astoria by Wilkes to care for the sick. Purser Waldron was also stationed there to bake 10,000 pounds of bread for the homeward voyage. Palmer was of a prominent Maryland family and had served in the navy as assistant surgeon since 1834. He went on to become medical director of the navy in 1871 and surgeon-general of the army the following year (ZB).*

[20] *Sir George Simpson (1792–1860), a Scot, was the longtime governor (1821–1856) of the Hudson's Bay Company in Canada. A great promoter of exploration in his jurisdiction, on this particular journey Simpson continued westward after leaving Oregon, traveling through Siberia, and eventually reached St. Petersburg; he later published* Narrative of a Journey round the World *(1847). Simpson met Wilkes, Hudson, and other members of the expedition at Fort Vancouver in August 1841 (Simpson 1973:58). Simpson brought news of the death of William Henry Harrison in April 1841.*

We are to sell the Schooner immediately after our arrival and I expect to finish the cruise in the Vincennes. As I cannot look for promotion in the Squadron, I will be better satisfied to go on board the V—— and prefer her to either of the Brigs: it will not be so pleasant to come down to a steerage again, after playing 1st Lieut. for a year and living in the Cabin, but I suppose that I can put up with it for six months.[21] It will be a very peremptory order, though, that ever sets me afloat again until my right shoulder shall be ornamented with a large gold swab.[22]

I am afraid I shall die of pure grief if I am not made Lieut. very soon; I am very spiteful now. 44 promotions, however, has cleared away the list famously. Another batch of the same number and I must be included. I fear the thing will slumber for a year or two and am miserable, to think so.

Have I ever mentioned to you that Captain Wilkes named a great big Island next door to Cape Horn "Reynolds Island" after *me*, who chanced to discover it while in the Launch. I am in excellent company, among Wollaston and Herschel Islands etc.; but the appellation may be considered as "Sir Joshua," or as J.N.R. the Explorer. To guard against this, I intend to have the fact put in all the Geographies, with an historical memoir of the distinguished young officer etc. etc., as soon as we get Home. This is all the fame I have gained![23]

[21] *Since the* Flying Fish's *full complement of fifteen or sixteen usually included only two officers, Reynolds thus became second in command or first lieutenant with responsibilities he would not have on the larger vessels. Wilkes felt that the schooner's small size did not require officers ranking higher than passed midshipmen to command it.*

[22] *A lieutenant in the navy wore a single gold epaulette according to the dress regulations of the period (U.S. Navy Department 1832:65; Tily 1964:77).*

[23] *See Letter No. 7, n. 11. The Wollaston Islands and Herschel Island, named for the prominent English scientists William Hyde Wollaston (1766–1829) and Sir William Herschel (1738–1822), both lie near Cape Horn. The two other Reynoldses are the great portraitist Sir Joshua Reynolds (1723–1792) and Jeremiah N. Reynolds (1799–1859), the Ohio journalist whose crusade for exploration of the polar seas was a principal early stimulus for the U.S. Exploring Expedition. William Reynolds, of course, also had a peak in Antarctica named for him (Letter No. 14, n. 14).*

I am certain that this letter is very incoherent and very stupid, but indeed I cannot help it. I am really unfit to attempt any thing like arrangement and the more I try to think, the more confused I become. If I could force myself into the humour, I should endeavour to give you some account of the Columbia River and the state of society there, but I must leave this until I see you face to face. I have scribbled away and covered the paper so that you shall *at least have a letter*, but I must beg your indulgence for its wretched style.

I have one matter to make particular mention of. My very intimate friend Dr. Guillou, now on board here as our guest and passenger, will most probably return home from Oahu; I have given him a letter to Father which he will forward to you in due time after his arrival, and which must be his introduction, for he has promised me to visit you as soon as he can leave his own family. You will take care of him for my sake, at first; when you know him, you will be sufficiently interested in himself. He is the most singularly gifted man I have ever had the fortune to meet with, and the more I see of him, the more do I wonder at and admire the extraordinary talents which he possesses. Test his information on almost any subject and you will wonder also and if the English language be too meager, try him if you can in French, Spanish, Italian, or in the dead tongues. But I will not praise him any more—you will be delighted to observe for yourselves.

His return home is caused by his difficulties with Captain Wilkes, who, commencing by injustice, has tyrannized, cheated and abused Dr. Guillou to an excess that will hardly be believed. I need scarcely say that the Dr. has my entire sympathy in the whole of this matter, and as there is all possible confidence between us, you can learn from *him* every thing that you might like to know from *me*.

I am very glad that you are to see him and I am sure you will all be very kind and attentive to him and make his stay with you as pleasant as possible. I have explained to him the out of the way situation of Cornwall and given him sailing directions for his guidance. When he forwards the letter, he will inform you when to expect him in Lancaster, where some one must meet him and be ready to take him to Aunt's house and our Home.

When we found the famous Tomatoes in the Fiji Islands, I did not forget Thomas and his garden, but procured as many seeds as I could. I hope we will succeed with them, for they are delicious beyond all telling—rich, juicy and sweet, with the *smell* and *somewhat*

the taste of the red *plumbs* of the tree by the cistern in our *old yard!* I
have ever borne my promise to Thomas in mind, but I regret that
these are the only things I have been able to procure. I early made
friends with the Horticulturalist on this account and if he had any
thing in his collection that would thrive at Home, I should be sure of
a sample. The fruits and vegetables of the Tropics will not answer for
our climate and we have scarcely collected beyond their limits. . . .[24]

I am sure that Aunt's establishment in Lancaster is a very pleasant
arrangement to you all and am equally certain it will be so, to me. It
always was strange to me to make my Home at the Hotel.[25]

I will remember Hal's *written* request to bring her a bird, but it will
have to be a dead one. The brilliancy of its plumage, however, shall
exceed that of any living warbler in all North America. If I am not too
poor in pocket, I will surely not forget any of the girls, but bring
them each a gift. I cannot promise, however. All the clothes I
possessed that were fit to wear went down in the Peacock, and I am
left nearly as destitute in the matter of a wardrobe as the poor fellows
who belonged to her; when she was wrecked, *they* did not save even
a second shirt.[26]

By the time I can fit myself again with the apparel becoming an
officer and a gentleman, I am afraid the balance on the Purser's
books will *not* be in my favour and if the extra pay be really taken
away from us, I shall come home as poor as I ever was when a
midshipman and very possibly in debt besides. It can't be helped,

[24] *The Fiji tomatoes were probably Solanum repandum (Forst.); the
species is edible and was thought to be a new discovery but later proved to
have been identified on one of Cook's voyages. That the tomatoes were
eventually planted in Cornwall is testified to by a letter from Reynolds to his
father in 1843, describing efforts of government horticulturists to grow
them in Washington (Reynolds 1843b). Reynolds refers to William Rich
(1800–1864), the expedition's botanist. See Eyde (1986) for a biography.*

[25] *John Reynolds had rented a house in Lancaster so that his younger
daughters could have a home while attending school. Jane and Kate were there
also, "attending to their French and music." This arrangement provided
Reynolds an office when in town; "Aunt" presided happily over all.*

[26] *En route to the Columbia, Reynolds had teased Knox, whose clothes
were all eaten by mice during the southern cruise, that his were in a snug
drawer of the Peacock.*

though—and the Government is a very honourable and a very generous Government, to be sure, and there is a great pleasure in serving it (even as a midshipman for 10 years, without any prospect of promotion) and exposing one's life in a hundred ways, and in working like slaves, and in absenting oneself from one's home, and in suffering from hunger and thirst etc., and all the time incited to perseverence by the stimulating consciousness that we may do all this and be dead and that if we finally survive to reach Home, we shall receive more kicks than half pence and be graciously permitted to live on the fat of the Land on 20 cents a day, until we can refund the money which the Government inveighed us into expending. There, excuse this ill nature, it escaped before I could stop it! Perhaps I am all wrong, perhaps the Government intend to indemnify us most munificently—grant us the Rocky mountains, or the like. . . .

Margy Krug's marriage was another surprise, but it reminds me that I have been long enough absent for young girls to grow into women, and that I must expect to find society somewhat changed.[27] I am quite anxious to get your letters for a history of these weddings etc., as Mother and the others merely mention their occurrence. I trust somebody will wait for me, for I entertain *at times* serious ideas of attempting matrimony as soon as ever I return. One very serious obstacle always intrudes itself, to ruin all my visions: I can not cipher out, by any means, how I could keep a wife when I am dependant upon such a proffession as the Naval service of the U. States, which not only is insufficient to keep me alone, but at times strips me naked and leaves me without a shot in the locker. This objection, you see, is a very stubborn one and I cannot get over it, so I very wisely forget the matter until some thing brings it to mind again when the same process of arithmetic is gone over and with the same result.

Honolulu, November 26th

We got safely to this place a week ago. Much to our disappointment Captain Wilkes arrived the same day—and he has not sold the Schooner, but takes her on and most probably I shall

---

[27] *Margaretta Krug (1822–1859) was Rebecca's younger sister, who married, at age eighteen, her first cousin Edwin Francis Shoenberger (1813–1905), of Pittsburgh and Sarah Furnace.*

finish the cruize in *her* now. I am satisfied to remain in her for 6 months longer and you *must* come and look at the little beauty as soon as ever we get Home! She has been refitted: new rigging, sails etc.

All our letters left 10 days before we arrived, for Manilla, where we shall find them shortly.

Excuse the abruptness of this closing, for we sail to morrow and I have not had an instant's leisure as yet. Knox has been sick and I have had to attend to every thing myself.[28]

I was very much and very agreeably surprised to find here a Lady who had seen Jane and Catharine and Father very frequently, and very lately. She was Miss *Turner,* an assistant preceptor at Mr. Girault's academy, and is now Mrs. Brewer, the wife of a wealthy and much esteemed merchant here. I took tea there the other evening. She said, as soon as ever I entered the room, "Oh, Mr. Reynolds, I should have known you any where from your resemblance to your sister Mary Jane." I suppose I ought to consider myself highly flattered—and hope that Jane will not be mortified. But you may be sure I was very much delighted to have a chat about my own folks, and I never had any thing of the kind to happen to me before.[29]

Jim Gibson is well and I wish his friends to be told of it.

[28] *Because May was unwell, Reynolds shared his "pleasant house" in Hawaii while the schooner was "turned bottom up." Then Knox took sick, which left Reynolds in charge of the refitting, with less time for galloping over the countryside. Blair was transferred to the* Vincennes; *Passed Midshipman Joseph P. Sanford (b. 1816) was to take his place (Journal 2:342, 344).*

[29] *Martha Turner had just arrived in Honolulu as the bride of Charles Brewer (1804–1885), a Boston sea captain who had become one of the principal merchants in the Hawaiian Islands. Blunt stayed, and Reynolds was also a frequent guest, at the house of Brewer's partner Henry A. Pierce: "House, horses, table and bed at one's disposal. . . . Pleasant are the memories I shall carry away of Oahu" (Journal 2:267). Pierce, future U.S. minister to Hawaii (1869), was related to Lieutenant James Alden (Journal 2:344). Monsieur Girault had founded Spring Villa Female Seminary in Bordentown, New Jersey, in 1837; Jane and Kate Reynolds and Isabel Coleman were pupils during 1839–1840.*

Good bye—God bless you all and in a little while I shall be too happy to take a resting spell at Home. Remembrances to all Friends.

Your affectionate Brother,

Wm. Reynolds

Miss Lydia M. Reynolds,
   Cornwall Furnace.

U.S. Schooner Flying Fish
Columbia River, August 10th 1841

My dear Father,

You will receive this letter by Dr. Charles
Guillou, late of the Expedition, and it will be the herald to you of a
visit from himself. He is *my friend* and has been my messmate and
companion during the most of this cruise. In parting with him now, it
is no slight consolation to me that he has promised me to go to
Cornwall as soon as he can leave his own family. Receive *him* as you
would *myself* and I am sure the pleasure his company will afford you
will show you in some degree the measure of enjoyment that his
society has given me. I wish you to have the happiness of knowing
him, and I am glad that *my own* arrival at home will be preceded by
one to whom I can refer you with the greatest confidence for any
information you may desire. Keep him as one whom I esteem more
than I can tell you, and if, while he remains at Cornwall, you will
contribute half so much to his happiness as he has to mine while *we*
have been together, I shall be content and will be glad that my debt
of friendly gratitude to him is partly repaid.

During this cruise we have all suffered much from the tyranny of
Captain Wilkes, who has proceeded to such extremes that unless he
be considered as insane, there can be no excuse for his conduct. He
has carried his shameful and malicious persecutions to an extent that
is almost beyond belief and he has made our servitude under him to
be more galling than can well be borne. All that promised so fair

when we set out, when his reputation was so high that many of us would not allow a word to be breathed against him, was soon dispelled and we have regarded him more as a monster than a man, as one who has done us all the Evil he could.

He has sent Home from the Squadron the very best among us all upon charges which he can never prove; he dismissed them to gratify his horrible spite and for no other motives less personal than this. The sympathy of almost every one of us who are left, attends those who have gone, while we every day find new occasion to regret their loss.

Among those who have been subjected to his displeasure is Doctor Guillou, who after having been deprived of his rank by having *a favorite* (junior to him) promoted over his head and after suffering various indignities, was finally given permission to return home from Oahu in December last. This permission was coupled with such terms that it was impossible to accept it, and Dr. Guillou has since then been a prisoner at large on board the Peacock. Now that *she* is lost, there will be a kind of dispersion among her Officers and it is likely that the Dr. will get Home before the *remnant* of the Squadron; it is with this hope that I write you this letter.[1]

---

[1] *Dr. Guillou delivered this letter to John Reynolds in April 1842, in Philadelphia. He had not left Oahu until nearly a month after the squadron's departure in November 1841. Since returning home, he had been "in almost daily expectation of being able to pay [the Reynolds family] a visit," but "occurrences" had prevented, or so Mr. Reynolds wrote his wife on 13 April when he forwarded his son's letter—the first they had received in a year. Had his family been aware of William's transfer to the Flying Fish just after he sealed Letter No. 17, they would have been spared much anguish when they read accounts of the Peacock's loss.*

Of Dr. Guillou, John Reynolds wrote: "He is quite an interesting young man and I think you will all be pleased with him. He will give you many particulars of the cruize which will surprise and interest you much. He says that William in the Flying Fish suffered more than those of his friends who were in the Peacock, but could do nothing for her relief and the next morning, when the fog rose so as to allow them to see where she had been the evening before, she was not to be seen. Luckily they saw one of the boats, after the fog cleared off, making for the shore and then had hopes that some, if not all,

Captain Wilkes has preferred charges against so many of his Officers (and they in return have done him the like favour) that the difficulties can only be settled by a General Court Martial, after our return. The Evidence in every case will I am sure be dead in favour of the Officers, but I wish you to ask Dr. Guillou to give you some history of his own case and the others, so that when you hear the particulars you will have a better idea of how things have gone on than I can furnish you by letter; and heretofore, in writing home, I have avoided this subject as much as possible, to save you from some uneasiness.

Whatever the result of these Court Martials may be, as long as they are pending men's minds will be busy with the merits and demerits of the different parties, and the individuals concerned will feel that there is an uncertainty in the public opinion (as well as about the verdict) which can best be relieved by the voices of their friends.

It has occurred to me that it would be of some benefit to Dr. Guillou if he were made acquainted with Mr. Buchanan, and I am sure that Mr. B. himself would derive great pleasure and interest from the conversation of my friend, whose intelligence and varied information I will not praise because it will delight you to observe for yourself. I know that this will be extremely gratifying to Dr. Guillou and I ask it of your kindness with the greatest readiness in the certainty that you will all be mutually pleased.

---

had been saved. But you must wait till I get home for any further details and until the Doctor comes up for full particulars" (J. Reynolds 1842).

Upon arriving in New York in July 1842, William received a letter from his mother, dated 12 June, telling him that the doctor had "come up" and that they were all "much pleased" with him. "He promised to visit us again, probably with you" (L. Reynolds 1842a).

Almost immediately upon his return to the United States from the expedition, Guillou was promoted to passed assistant surgeon. In subsequent years, he served with the East India and Mediterranean squadrons and at various domestic bases until his resignation as a surgeon in 1854, at which time he took over the post of surgeon at the American Hospital in Honolulu. It was there that he treated the invalided William Reynolds, as described in the Epilogue. Guillou died in 1897 (ZB).

I have told the Doctor that there is no rail road to Cornwall as yet, and he is aware of Aunt's establishment in Lancaster. He will forward you this from Philadelphia and inform you on what day to expect him in L—— where, of course, some of you will receive him. As I do not know whether Sam or John or James will be at Home, I shall give my friend a letter to Newton Lightner, as it will be more agreeable to him to have a companion of his own years.

And now my dear father, I once again commend my friend to your kind attentions and I think that ere he has been long gone from you, I shall be once more under your roof, myself: in this hope, which is in itself happiness,

I remain

Your affectionate Son

Wm. Reynolds

John Reynolds
    Cornwall Furnace

[*Outside wrapper:*] Forward by Dr. Guillou

Letter No. 20

U.S. Brig Porpoise
April 6th 1842
At Sea off Cape Good Hope

My dear Mother,

A vessel is near which we think must be bound *Home* and in anticipation I have got relieved from the deck to tell you of my good health and that we are *thus far* Homeward bound.

We left Sincapore on the 26th of February and seperated from the Vincennes when we cleared the Straits of Sunda. She stops at the Cape of Good Hope, and then for New York via St. Helena. We touch at St. Helena, and then for New York via Rio de Janeiro; the Vincennes will get Home several weeks *before us* and probably prior to the arrival of the vessel now in sight.[1] We do not hope to see N. York before the 1st of July. I expect to find *letters waiting me there,* to the care of the Lyceum.

I received many old letters in Manilla and Sincapore, and at Manilla received news of my promotion to a Lieutenant for which I am too happy.[2]

[1] *The American ship* Clarendon *was indeed bound for New York, from Canton (Journal 2:383), arriving before the* Vincennes.

[2] *The letter from Acting Secretary of the Navy J. D. Simms informing Reynolds of his commission is dated 21 September of the year previous (Simms 1841).*

I have mounted the *swab*.
In the greatest haste and with the greatest love

                                        Your affectionate

                                              William
                                        Lieut. U.S.N.

Mrs. L. M. Reynolds

[*Inside wrapper*] Report of the Clarendon: 30 March spoke the
Vincennes E. of Madagascar; 26 April the Porpoise left St. Helena.

[*Postmark:*] New York, Jun. 8

U. States Brig Porpoise
At Sea April 20th 1842

[No salutation]

We are now two days' sail from St. Helena, where we will make a very brief delay and then proceed to Rio de Janeiro, where we expect to arrive about the 7th May and leave again in five days for New York.

I wrote to you in November last from Oahu. We had a long passage to Manilla, as we deviated greatly from the direct track.[1] We

---

[1] *When the squadron left Hawaii on 27 November 1841, the* Flying Fish *was to proceed to Manila via the Caroline Islands; the intermediate stops were bypassed, however, because of a sprung mast and calm winds. The* Vincennes *sailed on a similar course between latitude 15 and 20 N, attempting to locate and fix previously reported islands and visiting Wake and the Northern Marianas. Meanwhile, the* Oregon *and the* Porpoise *were ordered to proceed farther north, through the Sea of Japan and the China Sea directly to Singapore.*

On parting with Wilkes and the Vincennes, *Reynolds recorded: "He sent us arms, stores, orders and Dr. Whittle. We were happy enough to get clear of him; and old Whittle, one of the very noblest fellows in the world, made up a most sociable mess of four miserable, discontented wretches as ever were seen." As usual, they were astonished at their orders—to proceed first to Strong (Kusaie) and Ascension (Ponape) islands in the Carolines before proceeding to Manila, where they were to arrive "by the 10th of January without fail." Despite the delay it would occasion, Reynolds managed to*

had hoped Captain Wilkes would be faithful to his promise to the men when he induced them to re-enter, "that they should all be discharged in the U. States on or before the 31st May 1842, unless prevented by an act of God." Now, however, we *gave up* this hope and resigned ourselves to be humbugged and delayed all the way home.

We anchored in Manilla on the 13th January, where I received a letter from Samuel and Lydia dated in February 1841, a few days later than those which came across the Land to the Columbia River, and this is the most recent news I have had of you. On the 21st we sailed and on leaving the Harbour boarded an American Ship four months from Boston, with papers announcing the Naval promotions in September last. I happened to see them first and as my eye fell on *my own* name among the Lieuts. I was absolutely choked with

----

summon up real enthusiasm for a visit to Ascension, a paradise complete with mysterious ruins, and to be acutely disappointed when Knox decided there was no time for such a survey. They pushed on toward Manila. Close now, during his night watch, Sanford saw surf, and then land. Knox and Reynolds dashed topside in their nightshirts; the schooner was in the rollers—they could see the bottom. Every man worked frantically, drenched constantly by the Niagara of water. Finally, the sails were set "amid great fear and effort." "The Schooner trembled, jumped, pitched . . . had she not been the most glorious model of a sea boat that ever was built, she could not have borne the sail an instant." Uncertain as to the outcome, Reynolds hurried down to the cabin for a life preserver; then "she came about! and we knew we were saved" (Journal 2:346–55).

There is not a word of this trauma in his letter home. "Of all the frights I ever had, this was the worst, and the Launch off Cape Horn, the Peacock among the Ice and all the unmentionable risks that have attended my seafaring left no such trace in my mind, nor alarmed me half so much while the danger existed. Roused out of a Sleep to be drowned in five minutes . . . the howling of the gale, the struggle of the vessel, and the terrific aspect of the Land and the Sea and the darkness of the night. . . . I had written home, too, from Oahu telling them that all possible risks were then fairly passed and that we trusted to have a safe and speedy passage to the U. States. Speedy is out of the question, and this tale of 'Cape Espiritu Santo' is yet to be told" (Journal 2:256–57).

surprize and joy. When I found my tongue, I *screamed* loud enough and went fairly wild. I did not expect it for three years to come.

We parted from the Vincennes to survey a shoal to the South of Manilla and entirely out of the route to Sincapore; after finding the shoal and waiting 10 days at an appointed Rendezvous without seeing the Vin. we kept on for Sincapore and arrived there on the 16th of February, instead of the 1st as we had expected, which would have given us the usual time for the direct run.[2] The Oregon and Porpoise had been laying in the harbour *26 days* and had almost given us up. On the 19th the Vincennes arrived and we learned they had been way down in the "Soloo Sea" surveying, as if time was of no account. Captain Wilkes insisted that he had ordered us to follow him there and had a Court of Enquiry on Knox for not doing so, which resulted in showing that he had given no such orders at all.[3]

[2] *After leaving Manila on 21 January, Wilkes ordered the* Flying Fish *to survey the Apo Shoal between Mindoro and Palawan islands, while he surveyed the coast of Panay. Wilkes then continued south through the Philippine Islands to the Sulu archipelago, where at Soung (today Jolo) he negotiated an agreement with the sultan of Sulu to protect and encourage American trade. The Sulu Sea was a shortcut for American ships in the China trade, yet the presence of pirates and treacherous currents made passage risky. Some six years before, the sultan had invited American commerce to his realm, in a letter addressed to a captain G. E. Ward of Salem and transmitted to the Department of State by another Salem merchant captain in 1837 (Amilbahar [1836]; Phillips 1837; N. L. Rogers and Brothers 1838; and Agreement Made by the Sultan of Sooloo 1842).*

[3] *According to Reynolds, two rendezvous points had been decreed. Because the* Vincennes *was not at the first, the schooner lay off Balabac Strait southwest of Palawan, the second point, from 20 January to 8 February "in a fever of impatience and disgust," and also in fear of the many shoals and of pirates. When Knox finally decided to proceed to Singapore, he had no idea the* Vincennes *was close to the eastward, thanks to the usual lack of communication; he thought the ship and the brigs would be well on their way through the Straits of Sunda on their way home. At the court of inquiry, the faithful Knox was accused of not looking for the* Vincennes *at still a third rendezvous. The "usual passage from Manilla to Sincapore during favourable monsoon is 7 or 10 days," but theirs was twenty-six days (*Journal *2:370–77).*

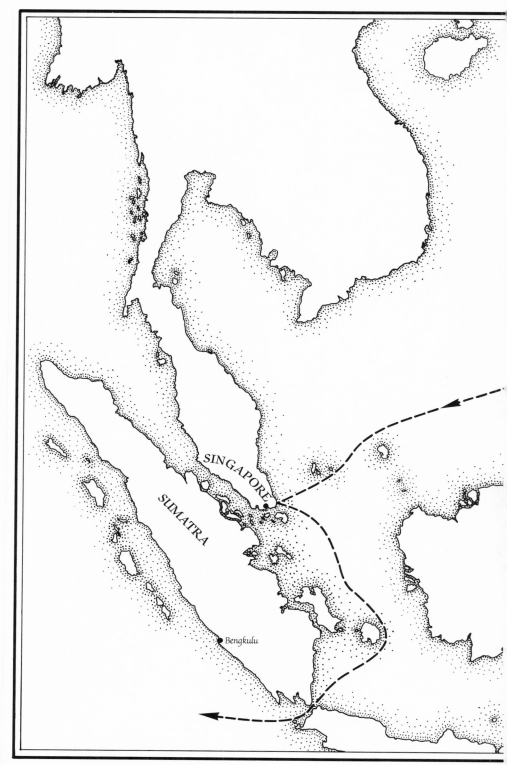

The Philippines and Singapore

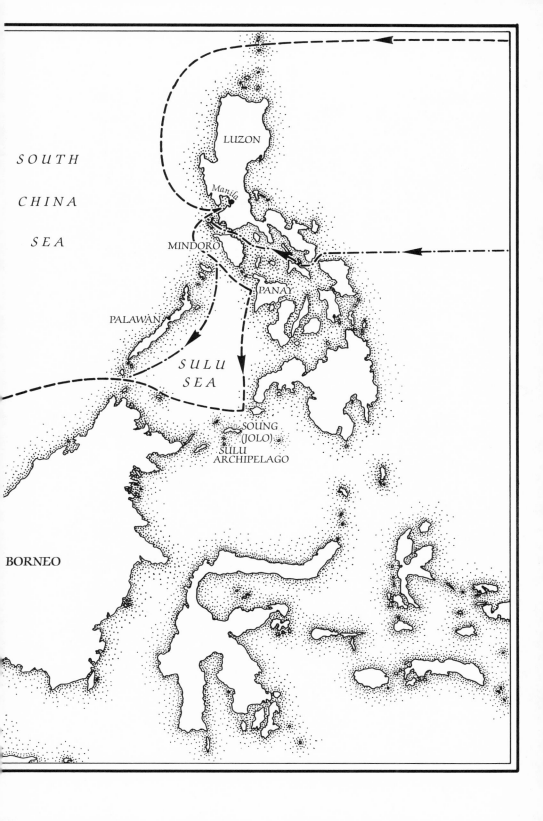

SOUTH

CHINA

SEA

LUZON

Manila

MINDORO

PANAY

PALAWAN

SULU
SEA

SOUNG
(JOLO)
SULU
ARCHIPELAGO

BORNEO

The Flying Fish was sold and I had the satisfaction, at last, to haul down her flag and deliver her up.[4]

I joined this Brig and on the 26th February we sailed from Sincapore, expecting that we would all meet at the Cape of Good Hope and then sail in company for home. Five days out, Captain Wilkes issued a general order recognizing our promotions and we mounted *the swab* accordingly. May came in for the Mastership of the Vincennes.

We cleared the Straits of Sunda on the 6th March and launched into the Indian Ocean quite glad to be free from Islands, shoals and surveys, and to have a clear sea around us at last. The Vincennes outsails the Brigs and in two days she was out of sight ahead; *the murder came out, now:* The Vin. alone was to touch at the Cape and then Home via St. Helena, as strait a course as can be run. The Brigs were to go *out* of their way *300 miles merely* to leave *word* at St. H. "*how we got on, as he would like to know,*" and then proceed to Rio de Janeiro to make some paltry magnetic experiments, which deviation will add four weeks' delay and keep us out until the first week in July.[5] The miserable reason for this is very plain: he did not wish to

---

[4] *Because Knox was both suspended during the inquiry and unwell, the charge of the schooner devolved on Reynolds "to clean her out, carry her on shore, and deliver her up. . . . The crew were unwilling to leave her for they were very much attached to her. . . . We left her together and I could not help feeling some sorrow at leaving her in the hands of strangers." She was "like a gallant horse that has carried you safely through the fight" (Journal 2:378). The sale of the* Flying Fish *realized $3,700. Howard I. Chappelle (1949:390) reports that the schooner "afterward became a notorious opium smuggler, under the name of* Spec.*"*

[5] *Despite his reluctance to touch at St. Helena, Reynolds was singularly impressed by the sole day spent there, 24 April. The last three pages of Journal No. 2 and the first six of Journal No. 3 are filled with the mystique of Napoleon's last dwelling place and its comical commercialization but above all with the "extraordinary thrill of pleasurable excitement" brought on by the unexpected presence of two young ladies, the British consul's daughter and a friend. It was as if "some good fairy had waved her wand over us—we were as happy as all enchanted mortals should be." Before returning to the brig, he*

be detained by sailing in Company, and in separating to *make sure* that we should not arrive home *before him,* he sends us away to Jericho. He saddled us, too, with another species of persecution by requiring us to "heave to" every day, to try the temperature of the Sea at 100 fths.' depth, which during the whole cruize has not been done 12 times. A more ingenious system of torture he could not have invented; it is enough to make us cry to see the sails taken in when they are swelling before a fair breeze, but we cannot help it, and all the relief we experience is in putting a slight malediction on the head of our *friend* and in reminding each other that it cannot last for ever.

If we could continue on, now, direct for the U. States, we could arrive there with ease by the 1st of June, but we are to pay now for having trusted to the promise of a man who is as reckless of truth and as destitute of honour as any rascal that ever breathed.

We expect to be clear of the Brig immediately on our arrival in New York, as we think they cannot have the conscience to detain the officers to strip her after the crew have all received their discharges; of course *they* quit her and work no more after the anchor's down, if they will continue quiet and placable for that long. We shall have no legal authority over them after the 21st May and they are all aware that a Commander in the Navy has recently been fined $100.00 for

---

"*told them truthfully this had been to me the very happiest day of the cruise.*"

The two brigs sailed into Rio on 12 May. "As we passed under the stern of the Old Delaware, I shoved off to board her to report our arrival to Commodore Morris. . . . The Delaware Officers looked at me as if I were a Natural Curiosity: they had not seen an Explorer *in full bloom. . . . The Commander remembered me and was very kind." Charles Morris (1784–1856) had commanded the Boston Navy Yard when Reynolds reported there for his first duty in 1832; the* Delaware, *too, was an old acquaintance, for he had sailed home in her in 1836.*

The task of the Porpoise *at Rio was to pick up five small boxes of specimens "light enough to be lifted by one hand." "The* Oregon *came for nothing, bought nothing, and went away as wise and as Empty as she came." Sunday, 22 May, they hove up anchor and the* Delaware's *"band played 'Sweet Home' as loud as they could blow" (Journal 3:10, 23).*

punishing a seaman whose time had expired. We have to trust entirely to their disposition for good or bad conduct, and a more disagreeable situation for the Commander and Officers cannot be imagined.[6]

I have determined, however, to remain in New York until I rig myself with a complete fit out of clothes, and so get that very important matter over at once; at present I have not a single garment decent enough to go ashore in. I suppose I shall stay there for 5 to 7 days and in that time will visit West Point.

This letter will be left at St. Helena for the Vincennes (it is *too* hard that we are reduced to writing *Home* by *her*) and I presume she will reach New York during the first week in June, or by the 10th at farthest; we cannot, until the 1st of July. I want you to have a letter awaiting me there in the care of the Lyceum with all the family news.[7] I hope to find letters in Rio up to January or February and, as you may suppose, I am very anxious to know whether Sam has left Cornwall and what has become of John and James; the rest of you are fixtures, I *know*.[8] I am very much afraid that John is in some out of

---

[6] *Reynolds wrote his father on 2 July on his arrival in New York, "in great Haste and confusion." "The men have all left the Brig, except 10 hands, and the Comod. kept us to look out for her and them. There are no funds here to pay them off, and I believe we are to be reduced to the necessity of borrowing money to buy our clothes and pay our way Home. It seems the extra pay hangs in a dubious scale, and as we have drawn so much of it, the Secretary has stopped all further payments until the matter is decided. I shall have no difficulty in procuring money here and suppose you will have enough of mine in your hands to repay it when I get Home" (1842).*

[7] *His mother's 12 June letter awaited William. After setting forth "all the family news," she offered some maternal advice: "I must beg, Dear Wm., if you have mustachios or any superfluous hairs on your face to have them removed before you come home, as your father dislikes them very much" (L. Reynolds 1842b).*

[8] *From the "3 or 4 letters" received in Rio, Reynolds had his "first intimation of Sam's establishment at 'Lucinda Furnace,' John's lieutenancy in the Artillery and Jim's commencement of the Law, etc. etc." Lydia and Jane's letter was as recent as February. They regretted exceedingly that John*

the way place where I shall not get to see him, but I have still some hope that this summer may bring us all together once more.

[*No closing*]

[*No addressee*]

[*Outside wrapper:*] John Reynolds, Esq.

[*Postmark:*] New York, Jun. 15[9]

---

would be stationed in Florida on William's return. Lydia wrote: "I do not believe you will know one of the family, but myself. Kate [seventeen] is very near as tall as I am, and so is Jane [eighteen], and they are both very pretty indeed. . . . R. Krug is still single and as much admired as ever" (Lydia and Jane Reynolds 1842). Reynolds actually failed to recognize his brother Sam when he and their cousin Sam Witmer came on board on 4 July and "had to ask 'which of you is it?' "

[9] The Vincennes arrived at St. Helena on 1 May, and she—and this letter—arrived in New York 10 June 1842.

Epilogue

Because Wilkes had sent the other ships to Rio for additional scientific specimens, the *Vincennes* reached New York City well ahead of them, arriving 10 June 1842. The *Oregon* arrived nineteen days later. Reynolds, now with the *Porpoise*, reached New York three days after that, on 2 July.

Having kept a careful accounting of the crew during the expedition, Reynolds recorded the final tallies. The expedition had left the United States with 346 crewmen of whom only 181 served to the end. Of the rest, 46 had deserted, 48 had left at Oahu because their enlistments had expired, and 71 had either died, were lost, or were sent home for one reason or another. To make up for the losses, Wilkes had added other personnel as needed so that the total number of enlisted men who served during the expedition was 524 (Stanton 1975:279).

Sadly, the voyage that had begun with such excitement and anticipation ended in bitterness and controversy. Instead of a hero's welcome, the explorers were met by a seemingly uninterested public, an unfriendly Congress, and doubts about their accomplishments in Antarctica. Wilkes attributed the lack of attention the explorers received to the Whig administration that had recently gained office and was "opposed to my receiving any honors or gratifications" (Wilkes 1978:520).

A harbinger of things to come was the death of Vendovi, who had remained a prisoner on board the *Vincennes* for almost two years. He survived the squadron's return to New York by only hours before dying in a naval hospital there. Although saddened by his death, the scientifics compensated for losing their living artifact by adding his skull to their collections.

More ominous for the reputation of the expedition was the antagonism between Wilkes and his junior officers. Even before the explorers returned, there had been rumors of discontent, which the *New York Morning Herald* confirmed three days after the *Vincennes* reached port: "We understand that there is to be a nice mess dished up in a short time in the shape of court martials, [and] courts of inquiry . . . in the eating of which nearly all of the officers of the Exploring Expedition are to participate with finger glasses and napkins" (1842). Would they participate? There would have been no keeping them away so certain were they that the arrogant Wilkes was finally going to receive his comeuppance.

One of the most interested spectators was Reynolds, who had managed to buy a new outfit and slip away for a brief visit home. He returned in time to attend the courts-martial, which began 25 July on board the man of war *North Carolina* at the Brooklyn Navy Yard. For the next three months, he and his fellow explorers listened intently to the testimony as the court heard the charges brought by Wilkes against Reynolds's good friends May and Guillou and Lieutenants Robert E. Johnson and Robert F. Pinkney.

The American public also looked forward to the courts-martial in hopes of learning something about what had been accomplished during the expedition. Up to now, commented one newspaper, its activities had been "like a sealed book" (Stanton 1975:283).

Expectations were great, but for the most part the trials were a disappointment to everyone except the defendants. The testimony revealed more about Wilkes than about the Exploring Expedition as a procession of his officers, testifying on behalf of the defendants, described him as "violent," "overbearing," "rude withal," "offensive," and "taxing forbearance to the last degree." Perhaps the most telling statement was by May, who wrote of Wilkes: "He who would survey the world must first sound the depths and shallows of his own character." The *New York Tribune*, in summing up the litany of petty grievances, suggested the courts-martial did little more than show "the excitability of Lieutenant Wilkes" (Stanton 1975:284).

The results of the court certainly served to vindicate the junior officers. May, charged with disrespect, was found guilty of disobeying an order—he had refused to remove a label from a box—and received a public reprimand. Pinkney was found guilty of writing disrespectful letters, among them one he attempted to send to the secretary of the navy; he received a public reprimand and was suspended from the service for six months. Johnson, charged with disobedience and wasting government property, was acquitted after only two days of testimony. Guillou had a tougher time of it because Wilkes had a lengthy list of offenses against the feisty doctor, whose main problem seems to have been a failure to adjust to naval discipline. The court ordered him dismissed from the naval service, but President John Tyler reduced the sentence to a year's suspension.

During a brief recess before the main attraction—the court-martial of Wilkes on charges brought against him by Pinkney and Guillou— Reynolds rushed back to Lancaster "to conclude" his marriage to Rebecca Krug. "I do not expect this announcement to surprise you much," Reynolds wrote his father on 14 August, "as I mentioned to you that if I could make such an arrangement, I should adopt it, without delay."[1] The marriage took place two days later; Lydia was a bridesmaid.

The following day Reynolds and his bride were in New York in time for the opening of Wilkes's court-martial.[2] The embattled commander faced seven charges brought against him by Guillou, including oppression, cruelty, disobedience of orders, illegal punishments, and conduct unbecoming an officer. Pinkney's four charges covered basically the same ground but with different specifications.

The most serious of Guillou's charges was that Wilkes had lied about sighting land on 19 January 1840. Only one enlisted man could recall discussing it with him on the morning in question, whereas several officers who had been on board the *Vincennes* that day could recall

[1] *Unless otherwise cited, quotations and information about members of the family are taken from correspondence and documents in the custody of Anne Hoffman Cleaver, Westfield, Indiana, and the Reynolds Family Papers at Franklin and Marshall College.*

[2] *The court-martial proceedings can be found in Records of the Hydrographic Office, RG 37, NA.*

nothing noteworthy having occurred. The situation looked bleak for Wilkes and the reputation of the expedition until Reynolds and his shipmate Henry Eld stepped forward. They could not say what Wilkes had seen from the *Vincennes* on 19 January, but they knew what they had seen from the *Peacock* three days earlier. "I went to the Main topmast Crosstrees in company with Lt. Reynolds as it was my custom to do every day while cruizing in those seas," Eld declared. "We both of us immediately exclaimed and I believe simultaneously—there is the land" (Stanton 1975:287).

The only charge against Wilkes that the court substantiated was that of illegal punishments. Navy ship captains could authorize a maximum of twelve lashes without benefit of a court, yet Wilkes had ordered more, sometimes as many as forty. The court found him guilty of ordering illegal punishments in seventeen instances and sentenced him to a public reprimand by the secretary of the navy. It was a mild rebuke but one that deeply stung the proud Wilkes, whose lengthy defense had stressed the many hardships he had faced. One of his most difficult challenges, he claimed, had been the "cabal" of officers formed "to thwart all the objects of the Expedition, which were not consistent with the ease of the gentlemen who composed it." Reynolds, whom Wilkes considered a member of the cabal, grumbled to his family that the defense had been "such a production as was to be expected from him—Arrogant, careless, dictatorial in its tone to the Court and full of malicious abuse [and] . . . taking a sly chance at us all" (Stanton 1975:288).

Reynolds remained ashore for more than a year after his return. Much of that time he lived with Rebecca in the Krug household, down the street from his family's temporary "town" house, where he enjoyed the life of a landlubber and was able, for the first time since joining the navy eleven years before, to celebrate his birthday and Christmas with the members of his "many headed" family. Even his brother John was home, now a lieutenant in the army and recuperating from a near fatal attack of "bilious fever" contracted in Florida.

The extended leave had both its high and low moments. While in Washington in January 1843 to "electioneer" among members of Congress for the "extra pay" that had been promised the explorers, he visited the Patent Office Building to see displayed there the specimens that had been collected during the Exploring Expedition. Wilkes, who

William Reynolds during the mid-1840s.
Courtesy Anne Hoffman Cleaver.

had charge of the specimens and was supervising the publication of the
scientific reports based on them, was also there. As luck would have it,
the two met, giving Reynolds "the supreme gratification"—he boasted
to Eld—"of cutting him dead. God everlastingly damn him!" Later that
month Reynolds was in Baltimore for the wedding of one his shipmates.
A dozen of his fellow explorers were also there, and they had "a merry
time" (Reynolds 1843a). The pleasant reunion with his family ended on
a sad note, however, with the unexpected death of his mother just as he
was about to return to sea duty. She was only forty-nine. Her grave

became the first of twenty-five in the family plot in the new Lancaster cemetery.

Hoping to give Rebecca a cruise to the Mediterranean, Reynolds applied for duty on board the frigate *Cumberland*, flagship of the Mediterranean Squadron. It was a welcome assignment because the squadron's winter headquarters at Mahon, Minorca, provided facilities for wives. When Rebecca arrived in November 1844, she found that her husband had rented "a very fine house . . . set amid flowers and orange trees, for which, with the furniture [they paid] $15.00 a month." To manage the household, Reynolds had the volunteer services of the retired steward of the *Vincennes*, who also loaned them the handsome table service from that ship given him at the end of the expedition. The young couple had many pleasant moments at Mahon as veterans of the Exploring Expedition continually gathered around their table to talk over "that never to be forgotten cruise." Rebecca's only regret was that William had so many friends she scarcely had an hour alone with him. "The officers think we are a pattern couple, but very unfashionable to be so much in love after being married for more than two years."

The years that followed were less tranquil. From the Mediterranean, Reynolds returned to Lancaster and spent another year in the Krug household. During this time, Rebecca's brother Harry, who had long been ill at home, finally died of consumption. Many of Reynolds's future physical problems, which included symptoms of that dreaded disease, in all probability stemmed from this long exposure.

Of more immediate concern to Reynolds was Wilkes, who, in 1845, had published the official history of the expedition. Titled *Narrative of the United States Exploring Expedition*, the five-volume work did not please Reynolds and other officers. Publishing passages from their journals without attribution was bad enough, but his use of the *Narrative* to even old scores was intolerable. As a result, Wilkes once again found himself embroiled in controversy with his fellow explorers, who this time managed to enlist the aid of several sympathetic congressmen in their cause.

One was the avid expansionist Thomas Hart Benton of Missouri, who questioned the validity of Wilkes's condemnation of the Columbia River as a safe harbor. Senator Benton noted that the condemnation was disputed by "the seventy days' labor of three young gentlemen, midshipmen in the expedition, whose numerous soundings show the diligence and the accuracy of their work—their names, Knox, Reynolds, and Blair" (Blair [1846]:4). The three "gentlemen" gleefully sided with Benton. Wilkes, never one to retreat from a fight, responded in kind. The result was a war of words that amused readers of the *Washington Union* from May to August 1846. Wilkes twice refuted his officers and was answered. Reynolds not only responded at length, but he also obtained the testimony of other expedition officers who questioned Wilkes's judgment.

Much more lively was the assault on Wilkes for using the *Narrative* to air charges against his officers that had supposedly been settled by the courts-martial. Thirteen officers signed a "Memorial" (1846), which was presented to the Senate by Benton and to the House of Representatives by Stephen A. Douglas on 11 January 1847. The memorialists, citing twenty-three pages of accusations against them, demanded the appointment of a congressional committee to investigate the "various allegations" made in the *Narrative* that affected their "private and professional honor and character." The Congress, instead, ordered the document printed and turned over to the Library Committee, the body that had authorized publication of the *Narrative*.

No investigation was forthcoming, but Wilkes did reply to the memorial. As could have been anticipated, his response was not very conciliatory, and it infuriated Reynolds, who told his father it was "full of false statements from beginning to end. He says *we* were the *insubordinates* and *cabalists* and that *he* and the *rest of the officers* did all *the work*." The irate lieutenant drafted fifteen pages of precise refutation which he sent to the chairman of the Library Committee, who evidently ignored it, thereby bringing the matter to a close.

When the war with Mexico broke out, Reynolds immediately asked for a combat assignment but was told that there was "no exigency" for officers. He eventually was assigned as second lieutenant to the *Allegheny*, 1,100 tons, the navy's first war steamer, which featured an experimental horizontal paddle system. Unfortunately, the vessel never performed to expectations. For months, it was bogged down in mud at the Memphis Navy Yard. From Memphis it went to New Orleans, where it received orders for an ocean test, but yellow fever struck the *Allegheny* before it had proceeded very far. With Reynolds and the ship's doctor the only officers fit for duty, the vessel put in at Key West and then limped to Norfolk, where she was taken apart and then rebuilt. By now, Reynolds had been named first lieutenant, but the promotion did little to ease his dissatisfaction at missing out on the glories of war, especially when he learned that May had been seriously wounded in the taking of Tabasco and his brother John had been breveted a captain for outstanding service at Monterrey; John capped that feat a few months later by being promoted to brevet major for bravery at Buena Vista.

Finally, in February 1848, the *Allegheny* left Norfolk for a shakedown cruise, going from Rio de Janeiro to Buenos Aires and back several times before returning. This time it was Reynolds who had problems, experiencing the ill health that was to plague him the rest of his life. He was "bled" for the first time, slept poorly, and suffered severe chest pains and soaking night sweats—symptoms he was to know for many years. "Wonder if I am to get the Conzumption and die!" he confided in his journal. "I have for the first time in my life become Melancholy! Whether these things are to wear off, or to wear me out, remains to be seen." This was in sharp contrast to the excellent health he enjoyed during the Exploring Expedition, when he boasted: "In one thing I have reason to be thankful. I have never been unwell, not for an hour, for the last five years and have not missed a single watch by day or night on account of my health. Among the Sea Officers, not another one has been so fortunate . . . and I think there can be little wrong in a constitution that has borne all the hardships, climates and privations of this cruize" (Journal 1:30).

Despite concerns about his health, Reynolds accompanied the *Allegheny* to the Mediterranean. Perhaps he hoped a sea voyage would improve his condition. If so, he was mistaken. A few days after his thirty-third birthday he had eleven leeches applied to his throat; his health remained poor throughout the voyage. Upon his return, his condition did not escape Rebecca's notice. She thought he looked thinner than ever and "not well." Having lost her mother, sister, and brother to consumption, she knew its symptoms all too well. The *Allegheny* also returned the worse for wear; a naval board condemned it to coastal service.

In March 1850, Reynolds began working for the Bureau of Construction and Repair but found the pace too much for him. His doctor recommended that he spend the winter in Florida, living in the open air as much as possible. The worried officer followed the prescription to the letter. He and Rebecca arrived in Palatka on the St. John's River in

William Reynolds and Rebecca Krug Reynolds during the 1860s. This picture of Commander Reynolds was taken at Hilton Head by the Tenth Army Corps photographer. Rebecca's, inscribed "Nov. 1862" on the back, was taken in Philadelphia, probably to send to William at Port Royal before she joined him there. Courtesy Anne Hoffman Cleaver.

November and took up residence in a boardinghouse for "gentlemen invalids," where they remained until mid-April. Having arrived in Palatka by boat, they returned on horseback—a favorite medical recommendation for the ailing of his day, second only to a "sea voyage." Nevertheless, his health remained precarious.

Determined to see if a protracted stay in a warm climate would not restore his health, Reynolds requested a year's leave of absence. In September 1851, he set sail for the Hawaiian Islands (Rebecca joined him the following year), where he leased one hundred acres at Malumalu on the east coast of Kauai—at one dollar the acre for fifty years—built a house, and tried his hand at farming. When that venture failed, he tried unsuccessfully to obtain a consulate in the islands. Meanwhile, his

health remained poor, and he feared that he would never be robust again. Although he received another year's leave from the navy, he did not have sufficient income to continue living on Kauai and so accepted command of the storeship *Fredonia*, stationed in Valparaíso. His command was short-lived because of continued ill health. He was detached and placed on the reserve list. Upon returning home, he inherited some money as a result of his father's death and obtained the post of naval storekeeper in Honolulu. Once again in Hawaii, William and Rebecca spent the winter with Dr. Guillou and his family and the following summer sold their home at Malumalu.

Notwithstanding the change in climate, poor health continued to plague Reynolds. In 1858 tumors developed in a leg, which became so swollen and inflamed that it had to be lanced—again and again. Dr. Guillou warned that amputation might be necessary. Reynolds managed to avoid that drastic step, but he felt he should be resigned to lameness, which could fluctuate from partial to entire for the rest of his life.

When the Civil War broke out, he wanted to be part of the action. Reynolds returned to Washington, where he met his brother John, now a brigadier general. Although John thought he looked "badly," William was determined to get afloat again. He spent most of 1862 relentlessly seeking a cure from doctors in Baltimore, Philadelphia, and Newport and lobbying for an assignment. In October, having been promoted to commander on the reserve list, he was given command of the storeship *Vermont*. The vessel was stationed at Port Royal, the base for the South Atlantic Blockading Squadron midway between Charleston and Savannah. For a time Rebecca lived with her husband on the *Vermont*, but she returned to Pennsylvania shortly before it was hit by a torpedo. Reynolds's pleasure at being in uniform once again was tempered by John's death, killed at Gettysburg by a Confederate sharpshooter on the first day of battle. "I do believe that as far as human infirmities ever allow, he was a man without guile and without reproach," William wrote upon learning the news.

When the war ended, Reynolds was commended by Admiral John Dahlgren for his service to the blockading fleet. This had been a great responsibility, Dahlgren noted, and its successful conduct was owing entirely to Reynolds's "intelligence and experience." Despite the strenuous duty, Reynolds had enjoyed good health for the first time in many years. His weight, which had been only 123 pounds in Valparaíso, was now 188.

Following the war, Reynolds sought reinstatement to the active list, which he succeeded in obtaining thanks to the aid of fellow officers. He was confirmed on 11 May 1866 retroactive to 25 April 1861. The news came while he was in command of the USS *Lackawanna* in New York harbor, bound for Honolulu. On the voyage he learned of his promotion to captain. His many friends in Honolulu welcomed the now healthy officer and his wife; not so the government. The pro-British and pro-native-rights king, Kamehameha V, and his advisers were highly suspicious of an American warship seemingly stationed indefinitely in Hawaiian waters and even more of her captain, whose advocacy of American annexation in the 1850s was well remembered. Hawaiian duty was strained. On 28 August 1867, Captain Reynolds took formal possession for the United States of Brooks Island. "It is exceedingly gratifying to me to have been . . . concerned in taking possession of the first island ever added to the domain of the United States beyond our own shores, and I sincerely hope that this instance will by no means be the last of our insular annexations," Reynolds wrote. The island is now known as Midway.

Reynolds's career now blossomed. Upon his return from Hawaii in 1869, he was named "President of Ordnance." The following year he was appointed a member of the Board of Visitors of the U.S. Naval Academy, named chief of the Bureau of Equipment and Recruiting, and commissioned a commodore. In 1873, he was promoted to rear admiral. He also served twice as acting secretary of the navy.

On the heels of these laurels came another tour of sea duty, this time as commander of the Asiatic Station. His flagship was the USS *Tennessee*, 3,281 tons (compared to the 700 tons of the Exploring Expedition's *Vincennes*). Rebecca shared his steam-heated quarters on board the flagship, and they enjoyed an idyllic life visiting various ports of call between China and Japan.

At every port there was much entertaining between ship and shore. The admiral and his staff were received by the emperor of Japan and the leading ministers of both Japan and China. Probably the most significant accomplishment of the cruise, however, was the reestablishment of friendly relations between Siam and the United States and her missionaries.

The grand tour ended abruptly at Yokohama in the summer of 1877, when Reynolds suffered a seizure and collapsed. A series of receptions had been organized for the Yokohama visit even though both the admiral and his wife had been unwell for some time. Reynolds had a bad cough, difficulty breathing, and trouble with his leg. Nonetheless, he seemed to enjoy the Fourth of July celebration and a reception for several hundred people. The next day, however, he was stricken by a "congestion of the brain" and lost consciousness for several hours. The ship's doctor declared him "unfit for duty" and recommended that he be sent home at the earliest opportunity.

Reynolds returned to Washington, D.C., where he lingered for another two years. During this time, he added a codicil to his will, stating his desire to be buried in the family lot in Lancaster "in a quiet and inexpensive manner . . . under the auspices of my Masonic Brethren." His death on 5 November 1879 came as no surprise, and he was buried as he desired. His walnut casket, covered with the American flag from the *Tennessee,* was displayed in the Masonic Hall on West King Street in Lancaster, only a few doors from the house he had quitted for the navy.

Reynolds died just twelve days short of completing forty-eight years of naval service. During his remarkable career, he had survived collisions with icebergs, cannibals, and storms at sea, somehow escaping the watery grave so common to sailors in the age of sail. Not so his beloved Rebecca, who once wrote: "I shall never love the sea except from shore." She drowned while on an excursion off Old Point Comfort, Virginia, on 12 April 1885.

ITINERARY OF WILLIAM REYNOLDS

on the U.S. Exploring Expedition, 1838–1842

1838

18 August	Departed Norfolk, Virginia (Reynolds assigned to *Vincennes*)
16–25 September	Funchal, Madeira
7 October	Porto Praia, Cape Verde Islands
23 November	Arrived Rio de Janeiro, Brazil

1839

6 January	Departed Rio de Janeiro
25 January–3 February	Rio Negro, Argentina
18 February–17 April	Orange Harbor, Tierra del Fuego (During this period, four of the ships made the first Antarctic cruise; the *Sea Gull* was lost)
15 May–6 June	Valparaíso, Chile
30 June–13 July	Callao, Peru (*Relief* detached from the squadron and headed home via Hawaii and New South Wales)

13 August–9 September	Tuamotu Archipelago
9–29 September	Tahiti and Society Islands
11 October– 10 November	Samoa Islands
29 November– 26 December	Sydney, New South Wales (Reynolds assigned to *Peacock*)
26 December	Second Antarctic cruise begins

1840

21 February–30 March	Sydney, New South Wales (The rest of the squadron in the meantime proceeded to New Zealand)
1–5 May	Tonga Islands
6 May–11 August	Fiji Islands
30 September– 2 December	Sandwich (Hawaiian) Islands (Reynolds assigned to *Flying Fish*. At this point, the *Porpoise* explored the southeast Pacific again, the *Peacock* and *Flying Fish* returned to the south central Pacific, and the *Vincennes* remained in Hawaiian waters)
11–20 December	Line Islands

1841

9 January	Phoenix Islands
18 January–3 February	Tokelau Islands
5 February–6 March	Samoa Islands
14–24 March	Ellice Islands (Tuvalu)
3 April–1 May	Kingsmill or Gilbert Islands (Kiribati)
2–9 May	Marshall Islands
14–21 June	Sandwich Islands
18 July–20 October	Oregon Territory (*Peacock* was lost; *Oregon* purchased. The other ships left Oregon for California before sailing for Hawaii)
17–27 November	Sandwich Islands

1842

13 January–ca. 6 February	Philippine Islands (*Porpoise* and *Oregon* bypassed Philippines for South China Sea)
16–26 February	Singapore (*Flying Fish* sold; Reynolds assigned to *Porpoise*)
24 April	St. Helena Island
12–22 May	Rio de Janeiro
2 July	Arrived New York (*Vincennes* had arrived 10 June)

Appendix B

Genealogy of William Reynolds's Family

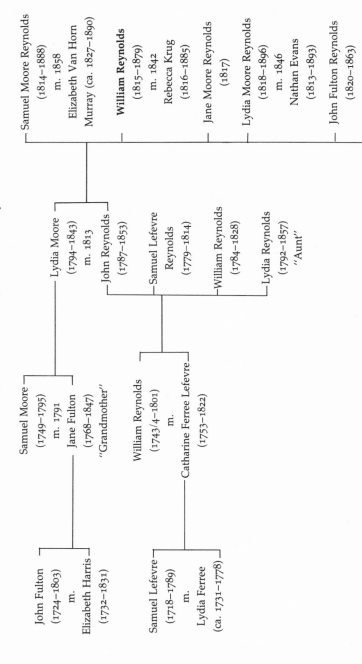

Samuel Moore
(1749–1795)
m. 1791
Jane Fulton
(1768–1847)
"Grandmother"

John Fulton
(1724–1803)
m.
Elizabeth Harris
(1732–1831)

William Reynolds
(1743/4–1801)
m.
Catharine Ferree Lefevre
(1753–1822)

Samuel Lefevre
(1718–1789)
m.
Lydia Ferree
(ca. 1731–1778)

Lydia Moore
(1794–1843)
m. 1813
John Reynolds
(1787–1853)

Samuel Lefevre
Reynolds
(1779–1814)

William Reynolds
(1784–1828)

Lydia Reynolds
(1792–1857)
"Aunt"

Samuel Moore Reynolds
(1814–1888)
m. 1858
Elizabeth Van Horn
Murray (ca. 1827–1890)

William Reynolds
(1815–1879)
m. 1842
Rebecca Krug
(1816–1885)

Jane Moore Reynolds
(1817)

Lydia Moore Reynolds
(1818–1896)
m. 1846
Nathan Evans
(1813–1893)

John Fulton Reynolds
(1820–1863)

James Lefevre Reynolds
(1822–1880)

Mary Jane Reynolds
(1824–1901) "Jane"

m. 1849

George Gildersleeve
(1822–1900)

Catharine Ferree Reynolds
(1825–1905)
"Kate" or "Cate"

m. 1854

Henry D. Landis
(1824–1895)

Anne Elizabeth Reynolds
(1827–1832)

Edward Coleman Reynolds
(1827–1828)

Edward Reynolds
(1829)

Harriot Sumner Reynolds
(1832–1898) "Hal"

Eleanor Reynolds
(1835–1923) "Elly"

Abbreviations

AHC	Personal collection of Anne Hoffman Cleaver, Westfield, Indiana
Letters WEE	Letters Relating to the Wilkes Exploring Expedition, National Archives
MV	Herman J. Viola and Carolyn J. Margolis, eds., *Magnificent Voyagers: The U.S. Exploring Expedition, 1838–1842.* Washington: Smithsonian Institution Press, 1985.
NA	National Archives and Records Service, Washington
RFP	Reynolds Family Papers, Archives and Special Collections Department, Shadek-Fackenthal Library, Franklin and Marshall College, Lancaster, Pennsylvania
RG	Record Group
WFP	Wilkes Family Papers, Manuscript Department, Duke University Library
ZB	ZB Files, Operational Archives, Naval Historical Center, Washington Navy Yard

Bibliography

Agreement Made by the Sultan of Sooloo at Soung, 5 February 1842
    1842   Box 21, Charles Wilkes Family Papers, Manuscript Division, Library of Congress.

American State Papers
    1861   *Naval Affairs.* Vol. 4 (1831–1836). Washington.

Amilbahar, Datu
    [1836]   Letter to G. E. Ward, undated. Box 1, Area File 10, RG 45, NA.

Appleman, Daniel E.
    1985   James Dwight Dana and Pacific Geology. In *MV*, pp. 89–117.

Badger, George E.
    1841   Letter to Charles Wilkes, 23 April. Roll 33, M149, Letters Sent by Secretary of the Navy to Officers, Navy Department, NA.

Bauer, K. Jack
    1969   *Surfboats and Horse Marines: U.S. Naval Operations in the Mexican War, 1846–48.* Annapolis: United States Naval Institute.

Bennett, Frank M.
    1900   *The Monitor and the Navy under Steam.* Boston: Houghton Mifflin.

Bertrand, Kenneth J.
    1971   *Americans in Antarctica, 1775–1948.* Special Publication 39. New York: American Geological Society.

Bethell, Leslie
    1970   *The Abolition of the African Slave Trade: Britain, Brazil, and the Slave Trade Question, 1807–1869.* Cambridge, Eng.: University Press.

Bingham, Hiram
    1981   *A Residence of Twenty-one Years in the Sandwich Islands, or the Civil, Religious, and Political History of Those Islands.* 1847. Reprint. Rutland, Vt.: Charles E. Tuttle.
Biographical Annals of Lancaster County, Pennsylvania
    1903   Chicago: J. H. Beers.
Blair, James, comp.
    [1846]   *Notices of the Harbour at the Mouth of the Columbia River. By the Commander and Other Officers of the Exploring Expedition.* [Washington.]
Blunt, Simon
    1841   Letter to William Reynolds, 3 April. Box 1, Area File 9, RG 45, NA.
Borthwick, Doris Esch
    1965   Outfitting the United States Exploring Expedition: Lieutenant Charles Wilkes' European Assignment, August–November 1836. *Proceedings of the American Philosophical Society* 69 (3): 159–72.
Boynton, Charles B.
    1867   *The History of the Navy during the Rebellion.* New York: D. Appleton.
Burr, Henry L.
    1939   *Education in the Early Navy.* Philadelphia: N.p.
Callahan, Edward W., ed.
    1894   *A History of the United States Navy from 1775 to 1894.* New York: D. Appleton.
Carmean, Edna J.
    1976   *The Colemans—Lebanon's Royal Family.* Lebanon, Pa.: Lebanon County Historical Society.
Cassin, John
    1858   *Mammalogy and Ornithology Atlas. United States Exploring Expedition.* Philadelphia: C. Sherman.
Chappelle, Howard I.
    1949   *The History of the American Sailing Navy.* New York: Norton.
Christie, E. W. Hunter
    1951   *The Antarctic Problem: An Historical and Political Study.* London: George Allen & Unwin.
Clark, Charles E.
    1977   *Maine, A Bicentennial History.* New York: Norton.
Clark, Charles M. H.
    1962–1973 *A History of Australia.* 3 vols. London: Cambridge University Press and Melbourne University Press.
Coletta, Paolo E., ed.
    1980   *American Secretaries of the Navy.* 2 vols. Annapolis: Naval Institute Press.

Congreve, William
1970   *The Details of the Rocket System: Showing the Various Applications of This Weapon, Both for Sea and Land Service, and Its Different Uses in the Field and in Sieges. . . . 1814.* Reprint. Ottawa: Museum Restoration Service.

Cook, James
1955   *The Journals of Captain James Cook on His Voyages of Discovery: The Voyage of the Endeavour, 1768–1771.* Edited by J. C. Beaglehole. Cambridge, Eng.: Hakluyt Society by the University Press.

Cooper, John M.
1946   The Yahgan. In *Handbook of South American Indians.* Edited by Julian Steward, 1:81–106. Smithsonian Institution, Bureau of American Ethnology, Bulletin 143. 7 vols. Washington: U.S. Government Printing Office, 1946–1959.

Craig, Robert D., and Frank P. King, eds.
1981   *Historical Dictionary of Oceania.* Westport, Conn.: Greenwood Press.

Darling, Frank C., ed.
1965   *List of the Officers of the Navy of the United States and of the Marine Corps from 1775 to 1900.* New York: L. R. Hamersly.

Daws, Gavin
1968   *Shoal of Time: A History of the Hawaiian Islands.* New York: Macmillan.

Delpar, Helen
1980   *The Discoverers: An Encyclopedia of Explorers and Exploration.* New York: McGraw-Hill.

Dickens, Charles
1938   *The Posthumous Papers of the Pickwick Club. 1837.* Reprint. New York: Heritage Press.

Dictionary of American Biography
1928–1936   20 vols. New York: Charles Scribner's Sons.

Dictionary of National Biography
1917   Leslie Stephen and Sidney Lee, eds. 21 vols. London: Oxford University Press.

Dobyns, Henry F., and Paul L. Doughty
1976   *Peru: A Cultural History.* New York: Oxford University Press.

Dodge, Ernest S.
1972   Aspects of Sino-American Trade in the Nineteenth Century. In *China and the Red Barbarians: American and British Relations with China in the Nineteenth Century.* London: National Maritime Museum.

1973   *The Polar Rosses: John and James Clark Ross and Their Explorations.* London: Faber and Faber.

1976   *Islands and Empires: Western Impact on the Pacific and East Asia.* Minneapolis: University of Minnesota Press.

Dulles, Foster Rhea
    1932   *America in the Pacific: A Century of Expansion.* Boston: Houghton Mifflin.

East India Marine Society, Salem, Mass.
    1834   Memorial . . . Praying That an Expedition Be Fitted Out by the Government to Make a Voyage of Discovery and Survey to the South Seas. 16 December. 23d Cong., 2d sess. Document 75. In J. N. Reynolds, *Pacific and Indian Oceans: or, the South Sea Surveying and Exploring Expedition: Its Inception, Progress, and Objects.* New York: Harper & Brothers, 1841.

Egle, William Henry
    1883   *History of Counties of Dauphin and Lebanon in the Commonwealth of Pennsylvania, Biographical and Genealogical.* Philadelphia: Everts and Peck.

Elits, Hermann Frederick
    1962   Ahmad bin Na'aman's Mission to the United States in 1840: The Voyage of al-Sultanah to New York City. *Essex Institute Historical Collections* 98:219–77.

Ellis, Franklin, and Samuel Evans
    1883   *History of Lancaster County, Pennsylvania, with Biographical Sketches.* Philadelphia: Everts and Peck.

Emmons, George Foster
    1853   *The Navy of the United States, from the Commencement, 1775 to 1853; with a Brief History of Each Vessel's Service and Fate as Appears upon the Record.* Washington: Gideon.

Erskine, Charles
    1985   *Twenty Years before the Mast.* 1890. Reprint. Washington: Smithsonian Institution Press.

Eyde, Richard
    1986   William Rich of the Great Exploring Expedition and How His Shortcomings Helped Botany Become a Calling. *Huntia* 6(2):165–96.

Fitzpatrick, Brian
    1946   *The Australian People, 1788–1945.* Melbourne: Melbourne University Press.

Freidel, Frank, ed.
    1974   *Harvard Guide to American History.* Rev. ed. 2 vols. Cambridge, Mass.: Belknap Press of Harvard University Press.

Fry, Howard Tyrrell, et al.
    1970   *The Significance of Cook's Endeavour Voyage, Three Bicentennial Lectures.* N.p.: James Cook University of North Queensland.

Galbraith, John S.
    1957   *The Hudson's Bay Company as an Imperial Factor, 1821–1869.* Berkeley and Los Angeles: University of California Press.

Gregory, Winifred, ed.
 1967 *American Newspapers, 1821–1936: A Union List.* . . . 1937.
     Reprint. New York: Kraus Reprint Corporation.

Grittinger, Henry C.
 1901 *Cornwall Furnace and the Cornwall Ore Banks, or Mine Hills.*
     Lebanon, Pa.: Lebanon County Historical Society.

Gutch, John
 1974 *Beyond the Reefs: The Life of John Williams, Missionary.* London:
     Macdonald.

Hamersly, Thomas H. S., ed.
 1882 *General Register of the United States Navy and Marine Corps* . . .
     1782–1882. . . . Washington: Thomas H. S. Hamersly.

Harris, Alex
 1872 *Biographical History of Lancaster County.* Lancaster, Pa.: E. Barr.

Herold, Amos L.
 1926 *James Kirke Paulding, Versatile American.* New York: Columbia
     University Press.

Hopkins, Manley
 1862 *Hawaii, The Past, Present, and Future of Its Island Kingdom.*
     London: Longman, Green, Longman, and Roberts.

Hudson, William L.
 1838 Letters to Charles Wilkes, 14 April and 19 May. Box 3, WFP.
 1838–1842 Journal. Vol. l. American Museum of Natural History, New
     York.

James, Preston E.
 1959 *Latin America.* 3d ed. New York: Odyssey Press.

Johnson, Daniel Noble
 1959 *The Journals of Daniel Noble Johnson (1822–1863), United States*
     Navy. Edited by Mendel L. Peterson. Washington:
     Smithsonian Institution Press.

Jones, Thomas ap Catesby
 1837 South Sea Surveying and Exploring Expedition. Suggestions
     Furnished by Commodr Thos. ap Catesby Jones, June 1st
     1837. Memorandum in roll 2, Letters WEE, M75, NA.

Kassell, Bernard M.
 1985 Iron Men and Wooden Ships: A Chronology, 1838–1842. In
     MV, pp. 257–65.

Klein, H. M. J.
 1924 *Lancaster County, Pennsylvania—A History.* 4 vols. New York:
     Lewis History Publishing Co.

Klein, Philip Shriver
 1962 *President James Buchanan, A Biography.* University Park:
     Pennsylvania State University Press.

Koepcke, Maria
    1983   *The Birds of the Department of Lima, Peru.* Rev. ed. Newton
             Square, Pa.: Harrowood Books.
Lancaster County Historical Society, Lancaster, Pa.
    1896–1970 *Journal.* Various issues.
Langley, Harold D.
    1967   *Social Reform in the United States Navy, 1798–1862.* Urbana:
             University of Illinois Press.
Lanig, Alexander
    1961   *American Sail: A Pictorial History.* New York: E. P. Dutton.
La Pérouse, Jean-François de Galoup de
    1968   *A Voyage around the World Performed in the Years 1785, 1786,
             1787, and 1788 by the Boussole and Astrolabe.* . . . 1799. Reprint
             in 2 vols. New York: Da Capo Press.
Leonhart, Joye L.
    1985   Charles Wilkes: A Biography. In *MV,* pp. 189–203.
Loomis, Albertine
    1951   *Grapes of Canaan: Hawaii 1820, the True Story of Hawaii's
             Missionaries.* New York: Dodd, Mead.
Loose, John Ward Willson
    1978   *The Heritage of Lancaster.* Woodland Hills, Calif.: Windsor
             Publications.
McEwen, W. A., and A. H. Lewis
    1953   *Encyclopedia of Nautical Knowledge.* Cambridge, Md.: Cornell
             Maritime Press.
McLoughlin, John
    1943   *The Letters of John McLoughlin from Fort Vancouver to the
             Governor and Committee.* 2d ser. 1839–1844. Edited by E. E.
             Rich. London: Hudson's Bay Record Society by the
             Champlain Society.
Machado, Deirdre Meintel
    1976   *Cape Verde and Its People: A Short History.* Washington: U.S.
             Office of Education.
Maclay, Edgar Stanley
    1906   *A History of the United States Navy from 1775 to 1901.* Rev. ed.
             3 vols. New York: D. Appleton.
Mariner, William
    1820   *An Account of the Natives of the Tonga Islands in the South Pacific
             Ocean, Compiled and Arranged from the Extensive Communications
             of Mr. William Mariner, Several Years Resident in Those Islands.
             By John Martin.* 1817. 1st American ed. Boston: C. Ewer.
Masterman, Sylvia
    1934   *The Origins of International Rivalry in Samoa, 1845–1884.*
             London: George Allen & Unwin.

May, William
    1840   Letter to Frederick May, 23 October. Box 1, Area File 9 and
                10, RG 45, NA.
    1841   Letter to William Reynolds, 9 May. Box 1, Area File 9, RG 45,
                NA.
Memorial of Officers of the Exploring Expedition, Praying the Investigation of
    1846   *Certain Statements and Allegations Contained in the Narrative of*
                That Expedition Affecting Their Characters. 29th Cong., 2d sess.,
                Senate Document 47.
Mendiburu, Manuel de
    1931–1935 *Diccionario histórico-biográfico del Peru.* 11 vols. Lima: Imprenta
                "Enrique Palacios" and Librería e Imprenta Gil.
Merrill, James M.
    1957   *The Rebel Shore: The Story of Union Sea Power in the Civil War.*
                Boston: Little, Brown.
Miller, Frederick K.
    1950   *The Rise of the Iron Community.* Lebanon, Pa.: Lebanon County
                Historical Society.
Morgan, George H.
    1877   *Centennial, the Settlement, Formation and Progress of Dauphin*
                County, Pennsylvania, from 1785 to 1876. Harrisburg: Telegraph
                Steam Book & Job Printing House.
National Geographic Society
    1981   *National Geographic Atlas of the World.* 5th ed. Washington:
                National Geographic Society.
National Cyclopedia of American Biography
    1892–1984 63 vols. New York: James T. White.
Naval Encyclopedia: Comprising a Dictionary of Nautical Words and Phrases;
    1881   *Biographical Notices and Records of Naval Officers. . . .*
                Philadelphia: L. R. Hamersly.
Nesser, Robert Wilden
    1909   *Statistical and Chronological History of the United States Navy,*
                1775–1907. 2 vols. New York: Macmillan.
Newman, Eric P., and Kenneth E. Bresset
    1962   *The Fantastic 1804 Dollar.* Racine, Wisc.: Whitman.
New York Morning Herald
    1842   13 June.
Nichols, Edward J.
    1958   *Towards Gettysburg: A Biography of General John F. Reynolds.*
                University Park: Pennsylvania State University Press.
Oman-U.S.A., 150 Years of Friendship
    1983   Washington: Embassy of the Sultanate of Oman.
Patterson, C. Meade
    1959   Firearms on the Wilkes Expedition. *Gun Report* 5:10–29.

Paulding, James K.
    1838   Letter to Charles Wilkes, 12 July. Letters to Officers, p. 353,
                roll 27, M149, Navy Department, NA.
    1839   Letter to Charles Wilkes, 29 March. Letters to Officers, pp.
                345–46, roll 28, M149, Navy Department, NA.
Paullin, Charles Oscar
    1907   Naval Administration under the Navy Commissioners,
                1815–1842. *U.S. Naval Institute Proceedings* 33:597–641.
Phillips, S. C.
    1837   Letter to the secretary of state, 1 July. Miscellaneous
                Correspondence, roll 82, M179, Department of State, NA.
Phillips, Wendall
    1967   *Oman: A History.* N.p.: Reynal.
Pickering, Charles
                Journal. Massachusetts Historical Society. Copy at the
                Philadelphia Academy of Natural Sciences.
Pillsbury, J. E.
    1910   Wilkes' and D'Urville's Discoveries in Wilkes Land. *U.S. Naval*
                Institute Proceedings 36:465–68.
Reynolds, Clark G.
    1978   *Famous American Admirals.* New York: Van Nostrand Reinhold.
Reynolds, Jane
    1841   Letter to brother William, 17 June. AHC.
Reynolds, John
    1842   Letter to wife, Lydia Moore, 13 April. AHC.
Reynolds, Lydia Moore (1794–1843)
    1842a   Letter to husband, John, 12 June. AHC.
    1842b   Letter to son William, 12 June. AHC.
Reynolds, Lydia Moore (1818–1896)
                Letters to brother William. AHC.
    1837   19 March.
    1838a   4 August.
    1838b   18 November.
    1839a   17 February.
    1839b   1 December.
    1840a   1 February.
    1840b   10 May.
    1840c   15 July.
    1840d   5 November.
    1841a   14 February.
    1841b   26 February.
    1841c   17 June.
    1841d   31 October.
Reynolds, Lydia Moore, and Jane
    1842   Letter to brother William, February. AHC.

Reynolds, William
    1832   Letter to father, John, 16 July. RFP.
    1836   Letter to sister Lydia Moore, 11 October. RFP.
    1838–1842 Journal on board the Vincennes, Chas. Wilkes, Esq.,
              Commander, Sea Account. 245 pp. RFP [cited as Public
              Journal].
    1838–1840 Journal of U.S. Ship Vincennes & Peacock, 1838, 1839, 1840
              . . . from the United States to the Fiji Islands. 370 pp. RFP
              [cited as Journal No. 1].
    1840–1842 Journal 1840, 1841, 1842—Peacock, Flying Fish, Porpoise—
              from Fiji Isds. to St. Helena. 388 pp. RFP [cited as Journal
              No. 2].
    1842   Private Notes from St. Helena to the U. States, via Rio de
              Janeiro from April to July 1842—U.S. Brig Porpoise—
              Homeward Bound. 31 pp. RFP [cited as Journal No. 3].
    1842   Letter to father, John, 2 July. RFP.
    1843a   Letter to Henry Eld, 22 January. Eld Papers, Western
              Americana Collection, Yale University.
    1843b   Letter to father, John, 5 July. RFP.
    1847–1849 Private Journal aboard U.S. Steamer *Allegheny*. RFP.
              Critique. Second draft, ms., undated. RFP.
    1857–1861 Account of Hawaiian Islands by Lieutenant William Reynolds,
              Naval Store Keeper, Honolulu. Logs and Journals of Vessels,
              subseries 80, entry 392, RG 45, NA.
    1866–1869 Remark Book of the *Lackwanna*, commanded by Capt. William
              Reynolds, on a cruise from New York to Honolulu and back
              to San Francisco. Officers' Letterbooks, subseries 129, entry
              395, RG 45, NA.
    1868   Letter to Thomas T. Craven, 26 September. This and other
              correspondence in Letters Sent by Capt. Wm. Reynolds,
              Lackawanna, Pacific Squadron, 1867–1869. 2 vols. Officers'
              Letterbooks, subseries 102, entry 395, RG 45, NA.
    1875–1877 Letters Sent by R. Adm. William Reynolds, *Tennessee*, Asiatic
              Squadron. 9 vols. Officers' Letterbooks, subseries 115, entry
              395, RG 45, NA.
Reynolds, William, J. S. Whittle, William May, and Simon F. Blunt
    1839   Letter to Charles Wilkes, 20 August. Box 1, Area File 9, RG 45,
              NA.
Ribeiro, Orlando
    1960   *A Ilha do Fogo e as suas erupções.* 2d ed. Lisboa: Junta de
              Investigaciones do Ultramar.
Rogers, N. L., and Bros.
    1838   Letter to Charles Wilkes, 16 July. Papers of Charles Wilkes,
              1837–1847, Microfilm MS-535, Kansas State Historical Society,
              Topeka.

Roscoe, Theodore, and Fred Freeman
    1956   *Picture History of the U.S. Navy.* New York: Charles Scribner
           and Sons.
Rosengarten, Joseph G., et al.
    1880   *Reynolds Memorial. Addresses Delivered before the Historical Society*
           of Pennsylvania upon the Occasion of the Presentation of a Portrait of
           Maj. Gen. John F. Reynolds, March 8, 1880. Philadelphia:
           Lippincott.
Ross, James Clark
    1847   *A Voyage of Discovery and Research in the Southern and Antarctic*
           Regions, during the Years 1839–43. 2 vols. London: J. Murray.
Rubincam, Milton
    1962   *America's Only Royal Family: Genealogy of the Former Hawaiian*
           Ruling House. National Genealogical Society.
Rupp, I. Daniel
    1844   *History of Lancaster County.* Lancaster, Pa.: G. Hills.
Shenk, Hiram H.
    1930   *A History of the Lebanon Valley in Pennsylvania.* Harrisburg:
           National History Association.
Simms, J. D.
    1841   Letter to William Reynolds, 21 September. RFP.
Simpson, George
    1847   *Narrative of a Journey round the World, during the Years 1841 and*
           1842. 2 vols. London: Henry Colburn.
    1973   *London Correspondence inward from Sir George Simpson, 1841–42.*
           Edited by Glyndwr Williams. London: Hudson's Bay Society.
    1975   The "Character Book" of Governor George Simpson, 1832. In
           Hudson's Bay Miscellany, 1670–1870, edited by Glyndwr
           Williams, pp. 151–236. Winnipeg: Hudson's Bay Record
           Society.
Smith, A. Thomas
    1843   Letter to Charles Wilkes, 31 May. Letters to Officers, p. 46,
           roll 37, M149, Navy Department, NA.
Smith, Archibald
    1839   *Peru as It Is: A Residence in Lima, and Other Parts of the Peruvian*
           Republic. . . . 2 vols. London: Richard Bentley.
Stackpole, Edouard A.
    1953   *The Sea-Hunters: The New England Whalemen during Two*
           Centuries, 1635–1835. Philadelphia: Lippincott.
Stann, E. Jeffrey
    1985   Charles Wilkes as Diplomat. In *MV,* pp. 205–25.
Stanton, William
    1975   *The Great United States Exploring Expedition of 1838–1842.*
           Berkeley and Los Angeles: University of California Press.

Stevens, Sylvester K.
    1945   *American Expansion in Hawaii, 1842–1898*. Harrisburg: Archives
                Publishing Company.
Tate, Merze
    1965   *The United States and the Hawaiian Kingdom: A Political History*.
                New Haven: Yale University Press.
Tily, James C.
    1964   *The Uniforms of the United States Navy*. New York: T. Yoseloff.
The Times Atlas of the World
    1983   Comprehensive ed. New York: Times Books.
Topham, Washington
    1930   Dr. Frederick May. *Records of the Columbia Historical Society*
                31–32:307–11.
Tschudi, Johann Jakob von
    1849   *Travels in Peru, during the Years 1838–1842, on the Coast, in the*
                Sierra, across the Cordilleras and the Andes, into Primeval Forests.
                New York: George P. Putnam.
Tyler, David
    1968   *The Wilkes Expedition: The First United States Exploring Expedition*
                (1838–1842). Philadelphia: American Philosophical Society.
United States. Defense Mapping Agency
    1978   Canal Beagle to Cabo de Hornos. Chart 22430.
    1978   Estrecho de Magallanes to Cabo de Hornos. Chart 22036.
    1980   Operational Navigation Chart, ONC, Sheet N-25. Ed. 3, Rev.
United States. Department of State
                List of U.S. Consular Officers, 1789–1939. 21 rolls, M587, NA.
United States. Laws, statutes, etc.
    1841   *Laws of the United States, in Relation to the Navy and Marine*
                Corps. . . . Compiled by Benjamin Homans. Washington:
                Printed by J. and G. S. Gideon.
United States. Navy Department
    1832   *Rules of the Navy Department, Regulating the Civil Administration*
                of the Navy of the United States. Washington: Printed at the
                Globe Office.
    1838   General Order, 22 June. Circular and General Orders, vol. 1
                (1793–1842), pp. 335–36, RG 45, NA.
    1848   *A General Register of the Navy and Marine Corps of the United*
                States. . . . Washington: Alexander.
    1959   *Dictionary of American Naval Fighting Ships*. Washington: U.S.
                Government Printing Office.
United States. Superintendent of Documents
    1911   *Checklist of United States Public Documents, 1789–1909*. 3d ed. 2
                vols. Washington: U.S. Government Printing Office.
Viola, Herman J.
    1985   The Story of the U.S. Exploring Expedition. In *MV*, pp. 9–41.

Viola, Herman J., and Carolyn Margolis, eds.
  1985   *Magnificent Voyagers: The U.S. Exploring Expedition, 1838–1842.*
            Washington: Smithsonian Institution Press.
Washington Globe
  1838   10 July, 1 August, and other issues from the period of the
            expedition.
Washington Navy Yard. Naval Historical Center. Operational Archives. ZB
            File.
Watson, George E.
  1985   Vertebrate Collections: Lost Opportunities. In *MV*, pp. 42–69.
Wilbert, Johannes, ed.
  1977   *Folk Literature of the Yamana Indians: Martin Gusinde's Collection
            of Yamana Narratives.* Berkeley and Los Angeles: University of
            California Press.
Wilkes, Charles
  1838   Letter to William L. Hudson, 5 June. Box 3, WFP.
  1839   Order to the Officers of the *Vincennes,* 20 August [copy]. Box
            1, Area File 9, RG 45, NA.
  1840a   Despatch 66, 10 August. Roll 6, Letters WEE, M75, NA.
  1840b   Letter to Jane Wilkes, 10 August. Box 4, WFP.
  1840c   Despatch 68, 11 August. Roll 6, Letters WEE, M75, NA.
  1842a   Despatch 104, June. Roll 6, Letters WEE, M75, NA.
  1842b   *Synopsis of the Cruise of the U.S. Exploring Expedition, during the
            Years, 1838, '39, '40, '41, & '42; Delivered before the National
            Institute, by Its Commander, Charles Wilkes, Esq., on the Twentieth
            of June 1842. To Which Is Added a List of Officers and Scientific
            Corps Attached to the Expedition.* Washington: Printed by P.
            Force.
  1845   *Narrative of the United States Exploring Expedition during the Years
            1838, 1839, 1840, 1841, 1842.* 5 vols. and atlas. Philadelphia:
            Lea and Blanchard.
  1850   *United States Exploring Expedition, during the Years 1838, 1839,
            1840, 1841, 1842. . . . Atlas of Charts.* 2 vols. Philadelphia: C.
            Sherman, Printer.
  1978   *Autobiography of Rear Admiral Charles Wilkes, U.S. Navy.* Edited
            by William James Morgan et al. Washington: Naval History
            Division, Department of the Navy.
Wilkes, John
  1816   Letter to James K. Paulding, 6 May. Box 1, WFP.

Index

Italicized page numbers indicate illustrations; "n" denotes a footnote.

THE NAVAL INSTITUTE PRESS is the book-publishing arm of the U.S. Naval Institute, a private, nonprofit professional society for members of the sea services and civilians who share an interest in naval and maritime affairs. Established in 1873 at the U.S. Naval Academy in Annapolis, Maryland, where its offices remain today, the Naval Institute has more than 100,000 members worldwide.

Members of the Naval Institute receive the influential monthly naval magazine *Proceedings* and substantial discounts on fine nautical prints, ship and aircraft photos, and subscriptions to the Institute's recently inaugurated quarterly, *Naval History*. They also have access to the transcripts of the Institute's Oral History Program and may attend any of the Institute-sponsored seminars regularly offered around the country.

The book-publishing program, begun in 1898 with basic guides to naval practices, has broadened its scope in recent years to include books of more general interest. Now the Naval Institute Press publishes more than forty new titles each year, ranging from how-to books on boating and navigation to battle histories, biographies, ship guides, and novels. Institute members receive discounts on the Press's more than 300 books.

For a free catalog describing books currently available and for further information about U.S. Naval Institute membership, please write to:

Membership Department
U.S. Naval Institute
Annapolis, Maryland 21402

or call, toll-free, 800-233-USNI.

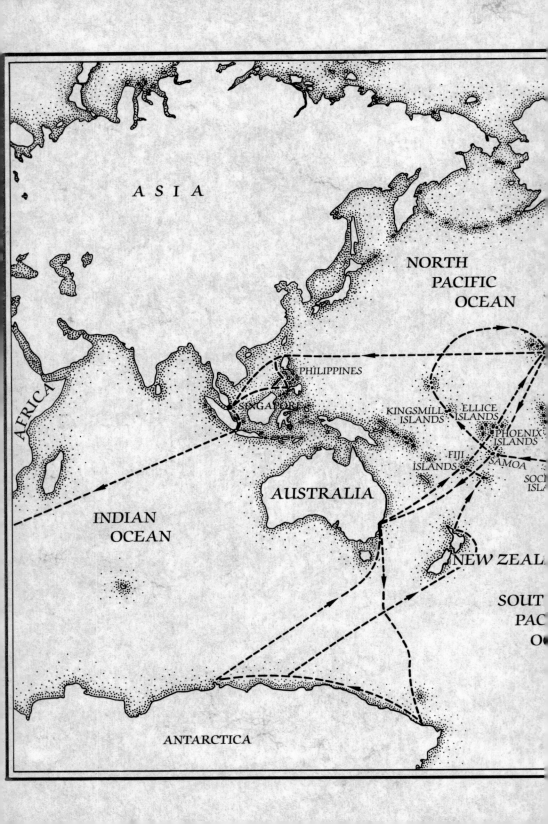

ASIA

NORTH
PACIFIC
OCEAN

PHILIPPINES

SINGAPORE

AFRICA

KINGSMILL
ISLANDS

ELLICE
ISLANDS

PHOENIX
ISLANDS

FIJI
ISLANDS

SAMOA

SOC
ISLA

AUSTRALIA

INDIAN
OCEAN

NEW ZEAL

SOUT
PAC
O

ANTARCTICA